DATE DUE

CAPITAL SOURCES

CAPITAL SOURCES

AND MAJOR INVESTING

INSTITUTIONS

By

WILLIAM C. HANSON

Financial and Investment Consultant

Formerly Economic Consultant to U. S. Department of State and U. S. Treasury Department

SIMMONS-BOARDMAN PUBLISHING CORPORATION

New York

Library of Congress Catalog Card Number: 63-21575
Manufactured in the United States of America

FOREWORD

The purpose of this publication is to provide a handy reference guide to all significant sources of capital, and to the major investing institutions. Virtually all types of banks, financing organizations, credit groups, special funds, underwriters, and moneyed institutions have been included. Coverage is also provided of the vast network of lending, financing, credit and guarantor agencies of the United States Government —the greatest banker in history. Likewise included is the complex of quasi-government international finance agencies—all located in Washington—which provide literally billions of dollars. These international banks are undergoing rapid change and expansion; consequently, many of their facilities have come into existence only recently.

For practical purposes, the book has been organized into three divisions or parts. Part 1 describes the various sources of capital and financial institutions. Part 2 is, in effect, a subject-index, listing a wide variety of purposes or objects of financing; then indicating the specific sources to be used. Part 3 provides lists of specific organizations or institutions, with names, addresses, and financial resources. Wherever possible or practicable, the names of financial officers to contact is also indicated. Needless to say, none of the component lists of such organizations claims to be all-inclusive. Space limitations alone would prevent such coverage; furthermore, it is doubtful whether any useful purpose would be served by attempting to list every organization in any field, no matter how limited or small. Consequently, the organizations and institutions listed have been selected with careful deliberation to represent those most likely to be useful for the majority of business and financial people using this book. In most instances, the organizations listed represent the leaders in their respective areas.

Many minds and hands have helped bring this book into being. The author is deeply grateful to those who have generously contributed ideas, suggestions, and no small degree of inspiration. Thus, the end result may be described as a consensus of the best-informed opinion in banking circles, the investment community, the industrial world, many government agencies, and elsewhere.

ACKNOWLEDGMENTS

Special acknowledgment is made to the following:

American Banker; *Louis Asterita, Deputy Manager, Robert G. Howard, Deputy Manager, Edgar T. Savidge, Deputy Manager,* American Bankers Association; The Library Staff of Chase-Manhattan Bank; Foreign Credit Insurance Association; Institute of Life Insurance; *Richard H. Grant, Director of Public Information,* Investment Company Institute; National Association of Mutual Savings Banks; National Association of Manufacturers; National Business Bureau; New York State Banking Department; *B. Colwell Davis, Jr., Executive Vice-President,* New York State Chamber of Commerce; also the following officials and agencies of the United States Government and quasi-Government institutions: *Arnold H. Dadian, Information Officer,* Agency for International Development; *Lucia M. Fraber, Information Officer,* Agricultural Stabilization and Conservation Service (Department of Agriculture); Bank for Cooperatives (Department of Agriculture); Bureau of International Commerce (Department of Commerce); Commodity Credit Corp. (Department of Agriculture); *R. Coleman Egertson, Acting Comptroller,* Office of the Comptroller of Currency (Treasury Department); *Eugene Wolfe, Information Officer,* Export-Import Bank of Washington; *W. Gifford Hoag, Chief of Information Services.* Farm Credit Administration (Department of Agriculture); *Robert E. Nipp, Information Officer,* Farmer's Home Administration (Department of Agriculture); Federal Deposit Insurance Corp.; Federal Farm Mortgage Corp.; Federal Intermediate Credit Banks (Department of Agriculture); Federal Land Bank Association (Department of Agriculture); Federal Reserve Bank of New York; *Elizabeth L. Carmichael, Assistant Secretary,* Federal Reserve Board; Federal Savings & Loan Insurance Corp.; House of Representatives, *Office of Hon. Frank J. Becker;* House of Representatives, Select Committee on Small Business; Housing & Home Finance Agency; *Joaquin E. Meyer, Director, Division of Information,* Inter-American Development Bank; *H. N. Graves, Information Officer,* International Bank for Reconstruction & Development (World Bank); *Elizabeth A. Burton, Agreements Officer,* International Cooperation Administration (Department of State); International Development Association; International Development Bank; *H. N. Graves, Information Officer,* International Finance Corp.; Office of Area Development (Department of Commerce); Office of Education (Department of Health, Education & Welfare); *William Chafin, Research Analyst, Frank M. Kleiler, Director, Office of Welfare & Pension Plans, Norris B. Sacharoff, Chief, Division of Reports,* Office of Welfare & Pension Plans (Department of Labor); Rural Electrification Administration (Department of Agriculture); Rural Telephone Administration (Department of Agriculture); Securities & Exchange Commission; Small Business Administration; U.S. Senate, *Office of Sen. Wright Patman.* Also to researchers *Norma R. Cook; Gary P. Hanson; Judy Mathuran; Laura Minnerly; Sue Minnerly.*

Table of Contents

Part 1

SOURCES OF MAJOR CAPITAL

Knowing how and where to locate capital is a powerful advantage in the business world today. Our whole economic system is fueled by capital, since money is needed in every phase of business operations—initially, to launch a new enterprise; then, to keep it going; and eventually, to help the business expand and to acquire new plants and equipment.

In the keenly competitive business world, the firm that has ready access to funds is often the one which can outstrip its rivals and forge ahead to the place of leadership. With adequate finances, it can hire all the needed management and production skills, enter new markets, and acquire the new equipment frequently needed to remain competitive. By the same token, many an otherwise sound organization, endowed with good management, skilled workmen and fine products, stays forever in a rut, or may even be dissolved because of one great handicap—it does not know where to go for capital funds. In this one respect alone, such a company lacks the "secret" of its more successful competitors.

Capital: The "Secret Weapon" of Successful Businesses

Significantly, studies by Dun & Bradstreet and other authorities show that one of the main reasons for business failure, year after year, is "undercapitalization." This is notably true of many small business firms; however, it is a condition which exists throughout the realm of business and affects even some fairly substantial corporations. "Under-capitalization" does not mean that a company is without funds; on the contrary, it may show a fair cash balance and a reasonably sound position

1

in its financial statements. "Undercapitalization" is a relative term; in its real sense, it means not having sufficient funds, or lines of credit, to meet all the needs and contingencies of business operation in today's fast-changing markets and technology.

A great deal of capital is mandatory to operate a business organization of significant size today, and, even among smaller firms, the amount of funds required is proportionately greater than ever before, This is precisely a reason—perhaps *the* reason—why the present great super-corporations keep growing in size, earnings, and affluence. They not only have abundant internal cash resources with which to finance their growth, plus their depreciation allowances and internal cash-flow, but they are expert in utilizing outside capital sources.

CAPITAL AND ITS AVAILABILITY

One of the interesting things about capital is that there is an abundance of it in the United States at present. Indeed, it is paradoxical that there exists a surplus of funds in this country—exceeding the demand—which is actually seeking qualified users. The very nature of capital demands that it be kept productive; above all, that it avoid idleness. There is a reservoir of available money and credit in the United States infinitely greater than in any other country in the world. One measure of this fact is that interest rates here are among the lowest in existence.

This supply of capital exists in many places. Some of it can be found in almost any community, even relatively small ones, in local banks, savings and loan associations, finance companies, and special investing companies. There are also huge concentrations of funds in certain kinds of organizations not generally known to the public. Usually such large sources of liquid assets are found in New York and other major financial centers. Nevertheless, much of this money backlog is available to qualified business firms in virtually any part of the country.

It is the purpose of this book to report on the various sources of capital in the United States which are accessible to small business firms and large corporations, to farmers, homeowners, and others seeking capital. Also included is information regarding funds available for charities, churches, hospitals, welfare projects, as well as educational and research programs.

In this survey, we are concerned primarily with the kind of capital needed by business firms and non-business organizations, rather than individual non-business borrowers. Thus, the emphasis is upon sources of medium-sized and large funds. Consequently, little or no coverage is given to "small loan" companies, credit unions, and other sources which cater chiefly to small personal loan requirements.

The sources of finance described in the following pages are many and varied: commercial banks, savings banks, savings and loan associations, insurance companies, mutual funds, pension funds, foundations and charitable trusts, labor unions, small business investment companies, government agencies, and specialized sources. Each of these sources is distinctive from the others. Each performs a particular function and supplies money, credit, or guarantees for a specific purpose or group of purposes.

It is vital, then, to recognize that different kinds of capital are earmarked for different purposes. Although, as previously mentioned, huge accumulations of capital are in existence, these funds break down into well-defined categories, as far as their investment objectives are concerned. For example, some capital will go only into government bonds or other highly conservative investments; other funds will be confined to real estate mortgages; still others will provide financial backing for a new business firm, etc.

Needless to say, it is important to know not only the various money sources, but the purposes for which the funds, in each case, might be obtainable. The object of this book is to provide both types of information.

How to Utilize Information Provided in This Book

The material in this book is organized in three sections. Section I discusses and describes the principal sources of capital and the main purposes for which they are available. Part 2 is classified according to the various purposes for which capital may be sought such as mortgage loans, farm financing, chattel mortgages, term loans, small business financing, etc. The object of Part 2 is to enable the user to locate, quickly and conveniently, the specific sources of capital for a particular purpose. The capital sources listed under each of the subject headings refer to lists which will be found in the next section of the book, Part 3. This section contains lists of individual banks, institutions, and organizations under each major group. In most instances, the amount of financial resources of each individual organization is indicated; moreover, names of officials to contact are provided wherever possible.

COMMERCIAL BANKS

When the need for capital or credit for business purposes arises, one instinctively thinks of the local community bank. The commercial bank is one of the most prolific sources of funds; however, it is doubtful that the average individual or the typical business man realizes the variety and scope of financing services which his local bank provides.

Of course, it is recognized that the local bank is in the "lending business," and most business men are familiar with the usual or more conventional type of loan such as loans for working capital, financing of inventories, loans to finance the purchase of automobiles, home appliances, and personal loans, both secured and unsecured. Secured loans are those based upon marketable securities, life insurance policies, government bonds, or other collateral with ready marketability. Unsecured loans are those granted entirely upon credit standing of the borrower, without tangible security of any kind.

It is also widely known that commercial banks are sources of funds for mortgages on residential, commercial, industrial or farm properties.

The nature of commercial banking is such that most loans are relatively "short term" in duration, that is, for periods up to, but not usually exceeding, 12 months. Mortgage loans are a conspicuous exception, and may run for periods of ten or more years.

While commercial banks have traditionally been excellent sources of capital, their lending capabilities were limited, for many years, to relatively short-term commitments. Needless to say, such restrictions were a hardship to many would-be borrowers who required longer-term capital for their business needs. This was specifically disadvantageous to smaller business firms because they could not secure longer-term funds in the major capital markets with the same facility as larger corporations; in many instances, the smaller firm could not secure long-term money under any circumstance.

In recent years, however, and particularly since World War II, the nation's commercial banks have evolved a unique form of lending which goes a long way toward solving the longer-term capital needs of business—large and small. This special kind of financing is the device known as the "term loan."

Term Loan Financing

A term loan may be defined as a loan to a business enterprise which is repayable, according to agreement between lender and borrower, over a period of more than one year. The maturity period of a term loan is approximately five years, although some term loans may run up to 10 to 15 years. Term loan financing has many advantages for the borrower, of which one of the foremost is that it helps many firms to compensate for equity capital deficiency in their businesses. This is notably the case with those firms which cannot readily or conveniently go to the investment capital markets for additional funds.

Term loans differ in many respects from loans customarily made by banks, since they are designed to fit special needs and requirements of a particular borrower. Since the term loan may not finally mature for some years, considerable attention is given by the banker to the long-range prospects of the borrowing company, its earning power, its ability to meet scheduled payments, the continuity and resourcefulness of its management, and its existing and future position in the industry of which it is a part. Because of the peculiar characteristics inherent in the transaction, and the length of time involved, the loan agreement contains reasonable safeguards in the form of affirmative and negative covenants as well as other provisions which must be mutually agreeable to the borrower and lender.

Term loans have a place among the assets of banks, the amount thereof in a particular bank being governed by the liquidity and maturity composition of the bank's assets, the character and stability of its deposits, and capital funds. Term loans are a logical substitute for many short-term loans that are made with full realization by both the borrower and the lender that repayment at maturity will probably not be convenient and that they may have to be renewed. Term lending may be considered a supplement to the customary bank function of short-term lending.

Not only is it possible for a single bank to make term loans for its own account, but a group of banks can participate in the arrangements. By means of this sharing with other banks, the customer's principal bank can arrange a term loan for a larger amount than it is able or willing to carry alone; *thus the individual bank can offer a local, regional, or even national financing service.*

Occasionally, banks, in arranging term loans, invite the participation of insurance companies. In such cases, these institutions usually share with the banks pro rata in any security and enjoy all the benefits set forth in the loan agreement. The proceeds of the loans may be required to modernize or erect new buildings, acquire existing facilities owned by others, acquire real estate, install new machinery or equipment in order to produce new products or reduce production costs on existing products, improve the means and methods of production and marketing, or carry larger inventories and receivables created by an expansion of sales.

Advantages of Term Loans to Borrower

The term loan has certain definite advantages to the borrower. First, it is a carefully negotiated loan on terms and conditions acceptable both to the borrower and to the lender. Second, it is based primarily on the borrower's ability to pay the loan from earnings. The objective, generally, is to extinguish the debt by the final maturity date of the loan. Third, the borrower is assured that there will be no call to accelerate payment provided there is adherence to the terms and conditions of the loan agreement. Fourth, since a term loan is a contract between a single borrower and one or a small group of lenders, it can be revised more readily and less expensively than can a typical indenture or the provisions of a preferred stock. Fifth, there is no registration expense in connection with a term loan, although the borrower as a general rule is expected to absorb the lender's legal fees and out-of-pocket expenses. Sixth, commercial banks have had wide experience with the financial and industrial problems of companies in many lines of activity; thus, the borrower is able to consult with, and obtain the advice of, persons who have a broad understanding of the problems confronting a business enterprise. Seventh, the direct and intimate relationship and the confidence established between the borrower and the lender when the loan is arranged continue throughout the arrangement. Thus, if new or unforeseen circumstances which affect the borrower's performance according to the original agreement are encountered, the lender, who is vitally interested in the borrower's progress, can readily agree to formal amendments or supplements which will recognize the altered conditions. This provides a high degree of flexibility.

Installment Loans

Another type of financing which has evolved in recent years is the installment loan for business firms. Installment loans are paid off in monthly (sometimes quarterly) installments, over periods ranging from about 12 to 24 months. In some instances, they may run for moderately longer terms. Thus, the installment loan is somewhat intermediate between the conventional short-term bank loan and the longer-duration term loan described above.

Installment loans may be granted for numerous purposes. The needs of small business may begin with individuals entering a new business, buying out or revitalizing an old one, or expanding a present business. Money for these purposes is often needed as capital and therefore may require a term longer than is provided under the conventional pattern of commercial lending.

In addition to supplementing working capital, some of the purposes for which small business will require banking assistance may be to build up inventory; to add new lines; to increase production; to expand or diversify business; to buy an interest in a business; to buy out a partner; to affect operating economies; to discount bills; to pay taxes; to meet payrolls; to carry accounts receivable or notes receivable; to finance shop equipment or machinery; to purchase store and office furniture, fixtures, and equipment; to buy special equipment for groceries, meat markets, drug stores, bakeries, laundries, dry cleaning establishments, restaurants, dairies, hotels, hospitals, physicians' and dentists' offices, etc; to finance trucks, trailers, buses, tractors, heating equipment, air conditioning equipment, commercial refrigeration equipment, and farm equipment; to make property repairs, improvements, modernizations; and to realize a wide range of other business purposes.

Qualifications for Installment Loans

Understandably, requirements vary depending on the type of loan desired; thus, it is worth noting what qualifications banks usually seek from applicants for installment financing. The American Bankers Association offers the following recommendations on this subject.

"The prerequisites for credit of this type may be summarized briefly as follows: (1) the borrower must be an excellent moral risk; (2) there must be evidence that he has the ability to operate his business on a sound basis; (3) the past record of the business or future propects must show sufficient probable income so that the borrower may repay the installment loan out of future income from his business; and (4) while a normal risk should be assumed on loans of this type, the necessary steps must be taken to insure the bank against a loss on the loan greater than can be profitably absorbed in the usual course of business.

"To further evaluate the credit, consideration should be given to the borrower's investment in the business. In other words, how much of his own money does he have invested in the business? What is the nature of the assets, and what are the liquidation values? It is advisable to check into the competitive situation, the location, terms of lease, and rental values. A satisfactory analysis and appraisal of these factors are an important function of this type of lending and should be weighed carefully.

"Through the pledging of fixed assets, which are practical to assign, the borrower shows evidence of good faith and the bank's position is improved in liquidating the loan. These assets may be in the form of machinery and equipment, real estate equities, automotive equipment, notes and accounts receivable, inventory, and liquid assets such as savings account passbook balances, cash surrender value of life insurance, assignable war bonds, stocks, and bonds. Once again, it must be realized that reliance is primarily on the man and only secondarily on the asset pledged, which is merely to assist in policing and controlling the loan.

"It is recognized that many a well-managed, credit-worthy business finds it impractical or inconvenient to meet the requirements for the conventional type of short-term loan. There are numerous concerns in this position, including manufacturers, distributors, retailers, and personal service firms. Accordingly, whenever possible, credit should be extended on terms arranged especially to fit the borrower's particular needs and circumstances.

"The opinion of many bankers is that the use of monthly installments of repayment better fits the needs of most borrowers and is one of the most desirable methods of handling this type of loan.

"Banks can adopt the same fundamental policies for small business that are followed in the field of installment lending, that is, provide credit to any reliable and capable borrower for any useful purpose. Applying the principle of term loans to small business risks will go far toward rendering this credit service to a greater number of businessmen in the country."

Interest rates on bank installment loans are usually relatively high due to the costs involved in making this type of loan. The rate, which varies among different banks, may range from an effective rate of 6 per cent to as much as 20 per cent per annum, with 12 to 16 per cent as the most common.

The following "case histories" illustrate the use of installment credit financing in actual situations:

1. A neighborhood grocer, having recently moved to larger quarters, needed additional stock to handle increased business. A loan of $1,000 not only solved his problem but also enabled him to maintain a stronger cash position.

2. A manufacturer, after a long search for a certain type of equipment, finally found what he needed, but the seller demanded "cash in full." A loan of $2,000 arranged on installment terms, repaid in 18 monthly installments, was the solution.

3. A hardware dealer saw profits ahead if he could immediately stock up on certain items at favorable prices, but he could not spare sufficient working capital to take advantage of the transaction. Solution: an installment loan of $1,076 repaid out of income in 18 prearranged monthly installments.

4. A small subcontractor on a construction job, operating with limited funds, needed additional material to complete his work, for which he could not expect payment for several months. Solution: a $500 installment loan paid for the needed materials and the loan was repaid in 12 monthly installments.

5. A retail store owner decided that extensive remodeling was essential to improve his service and maintain his competitive position but did not care to deplete his working capital. A modernization loan of $3,000 repayable in 36 monthly installments resolved this problem.

6. To handle a growing volume of business, a trucking company needed two additional trailers priced at $6,500 but could invest only $2,500 without impairing working capital. Solution: installment credit financing covered the balance of $4,000, repayable in 24 monthly installments.

Other Types of Bank Loans

Commercial banks make a variety of other loans to business men and companies, which differ mainly in terms of the security pledged as collateral:

Life insurance policy loans. These are loans secured by certain types of life insurance policies, where the "cash surrender value" of the policy bears a sufficient relation to the principal of the loan.

Chattel mortgage loans. A fairly common form of security for bank loans is a chattel mortgage. This instrument is an assignment of title to the bank of certain *tangibles*: machinery, office equipment, or other movable personal or business property.

Accounts receivable loans. For many years, non-banking sources traditionally provided most of the financing of loans secured by the borrower's accounts receivable; however, commercial banks more recently have been emphasizing this type of financing. Under this arrangement, the borrower—usually a manufacturer, wholesaler, or large retailer—pledges its accounts receivable, i.e., the sums of money owed to it by its various customers or clientele. Loans may be made by the bank against "open accounts," or the ledgers of the borrower, or against notes receivable, viz., IOU's made out to the borrower from its own customers as evidence of their debt.

Warehouse receipt loans. Frequently, bank loans are made on the security of goods or commodities which are in a commercial warehouse (or which can be placed there for the purpose). Salable merchandise, properly deposited in a recognized warehouse, is evidenced by an instrument known as a "warehouse receipt," which conveys title and accessibility to the material in storage. A warehouse may be either a public or a field warehouse. A public warehouse is an establishment operated by persons engaged in the business of storing of goods for the general public under laws of the particular state which regulate such agencies. A field warehouse is a segregated storeroom or building operated by a field warehouse corporation upon the premises of the company using the inventories pledged under the loan.

Although the warehouse receipt may be negotiable or nonnegotiable, the former is preferred as a basis for bank financing. The status of warehouse receipts is clearly defined in the Uniform Warehouse Receipts Act adopted by all 50 states, and such instruments qualify as excellent collateral for bank financing.

Mortgage loans. Bank loans secured by pledge of real estate are among the most familiar and universal forms of financing. Until 1913, state-chartered banks were the principal mortgage-lenders in the commercial banking field due to stringent restrictions on the activities of national banks in this area. However, the national banks began to enter the mortgage market on an impressive scale in 1913 when the Federal Reserve Act permitted them to grant loans on farms. In 1916, they were given the further right to make loans on improved, unencumbered nonfarm real estate. State banks continue to provide a substantial amount of mortgage financing, in accordance with statues in the respective states.

Collateral loans. Another form of secured loan is the type made on the pledge of U.S. government bonds, corporate bonds, or stocks pledged as collateral. The essential point is that the security or securities pledged must have ready marketability. Loans of this kind are made on about 50 per cent of the market value of the security in question, less than this in some cases, more in others. Highest loan ratios are granted on U.S. government securities. In all collateral loans, the borrower is expected to put up additional collateral, or to reduce his loan proportionately, in the event of a substantial decline in the market value of the pledged securities. Collateral loans are usually subject to the restriction that they are "non-purpose" transactions; that is, that the proceeds will not be used to purchase additional securities either on listed stock exchanges or in the over-the-counter market.

A special kind of collateral loan is the "call loan," a means of borrowing widely used in Wall Street and other principal investment centers. This type of loan is secured by stock exchange collateral consisting of stocks or bonds. The "call loan" is so named because it is a demand loan, which can be terminated ("called") at the option of either borrower or lender almost at any time. Technically, such loans can be called until about 3 o'clock in the afternoon of any business day, but actually the call is rarely made after 12 o'clock noon.

This type of loan is often a convenient way to raise funds for brief periods or to accommodate a company during a temporary cash shortage. Because of their strongly secured position and liquidity, call loans are popular with banks. Borrowing costs, which are comparatively moderate, are quoted daily on all financial pages.

Expanded Financing Facilities Through Correspondents and Credit Groups

An interesting aspect of contemporary American banking is the trend toward "credit groups," whereby a number of individual commercial banks work cooperatively in arranging financing. Nearly all commercial banks in the nation today have well-developed "correspondent" relations with other banks, both locally and in the larger financial centers. This correspondent network enables even smaller banks in remote areas to render better service and to handle more and larger loans. If a bank is unable to make a loan of the size requested, it may offer all, or part, of the loan to other banks in the community or in neighboring cities. This "share the loan" policy has been an effective means of providing funds to many communities, and to borrowers, which might otherwise have been deprived of such financing.

As an additional means of assuring that adequate credit will be accessible at all times, the nation's commercial banks have organized over 50 credit groups throughout the country, with commitments approximating one billion dollars. The groups do not initiate loans on their own, but they handle loans which individual banks are unable to make for legal or policy reasons.

Farm Loans and Credit

Commercial banks are a more important source of capital and credit for farmers, livestock men, and other agricultural interests than is generally realized. Substantial amounts of capital are needed in farming and allied operations today, just as in other industries and occupations. The nation's commercial banking system provides a considerable amount of the needed funds. Close to $7,000,000,000 in loans to farm borrowers are presently outstanding with commercial banks, of which some $5,000,000,000 are non-real estate loans, the remaining $2,000,000,000 representing farm real estate transactions.

Although banks in the predominantly agricultural states are the heaviest lenders to farm and allied interests, a number of town and city banks also are active in such financing. A survey by the American Bankers Association discloses that about 92 per cent of the commercial banks throughout the nation reported having farm loans outstanding.

Several types and forms of financing are available to farmers through their banks. Credit needs of farmers differ from those of many other borrowers because of the nature of their business. Loans for periods of 90 or 120 days are too short to finance many crop or other operations. Banks have recognized this by providing loans up to a year or more. The rapid growth in farm mechanization has led to a decided increase in investments in farm machinery on a typical commercial farm. Not only has the use of machinery become universal, but the numbers, kinds, and complexities also have grown rapidly. These, coupled with rising price trends, have added to costs of acquisition. According to the Balance Sheet of Agriculture for 1960, machinery and motor vehicles made up the largest item in non-real estate assets with a total of $18.4 billion. Live stock, which came next, showed a total of $16.2 billion.

The cost of a major machine such as a tractor or combine is too large to make it reasonable to expect that it can be paid for out of the returns of one year. The same is true of purchases of livestock to build a herd. A loan for only one year will not meet the need unless the farmer has delayed the purchase until he has accumulated a large share of the cost or unless the loan is renewed for additional periods. In the former instance, the farmer is deprived, for a period, of the income which would be added by the machine or other assets. In the latter case, there may be uncertainty with respect to renewals.

This has given rise to an increasing number of intermediate-term farm loans. Such loans may be made up to periods of three to five years, usually with provisions for monthly, seasonal, or other periodic repayment.

Financing Foreign Trade

Commercial banks play a vital role in financing the nation's import and export trade. Most of this activity is undertaken by the foreign departments of the larger banks in New York, Philadelphia, San Francisco, and other major financial centers because of their historic association with international trade. However, it is now possible to arrange for foreign trade financing through almost any local commercial bank, which can then refer the request to its correspondent institutions in major banking cities.

The principal banking instrument used in international trade is the letter of credit, of which there are several varieties. The traveler's letter of credit is used primarily by tourists, noncommercial travelers, and, very often, by small business interests in limited transactions. The commercial letter of credit is used in international trade transactions. It may be revocable or irrevocable; payable in U.S. dollars or in any other currency; divisible or non-divisible; conditional upon execution of certain attendant documents, or non-conditional, in which instance it is virtually a sight draft or money order. The letter of credit is a highly flexible and adaptable banking device which may be used in numerous ways to suit a variety of circumstances. Thus, it may be utilized to serve as a bid bond or advice of authority to pay.

Other instruments employed in international trade are bankers' drafts, bills of exchange, and correspondents' orders to transfer dollars (or other currencies). Commercial banks with foreign trade departments also assist in obtaining import and/or export insurance and in arranging the various licenses, insurance coverage, forms, and documents involved in international commerce. The larger banks also have foreign exchange departments which purchase and sell world currencies.

Foreign trade financing, like most other aspects of banking, is far from a static operation. Here, as elsewhere, in banking, change and progress are evident, and new financing facilities are being developed. An historic "breakthrough" in international trade financing has resulted from an arrangement whereby the commercial banks may now work with the Export-Import Bank of Washington to provide far greater foreign trade financing than ever before. As a result of this innovation, virtually every commercial bank in the nation, large or small, can now participate in providing funds and finance for overseas trade. The details of this new arrangement are described in a later section of this book under "United States Government Sources of Capital, Credit and Guarantees," in the subsection referring to the Export-Import Bank of Washington.

"Edge Act" Bank Affiliates and Overseas Branches of U. S. Banks

American commercial banks are becoming increasingly active in providing funds for various overseas businesses and activities. Major institutions such as Bank of America, Chase Manhattan Bank, First National City Bank of New York, and others, have branches in many European, Latin-American, Asian, and African nations. These branch banks provide a variety of loans and credits to business men and corporations in the areas in which they are established. For the most part, such financing is relatively short-term or intermediate-term, corresponding to the kind of lending provided by U.S.A.-based banks.

In recent years, particularly since the end of World War II, some leading banks have been establishing separate corporate affiliates for lending operations abroad, principally to meet the need for longer-term capital and investment-type financing. These subsidiaries are the "Edge Act" banks, named after the Edge Act of 1920 enacted by Congress, which permitted U. S. banks to extend their service abroad in this manner.

FOREIGN COMMERCIAL BANKS

The importance of the American banking system in supplying financing of various kinds has already been indicated. Foreign banks are also significant sources of capital for certain purposes, not only within their own borders, but to Americans and others as well. Some of the leading commercial banking institutions in Canada, Western Europe, and Japan have resources approaching, or exceeding, the equivalent of billions of dollars. These huge banks play a profoundly important role in the economic life of their respective countries, and, in some nations, engage in activities beyond the realm of commercial banking.

The great majority of American business firms will find that their financing requirements can be completely accomodated by domestic banks. However, a certain number of U. S. firms doing business abroad sometimes wish to supplement their domestic banking facilities with overseas bank affiliations. For such clients, foreign banks can be helpful in several ways: (1) arranging letters of credit and other forms of foreign trade financing; (2) providing credit reports on firms domiciled within their nation's borders; (3) arranging introductions to other business firms in their areas of operation; (4) receiving deposits of special accounts; (5) sometimes providing capital in a consortium with other financing groups in their own country or in neighboring countries.

Among foreign institutions, Swiss banks have become legendary for certain specialized accommodations which they provide. The Swiss banks have gained worldwide recognition for their confidential handling of "anonymous" deposit accounts and for their ability to provide large capital, on occasion, to American interests for large corporate and securities transactions. It is a well-known fact in the world of international finance that the Swiss banks are custodians for vast amounts of funds on deposit in "confidential" accounts. This money, or a part of it, is loaned throughout the world for various purposes.

TRUST COMPANIES AND BANK TRUST DEPARTMENTS

One of the largest concentrations of private capital is the money, securities, and other property tied up in trust funds. It is reliably estimated that the total value of trust funds exceeds $58,000,000,000, while some authorities believe that it may be $60,000,000,000 or more.

A trust fund, which is an entity strictly regulated by laws in each state, is created by either one of two instruments: (1) a will or (2) a trust agreement. The individuals or institutions designated to administer the trust fund are known as trustees. About 130 years ago, a specialized class of corporate trustee developed, known as the trust company, which has become increasingly important in the handling of trust funds. Many commercial banks have also established trust departments, which perform the same function.

Trustees, whether individual or corporate, have a weighty responsibility to administer the funds under their supervision with complete integrity and to preserve the capital value of the trusts to the best of their ability. Just how the trustees invest the funds under their care depends upon the terms of the will or trust agreement. If the will or trust agreement specifies the manner in which funds are to be employed, or the types of investments to be made, the trustees are obligated to follow these terms and provisions. If the document does not specify the types of investments to be made, the trustee must then observe the state laws governing such fiduciary investments. There has been increasing tendency in recent years on the part of states to permit use of the "prudent man rule" in administering trusts, that is, to permit the trustee to use a certain amount of discretion by selecting those securities which a "prudent man" would be expected to choose in the supervision of funds.

As a general rule, trustees tend to invest in the more conservative type of corporate bonds, preferred and common stocks, as well as in federal, state and municipal obligations. Investments are also made in real estate mortgages backed by substantial property values. In Part 3, trust companies are included in the list of commercial banks.

MUTUAL SAVINGS BANKS

Mutual savings banks are a unique type of financial institution. They are true "banks" in the sense of accepting deposits and making certain kinds of loans and investments; nevertheless, they differ from commercial banks in several ways. The mutual savings banks accept savings deposits, which are essentially long-term commitments, but do not provide for "demand" or checkbook accounts. They may not make the wide variety of commercial and personal loans which is the normal function of commercial banks.

Mutual savings banks rank among the major capital sources in the nation. At the start of 1963, there were 512 savings banks with more than $41,000,000,000 in deposits and over $46,000,000,000 in total assets.

The mutual savings banks are primarily and preeminently a source of funds for *real estate mortgage loans*. This is illustrated by the fact that the savings banks now have some $32,000,000,000 invested in mortgage loans, representing roughly three-quarters of their assets. *Since 1952, the mutual savings banks have channeled a larger volume of savings into federally-underwritten mortgages than any other type of lender.* They are the largest holders of VA loans, and the second largest holders of FHA loans.

Most savings banks tend to make mortgage loans on properties within a 25- to 50-mile radius, but they will also invest in out-of-state mortgage loans. Mortgage loans are made to individual homeowners as well as to owners of commercial and industrial properties.

In addition to mortgages, the mutual savings banks invest in U. S. government securities, state and municipal obligations, and high-grade corporate securities. A detailed list of specific securities in which savings banks may invest are published by the banking departments of the various states in which mutual savings banks are located.

FACTORING, FINANCE AND COMMERCIAL CREDIT COMPANIES

Another source of business capital is represented by the complex of financing organizations which includes factoring, commercial finance, and sales finance companies. Also included in this non-banking financial area are two closely related types of organization: (1) personal finance firms and (2) consumer finance agencies. But since the last two media are chiefly sources of relatively smaller funds or credit and cater to small individual financing needs, they are considered outside the main province of this publication.

The three major groups enumerated above occupy a unique place in the American financial scene. They are outside the realm of commercial banking; yet, they both augment the services of commercial banks and in some areas compete with them. At the same time, they are among the best customers of the commercial banks, for it is from the latter source that these agencies secure much of the funds which they re-lend to to their own clientele.

These non-banking lending organizations have come into existence for various reasons. Perhaps the chief one is that they offer certain services and functions which commercial banks may not, by law or by policy, provide. In many cases, these agencies provide highly specialized kinds of financing, of a type not ordinarily available in the banking system. The impression exists that these organizations will assume financing risks that are substandard or unduly hazardous from a commercial banking standpoint. This is sometimes true, but not predominantly so. In fact, commercial banks, in recent years, have begun to compete more aggressively with these concerns in the "borderline" areas where they can offer the same, or similar, facilities.

As indicated, there are certain classes and kinds of financing which, although unacceptable by commercial bank standards, will be considered by these organizations. It must be remembered that banks lend funds received from their depositors; thus they are under strict legal restraint, as well as a heavy moral responsibility, regarding the handling of such moneys. The non-banking financial organizations have no such responsibility; or, at least, they have a different kind of responsibility. Their capital funds are provided by stockholders or proprietors, who stand in a different position from depositors of a bank. Moreover, these firms secure much of their additional lending capital by borrowing directly from the commercial banking system or from other prime sources. Furthermore, these concerns are permitted wider latitude than is permissible under federal and state banking laws.

Factoring Companies

From an historic standpoint, factoring is the oldest of non-banking institutions, dating back to earliest colonial times. Through the centuries, various changes have occurred in the number and scope of services which factors provide; however, their main function has been to supply financing to business firms through the purchase of accounts receivable. This, in fact, is the essence of factoring, and it is that which distinguishes the factors from other non-banking organizations which also finance receivables.

The factor usually purchases outright the open accounts receivable of its client, thus making funds immediately available. The factor also assumes complete responsibility for collection of the receivables thus purchased and notifies the debtors whose accounts have been assigned that the purchase has transpired. Factoring has long been associated with the textile industry, where it became a widespread practice for mill operators to secure funds through the assignment of their receivables. Gradually, the practice expanded to other fields.

Today there are roughly two dozen of the "old-time" factors in business, some of which have a century or more continuous existence. They are mostly located in New York City, which has long been a factoring center. With these veteran firms, factoring is either their sole business or a principal phase of it. However, a good deal of the factoring today is done by firms which are diversified by having other financing activities.

Factoring is not the most economical method of securing funds, but at least it does provide ready capital in instances where other financing might not be available or feasible. Borrowing costs vary widely with this type of financing depending on many elements involved, notably the amount of funds and the length of time the funds are in use. A study by the Federal Reserve Board in 1957 disclosed that the finance charges in factoring were equivalent to annual lending rates of 6.4 to 45.4 per cent, with a median of 14 per cent. Generally, borrowing costs run between 10 and 24 per cent—expressed in terms of cost per annum—for this type of financing.

Commercial Credit Companies

An important segment of the non-banking financing industry is represented by commercial credit companies, which are also known as discount or finance firms. Such companies differ from factors mainly in that they do not *buy* accounts receivable; furthermore, they usually do not assume the responsibility of collection from the account involved. Essentially, the commercial credit company lends money secured by a pledge of accounts or notes receivable but does not buy them outright.

There are two arrangements under which such financing is provided: (1) the notification basis and (2) the nonnotification basis. Under the notification basis, the commercial credit notifies the account involved that the account has been pledged and directs the debtor to make payment to the commercial credit company. On the nonnotification basis no notification is made to the account, and the borrower assumes the responsibility of collection and ultimate repayment of its loan to the finance company. At present, most commercial credit companies provide funds on the nonnotification basis.

Borrowing costs in nonnotification financing are usually calculated upon the average daily balance outstanding at a stated per diem rate. The prevailing range is about 1/40 to 1/52 of 1 per cent per day. In those instances, which are numerous, where the sum advanced is about 90 per cent of the face value of the account, a rate of 1/40 of 1 per cent per day is approximately 10 per cent per annum. As in other types of financing, actual percentage costs vary here since much depends upon the amount of the funds involved, the time element, and the credit standing of the borrower and the accounts pledged. A borrowing rate equivalent to 10 to 12 per cent per annum is fairly prevalent in non-notification financing.

Although lending on receivables is their distinctive and main activity, many commercial credit concerns today have advanced into other areas such as providing inventory loans, financing installment equipment purchases, and installment consumer sales.

Sales Finance Companies

Sales finance companies specialize in buying installment receivables at a discount; hence, they are also known as "discount" firms. These organizations have provided and continue to provide, a considerable amount of the funds which have made installment selling possible. With the enormous growth of installment selling since the 1920's sales finance firms have grown both in number and affluence; in fact, it is estimated there are well over 1,000 such companies in the United States today. Most of them handle a variety of accounts stemming from the sale of *durable* goods, automobiles, farm equipment, office equipment, machinery, etc., as well as *consumer durables* such as furniture, jewelry, household electrical appliances, etc.

This type of financing is a quick and convenient way for manufacturers or dealers to obtain funds. An automobile dealer or a retail furniture store, for example, sells (or "discounts") the installment contracts received from his customers to the sales finance agency, which pays immediate cash thus augmenting the borrower's working capital. Ordinarily, the customer who purchased the merchandise or equipment is directed to make installment payments to the finance firm.

Today, many of the large commercial credit companies also maintain a department which handles this type of financing. An increasing number of commercial banks have been penetrating this field, offering more competition to the sales finance companies.

Because this field is—and will likely continue to be—so competitive, prospective borrowers should do some judicious "comparison shopping" among the various sources before accepting a final offer. Borrowing costs, generally speaking, are lower today on the average than was the case some 15 or 20 years ago; nevertheless, there is still wide variation. Finance charges are usually quoted as a per cent per month on the unpaid balance. Borrowing costs run the gamut from around 5 to 6 per cent to as much as 8 to 10 per cent. Here, as elsewhere, top-rated borrowers are able to obtain on an annual equivalent basis preferential financing rates.

SAVINGS AND LOAN ASSOCIATIONS

Savings and loan associations (also known as "building and loan" associations) occupy a special place in the banking world. Resembling commercial and savings banks in some respects, they differ fundamentally from them in others. Like banks, these associations accept savings accounts from the public, although such deposits are technically regarded as "shares" in the institution. The income paid to owners of savings accounts (shareholders) is called "dividends"— corresponding to the "interest" paid on a bank account. Usually it is payable in a similar manner, i.e., at a designated rate and on specified dates—quarterly, semiannually, etc.

One of the major differences between savings and loan associations and banks lies in their basic field of operation. Whereas commercial banks are permitted to make a variety of business and personal loans, the associations concentrate on one type of lending—the granting of mortgage loans on residential and nonresidential income-producing property. In this specialized area, the savings and loan associations render a valuable service to the community by helping millions of families to finance the purchase of their homes.

Thus, these mutual associations are one of the prime sources of funds for mortgage financing. The average S & L association invests about 80 to 90 per cent of its assets in mortgage loans; the balance is usually kept in U.S. government securities as a safety and liquidity reserve.

Savings and loan associations are located throughout the United States. Some are insured by an agency of the federal government; others are not. It is noteworthy that several of the largest S & L's are based in California, where they have played an important role in financing the rapid expansion of home building in that state. Some of the oldest and most substantial associations are also established in New York and other eastern cities.

LIFE INSURANCE COMPANIES

Life insurance companies rank high among the financial institutions of the United States, with assets in excess of $134,000,000,000 on January 31, 1963. Insurance companies are important sources of capital not only because of their tremendous resources, but because of the numerous ways in which they can provide funds for diverse purposes. These institutions are a prolific source of capital for individuals, homeowners, farmers, small business firms, and large corporations. The insurance companies also provide substantial amounts of investment money annually to federal, state and local governments. Thus, it can be said that insurance firms provide financing for almost every segment of our economy.

Individual borrowers can secure funds from life insurance firms through personal loans secured by the borrower's life insurance policy. In such instances, a loan is made up to about 80 per cent of the "cash surrender" value of the policy.

Small business financing has become an activity of increasing importance with insurance firms in recent years. Such financing may assume one or more forms: a loan secured by the borrowing company's physical assets; an advance made upon insurance on the life of one or more proprietors; or, in some instances, "private placement" of a note or bond of the borrower for a certain term of years.

Financing of *real estate and mortgages* is another major activity of insurance organizations. Mortgage loans are made to individual homeowners, farmers, business firms, and builders. Among the several classes of non-farm mortgage loans are FHA, NHA, VA and "conventional" mortgages. Moreover, insurance companies invest directly in real estate of many kinds, of which the most popular is income-producing.

Insurance companies are a most important fountainhead of capital to *corporations*. It is noteworthy that over half of the total assets of the insurance industry is invested in common stocks, preferred stocks, and bonds of various kinds. Insurance companies purchase securities in several ways: in the open market, that is, through investment brokers or by direct negotiation with the corporation seeking financing. The latter method, which is known as "private placement," is an increasingly important method in securing corporate funds.

The following table entitled "Investments of U.S. Life Insurance Companies" provides a summary of the various types of and classes of investments held by these institutions.

TABLE 1

INVESTMENTS OF U. S. LIFE INSURANCE COMPANIES

(000,000 Omitted)

	TYPE OF INVESTMENT		ACQUIRED		HELD		CHANGE IN HOLDINGS
			Jan. 1963	Jan. 1962	Jan 31, 1963	Jan 31, 1962	Dec. 1962-Jan. 1963
BONDS	Government	U. S.	$ 490	$ 517	$ 6,312	$ 6,358	$+123
		Canada	141	12	566	294	+139
		Other	—	0	230	188	—
	Non-Guaranteed Federal Agency		15	41	100	119	— 1
	State, Provincial, Local						
	U. S.	Direct & Guaranteed	10	13	1,090	1,101	— 3
		Special Rev. & Other	58	50	2,998	2,830	+ 31
	Foreign	Direct & Guaranteed	49	3	1,360	1,137	+ 48
		Special Rev. & Other	2	—	25	18	+ 2
	World Bank & Other International Agency		2	—	271	244	+ 2
	Railroad	U. S.	2	8	3,542	3,650	— 16
		Foreign	—	—	19	19	—
	Public Utility	U. S.	48	30	16,535	16,210	+ 23
		Foreign	8	1	829	785	+ 7
	Industrial & Miscellaneous						
	U. S.	One Year or Less at Issue	553	517	525	418	+184
		All Other	184	386	28,195	26,673	— 8
	Foreign		58	91	1,847	1,596	+ 29
		TOTAL	1,620	1,675	64,444	61,649	+560
PREFERRED STOCKS	U. S.	Railroad	—	—	64	63	—
		Public Utility	7	3	1,496	1,415	+ 5
		Bank, Trust & Ins.	—	—	18	11	—
		Industrial & Misc.	5	3	665	630	—
	Foreign		—	—	4	4	—
		TOTAL	12	6	2,247	2,123	+ 5
COMMON STOCKS	U. S.	Railroad	—	—	24	27	— 1
		Public Utility	7	6	671	623	+ 6
		Bank, Trust & Ins.	32	15	549	466	+ 33
		Industrial & Misc.	19	24	1,662	1,531	+ 11
	Foreign		1	1	84	69	+ 2
		TOTAL	59	46	2,990	2,716	+ 51
MORTGAGES	Farm		66	65	3,398	3,170	—
	Non-Farm	FHA	122	128	10,309	9,766	+ 52
		NHA	6	6	348	289	+ 5
		VA	48	34	6,397	6,541	+ 3
		Conventional	405	332	26,751	24,633	+163
		TOTAL	647	565	47,203	44,399	+223
REAL ESTATE	Company Used		12	8	1,182	1,141	— 70
	Investment	Residential	—	1	409	413	— 1
		Commercial	21	11	2,502	2,413	+ 98
	Other		3	11	61	51	+ 3
		TOTAL	36	31	4,154	4,018	+ 30
POLICY LOANS			120	121	6,245	5,784	+ 31
CASH			xxx	xxx	1,283	1,293	—128
OTHER ASSETS			xxx	xxx	5,445	5,571	+ 70
TOTAL			$2,494	$2,444	$134,011	$127,553	$+842

Source: Institute of Life Insurance. Totals for U. S. companies estimated on basis of reports from life insurance companies representing over 94% of all assets. The amounts shown represent book values for all items except "Other Assets" and "Total." The change in holdings for the month may sometimes be greater than acquisitions for a particular item due to rounding, write-ups and other adjustments. 1962 figures have been revised.

INVESTMENT COMPANIES

Investment companies represent one of the largest and fastest-growing concentrations of capital in the United States today. There are two kinds of investing companies: the so-called "open end" variety, more popularly known as "mutual funds," and the "closed end" type. Both kinds of organization perform essentially the same function, i.e., investing their stockholders' funds in a diversified portfolio of securities, maintaining constant supervision over these portfolios and distributing dividends and realized capital gains to shareholders.

The growth in investing companies in terms of assets, earnings, and number of shareholders, has been phenomenal. At the close of 1962, investment companies of both varieties had assets totaling $25,000,000,000.

With such substantial assets and with still further gains anticipated for years to come, these institutions are obviously becoming an important reservoir of capital. However, it must be recognized that investment company funds are available only for certain purposes. Investment companies do not make business loans in the sense that commercial banks do, nor do they normally make funds available to small business firms or individuals. Today, the majority of investment companies operate under the provisions of the Investment Company Act of 1940, which lays down basic guidelines of fund management, although the Act does *not* specify the quality, type, or variety of securities in which these companies may invest.

The basic factors determining the type and range of investments made by the individual investment company are the provisions of its corporate charter and its fundamental investment objectives. Despite wide varation concerning investment policies among the individual companies in this field, most of them currently tend to avoid speculative or marginal securities. The bulk of the majority of investment portfolios consists of medium-quality to high-grade corporate issues.

Thus, by the very nature of their operations, the investing companies offer a prime market for corporate securities. Just which securities a given investment company may purchase at a particular time is determined largely by its charter, its basic investment objectives, and various other considerations. Some funds are *diversified,* which means that they will invest in a variety of corporations in different industries. Others are *non-diversified or specialized funds,* and they concentrate their holdings in particular industries such as electronics, chemicals, utilities, natural resources or other specialties. Before approaching any investing company as a prospective source of capital, it is essential to learn as much as possible about the fund's basic investment philosophy and objectives, and to secure a recent prospectus describing the particular fund's investment portfolio.

It is possible to get a general idea of how some of the big funds are investing their resources from a survey recently undertaken by the Investment Company Institute of New York:

"Common stocks of financial institutions, public utilities and oil companies held top positions in mutual fund portfolios in 1962 just as they have for the past decade.

"The Investment Company Institute, in a survey of mutual fund members' holdings in 27 industry groups, reported that stocks of financial institutions, including banks and insurance companies, constituted 15.6 per cent of the total value of common stock holdings.

"This industry group was also first in 1961 with 14.9 per cent of the total value of common stock holdings and second in 1960 with 11.9 per cent.

"Second largest holding among the industry groups, the Institute reported, was public utilities with 14.1 per cent of the total value of common stock holdings. This group was second in 1961 with 13 per cent and first in 1960 with 13.5 per cent.

"Common stocks of oil companies were third among the industry groups in 1962 with 13.4 per cent of the value of common stock holdings. Oil companies were third in 1961 with 10.1 per cent, third in 1960 with 11.3 per cent and first in 1959 with 11.8 per cent.

"Chemical industry common stocks ranked fourth with 5.3 per cent, as they were in 1961 with 6.6 per cent, and in 1960 with 6.3 per cent. Office equipment common stocks ranked fifth in 1962 with 4.7 per cent, fifth in 1961 with 5.3 per cent, sixth in 1960 with 4.5 per cent and 14th in 1959 with 3.2 per cent.

"Others in the top ten with percentage of total value of common stock holdings by mutual funds were: Electrical and electronics equipment, excluding radio and television, 4.4 per cent; automobiles and accessories, excluding tires, 4.1 per cent; retail trade, 3.3 per cent, drugs, 2.9 per cent and metals and mining stocks 2.7 per cent.

"The survey was based on the financial reports of 20 major mutual funds representing 60 per cent of the assets of the industry.

"Changes in ranking from 1961 to 1962 noted by the Institute survey included: Electronic and electrical equipment from eighth to sixth place; retail trade from fourteenth to eighth, and food and beverages from sixth to tenth place.

"The Institute pointed out that changes in the value of common stock holdings in various industries result from several factors. Holdings reflect not only decisions of the professional managers of the mutual funds to purchase or sell various stocks but also the ups and downs of stock prices.

"A percentage rise or decline of an industry holding can be caused by stock prices in an individual industry moving faster or slower than prices in general, or in the opposite direction as well as by changes in the holdings by the mutual funds.

"The Institute noted that the mutual funds surveyed showed wide differences in their common stock holdings, reflecting various management policies and investment objectives. There was no mutual fund that held stocks in all 27 industries, nor was there any one industry represented in the portfolios of all the mutual funds studied.

"These variations are caused by the fact that there are different types of mutual funds, with differing long-term investment objectives. Varying objectives can mean different valuations of particular industries as well as of individual company stocks with an industry.*

INVESTMENT BANKERS AND UNDERWRITERS

One of the prime sources of capital for corporations, municipalities, governments, and other organizations is the investment community. This is a complex of investment bankers, underwriters, brokers, organized exchanges, and unlisted securities markets. The investment community is often referred to as Wall Street, because much of the nation's and the world's financing activity is centered in New York; however, investment banking and brokerage facilities are also available in various other cities from coast to coast, thus comprising a nationwide financing network.

Through the facilities of the investment community, corporations and governmental borrowers raise billions of dollars annually. In 1962, for example, corporate financing in the form of public underwriting amounted to approximately $6,900,000,000. This figure compares with $8,200,000,000 in 1961, and $7,200,000,000 in 1960. The all-time record to date, incidentally, was $9,066,000,000 in 1957. The comparatively lower volume for 1962 is attributed to the severe market decline in the spring

---

* The Investment Company Institute.

of that year, which resulted in the cancellation or deferral of many underwriting plans. However, an impressive recovery in securities markets began in the early months of 1963, which, with an attendant return of investor confidence, has gradually effected healthier conditions in the public underwriting market. Consequently, corporate underwritings for 1963 to 1964 should compare favorably with 1962 results.

The investment community is also the principal medium for large-scale financing by the United States government as well as the various states, cities, towns, villages, school districts, water districts, turnpike authorities, and numerous other agencies which constitute the "public" or governmental borrowing clientele. Foreign governments, municipalities, and corporations also obtain substantial funds each year from the American investment community.

In considering the investment community as a source of financing, it might be helpful to consider the following facts. Investment bankers and underwriters seldom utilize their own funds in providing capital; instead, they perform the very valuable function of securing funds from "outside" sources, which include the general public and investing institutions such as those listed in Part 3 of this book. The bankers obtain funds through the process known as a "public offering" or "public underwriting," which means that they offer the corporation's securities to numerous investors—ordinarily thousands of them. An alternative method of securing funds, which is practicable in some cases but not in others, is the "private placement" arrangement. A "private placement" is the sale of the bonds, notes, common stock or preferred stock of a corporation to one, or a very few, institutional investors such as life insurance companies, corporate pension funds, or other capital sources. Some of the huge corporations make such arrangements directly through their own contacts and facilities, although most of the private placement currently taking place is done through, or with the assistance of, investment bankers or underwriters.

When feasible, the private placement method renders distinct advantages to the corporate borrower. The costs involved are usually considerably less than with "public offerings," because much legal expense and SEC filing charges are thus avoided. Private placements are specifically exempted from the registration provisions of the Securities Act of 1933, whereas public corporate offerings with the exception of issues under $300,000 must be fully registered. Private placements are effected through negotiation, either by the issuer, or more usually by the investment banker, with the institutional investor. Under such circumstances, the financing provisions can be custom-tailored and adapted to the requirements of both investor and issuer to an extent not possible with public issues.

Another distinct advantage of private placements is that such negotiations can be transacted confidentially, since the borrower is able to disclose certain information to the investor institutions which he may not wish to divulge in a public underwriting; or the information may be of such nature that it might not be acceptable under the very stringent regulations covering disclosure of facts in the prospectus required in public issues. Furthermore, when and if the time should come to refinance the initial private placement, to modify the terms, or to secure additional funds from the same source, the flexibility with which such arrangements can be made is truly advantageous.

Considering these benefits, it is not surprising that the private placement method of financing has been gaining in popularity in recent years. According to a survey made by "Investment Dealers Digest," the total volume of funds secured by private placement reached an all-time high of $5,864,785,800 in 1962, compared with the previous record of $5,363,818,672 in 1961. What makes this increase all the more impressive is that the volume of *public underwritings,* as already noted, declined perceptibly in 1962. Many observers predict the significant growth of private placement financing in coming years; however, this does not imply that the public underwriting method will take second place. Each method is suited to particular purposes and specific situations. Consequently, both will continue as important media for obtaining capital funds.

Financing By Public Underwriting

As already noted, the raising of funds by public offerings or public underwritings has been, and still is, one of the prime methods of corporate financing. When corporations come to Wall Street, or more correctly described, the financial community, for funds, they are seeking a different kind of capital than they usually secure from commercial banks or other sources. The financing provided by the investment community is predominantly long-term in nature, whereas that obtained from the commercial banking system is essentially short-term. Furthermore, the funds secured from investment channels become part of the capital structure of the issuing corporation and are reflected as such on the corporation's balance sheet.

Corporate financing via public underwritings has been a time-honored, proven method of securing funds for almost the last two hundred years in Western Europe and the United States, and particularly since 1800 in this country. In the period from about 1800 until the Civil War, the investment bankers of the United States were important agencies in selling to the investing public shares in the many new banks being formed, in railroads, canals, water systems, and various manufacturing industries. Moreover, during the crucial days of the Civil War, the investment bankers played a vital role in helping finance the U.S. Treasury's borrowing operations, as well as meeting the capital needs of private industry. In the decades following the war, the investment community gained enormously in stature, maturity and prestige, and Wall Street—literally and figuratively—began to assume international status.

The era of great industrial growth in the postwar years opened new channels of financing for the nation's underwriters. This was the period of vast expansion for the country's railroads, of the rise and growth of major industries such as steel, gas utilities, large-scale mining and steam power. From the end of the Civil War until the advent of World War I, the nation's investment bankers gained worldwide prominence in raising funds, mostly in the form of stock and bond offerings, for American industry. During World War I, with the need for financing the nation's allies, the investment community became truly international and has remained so ever since. Wall Street began to surpass London as the world's leading investment center soon after World War I, and it has become indisputably the global investment mart since the second World War.

With almost two centuries of experience, the investment community is obviously well equipped to provide capital funds to industry, whether in the form of private placement or public offerings. Regardless of the method used, the fundamental method of securing funds is by the sale of the issuer's (corporation's) securities to outside investors. The securities thus sold are either bonds, notes, common stock, preferred stock, or, sometimes, such specialties as "rights."

"Firm Underwriting" versus "Best Efforts"

When a corporation seeking investment capital approaches an underwriter on prospective financing, the underwriter may offer one of two alternative contractual arrangements. A "firm underwriting" is an arrangement whereby an investment banker, or a syndicate of several banks collaborating, agrees to purchase the entire security issue, contracting to pay the full purchase price (less certain costs and commissions) on a specified date. Firm underwritings are almost always employed in public offering of securities of large corporations, as well as numerous medium-sized and lesser corporations. Approximately 75 per cent of all public offerings in recent years have been firm underwritings.

A quite different contractual basis is the "best efforts" method of underwriting. In contrast with the firm underwriting whereby the underwriter or syndicate virtually guarantees the success of the offering, under the best efforts basis, everything is contingent. The best efforts device is exactly what the term implies i.e., the underwriter (or syndicate) will use his best efforts to assure completion of the financing. He agrees to endeavor to sell the issue to the public in exchange for an option (exclusive) to purchase the issue and an agency (also exclusive) to sell the securities. Under some best efforts terms, the issuer agrees to accept the proceeds from any portion of an issue if the entire issue is not sold. Other best efforts contracts provide that, if the entire issue or a majority of it is not sold, the purchase subscriptions will be refunded to the investors and the entire issue will be cancelled.

Best efforts offerings represent approximately 25 per cent of all public underwritings, but are far less prevalent than prior to World War I. Nowadays, this method is confined mostly to speculative and semi-speculative offerings, as well as other situations where the underwriter may be uncertain as to the possibility of marketing the entire issue. Many of the smaller securities flotations of the "Regulation A" type, of $300,000 or less, are on the best efforts basis.

Technical Aspects of Investment Underwriting

Raising capital through a public underwriting is a complex affair, involving many legals aspects and complications. Thus, when a corporation decides to utilize this method of financing, two fundamental, but indispensable, steps must be taken: first, to secure the services of a competent attorney and accountant, and second, to select a reputable underwriting firm. The utmost care should be taken to ensure that the underwriter selected is professionally competent and reputable in the financial and investment community. As in the selection of any other service, it is a good idea to do some discreet comparison shopping through exploratory talks with more than one prospective underwriter and subsequently to examine outside sources for opinions on the several prospective firms. However, after a firm has been selected and an agreement (even an oral one) has been made, the chosen underwriter thereafter has exclusive agency for the proposed transaction.

The offering of securities to the public is strictly regulated by federal and state law. The Securities Act of 1933, as enacted by Congress, provides for "full and fair disclosure of the character of securities sold in interstate and foreign commerce and through the mail and to prevent fraud in the sale thereof and for other purposes." The main objective of the Act can best be expressed by saying that it requires full, clear, and truthful disclosure of all essential facts pertaining to the offering. Severe penalties are involved for any willful violation of the Securities Act.

To accomplish the goal of such "full disclosure," the law provides for a *prospectus* or printed summary of essential information of the proposed public offering to be made available to the public. For public offerings in excess of $300,000, a detailed, comprehensive document called the "registration statement" is also mandatory.

Exemptions for Certain Small Offerings

Security issues not exceeding $300,000 are given special consideration under federal law. Because of the relative small amounts involved, or the limited nature of such financing, registration is not deemed essential to the public interest or to the protection of investors. The Securities & Exchange Commission has provided for exemption of five types of small offerings which are indicated here:

Regulation A. A general exemption for issues up to $300,000 for issuers. Limited to $100,000 for controlling stockholders.

Regulation A-R. Special exemption for bonds and notes secured by first liens on family dwellings up to $25,000.

Regulation A-M. Special exemption for assessable shares of mining companies up to $100,000.

Regulation B. Exemption for fractional undivided interests in oil or gas rights up to $100,000.

Regulation B-T. Exemption for interests in oil royalty trusts, or similar type of trusts, or unincorporated associations, up to $100,000.

COMMERCIAL PAPER UNDERWRITERS

One of the most convenient and economical methods by which qualified companies can raise short-term funds is through the medium of "commercial paper." This type of financing, which has provided American business firms with operating capital since the early 1800's, is employed by many substantial companies today.

In essence, this method of borrowing is very simple. First, the business firm seeking funds contacts one of the commercial paper underwriters to ascertain whether it qualifies for this kind of financing. It should be emphasized that not all firms qualify for issuance of commercial paper; the borrower must be a well-established business with a strong credit rating; moreover, he must meet certain specifications as to earnings, assets, etc. There are sound reasons why such standards must be maintained. Companies qualified to do this kind of financing represent the "elite" of the business world, which does not necessarily mean they are the largest companies, but rather those whose credit standing is beyond question. When it is considered that this kind of borrowing is done in the form of unsecured promissory notes, it is obvious that the issuer's "promise to pay" must be universally recognized.

After contacting the underwriter, the borrower, if qualified, then arranges to obtain a specified amount of funds. A promissory note for the agreed-upon sum is sold, at a small discount from face value, to the underwriter, who, in turn, resells the note (or notes) to commercial banks, institutions, and other purchasers. Such promissory notes are always for relatively short periods, viz., 30 days, 60 days, 3 months, 6 months, etc. Maturities rarely exceed 9 months, or 270 days, because the essential nature of "commercial paper" is its short duration and self-liquidating character. When the notes come due, the borrower simply repays the underwriter, or, if by prior arrangement, the holder in due course.

This distinctive kind of financing has many advantages, among which are ease and relative simplicity. Flexibility is another desirable feature, since the borrowing operation can be adjusted to meet whatever short-term financing the issuer may require at a given time. Arrangements can be also made to issue new notes for the same amount as the original loan, when the original notes come due. In this manner, the borrower may obtain a "revolving credit," which may by mutual agreement, be extended over lengthy periods of time.

Not the least of the advantages is the relatively low cost of financing. In the great majority of cases, raising funds via commercial paper costs less than obtaining the same sum from commercial banks. Occasionally, the costs may be as much as 25 or 50 per cent below bank rates. It may be asked why this differential exists. There are several reasons. First, as already indicated, companies qualified to issue commercial paper represent an "elite" group in the business world. Thus, as top quality clients, they would be entitled to preferential rates in any event. Secondly, this kind of borrowing does not involve the use of "compensatory balances" which many commercial banks require in granting large commercial loans. Third, there is relatively little overhead or operating cost on the part of the underwriter; thus, the benefits of the economy of operation redound to the borrower.

As cost-saving is one of the chief advantages of this kind of financing, some comments on rate structures are in order at this point. *The short-term commercial paper of the largest, top-rated corporations commands the lowest interest rates in the money market, second only to the U.S. Treasury itself!* The very select issuers of commercial paper, representing the strongest U.S. corporations, are known as "prime borrowers," and thus are entitled to the lowest borrowing rates. Their notes are called "prime commercial paper" in the money market, and they are bought by commercial banks and other institutions. Ordinarily, the rates they pay for borrowing are about one-eighth of a point over paper of comparable maturities of the U.S. Treasury. In other words, Treasury Bills—the government's shortest term paper—set the rates for all other paper in the short-term market, and "prime paper" follows very closely.

Borrowing rates in the short-term money mart fluctuate, within small limits, almost daily. As such minor variations occur, there is a corresponding adjustment, day by day, on the rates of new commercial paper coming to market. The "going rate," or prevailing interest charge, on commercial paper can be quickly and easily ascertained. Each day, leading journals like *The New York Times* and *The Wall Street Journal*, quote the borrowing rate for commercial paper. Virtually every commercial bank in the nation can quote rates upon request.

Needless to say, "prime rates" apply only to "prime borrowers." Other borrowers, even if they qualify for commercial paper financing, must pay correspondingly higher rates since their size and credit standing vary from those of the "prime" concerns.

SMALL BUSINESS INVESTMENT COMPANIES

One of the most significant developments in the capital market in recent years has been the rise of small business investment companies, popularly known as "SBIC's."

For years, one of the major problems of small business has been a shortage of long-term financing for plant, equipment, and other expansion needs. Whereas larger corporations could obtain such funds from investment capital markets, the average small business found it difficult to secure capital from such sources advantageously, if, indeed, it could obtain such funds at all.

In an effort to help relieve this problem, the Small Business Investment Act of 1958 was enacted by Congress. Under this legislation a new government agency, the Small Business Administration, was established, which is authorized to license and regulate a new type of financing institution—small business investment companies.

The number of small business investment companies organized and licensed by the Small Business Administration has grown rapidly in recent years. More than 700 such firms were in operation by the middle of 1963. All indications are that this new form of capital source will become an increasingly important factor in business financing in the years ahead.

Equity Capital Financing of Small Businesses

A major function of a small business investment company is to provide a source of needed equity capital for small business. Equity capital may be provided by an SBIC to an incorporated small business through the purchase of its equity securities—that is, *stocks of any class*, and *bonds or debentures* providing a participation in equity securities either through conversion or through accompanying warrants or options, subject to regulations of the Small Business Administration.

Where *convertible debentures* are used as the instrument of financing a small business, they must:

1. Bear interest and contain such other terms contracted for between the SBIC and the small business. The rate of interest may not exceed the maximum rate permitted by local laws; moreover, where no state limit is fixed, the maximum cost to the borrower shall not exceed a cost approved by SBA.

2. Be callable, in whole or in part, upon three months' notice, under conditions agreed upon between the borrower and the SBIC.

3. Be convertible, at the option of the small business investment company, or a holder in due course, up to and including the effective date of any call by the issuer, into stock of the small business at the sound book value of such stock, determined by the parties at the time of issuance of the debentures. In determining the value of the stock, all pertinent factors are to be considered, including the actual value of the assets of the small business and the relationship of its earnings to its invested capital.

4. Limit conversion privileges to the extent that debentures may not be converted into other equity or debt securities which carry additional conversion rights.

The SBA permits an SBIC to supply capital to a small business by means of any equity financing arrangements. However, SBA prohibits the issuance of additional stock purchase warrants or options and additional conversion privileges on stock or warrants or options obtained through conversion.

Long-Term Loans To Small Business

Small business investment companies may make *long-term loans to incorporated and unincorporated small businesses* in order to provide funds needed for sound financing, growth, modernization and expansion. Long-term loans, as used herein, mean loans with final maturities of not less than 5 years and not more than 20 years. However, this requirement will not preclude the making of *incidental shorter-term loans* under certain conditions when necessary to protect the interests of the investment company.

SBIC's long-term loans must be of such sound value, or so secured, so as to assist repayment reasonably. They may bear interest at rates agreed upon between the SBIC and the borrower. However, the rate of interest may not exceed the maximum rate permitted by local law; where no local limit is fixed, the interest rate charged must be within the rate limits set forth in the SBIC's proposal for a license.

Maturities of these loans as previously indicated may not exceed 20 years, except that the maturity may be extended, or the loan renewed, for additional periods not surpassing 10 years, if the investment company finds that extension or renewal will aid in the orderly liquidation of the loan.

The following specific recommendations for securing financing from one or more of the SBIC's are from a publication of the Small Business Administration:

Obtaining SBIC Financing

When considering a small business investment company as a source of funds for your business, you should become familiar with the Small Business Investment Act of 1958 and the SBA regulations issued under the Act. If you plan a public stock offering, you should know also the requirements of the Investment Act of 1940 and the Securities Act of 1933. Furthermore, you should be familiar with procedures to be followed in obtaining financing from an SBIC, and with the financial instruments (notes, debentures, capital stock, etc.) that will be involved in obtaining financing. A knowledge of the advantages that expansion of your operations and access to management skills may bring to you is also a necessity.

Because the SBIC to which you may go for funds will require specific knowledge about your operation, you should know your own company's financial position and requirements well. It would be advisable to consult your staff accountants, engineers, counsel, banker and others. Be well prepared before entering into negotiations with an investment company by having a complete knowledge of your own organization—its condition, needs, and future planning—and detailed justification (including specific purposes) for the desired financing.

The Borrower's Relationship With The SBIC

When you consult with a small business investment company, its management will discuss with you the size standards and other criteria which determine whether your firm qualifies as a "small business" for financing under the Small Business Investment Act. They will study your financing requirements and the prospect of your meeting obligations which they may suggest as a plan for financing your needs.

The Small Business Administration will not supervise any negotiations between you and the investment company. Furthermore, any agreement you subsequently reach will be strictly between you and the SBIC. Like your own firm, it is a private enterprise, organized for profit, and serves much the same function for small businesses as an investment banking house does for large corporations. Consequently, any transaction undertaken will be purely a private business arrangement between you and the company, and will have no direct connection with SBA or any other agency of the federal government.

The SBA's functions in this program are:

1. To license the private investment companies to operate in accordance with the Small Business Investment Act of 1958.

2. To furnish them with funds which they may require under the Act.

3. To regulate their activities.

In approaching a small business investment company for financing, you should know what types of financing are available, which ones the SBIC is permitted to offer, and what other services it is permitted to render under the Small Business Investment Act of 1958.

Under the Act and SBA's regulations, an SBIC may finance your small business through the following methods (including combinations thereof):

1. By the purchase of your convertible debentures.

2. By the purchase of capital stock in your company with or without stock purchase warrants to acquire additional stock.

3. By the purchase of debt securities with or without warrants to purchase stock.

4. Any other acceptable instrument of equity financing.

5. Through long-term loans to your business.

If you need more funds than one small business investment company can extend, it may be possible for the SBIC to have other SBIC's participate in a loan or in purchase of your debentures.

Convertible Debenture Financing

Debentures purchased from you by a small business investment company are to be convertible (up to the face value of the debenture) at the SBIC's option into stock of your company at a price per share determined by you and the SBIC, when the debentures are issued.

This conversion figure is described in the Small Business Investment Act as the "sound book value" of the stock and may consider a comparison of net assets to earnings and other relevant criteria.

The debentures must state a minimum maturity of five years but must also contain a clause which permits the borrower to prepay them on any interest date, on three months' notice of intention. However, the holder of debentures may convert these into stock up to the actual "call" date.

All other terms of the convertible debenture plan such as interest rate, plan of repayment and minor details must be agreed upon through negotiation between the borrower and the SBIC.

The SBIC is authorized to require, as a condition of any indebtedness, that the borrower does not enter into any "outside" debt financing during the term of the obligation without giving the SBIC the first opportunity to provide such financing. However, the SBIC must permit the borrower to purchase on "open account," and establish similar short-term credit, subject to agreement between borrower and the company. Other standard terms and conditions as to the borrower's operations and management may be required by the SBIC to protect its investment.

In considering the convertible debenture type of financing, the borrower's counsel should advise fully of state and other laws concerned, and the borrower should be well prepared technically in other respects as well to make an effective presentation to the investment company.

In order to issue convertible debentures, the borrowing firm must be a corporation. Therefore, if it is a partnership or a proprietorship and does not wish to incorporate a long-term loan is the only means of financing available to it from SBIC's.

Stock Warrants Involved In Some Cases

Capital stock sold by the borrowing company to an SBIC may constitute the entire equity the SBIC may have in the borrower's company. It is possible, however, that the SBIC will require that the stock carry warrants to purchase additional stock in the business at a price or prices set by mutual agreement.

It should be remembered that in the purchase of a straight equity in a company for the funds supplied, the SBIC is taking a risk when it assumes that the company will prosper sufficiently to justify the investment in capital stock.

If the SBIC wishes to supply capital for debt securities carrying a low interest rate, it may wish the debt securities to carry warrants to purchase capital stock at agreed prices.

Stock Options

In the purchase of equity securities, debt securities, or other securities evidencing a debt, the SBIC may wish to include options to purchase stock in amounts and at prices considered agreeable. These are legitimate transactions, which may be contracted for on agreed conditions.

In no case, however, may a transaction between the SBIC and the small business be consummated where securities carrying conversion privileges into stock or other instruments include *additional* conversion rights.

Long-Term Loans

If the borrowing firm is incorporated, and an SBIC makes a *loan* to it (as opposed to convertible debenture financing) the SBIC may not acquire stock or other proprietary interest in the corporation except through foreclosure on any equity securities pledged as collateral.

If the borrowing firm is *not* incorporated, only long-term loans (5 to 20 years) under Section 305 of the Small Business Investment Act are available to it. In this situation the borrower would probably be asked to arrange reasonable security and a mutually satisfactory schedule of repayment. The Small Business Administration's regulations provide that the borrower must be permitted to prepay all or any part of such loans on any interest payment date, if it should wish to do so. Prepayment penalties may, however, be included in financing contracts.

Other SBIC Services

Regardless of whether the borrower is incorporated, and of the type of financing it may arrange, its financing relationship with the investment company would give it access to management skills possessed by representatives of the SBIC. These skills may be very important to the borrower as it grows and enters new markets and areas, and encounters new competitors. The borrower should, therefore, inquire into the management consultant and advisory services which the SBIC is prepared to offer (for which a fee may be charged). The investment company may wish to put a representative on the borrowing company's board of directors to advise and consult with it, as well as to keep fully informed of the borrower's progress. Many small businesses may welcome and profit by such an association.

Limitations on Financing

It should be stressed that the Small Business Administration does not normally permit a financing arrangement under which the SBIC will acquire equity ownership exceeding 49 per cent of the business being financed.

A small business may not re-lend funds obtained from a small business investment company, or re-lend funds released in its accounts as a result of SBIC financing. Therefore, if the borrowing concern is a loan or mortgage company, or other type of credit or financing organization, it is not eligible for financing from an SBIC.

PENSION FUNDS

One of the great changes in the American way of life in this generation is that many millions of people are now covered by pension or retirement programs. Significantly, millions more are being added to the pension rolls annually. Consequently, the combined pension funds of the United States have grown into a financial colossus in recent years.

A report issued by the Office of Welfare and Pension Plans of the Department of Labor discloses that there were 120,510 welfare and pension benefit plans in operation at the end of the calendar year 1960 (latest period for which full data were compiled). Assets of these systems totaled $33,400,000,000 at the close of 1960. Moreover, reserves held by insurance companies to guarantee payments under insured pension and benefit retirement plans amounted to $18,800,000,000. The aggregate figure of $52,200,000,000 represented a gain of some $4,500,000,000 over 1959.

Already representing a huge concentration of capital, the pension funds continue to grow at an average rate of about 10 per cent per annum. There are indications that this pace of growth is likely to be maintained for some years to come. Within another decade, the pension treasuries—already greater in assets than all the mutual savings banks of the nation—may be approaching the life insurance companies in respect to total capital controlled.

Although there are many types of pension funds, the two main divisions (for the purposes of this publication) are corporate pension funds and labor union pension funds. Both types are covered in Part 3.

Pension funds are among the largest actual and potential sources of major capital in our economy today. Most of the pension treasuries invest their trusteed funds in relatively conservative securities: government, state, and local bonds; high-grade corporate securities; mutual funds, etc. A number have become substantial investors in real estate and mortgages. In some cases, notably the large labor union funds, the construction of low-rental housing has been undertaken not only as a source of income but to benefit members of the union.

It should be noted that labor unions control substantial capital in the form of cash and other assets in *their treasuries and special funds, in addition to the holdings in their pension programs.* The unions have become increasingly wealthy in the last two decades, and the capital under their control continues to amass. Therefore, a list of labor unions and other labor organizations, designating treasurers and other financial officers, has been included as an adjunct to the pension fund list in Part 3.

FOUNDATIONS AND CHARITABLE TRUSTS

Although not popularly known, the thousands of charitable trusts, foundations, and benevolent funds have become huge reservoirs of capital. In fact, these agencies have assumed a significant economic and financial role. Not only have the trusts and foundations grown in number, but in assets controlled, investments, as well as in other respects. According to data compiled by the Internal Revenue Service, there were 45,124 tax-exempt foundations at the close of 1960 (latest year available), compared with 12,295 at the end of 1952. The present total, according to best estimates, exceeds 46,000.

Numerically, the great majority of these foundations and trusts are relatively small, mostly local, and established for specified limited purposes. Conversely, about 500 such institutions—or a little more than 1 per cent of the total—are of appreciable size, with assets running in the multimillions and, in some cases, in the billions. Issued in December, 1962, a report by the Select Committee on Small Business of the House of Representatives covers 534 foundations and trusts with assets of $10,000,000,000 at the close of 1960.

As a source of capital, trusts and foundations are unique. Unlike any other financial institution, the benevolent funds have not been established for commercial lending or investing. Primarily, they exist to perform a benevolent community service. The foundations annually distribute considerable sums in the form of grants to charitable programs, hospitals, health improvement projects, youth benefits, scientific research, educational institutions, and multifarious public benefits.

In approaching foundations or charitable trusts as prospective capital sources, the first thing to ascertain is the main interest, or group of interests, of the particular fund in question. Relatively few foundations are really identical in their areas of interest. Rather, this is a field distinguished by a diversity of interests; in fact, there are practically as many funds as there are areas of interest or specified fields of service.

Part 3 of this book lists a selected group of foundations and charitable trusts, representing the largest such entities prevalent today. All the funds selected have assets of approximately $10,000,000 and upward. The areas of interest for each fund as far as can be ascertained are summarized under the caption "Main Purposes." Although these summaries indicate the general area of interest, they are not completely descriptive of the individual foundation's range of interest in every case. Actually, a number of the funds have interests which transcend the brief descriptions offered, particularly regarding the larger foundations and trusts.

If the basic area of interest, as shown by the caption, corresponds to the object for which funds are sought, the seeker of funds should then direct an inquiry to the financial officer of the fund whose name is given (in most instances) requesting fuller information on the various fields of endeavor in which the fund is interested. After receiving and studying this broadened information, the person or group seeking funds can then submit the proposal more effectively.

In addition to their benevolent activities, the charitable trusts and foundations also serve as a huge source of funds for investments, financing, and loans of various kinds. The aforementioned report of the Select Committee on Small Business of the House of Representatives shows that the foundations employ their funds in diverse investments: government, state and municipal bonds; corporate obligations; preferred and common stock; real estate and mortgages; sale/leasebacks of real estate properties; and loans of various kinds. Some of the foundations lend money to individuals; others to corporations and business firms; and still others to foreign corporations and governments.

COLLEGES, UNIVERSITIES AND CHARITABLE INSTITUTIONS

Colleges, universities, and other "endowed" institutions in the aggregate control billions of dollars in liquid funds. Therefore, a list of such institutions with endowments exceeding $1,000,000 is included in Part 3 of this book. Often, such institutions are prime markets for seasoned investment securities, private placements, and special financing.

The financial resources of the endowed institutions can best be ascertained by noting two essential items: its endowment and its "gifts for capital purposes." The figure on endowments is occasionally indicated by its book value or by market value of its investments; in some cases, by both.

Also included is a list of charitable annuity societies and major fraternal benefit organizations. Organizations of both types are sources of funds for conservative investments.

CHAMBERS OF COMMERCE AND INDUSTRIAL FOUNDATIONS

Chambers of Commerce and similar trade development groups have also become significant sources of capital for certain purposes in the years following World War II. By definition a Chamber of Commerce is a cooperative business group which has as its function the promotion of trade and business for a particular industry, community, or area.

Chambers of Commerce sometimes make direct loans or advances to business men or companies seeking to locate in their area of activity, or they may render financial assistance to established local firms wishing to expand their operations. As a general rule, though, Chambers of Commerce are indirect rather than direct capital sources, since they usually secure funds for borrowers from other sources in the community. Chambers of Commerce sometimes contact numerous local affluent citizens to form a sort of investment syndicate to finance a new company coming into the area or to help an existing firm to acquire new plants and equipment.

In the past decade or two, a special kind of financing agency at the local community level has emerged—the industrial foundation. Usually, these foundations are created by the local Chamber of Commerce or work closely with it.

Industrial foundations are privately sponsored community agencies which make investments out of their own funds, bring enterprises in need of capital to sources of funds seeking investment, or otherwise aid business in obtaining money. For the most part, they are nonprofit organizations. Stockholders and whole communities benefit from their operations through increased business generated by new payrolls and other new or additional business expenditures.

Extent and Use of Industrial Foundations

The use of the industrial foundation type of community industrial financing program has assumed enormous proportions in recent years.

This type of industrial financing is not new, however, since several foundations have been in operation for more than 20 years. The rapid increase in the number of foundations indicates the emphasis currently being placed on community financing programs by many cities in their desire to acquire new payrolls. The amazing success of many foundations is responsible for the increased activity in this field.

Business executives planning plant locations are attracted by cities that have materially and publicly expressed their desire for new industry. Although some of these executives do not intend to accept aid from any foundation, they feel that the very existence of a foundation is prima facie evidence that their enterprise would be welcomed and accorded loyal support by the community. Others are seeking plant sites already developed to the point where paving, grading, utilities, and railroad sidings are provided. Many firms do not want to invest money in brick and mortar; they want to lease their buildings for long periods of time.

Industrial foundations provide for such firms by *building or buying suitable plants* which they lease to new industry. Other foundations *provide loans* to firms by accepting a type of risk more marginal than that desired by banks, and some foundations also lend for longer periods and in larger amounts in ratio to the value of security than is customary with banks.

Services Provided

In realizing their primary purpose of attracting new industries or financing the expansion of enterprises already located in the community, industrial foundations provide the following services:

Buying, developing, and selling industrial sites. Many communities have experienced difficulty in finding suitable industrial sites at reasonable prices after a prospective industry has indicated a strong interest in locating in their city. The asking price usually spurts upward when the landowner learns that some company is interested in his land. Consequently, communities occasionally lose new industries to competing cities.

The foundation that owns good industrial land is in a strong position to quote attractive sales prices immediately to a prospective manufacturer. This is advantageous to both the community and the new producer. Neither party need delay nor terminate negotiations because of lack of land at a satisfactory price.

Buying and building plants for lease or sale. Most of the foundations erect buildings for lease or for sale. The financial terms of the contracts are almost always negotiated with each enterprise, thus varying in their details. A number of foundations lease with option to purchase. These arrangements are similar to those described in the sale and lease-back deals practiced by insurance companies.

Some foundations help industries by contracting for a lower rate of return on their plant investment than would be customary through ordinary business channels. A few foundations even offer free use of their buildings to new industries.

The foundations that provide buildings for industry through lease arrangements are performing a business service. Numerous business firms either cannot obtain the capital for plants or do not wish to tie up their money in real estate. By obtaining their plants on a lease basis, these firms have more money available as working capital and may charge off their rental payments as operating expenses, a procedure which may reduce their income taxes. In addition to making possible increased payrolls for the community, the average foundation is earning a return on its investment.

Providing funds for loan to or investment in industries. The industrial foundations that lend funds to industry usually do so by making outright loans, or by purchasing stock in the aided firm. One advantage of the direct loan method is that repayments are usually made over a period of time. The foundation has incoming funds for reinvestment more quickly than if it had to wait for repurchase of the stock. An advantage of the stock purchase method is that the value of the stock increases as the business prospers. The risk of failure, however, may deter the manager of the foundation from assuming ownership obligations.

Funds lent to new industry are generally used to buy land or buildings. Funds lent to established industry are used primarily for refinancing, supplementing working capital and purchasing new plant equipment.

Giving managerial, engineering, and other counseling services to small business. Most firms, and small enterprises in particular, consider it almost impossible to excel in all phases of management which are essential for efficient and profitable operations. An industrial foundation is able to provide expert advice and offer profitable suggestions to such firms by pooling the knowledge of the businessmen of the community.

In performing these business functions, the industrial foundations are not encroaching upon a bank function. Industrial foundations are organized to take risks that no bank is prepared to encounter. Loans are usually for a longer period than banks are able or willing to make. Furthermore, they are ordinarily for a higher percentage of the value of the property than banks consider reasonable. In dealing with a young business, payments may cover little more than the interest charges during the first year. The business can, in this way, stretch its working capital to the utmost, which it cannot do in borrowing from the typical bank. Moreover, banks hesitate to grant such loans because, if the business should fail, vacant factory property might become a problem.

In addition to the real estate and lending operations of the foundations, many community agencies *give subsidies in the form of free land, free use of buildings, or free water and other utilities.* Some states and cities have laws which enable foundations to offer exemption from property taxes.

Financial Policies of Industrial Foundations

The most common methods utilized by foundations to protect their investments involve taking a mortgage on the land, buildings, or machinery; requiring a representative of the foundation to be elected to the firm's board of directors; limiting the amount of funds that can be invested in any one firm; and limiting loans to a maximum percentage of the paid-in capital of the assisted firm.

The funds of a foundation are usually raised by solicitation of everyone in the community or of selected businessmen. The three principal methods of payment employed are subscriptions payable in cash when the full capital amount is subscribed; subscriptions payable in cash upon call; or subscriptions payable periodically in agreed amounts.

The typical foundation is a nonprofit corporation. Nonprofit foundations measure success not in dividends to stockholders but in the payrolls developed or maintained within the area. Many of them operate, as nearly as possible, on a cost basis in order to make the best contracts with industry.

The added funds obtained from business transactions are usually plowed back into the foundation. Over a period of time the capital of the foundation is increased considerably, thereby enabling a larger scope of operations without requiring another campaign for funds.

Industrial foundations have directed the final selection of a surprising number of plant locations in recent years. Assistance to local industry has enabled a large number of firms to expand; consequently it has contributed to greatly increased payrolls for the community.

TRADE AND INDUSTRY ASSOCIATIONS

Somewhat similar to Chambers of Commerce is another type of cooperative trade group, the trade and industry associations. A trade or industry association generally represents companies within a particular industry or a particular market, and works to advance the interests of its constituents. Some trade associations are local or regional, whereas others operate on a national or even international scale. The larger associations which maintain offices in Washington or New York, usually carry on substantial public relations programs on behalf of their constituents.

Trade associations can occasionally provide capital assistance to organizations in their respective fields of operation, or in the particular market or industry they serve. Usually, however, they are indirect sources of financial assistance. The executive secretary or similar official of a trade association is a person normally in touch with financial interests and can sometimes be helpful in arranging financing for firms in the particular industry he represents. As a general rule, however, it must be recognized that a trade association will not provide capital or other assistance to one company which may prejudice its competitors in the same line of business. Usually financial aid is extended with the object of promoting the interests of the industry as a whole. Periodically there are some exceptions to this rule particularly in the cases of smaller firms with special problems.

UNITED STATES GOVERNMENT SOURCES OF CAPITAL, CREDIT AND FINANCIAL GUARANTEES

The United States government, comprising various departments, agencies, and federal corporations, is literally the largest business enterprise in the world. The government is also the greatest banker in history, providing capital and credit, guarantees and financial aids, for innumerable purposes, to the extent of billions of dollars each year.

As a result of Congressional legislation and executive orders, chiefly over the past 30 years, a vast complex of lending and financing agencies has been established, which are direct and indirect sources of funds for individuals, business firms, banks, foreign trade groups, farmers, and international development projects.

Some of the more important agencies providing capital or credit are described in the following pages.

Commercial, Industrial, and Financial Loans

The Federal Reserve System. The Federal Reserve System consists of a Board of Governors (7 members), the 12 Federal Reserve banks and their 24 branches, and some 6,100 member banks. The principal loan function of the Federal Reserve banks is to extend credit to member banks. However, the Reserve banks also act as fiscal agents under the Board's Regulation V and the Defense Production Act of 1950 in a loan guarantee program to expedite defense contracts.

V-LOANS. The purpose of this type of loan is to facilitate and expedite the financing of contractors, subcontractors, and other persons having contracts or engaged in operations deemed necessary by the guaranteeing agencies (Departments of Army, Navy, Air Force, Interior, Agriculture, Commerce, the General Services Administration, Atomic Energy Commission, and National Aeronautics and Space Administration) for the procurement of materials or the performance of services for national defense.

Terms. Loans are actually made by private banks, with a designated portion guaranteed by the procurement agency most concerned. The guaranteed portion can run up to 100 per cent. The fee is based on a sliding scale, making it advantageous to request as small a guarantee as possible.

EMERGENCY FINANCING. The regional Federal Reserve banks are also authorized to *lend directly to business enterprises* where the latter cannot get money from the usual sources on reasonable terms. These loans, which are presently limited to five years or less, are for working capital purposes only. The loans are available only to established businesses. New concerns cannot be accommodated.

The regional Federal Reserve banks may also enter into commitments with commercial banks and other financial institutions to participate in their business loans. This means that if a local bank cannot make a loan on its own, it may be able to do so in cooperation with one of the regional Federal Reserve banks.

Treasury Department. Loans under Section 302 of the Defense Production Act for materials and services for national defense can be made upon certificate of essentiality issued by the director of the Office of Emergency Planning. Loans under Section 409 of the Federal Civil Defense Act for projects necessary for civil defense purposes can be made only upon the issuance of a certificate of necessity by the secretary of Defense.

Federal Home Loan Banks. Under the supervision of the Federal Home Loan Bank Board, 11 district Federal home loan banks fulfill the reserve credit needs of some 4,800 member savings and loan associations, cooperative banks, and savings banks. The funds of these district banks come largely from their capital (which is owned by the member institutions), the sale of obligations in the market, and deposits of excess cash of their members. *Purpose:* The district banks lend only to their member institutions to meet the seasonal and emergency credit requirements of these institutions and to maintain an adequate flow of home loan funds in every state.

Terms: Long term loans (up to ten years) of member institutions of the Federal Home Loan Bank System are secured by either home mortgages or government bonds. Short-term loans for periods up to one year may be so secured or simply unsecured. Interest rates vary in the district banks.

Where to Apply: Member institutions of the Federal Home Loan Bank System may apply for loans to their district federal home loan banks.

Small Business Administration. The role of the Small Business Administration in licensing and regulating small business investment companies, as sources of capital, has been previously described in this publication. In addition to the financing which qualified small business firms can obtain from the SBIC's, it is possible to secure funds directly from the SBA under certain specified conditions. The following is a summary of the more usual circumstances under which direct assistance can be obtained from the SBA:

BANK PARTICIPATION LOANS. Through its bank participation plan, SBA cooperates with private lending institutions in meeting the credit needs of small firms. Often a bank is willing to make a loan to a small firm if SBA participates in it, i.e., purchases (immediate participation) or agrees to purchase on demand (deferred participation) a share of it. SBA may participate up to 90 per cent of the amount of the loan. This participation may be immediate or deferred, as the bank may elect. The agency cannot enter into an immediate participation, however, if a deferred participation is available.

In an immediate participation loan, the agency purchases immediately from a bank, or sells to a bank, a certain percentage of a loan which has been approved by both it and the bank. The loan may be serviced either by the bank or by the Small Business Administration.

In the case of a loan in which the agency agrees to participate on a deferred basis, the participating financial institution makes and administers the entire loan, with the SBA agreeing to purchase from the bank, at any time during a stated period, a fixed percentage of the then-outstanding balance.

Terms: SBA business loans generally are repayable in regular installments, usually monthly, including principal and interest. Interest is charged only on the actual amount borrowed, and for the actual time the money is outstanding. All or any part of the loan may be repaid without penalty before it is due.

The maximum maturity of an SBA business loan is ten years; however, working capital loans generally are not made for longer than six years.

Maximum loan maturities and interest rates for SBA loans are established by Congressional limitations. The maximum term on regular SBA business loans, at the time of printing this book, is ten years. A term less than permitted by statute may be applied to loans used for working capital and in some other instances. The maximum interest rate on regular SBA business loans, at this printing, is 5½ per cent, with a minimum of 5 per cent permitted only in the event a participating lender reduces its rate to 5 per cent or less.

A private lender may set a higher interest rate than is permitted by SBA on its share of a participation loan, if the rate is legal and reasonable. It also may set a higher rate than SBA on its share of a deferred participation loan, the higher rate on the SBA share to apply until SBA is called upon to purchase its agreed-to share. If a private institution sets a lower rate than SBA's statutory rate on its share, the interest rate on the SBA portion shall be the same as that of the lender. However, in no event may the SBA rate be less than that permitted by statute.

A lower SBA interest rate on business loans is permitted in certain "redevelopment areas" designated in accordance with the Area Redevelopment Act (PL 87-27), and in "areas of substantial labor surplus" designated by the Department of Labor.

Full particulars on maximum maturities and interest rates are obtainable from the nearest SBA field office.

Where To Apply: All applications for business loans should be filed with the Small Business Administration's field offices. (See list of SBA field offices in Part 3.) Financial specialists in these offices are available to discuss financial problems with small business owners and managers and to assist them in preparing and filing loan applications.

Amount: The maximum SBA share in a bank participation loan to any one borrower is $350,000. Exceptions to the $350,000-limitation are loans made to corporations formed by "pools" or groups of small business concerns (1) to obtain raw materials, equipment, inventory or supplies for use by members of the group, or (2) to obtain the benefits of research and development for the members of the group, or (3) to establish facilities for such purposes. The maximum pool loan is $250,000 multiplied by the number of small firms which have formed and capitalized the pool corporation. (The interest rate on pool loans is 5 per cent on the share which the SBA has provided.)

DIRECT LOANS. Where a private lending institution will not make the full loan and will not participate, SBA may make a direct loan. Terms for direct loans, including repayment, maturity, interest, and amount, are the same as for bank participation terms. Similarly, applications for direct loans should be filed at the SBA's field offices.

DISASTER LOANS. Three types of disaster loans are granted:

a. *General Disaster:* This type of loan is made to individuals, business concerns (including proprietorships, partnerships, corporations, cooperatives, or other business enterprises), and nonprofit organizations such as churches and charitable institutions, to repair and rebuild homes and businesses, which have suffered physical damage from floods, tornadoes, hurricanes, and similar catastrophes, and whose location has been declared a "disaster area" *by the Administrator of the Small Business Administration* for purposes of receiving financial assistance, provided they have suffered tangible business or nonbusiness property loss, whether real or personal, as a result of such catastrophe.

Loans will *not* be made to repair or replace damaged or destroyed summer or winter cottages, camps, lodges, or other residential property occupied by the owner exclusively for recreation or relaxation. However, if the property is primarily rental property constituting an important source of income for the owner, a rehabilitation loan will be considered.

b. *Drought and Excessive Rainfall:* Such loans are made to assist small business concerns which have suffered economic injury due to drought or excessive rainfall and whose location has been designated a "disaster area" by the President or the Secretary of Agriculture as a result of excessive rainfall or drought, provided they can show substantial economic injury resulting from such causes.

Farmers and stockmen are not eligible for disaster loans from SBA, but should apply instead to theFarmers' Home Administration.

c. *Displaced Business Loans:* Disaster loans of this type may be made when a determination has been made by the SBA that a small business concern has suffered, or will suffer, substantial economic injury as a result of displacement by a federally-aided urban renewal or highway construction program, or by other construction conducted by or with funds provided, in part or whole, by the federal government.

Bank Participation Disaster Loans: The SBA may participate with private lending institutions in disaster loans on an immediate or deferred basis and to the same extent as in the business-loan program. The SBA share may not exceed 90 per cent.

Terms: All three types of disaster loans generally are to be repaid in equal monthly installments, including interest, usually beginning not later than 5 months after date of the note. The final maturity of a loan is based on the borrower's ability to repay, but by law may not exceed 20 years.

The interest rate on SBA loans made as a result of damage suffered from a physical disaster or because of economic injury due to drought or excessive rainfall is 3 per cent per annum. When a bank participates with SBA in a disaster loan for the purpose of home repair or construction, the interest rate on both the SBA and bank portion of the loan is limited to 3 per cent per annum. However, on other than home loans, the bank may fix the rate on its portion within reasonable limits.

Although displaced business disaster loans may likewise be for 20 years, interest rates are established on a statutory formula based on the average annual interest rate on all interest-bearing obligations of the Treasury plus ¼ of 1 per cent. Interest on these loans, at time of printing this Aid, is 3½ per cent. A bank participating in this type of loan may likewise charge a higher rate of interest on its share, provided the rate is reasonable.

Amount: There is no limit on the amount of an SBA disaster loan. However, for a general disaster, *a loan cannot be for more than the actual tangible loss* suffered as a result of the disaster, less any amount the disaster victim has recovered from insurance or obtained from any other source such as the American Red Cross for purposes of rehabilitation. For drought or excessive rainfall disaster, loans may be used to provide ordinary working capital, to replenish normal inventories, and to pay financial obligations (except bank loans) which the borrower would have been able to meet had it not been for the loss of revenue resulting from the disaster conditions in his area.

LOANS under the Small Business Investment Act of 1958, as amended. This Act provided for the lending of funds to development companies and small business investment companies:

a. *Development Company Loans:* The SBA is authorized to make loans to assist small business under a program designed to stimulate the flow of private equity capital and long-term financing of the operations, growth, expansion and modernization of small business concerns.

Section 501 of the Act authorizes SBA to make loans to state development companies. The proceeds of these loans are to be used only to provide equity capital or make long-term loans, or both, to small business concerns. A Section 501 loan may be made for a period of 20 years, with interest at 5 per cent per annum. The total amount of loans may equal the total amount borrowed from all other sources.

Section 502 of the Act authorizes SBA to make loans for plant construction, conversion, or expansion, including the acquisition of land, to state and local government companies, either directly or in participation with banks or other lending institutions. The proceeds of such loans must be used solely to assist an identifiable small business concern. Loans of this type made to a development corporation are limited to $350,000 for each small business concern assisted; the maturity may not exceed 25 years, with interest at 5½ per cent per annum, provided, however, that where the interest on the share of the participating bank or other institution is less than 5½ per cent, then the rate on SBA share will be the same, but not less than 5 per cent.

Where a Section 501 or 502 loan is made subsequent to April 4, 1961 to a state or local development company for the benefit of a small business concern which will use the plant in the establishment or operation of its business located in an area of substantial labor surplus, the interest rate on such a direct loan to the development company and on SBA's share of such a loan made in participation with another lending institution shall be 4 per cent per annum.

Full particulars are available in SBA field offices.

Maritime Administration. This Administration is a source of financing for various marine purposes.

INSURED LOANS. The Maritime Administration insures construction loans and/or mortgage loans to aid the private shipowner in the financing of construction, reconstruction, or reconditioning of vessels. When such insured loans are made to a United States shipowner by a private financing institution for the construction, reconstruction, or reconditioning of vessels, the Maritime Administration is authorized to insure 75 per cent or 87½ per cent of the total cost according to eligibility under the law. Interest rates charged on such loans may not be more than 5 per cent, except in special circumstances when no more than 6 per cent may be charged. Security is a preferred ship mortgage. The maximum mortgage period is 20 years for tankers and other liquid bulk carriers, and 25 years for other vessels. Eligible vessels under the authority of the Maritime Administration include all types of commercial vessels, except fishing vessels which are under the jurisdiction of the Bureau of Commercial Fisheries, Department of Interior. *Where to Apply:* Maritime Administration, Washington 25, D. C.

DIRECT LOANS. Mortgage aid is authorized by direct loans from the Maritime Administration for the construction, reconstruction and reconditioning of vessels to be used in the foreign commerce of the United States; however, appropriations for such loans have not been available for several years. *Where to Apply:* Maritime Administration, Washington 25, D. C.

Area Redevelopment Administration. The Area Redevelopment Act (P.L. 87-27) provides for loans and grants to businesses or public bodies in designated redevelopment areas. Such assistance is intended to stimulate new permanent employment, thereby alleviating unemployment and underemployment. *Where to Apply:* Administrator, Area Redevelopment Administration, Washington 25 D.C.

Commercial and Industrial Loans: Under Section 6 of the Act these may be for as long as 25 years. Current interest rate is 4 per cent. Maximum participation by ARA is 65 per cent of aggregate project cost. At least 5 per cent of such cost is to be supplied by nongovernmental sources as equity capital, and not less than 10 per cent of such cost is to be supplied by the state, local political subdivision thereof, or other area organization nongovernmental in character. Funds from non-federal sources which comprise not less than 15 per cent of the aggregate project cost must be subordinated to federal financial assistance and are repayable only after such obligation has been retired. Assistance is provided only after evidence of nonavailability of funds elsewhere at reasonable terms. Funds for operating capital are prohibited and funds for machinery and equipment are provided only if there is a demonstrated need.

Public Facility Loans and Grants: Under Section 7 of the Act, public facility loans may be for as long as 40 years. Current interest rate is 3⅝ per cent. Public facility grants may be provided under Section 8. Such loans and grants are to provide needed public facilities upon which business expansion and resulting new permanent employment depend. Grants are limited to that portion of a project which cannot be supported by a loan.

Other Assistance: The Act provides for occupational retraining and technical assistance as may be required to accomplish its basic aims.

Agricultural Loans

Farm Credit Administration (Cooperative Farm Credit System). The Farm Credit Administration supervises and coordinates a cooperative credit system for agriculture. Farmers and their cooperatives can obtain long-, intermediate-, and short-term credit needed in their operations through the banks and associations of this system. Loan funds come mostly from the sale of bonds and debentures to investors. These securities are *not* guaranteed by the U. S. government. The system operates cooperatively with each farmer or farmer-cooperative borrower owning capital stock. Its three credit services are provided through:

a. Twelve federal land banks and about 750 federal land-bank associations, all owned by farmers.

Farmers and stockmen, including farming corporations, obtain land-bank loans through local federal land-bank associations. *Purpose:* To refinance farm debts, to enable purchase of land, equipment, and livestock, and for other agricultural purposes. *Terms:* Up to 65 per cent of the appraised normal agricultural value of the farm plus the amount of stock the borrower is required to purchase in connection with the loan at an interest rate of 5½ per cent in ten Farm Credit Districts, 5¾ per cent in one district, and 6 per cent in one district (April 1, 1962). *Where To Apply:* A federal land-bank association.

b. Twelve federal intermediate-credit banks and 494 production credit associations:

1. The intermediate-credit banks, besides supplying most of the short- and intermediate-term funds used in the lending operations of the production credit associations, extend credit to various other lenders by the purchase or discount of their loans made for agricultural purposes. *Purpose:* To provide credit at reasonable rates of interest to agricultural lenders, and to supervise and assist the production credit associations.

2. The production credit associations make and service PCA loans. Over 450 of these cooperative organizations of farmers and stockmen are completely member-owned. *Purpose:* To provide short- and intermediate-term credit for all types of farm and ranch operation. *Terms:* Loans are made for periods up to five years. Interest rates vary by associations. *Where To Apply:* Local production credit association.

c. Banks for cooperatives. Twelve regional banks make loans to farmers' cooperatives. They are assisted by a central bank in financing large loans. To be eligible for loans, a cooperative must be an association in which farmers act together in marketing farm products, purchasing farm supplies, or furnishing farm business services. *Purpose:* To provide a permanent source of credit for farmer cooperatives in the form of commodity, operating capital, and facility loans. *Terms:* Interest rates vary by banks and by type of loan but cannot exceed 6 per cent. *Where To Apply:* Regional bank in the Farm Credit District in which the cooperative is located.

Rural Electrification Administration. The REA offers loans for three purposes: (1) to finance the construction of electric power lines and other facilities to provide electric service to unserved people in rural areas, (2) through its electric borrowers, to assist consumers in financing purchases of wiring, plumbing, and electric appliances and equipment, and (3) to finance the improvement and extension of telephone lines and other telephone facilities in rural areas. *Terms:* Loans are made for a maximum period of 35 years, at 2 per cent interest. The long-term electric loans are available to nonprofit cooperatives, to power districts and other public agencies, and to electric companies. Telephone loans are available to telephone companies and to nonprofit cooperatives and mutual associations. *Where to Apply:* Rural Electrification Administration, U.S. Department of Agriculture, Washington 25, D. C.

Farmers' Home Administration. The Farmers' Home Administration provides agricultural loans to deserving farm families who are unable to obtain needed credit from private and cooperative lenders. Loans are also available to residents in small rural communities to improve housing and to obtain water. Credit is furnished at reasonable rates and terms, and each loan is accompanied by technical farm and financial management advice.

OPERATING LOANS. *Purpose:* To enable operators of not larger than family farms to purchase livestock, equipment, seed, feed, fertilizer and finance other farm and home needs. *Terms:* Repayable within 7 years with a possible 5-year renewal period at 5 per cent interest. Borrower's total principal indebtedness for operating loans may not exceed $35,000. Security consists of first lien on crops and items purchased or refinanced and best lien obtainable on other chattels necessary to adequately secure the loan.

FARM OWNERSHIP LOANS AND SOIL AND WATER CONSERVATION LOANS MADE TO INDIVIDUALS. *Purpose:* Farm ownership loans may be made to applicants who will become owner-operators of not larger than family farms to acquire, enlarge, or improve farms or farm buildings and refinance existing indebtedness. Soil and water loans may be made to tenants or farm owners for land and water development, use and conservation. *Source of Loan Funds:* Loans may be made from federal funds or from private funds provided by other lenders and insured by the agency. *Terms:* Repayable within 40 years at 5 per cent interest. Borrower's total principal indebtedness on farm at time loan is made may not exceed $60,000 or normal value of security, whichever is less. Security consists of mortgage on the farm, or chattels, or other suitable security.

FARM FORESTRY LOANS. Purpose: To enable eligible farmers to carry out better forestry management practices, to expand their forest resources, and to convert crop land to forestry uses. *Sources of Loan Funds:* Loans are made from funds otherwise available for farm ownership, operating, and soil and water conservation loan purposes. *Terms:* Farm ownership and soil and water conservation loans are repayable over periods up to 40 years at 3 per cent interest. Operating loans are repayable over periods up to seven years at 3 per cent interest. Maximum amount that may be loaned for farm ownership and soil and water conservation purposes is $60,000 or value of security offered by farmer, whichever is less. The maximum operating loan indebtedness is $35,000.

SOIL AND WATER CONSERVATION LOANS TO ASSOCIATIONS. *Purpose:* To enable nonprofit groups of farmers and rural residents such as irrigation, drainage and water supply districts, cooperative water users' associations, mutual water companies, soil conservation districts and municipalities to develop water supply systems for irrigation, household and livestock use; to drain farm land and to carry out soil conservation measures. *Source of Funds:* Loans may be made from federal funds or from private funds provided by other lenders and insured by the agency. *Terms:* Repayable within 40 years. Interest rate on direct loans 4½ per cent and interest rate on insured loans varies but may not exceed 5 per cent. An association's total indebtedness cannot exceed $500,000 on a direct loan and $1,000,000 on an insured loan. Security consists of mortgage on the group's facilities; or bands or notes pledging taxes, assessments or revenues if they meet statutory requirements.

RURAL HOUSING LOANS. *Purpose:* To enable farm owners and owners of nonfarm tracts in rural areas and small rural communities with populations of not more than 2,500 to construct, improve, or repair rural homes and related facilities, or farm service buildings, or fallout shelters, or to provide water for farmstead and household use. *Source of Loan Funds:* Loans to individual owners to provide housing for themselves or their tenants are made from federal funds. Insured loans may be made to individual farmers, groups of farmers, and public or private nonprofit organizations to finance housing facilities for domestic farm labor. *Terms:* Repayable within 33 years. Interest rate is 4 per cent except that loans for domestic farm labor bear 5 per cent interest. A home built with loan funds may usually not exceed 1,400 square feet of living space. Security consists of mortgage on farm or nonfarm tract to be improved, and by mortgage on other property when necessary to adequately secure the loan.

EMERGENCY LOANS. *Purpose:* Loans are made to eligible farmers in areas designated by Secretary of Agriculture where natural disasters such as floods and droughts have brought about a temporary need for credit not available from other sources. Loans may also be made outside of designated areas to farmers suffering a production loss from a natural disaster affecting only one or a few farms, for the purchase of feed, seed, fertilizer, replacement equipment and livestock and for other items needed to maintain normal operations. *Terms:* Loans are scheduled for repayment when income from crop or livestock financed is normally received. Interest rate is 3 per cent and size of loan depends upon system of farming to be financed and actual needs of applicant. Security consists of first lien on all crops, livestock and equipment financed with loan funds and when necessary, best lien obtainable on other assets owned by applicant.

WATERSHED LOANS. *Purpose:* To enable local organizations such as soil and water conservation districts, irrigation districts, drainage districts, flood prevention or control districts, municipal cooperations and similar public bodies to plan and carry out works of improvement which protect and develop land and water resources in small watersheds. Types of improvements include the financing of local costs for flood control dams and reservoirs, water supply reservoirs, rural water supply and distribution systems, diversion dams, irrigation canals and drainage facilities. *Terms:* Total indebtedness for all watershed loans for any one watershed project may not exceed $5,000,000, repayable within 50 years. Interest rate, which is set at beginning of each fiscal year, is 2.742 per cent for 1962.

Commodity Credit Corporation. Commodity Credit Corporation offers three types of loans: price support, farm-storage facility, and mobile dryer equipment. For all three types, applications may be made to the local county office of the Agricultural Stabilization and Conservation Service, U. S. Department of Agriculture.

PRICE SUPPORT. *Purpose:* To provide farmers a cash return on their farm warehouse-stored commodities at the support level when market prices are below that level, and to promote orderly marketing. These loans are made direct to farmers or through financial institutions. *Terms:* The loans are nonrecourse (paid by the delivery of the collateral or repayment of the principal plus interest. Three and one-half per cent interest is charged when the loan is not repaid and the commodity is delivered to the CCC. Security is provided by the commodity itself.

FARM-STORAGE FACILITY LOANS. *Purpose:* To construct or expand farmstorage facilities. *Terms:* Farm-storage facility loans are made directly to farmers or through lending agencies at the interest rate of 4 per cent for a period of five years. Loans are made up to 95 per cent of the cost of the new facility. Security is provided by a mortgage on facility or a severance agreement (permission for the building to be removed from the land in case of default). Such loans are not available to individuals or corporations wanting to install commercial facilities such as a public grain elevator.

MOBILE DRYER-EQUIPMENT LOANS. *Purpose:* For the purchase of new mobile dryer-equipment (mobile dryers, air circulators, ventilators, tunnels, and fans) to be used to keep stored grain in proper condition. *Terms:* Direct loans to farmers or through lending agencies bear interest at the rate of 4 per cent for a period of three years and are payable in three annual installments. Security is provided by a chattel mortgage on the equipment. Such loans are not available for the repair or maintenance of existing equipment, the purchase of secondhand equipment, or for the purchase of equipment to be used in connection with any commercial operation.

Housing and Community Development Loans

The Housing and Home Financing Agency is responsible for the principal federal activities concerned with housing and community development. HHFA Regional Offices are located in New York City, Philadelphia, Atlanta, Chicago, Fort Worth, San Francisco and San Juan. HHFA programs are administered by the following HHFA constituents:

Office of Transportation. The Office of Transportation, HHFA administers the Mass Transportation Loan Program. These loans are made to public agencies to assist in financing mass transportation facilities and equipment. *Terms:* Interest rate varies in accordance with a statutory formula; the rate as of May 1, 1962, was 3⅝ per cent. No loans may be made with maturity dates in excess of 40 years. *Where to Apply:* Office of Transportation, Housing and Home Finance Agency, Washington 25, D. C.

Community Facilities Administration. The following four programs are administered by the Community Facilities Administration. For all four, applications may be made to the regional director of Community Facilities in each of the HHFA Regional Offices. Information is available from the HHFA Regional Offices or from the Community Facilities Administration, Washington 25, D. C.

ADVANCES FOR PUBLIC WORKS PLANNING. The CFA makes advances to non-federal public agencies for planning of public works. *Terms:* Interest-free; advance becomes due when construction begins.

COLLEGE HOUSING LOANS. These loans are made to institutions of higher learning to construct student and faculty housing and related facilities, and to public or nonprofit hospitals for housing student nurses or interns. *Terms:* Interest rate is established at the beginning of each fiscal year; the rate until June 30, 1962 is 3⅝ per cent; amortization period may be as long as 50 years.

PUBLIC FACILITY LOANS. These loans are made to small communities (and some larger communities in redevelopment areas) to finance needed public works. Loans must be sound and so secured as to reasonably assure repayment. *Terms:* Interest rate is established at the beginning of each fiscal year; the present rate is 3⅝ per cent, except in redevelopment areas where it is 3⅜ per cent. Maximum amortization period is 40 years. Loans may be made only when financing is not otherwise available on reasonable terms.

SENIOR CITIZENS HOUSING LOANS. These loans are made to nonprofit corporations, certain public bodies and consumers cooperatives for the construction of rental housing for occupancy by persons 62 or older whose income is too high for public housing but too low for conventional housing. *Terms:* Interest rate is established at the beginning of each fiscal year; the rate until June 30, 1962 is 3⅝ per cent; maximum amortization period is 50 years.

Public Housing Administration. The Public Housing Administration makes temporary, short-term loans for local housing authorities for the development and construction of low-rent public housing, the occupancy of which is limited to low-income families unable to afford decent, safe, and sanitary private housing in the locality. PHA may lend up to 90 per cent of the project's cost. *Terms:* Interest rate varies, since it is set at not less than "the going federal rate" as determined semiannually by the Secretary of the Treasury. *Where to Apply:* PHA regional offices in New York City, Atlanta, Chicago, Fort Worth, Philadelphia, San Francisco and in Santurce, P. R.

Urban Renewal Administration. The Urban Renewal Administration aids local communities in carrying out comprehensive urban renewal programs by providing loans and grants to accomplish rehabilitation or redevelopment in slum and blighted areas. *Loan Terms:* Interest rate varies, since it is set at "not less than the going federal rate" at the time.

The URA also provides grants for metropolitan and regional planning and for planning in smaller communities; for preparation of comprehensive community renewal programs; for demonstration programs to test new techniques and methods of blight prevention and elimination; and for acquisition of land to be used as permanent open-space. *Where to Apply:* HHFA Regional Offices, or Urban Renewal Administration, Washington 25, D. C.

Federal Housing Administration. The Federal Housing Administration operates the programs of insurance authorized by the National Housing Act. These programs provide against loss on specific types of loans made by private lending institutions for housing purposes. The premium charge for this insurance is currently 0.5 per cent annually on the unpaid balance. *FHA does not lend money, and it does not plan or build housing.* It does, however, approve the lending institutions which can make the various types of loans that it insures. Although the general term of the loan is a matter to be decided by the lending institution, FHA must approve specific items such as the maximum interest rate permitted, amount of down payment, amortization period, minimum construction standards, and appraised value. In Titles I, II, and VIII of the Act, specific rates of interest or limits are defined for the various types of insured loans. *Where to Apply:* Persons interested in obtaining an insured FHA loan should direct their inquiry to an approved FHA lending institution. Information is also obtainable from the 76 FHA insuring offices and 17 service offices located in principal cities.

TITLE I. This title provides for insurance on loans up to $3,500 maximum made to finance alterations, repairs, and improvements to homes and other property, and for the building of new small nonresidential structures. Authority to insure new loans of this type expires September 30, 1965. The maximum finance charge as of publication of this book is $5 per $100 per year for the first $2,500; and $4 per $100 per year for the next $1,000.

TITLE II. This title of the Act contains sections which authorize government insurance on mortgage loans for single family housing, multi-family housing, rental and cooperative housing, housing for elderly, nursing homes, housing rehabilitation, servicemen's housing, experimental housing, trailer parks and courts, and some other special categories of housing. Interest rates for the insurance programs enumerated under the various Sections of Title II are subject to change and presently range from 5¼ to 6 per cent.

TITLE VIII. This title of the Act contains sections which provide for insurance on mortgage loans for rental housing for military personnel at or near military installations (financing such housing); housing for sale to essential civilian employees at research or developmental installations of the military departments or NASA; and, sale and rental housing for military, essential civilian personnel of armed services, and construction employees in impact areas. Interest rates for these insurance programs are subject to change and presently range from 4½ to 5¼ per cent.

Veterans Loans (Veterans Administration)

The Veterans Administration guarantees or insures real estate and non-real-estate loans made by private lending institutions to eligible

World War II and Korean conflict veterans. Under certain conditions, it also makes direct home loans to them.

Purpose: To assist veterans in the purchase, construction, alteration, improvement, and repair of home, farm, or business real estate, and the acquisition of supplies, equipment, and working capital. *Terms:* The loan may be short-term (five years and under), or long-term (amortized). If the maturity is five years or less, no payments on principal are required until maturity. With a long-term loan, a definite monthly payment is required which will pay off the principal plus interest over the period of the loan. *Where to Apply:* Application for VA loans, other than those that are direct, should be made to banks and other private lenders.

To obtain information relative to eligibility and duration of entitlement rights to receive a VA loan, a veteran should contact his nearest VA office.

Generally, long-term loans are guaranteed and short-term non-real-estate business and farm loans tend to be insured. If guaranteed, or if for real estate purposes, the interest rate on the loan may not exceed 5¼ per cent per annum under present law. If insured, 15 per cent of each loan is credited by the VA to an insurance account of the lender, limited by the entitlement available to the veteran borrower, from which the lender is paid for losses on such insured loans up to the amount of the insurance account. Interest on a non-real-estate insured loan may not exceed 5.7 per cent per annum, or 3 per cent discount.

REAL-ESTATE LOANS. A home or business real-estate loan may be repaid up to 30 years, and a farm real-estate loan up to 40 years. The VA guaranty may not exceed $7,500, or 60 per cent of a loan for the purchase, construction, alteration, improvement, or repair of residential property which the veteran will, or does, occupy as his home. Nonresidential real estate (farm or business) loans may be guaranteed up to a maximum of $4,000 or 50 per cent of the loan. The purchase price of property (real or personal) being acquired with the proceeds of a guaranteed or insured loan may not exceed the reasonable value as determined by the administrator of Veteran Affairs.

NON-REAL-ESTATE LOANS. These are for the purchase of property other than real estate, such as machinery, tools, equipment, livestock, and working capital required in the operation of a farm or business. This type of loan may be repaid in up to 10 years and may be guaranteed by VA up to a maximum of $2,000 or 50 per cent of the loan.

DIRECT LOANS. Under certain conditions the VA makes direct loans to veterans for the purchase, construction, alteration, improvement, and repair of residential property (including a farm residence) which the veteran will, or does occupy as his home. Direct loans are not authorized for purposes other than to provide the veteran with a home. Such loans may not exceed $15,000 and may only be made in specified direct-loan areas. The interest rate on a direct loan is 5¼ per cent per annum, the same as a guaranteed home loan, and may be repaid in up to 30 years. The security is, generally, the property being acquired with the proceeds of the loan.

Natural Resources Loans (Department of Interior)

Bureau of Reclamation

SMALL PROJECTS. Loans and grants up to a maximum of $5 million are made by the Bureau of Reclamation to certain types of organizations for the development of small reclamation projects in the 17 western states and Hawaii. Such projects must be primarily for irrigation, including drainage, but may include as incidental purposes: commercial power, flood control, and fish and wildlife conservation.

FEDERAL RECLAMATION PROJECTS. Several types of loans may be obtained by the local contracting organizations on Federal Reclamation projects. The Bureau of Reclamation lends appropriated funds to such organizations in order to undertake certain types of construction. These loans and their purposes are as follows: distribution system loans to construct a local organization's own irrigation distribution system in lieu of construction by the bureau; drainage and minor completion loans to undertake work that would normally be delayed; rehabilitation and betterment loans to reconstruct and improve a local organization's facilities when it is not practical to do it as a part of the normal operation and maintenance of the project. *Where to Apply:* Regional offices of the Bureau of Reclamation.

Bureau of Commercial Fisheries. The Bureau of Commercial Fisheries makes loans for financing and refinancing operations, maintenance, replacement, repair, and equipment of fishing gear and vessels, and for research into the basic problems of fisheries in instances where the necessary credit is not otherwise available on reasonable terms. *Terms:* Loans bear 5 per cent interest and mature in not more than 10 years. Security is fishing vessel, equipment, and gear, but other security may be required. *Where To Apply:* Branch of Loans and Grants of the nearest regional office of the Bureau of Commercial Fisheries, U. S. Department of Interior.

Bureau of Indian Affairs. Loans through the Bureau of Indian Affairs are confined, insofar as possible, to Indians, Eskimos, and Aleuts who have no other source of financing available.

The purpose of these loans is to encourage industry and income-producing enterprises, and for the education of certain Indians needing funds for that purpose. *Terms:* Interest rates on direct loans made are: 2 per cent on loans to organizations for relending, 4½ per cent on loans to finance businesses, 2 to 5 per cent on loans to finance businesses and to cooperative associations, 4 to 5 per cent on loans to individuals for other than educational purposes, and 3 per cent on loans to individuals for education. *Where to Apply:* Individuals, cooperatives, etc. go to their local Indian relending organization or to the Indian Agency superintendent.

QUASI-GOVERNMENT INTERNATIONAL FINANCE AGENCIES

The United States government has played an important role in the establishment of six international development organizations, and, in two instances, has been the sole sponsor. Four of these programs have been established since 1956. All of the agencies *are sources of credit for development purposes, and all are able to provide technical assistance to borrowers.* None of these institutions is in direct competition with regular banking facilities. The six international institutions differ from one another, however, with respect to the average size of operations, the characteristics of borrowers, credit terms available, and the sources of funds utilized.

The World Bank

The International Bank for Reconstruction and Development, or World Bank, which operates on a multilateral basis, is the largest and best-known development institution. The World Bank was formed in 1944, simultaneously with the International Monetary Fund, at the Bretton Woods conference. The present membership of the World Bank, with the exception of Yugoslavia, is located outside the Communist Bloc of nations.

Although nearly all credit extended by the World Bank immediately following World War II was for the reconstruction of countries in

Europe, no new loans have been made for this purpose since the beginning of the 1950's. The World Bank extends credit to the governments of underdeveloped member countries, primarily *for specific projects*, e.g., the construction of electric power and transportation facilities. At the beginning of fiscal year 1963, World Bank loans outstanding totaled $6,500,000,000. (Except where otherwise noted all subsequent data refer to the fiscal year which ended on June 30, 1962.)

If the borrower is not a government, the Bank requires the guarantee of the member government concerned. Normally, it finances only the foreign exchange costs involved in the purchase of imported goods and services and expects the borrower to meet local costs, usually more than half the total, out of other resources.

The loans made by the Bank are amortized over a period of years determined by the type of project being financed. The Bank lends at the current cost of borrowed money, plus a 1 per cent per annum special reserve charge and about ¼ per cent per annum for administrative expenses. The rate has varied from 3 per cent to 6¼ per cent and currently is 5¾ per cent. The Bank does not distinguish between borrowers as to the rate of interest charged. There have been no losses on loans to date.

The World Bank also enlists the direct participation of private investors in its loans. By getting them to participate in new loans and selling them portions of loans from its portfolio, it has replenished its funds available for development financing. Sales to private participants are without recourse to the Bank.

The Bank has also been a prime mover in establishing privately owned industrial development banks in a number of countries. These institutions assist in the financing of small and medium private industrial enterprises, make available technical and managerial assistance to industry, and serve as a focus for the development and growth of markets for industrial securities.

Capital stock of the World Bank is based on subscriptions of the member governments, with the amount of subscription varying with the size of the individual nation. The United States subscription amounts to 31 per cent of the total. Only 10 per cent of capital is paid-in, however, and thus the bulk of the Bank's subscribed capital, or 90 per cent, assumes the form of a guaranty fund to be drawn upon when necessary to meet obligations arising out of credit extended or guaranteed by the Bank.

The requirements with respect to the paid-in portion are uniform: each member is to pay 1 per cent of its subscription in gold, and nine per cent in dollars or in its own currency. The means of payment for the callable portion of capital, however, can be in gold, local currency, and/or dollars.

Total paid-in capital of the Bank at the end of fiscal 1962 was $2,000,000,000. The major source of funds available to the Bank is borrowed capital, obtained by the sale of long-term bonds. Such capital outstanding at the end of fiscal 1962 amounted to $2,500,000,000.

International Finance Corporation

In order to fill development credit needs not covered by World Bank activities, two affiliates were formed in recent years. The first of these is the International Finance Corporation, established in 1956. The chief characteristics that distinguish the IFC from the World Bank are that it provides capital funds in relatively smaller amounts than the World Bank does, and that it lends to private enterprises directly without government guarantee of repayment. So far, the investments of IFC have been components of larger financing transactions, helping usually to complete projects in which private investors have provided substantially more than the IFC commitment. The IFC, in effect, is similar to an investment banker in that both *underwrite security issues*. In addition, it should be noted that the 63 member countries of IFC also belong to the parent body, the World Bank, and that investment commitments of the IFC at the end of fiscal 1962 totaled $62,500,000.

IFC participates in projects in association with nationals of the country in which the project is located, or with foreign private investors, or a combination of the two. It does not invest in government-owned or government-operated undertakings, but its participation in an enterprise in which some public funds have been invested is not precluded if the project is essentially private in character.

Any enterprise in which IFC invests must be designed to make a useful contribution to the development of the economy of the member country in which it is located. IFC requires assurance that private investors will put up most of the necessary capital and that sufficient investment funds are not available elsewhere on reasonable terms. IFC does not engage in operations that are essentially for purposes of refunding or refinancing, nor does it finance exports or imports. And IFC does not invest in public utilities, such as electric power and transportation, in real estate development, such as housing and hotels, nor in irrigation, reclamation or drainage projects.

As a rule, IFC's share of the required financing is limited to 50 per cent of the total. The agency usually keeps its investment within the $500,000 to $4,000,000 range. It may invest without tangible security. As a matter of principle, it will not exercise voting rights on stock it holds and ordinarily does not seek representation on a company's board of directors.

IFC has no uniform interest rates for its loans. The rate for each investment is governed by relevant circumstances, such as the risks involved and the prospective over-all return on the investment. The agency charges a commitment fee of 1 per cent per annum of the undisbursed portion of its obligation.

International Development Association

The second affiliate of the World Bank, the International Development Association, began operating in January 1961 to provide capital to its 62 member governments on more liberal terms of repayment and to help finance a wider range of projects than its parent institution is permitted to support. The IDA can finance projects of high developmental priority such as housing and sanitation facilities. Thus, the activities of IDA cover a broader range of investments than those of the World Bank. Loan commitments outstanding as of the end of fiscal 1962 totaled $235,000,000.

The primary purpose underlying the establishment of IDA was the creation of a supplementary source of development capital for countries whose balance of payments prospects would not justify their incurring, or continuing to incur, external debt entirely on conventional terms. The financial terms attaching to IDA credits have, therefore, been designed with due regard to this purpose.

IDA credits are repayable in foreign exchange, but on very lenient terms. In each of the credits so far made, a government has been the borrower; the credits are repayable over a period of 50 years, free of interest; there is a ten-year period of grace, following which 1 per cent per annum is repayable over the next ten years, and 3 per cent per annum over the final 30 years. To help meet IDA's administrative costs, a service charge of three-quarters of 1 per cent per annum is payable on amounts withdrawn and outstanding. Compared with conventional loans, these terms bring substantial alleviation to the repayment obligations of borrowing countries and bear much less heavily on their balance of payments.

It was not intended that these concessionary terms of IDA financing should result in the extension of financial subsidies to the actual projects on which IDA funds are employed, or that IDA funds should be used to finance a project which could not satisfy normal criteria of economic and financial viability. Hence, a project submitted for IDA financing is expected to meet the same technical, economic, financial, and administrative standards as the World Bank itself would look for if the Bank were making a loan for that project on conventional terms. Furthermore, in the case of revenue-producing projects, IDA requires that the proceeds of the IDA credit be invested in the project on a normal business-like basis and that the price of the goods or services produced by the project be fixed at levels which will make the investment remunerative.

If the proceeds of an IDA credit were passed on to the agency executing a revenue-producing project at the concessionary terms obtained by the borrowing government itself, the effect would be to give the project a substantial financial subsidy. This was no part of IDA's purposes and would encourage the waste and misdirection of scarce investment funds. IDA therefore requires that the borrowing government, if it re-lends the proceeds of an IDA credit for investment in a revenue-producing project, will do so on terms which will impose on the agency executing the project the normal financial discipline with regard to the fixing of rates and charges to consumers.

It remains, of course, a matter of judgment whether and to what extent a project should be put on a revenue-producing basis, and what should be regarded as suitably business-like re-lending terms, taking into account such factors as the existing pattern of interest rates in the borrowing country.

Inter-American Development Bank

The Inter-American Development Bank, unlike the World Bank and its affiliates, is a regionally-oriented institution. The IADB was organized early in 1960 by the 20 members of the Organization of American States for the purpose of providing an additional source of capital to help promote the economic growth of Latin America.

IADB lends both to government entities and indirectly to private enterprises through local development institutions. As of the end of fiscal 1962, loan commitments outstanding amounted to $271,000,000.

It should be noted that the callable portion of capital serves primarily as financial backing for bond issues.

To carry out its objective, the Bank is authorized by its charter to: (1) promote the investment of public and private capital for development purposes; (2) utilize its own capital, funds raised by it in financial markets, and other available resources, for financing the development of the member countries, giving priority to those loans and guarantees that will contribute most effectively to their economic growth: (3) encourage private investment in projects, enterprises, and activities contributing to economic development and supplement private investment when private capital is not available on reasonable terms and conditions; (4) cooperate with the member countries to orient their development policies toward a better utilization of their resources, in a manner consistent with the objectives of making their economies more complementary and of fostering the orderly growth of their foreign trade; and (5) provide technical assistance for the preparation, financing, and implementation of development plans and projects, including the study of priorities and the formulation of specific project proposals.

Ordinary operations. With its ordinary capital resources the Bank may make or guarantee loans to a member country, to the latter's government or its political subdivisions, or to a private enterprise within a member country. These loans are used to finance development projects, including those forming part of national or regional development programs and are repayable in the currency or currencies in which they are made.

Special operations. The Bank uses the Fund for Special Operations to make loans on terms and conditions suitable for dealing with special circumstances which may arise in specific countries or with regard to specific projects. Such loans may be repayable in whole or in part in the currency of the member country in which a project is being financed. Portions not repayable in local currency must be repaid in the currency or currencies lent.

Projects considered for financing. Although the Bank has no predisposition to favor particular categories of development projects, it does seek to give priority to undertakings which in its opinion will make the most effective contribution to the economic growth of its member countries. The Bank does not make loans for the purchase of established enterprises, for refinancing operations, or for working capital.

Because of the size of its resources, the Bank by itself does not finance large-scale projects. It can, however, participate with other financial institutions in financing such projects.

Social progress trust fund. The Bank also administers the Social Progress Trust Fund, which consists of $394 million of the $500 million fund established in 1961 by the United States government to stimulate social development in Latin America as part of the Alliance for Progress program. Detailed information on the operations and administration of the Social Progress Trust Fund is available from the Bank.

Criteria employed in making loans. In making loans or guarantees the Bank is guided by the following criteria:

Loans are made principally for financing specific projects. The Bank, however, also makes or guarantees loans to development institutions or similar agencies in order that they may relend the proceeds to finance specific development projects whose requirements are not large enough to warrant a direct loan from the Bank.

The Bank takes into account the ability of the borrower to obtain financing from private sources on terms which, in its opinion, are reasonable. It also pays due regard to the capacity of the borrower and his guarantor, if any, to meet their obligations.

The Bank lends foreign currency to cover local costs only under special circumstances, particularly when the project is expected to increase, directly or indirectly, the demand for foreign exchange in the country in which the project is located.

It grants loans in local currency to cover domestic costs in connection with a loan in foreign currency. As a general rule, it is not the Bank's policy to grant loans in local currency solely to defray local costs. However, it may do so if the borrower cannot furnish the necessary financing or if he cannot find appropriate domestic sources of financing within the country.

The Bank only finances projects in which the eventual borrower has made or plans to make a substantial investment. As a general rule, and in the absence of a special justification to the contrary, it finances no more than 50 per cent of the cost of a project. In the case of loans to governments, consideration is given to the contribution being made by the country to the total development effort.

In making loans to a private enterprise the Bank need not require a guarantee of repayment by the country in which the investment is made, although it may do so when circumstances warrant. The Bank does not extend loans or guarantees if they are unacceptable to the government of the country in which the project is proposed.

It is not the policy of the Bank to include in a loan granted any amounts designed to cover expenditures or obligations of the borrower incurred prior to the time of formal signing of a loan contract, including reimbursements for suppliers' contracts entered into prior to such time.

Acknowledgement of receipt of an application, its study by Bank officials, their requests for additional information or discussions with prospective borrowers about conditions or guarantees, do not bind the Bank in any way to approve the loan requested. The approval of a loan is a function of the Board of Executive Directors of the Bank, and a loan is not considered approved until the Board adopts a resolution to this effect.

The Bank may attach such other conditions to the making of loans or guarantees as it deems appropriate, taking into account both the interest of the members directly involved in the particular loan or guarantee proposal and the interests of the members as a whole.

Applications for loans. The Bank has no formal application forms. Rather, it encourages prospective borrowers to make preliminary inquiries, either in person or by mail. On the basis of these, it is possible for the Bank and the prospective borrower to determine the feasibility of conducting detailed negotiations. The Bank deals directly with the borrower or his fully authorized representative.

In order for the Bank to give adequate consideration to a loan application, the prospective borrower must provide the following information in writing: (1) The name, address and form of organization of the applicant. If the application is by a public entity other than the national government, it must specify the financial and legal relationship to such government. (2) A general description of the project. This should state whether it is a new undertaking or an expansion or improvement of an existing activity. (3) A plan of operations related to the activity to be developed, including, where appropriate: (a) kind and amount of products and services; (b) proposed markets and anticipated sales volume (the basis of estimates should be specified); (c) the type and source of raw materials; (d) available transportation and other pertinent services; and (e) plans for management. (4) The estimated cost of project, by principal items, listing local and foreign exchange costs separately. (5) The amount of loan requested, specific proposed uses of the loan funds and proposed repayment schedule, with a statement whether the financing is being or has been requested elsewhere. (6) The amounts and terms of other proposed financing and possible sources of funds, including the applicant's own contribution. (7) The estimated financial results, including projected annual income, expenditures and profits during the first three years of operation and financial reports for the past three years. These should include balance sheets and profit and loss statements. Applicants may use forms available from the Bank for this purpose. (8) Studies of costs, markets, prices of competing products or services, engineering surveys, and any other available information which will help to establish the economic and technical feasibility of the project. If all the pertinent data are not available, the applicant must indicate his plan for providing such information. (9) The applicant should indicate whether he desires the collaboration of the Bank's Technical Assistance Division and, if so, whether he is in a position to finance or share in the financing of such assistance.

Private firms must supply the following additional information: (1) efforts made to secure capital elsewhere; (2) a list of stockholders who own more than 10 per cent of the capital stock; and (3) bank and other business references.

After the initial study of the application, the applicant will be informed whether the Bank wishes to give further consideration to his request. If so, it will provide the applicant with a detailed outline of the additional information which must be received before a final decision is made.

Export-Import Bank

The Export-Import Bank was originally established in 1934, but its present form of organization dates from the end of World War II. The Ex-Im Bank is a U. S. government-owned corporation whose major function is to facilitate U. S. trade. Ex-Im had an initial capital of $1,000,000,000 paid-in by the U. S. Treasury, and may borrow, on a revolving basis, up to $6,000,000,000 from it. Ex-Im extends credit of varying maturities and/or provides guarantees on loans made by other institutions. *Credit is extended to both private enterprises and governments for the purchase of capital machinery and equipment.*

Ex-Im Bank seeks to stimulate and facilitate U.S. foreign trade by making (1) direct dollar loans for the purchase of U.S. goods and services, (2) guarantees and writing insurance on export transactions, and (3) medium-term exporter credits. It can assist export sales to customers in both developed and less-developed countries.

The Export-Import Bank is especially interested in making its facilities available for small transactions as well as large. Its smallest transaction to date has been $500. In recent years, more than 80 per cent of its exporter transactions were for less than $100,000, and 25 per cent were for less than $10,000. Most of the loans have covered the sale of capital equipment, agricultural machinery, and commodities such as cotton.

Ex-Im Bank will not give its help in any undertakings for which, in its judgment, private capital is available on reasonable terms. It welcomes and encourages commercial banks and other private institutions as participants in new loans and as purchasers of existing loans from its portfolio.

Agency for International Development

United States bilateral long-term credit is also extended through the Agency for International Development. AID was established by the United States government in the fall of 1961 in an attempt to help streamline the United States's contribution to the economic growth of underdeveloped areas. Long-term credit, as one part of AID, represents a continuation of the Development Loan Fund which was established by the Mutual Security Act of 1957. *Development credit under both programs has been extended to public and private enterprises for the purchase of goods and services produced in the United States.* Development loan commitments by AID totaled $1,300,000,000 in the fiscal year 1962. Note that, in contrast to the other development institutions, funds available to AID are based on annual appropriations by Congress and thus can *not* be committed to borrowers for years in advance.

A.I.D. is placing a greater emphasis than predecessor foreign assistance agencies upon sound country plans and self-help measures as pre-conditions for development assistance. It encourages, in particular, those investment proposals which will do the most to speed development of the friendly less-developed countries. There are far greater resources at the disposal of private enterprise than can ever be applied to such development by governments.

A.I.D. favors joint-venture type investments with local capital because this type of enterprise is most likely to result in a transfer of entrepreneurial, technical, and management skills to the country itself. Further, A.I.D. believes it is wisest in the long run for U.S. investors to identify their interests closely with those of the citizens of the country in which they operate. In view of the desire to mobilize scarce foreign exchange resources, those investments which are accompanied by dollar capital, in addition to management and technical know-how, are preferred. The sale of packaged plants, or the provision of so-called "turn-key" jobs, usually takes a lower priority position than those proposals in which there is a sizeable private equity contribution in relation to debt.

Consistent with A.I.D.'s objectives, several programs of particular interest to businessmen are receiving immediate attention and emphasis: (1) sharing the cost of conducting investment surveys undertaken by U.S.-owned business firms; (2) authorizing dollar development loans to private borrowers; (3) administering the PL 480 local currency (Cooley) loan program formerly handled by the Export-Import Bank; and (4) administering the broadened investment guaranty program.

Investment survey program. The purpose of the investment survey program is to encourage potential investors to identify specific investment opportunities in less-developed amicable countries which they might not otherwise investigate.

A.I.D. has authority, under Section 231 of the Foreign Assistance Act of 1961, to participate in up to 50 per cent of the cost of approved surveys which explore the feasibility of contemplated private investments in developing countries which will contribute to the achievement of A.I.D. objectives.

If the prospective investor then proceeds with the investment (following the survey), he will repay A.I.D. those funds which may have been advanced to him. The investor will retain exclusive rights to the survey.

But if the prospective investor *does not* undertake the investment studied, the survey will then become the property of the United States government. In this case, the investor is entitled to A.I.D. participation, providing he has complied with the terms and conditions of the participation agreement. He is then under no obligation to repay any such advances to A.I.D.

Note: A.I.D. participation in an investment survey in no way implies that the U. S. government will provide the investor with further financial assistance. Subsequent applications from the same investor for loans or guaranties will be considered separately on the basis of their respective merits.

Prospective investors eligible to participate in the A.I.D. investment survey program are persons who are citizens of the United States or any corporation, partnership, or other association substantially beneficially owned by U. S. citizens. The survey may be made either by the prospective investor or by a qualified independent contractor engaged by the prospective investor.

TERMS AND CONDITIONS. Within the limits of funds available, A.I.D. may participate in the financing of investment surveys which meet the following criteria: (1) There must be reasonable prospects that the survey will result in an investment. (2) The investment must contribute to the achievement of A.I.D.'s objective of furthering economic development of a less-developed friendly nation. (3) The investment must be consistent with the host country's development program.

NATURE OF SURVEYS. Surveys will normally explore and analyze the economic and technical feasibility of proposed investments. They will usually include analyses of the potential market, plant location, raw materials availability, labor supply, availability of qualified personnel, profitability and other financial considerations (capital requirements), and potential contribution of the investment to the host country's economy.

Surveys of extraction opportunities—including those ascertaining the existence, location, extent or quality of any deposit of ore, oil, gas, or other mineral, and those determining the feasibility of mining or other extraction of any such mineral or the processing of it to the stage of commercial marketability—are *not* eligible for A.I.D. participation.

How A.I.D. SHARES IN SURVEY FINANCING. For acceptable investment survey proposals, A.I.D. will normally share in the financing on the following basis:

1. A.I.D. will undertake to reimburse the prospective investor an amount not to exceed 50 per cent of the total allowable cost of an approved investment survey, as defined in the investment survey grant document. Total allowable cost, which may include both dollar and local currency expenditures, may include: (a) salaries of personnel at their normal rate of pay for the time spent on the survey, (b) expenditures for subsistence and travel, (c) communications, and (d) indirect costs which A.I.D. agrees are allocable to the survey.

2. Payment may be made after the survey is completed, or if

appropriate, provision may be made in the grant document for interim payments (pay-as-you-go).

3. The grant document will provide an appropriate period of time after completion of the survey for the investor to decide whether to invest.

4. If, within the agreed period of time, the decision is made to proceed with the investment, the costs may not be shared by A.I.D. (and the prospective investor will reimburse A.I.D. any funds paid to him by A.I.D.).

5. If, within the agreed period of time, the potential investor has decided *not* to invest (or has not decided to invest by the end of this period), he shall provide A.I.D. with copies of a professionally acceptable survey which then becomes the property of the U.S. government. In such event, A.I.D. also shall have access to, and obtain copies as desired of, relevant underlying correspondence, memoranda, working papers, documents and other materials gathered in connection with the survey. A.I.D. may then utilize the survey for any appropriate purpose.

How to Apply. Inquiries regarding the program in general should be directed to: Office of Development Finance and Private Enterprise, A.I.D., Washington 25, D. C. Inquiries regarding investment surveys in a specific country should be directed to the appropriate regional office of A.I.D., Washington 25, D. C. (See Part 3 Exhibit I for a listing of A.I.D. regional offices in Washington.)

Letters of application (there is no special application form) for A.I.D. participation in investment surveys should be addressed to the appropriate regional office of A.I.D., Washington 25, D. C. Send four copies of the application. The letter of application should be submitted at least 30 days prior to the contemplated start of the survey and should include the following information:

1. Applicant's full legal name, address, nature (whether corporation, partnership, etc.), and the country in which organized or incorporated.

2. Description of projected investment.

3. Scope of survey and estimated cost (breakdown of principal components).

4. Names and qualifications of persons who will conduct survey.

5. Proposed plans for the implementation of the investment project.

6. Statement indicating the ability of potential investor to finance the investment opportunity to be surveyed.

7. Proposed time schedule, including date by which investment decision will be made.

8. To the extent known, relationship of investment project to the over-all economy and development program of the host country.

Dollar loans. A.I.D. has authority, under Section 201 of the Foreign Assistance Act of 1961, to make dollar loans to private (as well as public) enterprise, both United States and foreign. It is A.I.D. policy to encourage those investments which contributed to the economic development of a less-developed friendly country in which the investment is to be made, with emphasis on assisting long-range development plans.

Dollar development loans may be made only where there are reasonable prospects of repayment. Normally, U. S. dollar loans are to be used to cover the U. S. procurement component of the project, with few exceptions permitted.

As required by statute, the administrator of A.I.D., before authorizing loans, must consider the availability of financing from other free world sources on reasonable terms. So, a prospective borrower should investigate a number of private and other public institutions before making formal application to A.I.D. In general, the other public agencies also require that the borrower first seek financing from private financial sources. Hence, potential borrowers should initially consult their regular banking relationships. If dollar financing is not available on reasonable terms from private or other public sources as outlined above, then application to A.I.D. may be made by private firms or individuals.

Loans may be made to private firms or individuals seeking to expand existing enterprises and to firms or individuals planning to establish new enterprises. Applicants need not be residents of the country where the enterprise is located.

The projected new investment, or expansion or diversification must be acceptable to the government of the country in which it will be made, and it must clearly contribute to the economic development of the country. Therefore, it is advisable to discuss acceptability of the project with both the host country government and the A.I.D. Mission in that country in advance of making formal application to A.I.D. In countries where the government requires prior licenses or other approvals of an industrial enterprise, prospective applicants should obtain such assurances from the appropriate government ministries *before* submitting their application to A.I.D.

TERMS AND CONDITIONS

1. The project must give reasonable promise of contributing to the development of economic resources or increasing the productive capacities of the country concerned.

2. It must be consistent with the other development activities being undertaken or planned for the country. Necessarily, A.I.D. is limited to financing only those activities which occupy a relatively high priority position in a country's development program.

3. The project must be economically and technically sound, with reasonable prospects that it will pay out satisfactorily.

4. The project must not compete (within the meaning of section 620(d) of the Foreign Assistance Act, 22 U.S.C. Sec. 2370(d) with U. S. enterprises, especially with enterprises in areas of the United States with substantial labor surpluses.

5. The proceeds of the loan must be used to finance the dollar costs of the project except where, for good cause, A.I.D. agrees otherwise.

6. Procurement will be limited to goods and services of United States origin, with few exceptions permitted.

7. Loans are generally made directly by A.I.D. to the private borrower at an interest rate of 5¾ per cent. While principal and interest are owed in dollars, arrangements may be made for repayment of principal and interest in local currency (dollar denominated) to the local government which, in turn, arranges to pay A.I.D. in dollars.

8. Borrowers must agree to follow normal commercially acceptable business practices to assure that the prices paid for goods financed under A.I.D. loans are reasonable and that contracts are awarded on an appropriate competitive basis.

HOW TO APPLY. Inquiries regarding the program in general should be directed to: Office of Development Finance and Private Enterprise, A.I.D., Washington 25, D. C. Inquiries regarding dollar development loans to private borrowers for operations in a specific country should be addressed to the appropriate U. S. A.I.D. Mission or to the proper regional office of A.I.D., Washington 25, D. C.

Letters of application (there is no special application form) must be in English. Six copies should be sent to the U. S. A.I.D. Mission in the appropriate country or to the proper regional office of A.I.D., Washington 25, D. C.

The letter of application should include the following, where applicable.

1. Applicant's full legal name, address, nature (whether corporation, partnership, etc.), and the country in which organized or incorporated.

2. A brief biographical sketch of the principal owners, directors, officers, and managers, including the percentage of United States and other ownership. Indicate the extent of management's experience and qualifications.

3. The amount of the loan requested from A.I.D. and a statement showing the specific uses to be made of the funds to be borrowed—buildings, machinery, services and equipment, etc.

4. The desired repayment period (in the form of a tentative repayment schedule).

5. If the enterprise is already in operation, submit (a) a current balance sheet and balance sheets for the prior three years, including statements of surplus; (b) a profit and loss statement for the past five years; (c) a statement of sources and uses of funds; and (d) a current cash flow statement, together with similar statements for the past three years. All financial statements should be audited if possible. Otherwise, they should be signed by an officer of the applicant.

6. All applicants must submit pro-forma balance sheets, and profit and loss and cash flow statements estimated for future years until operations become fully developed with debt servicing stabilized. Such statements should indicate clearly the assumptions made in the projections and the bases of these assumptions.

7. The name(s) of the applicant's bank(s).

8. The total cost of the proposed project (including all equity investment contemplated), and the amount of, sources of, security for, and repayment terms for all proposed borrowing and other financing.

9. Any preliminary engineering, economic, and market studies already made which are pertinent to the proposed loan, including (a) the volume and kind of end products or services which would be produced; (b) the source of the required raw materials; (c) the markets to be supplied, and the competition, if any; (d) the transportation available for raw materials and finished products; and (e) a forecast of production costs.

10. A description of the efforts which have been made to raise the required capital from other free-world sources and the terms, if any, on which such capital is available.

In short, a request for a dollar loan for a project should be supported by any and all information necessary to determine the equity participation, economic justification, technical feasibility, and cost; by a description of how the engineering, purchasing, construction, and management of the project will be carried out, and by appropriate financial projections. It should be made clear whether it is planned that consulting services will be utilized, and, if not, the reasons should be stated.

The length of time required by A.I.D. to process an application will vary, depending upon the nature of the proposal. However, as a general rule, the more completely documented the submission, the more quickly processing will be completed.

In the light of the large volume of applications to A.I.D., and in view of the limits on its resources, it is obvious that A.I.D. will not be able to extend credit for all the worthwhile proposals submitted to it for consideration. But all applications will be acknowledged after they have been subjected to preliminary review by the appropriate regional office within A.I.D. and by the U. S. A.I.D. Mission in the field. If an application cannot be considered within a reasonable time, the applicant will be so notified.

Local currency loans. Under Section 104(e), Title I of Public Law 480, the Agricultural Trade Development and Assistance Act of 1954, up to 25 per cent of the foreign currencies received by the U. S. government in payment for surplus agricultural commodities may be lent to qualified borrowers to develop business and expand trade. These local currency loans, usually referred to as "Cooley loans," are named after Congressman Harold D. Cooley, who sponsored the amendment to Public Law 480 setting aside some of the proceeds of certain surplus sales for relending to U. S. private businesses. This program, formerly administered by the Export-Import Bank of Washington, was transferred to A.I.D. on January 1, 1962.

Local currencies may be loaned to (1) U. S. firms or their branches, subsidiaries, or affiliates for business development and trade expansion in the foreign country, or (2) either U. S. firms or firms of the local country for expanding markets for, and consumption of, U. S. agricultural products abroad.

TERMS AND CONDITIONS. The currencies are available in countries where the United States has sold surplus agricultural commodities. The currencies may be used by the borrower to develop his business and to expand trade by financing such local costs as expansion of plant and equipment, land acquisition, working capital (in most of the countries), industrial training, and other normal costs of operations.

Cooley loans may not be made for the manufacture of products which would be exported to the United States in competition with U. S.-made products, and they may *not* be made for the production of commodities which would be marketed in competition with U. S. agricultural commodities. Cooley loans to foreign firms (non U. S.-affiliated borrowers) may only be made if they will be used to expand markets for U. S. agricultural products.

A.I.D. Cooley loans usually bear interest at rates comparable to those charged by local development banks. Maturities are related to the purposes of financing. Loans are repayable in the currency borrowed, without maintenance of value. In some cases, a guaranty of loan repayment may be required.

In countries where there are not sufficient Cooley funds to meet the demand, A.I.D. may impose priorities. Data on the availability of Cooley funds are periodically published in A.I.D. press releases. Persons wishing to receive these releases regularly may request that their names be included on the mailing list by writing to: Office of Development Finance and Private Enterprise, A.I.D., Washington 25, D. C.

How To Apply. Inquiries regarding the Cooley fund program in general or the availability of Cooley funds in a given country, should be directed to: Office of Development Finance and Private Enterprise, A.I.D., Washington 25, D. C. Inquiries regarding Cooley loans to private borrowers for operations in a specific country should be addressed to the appropriate U. S. A.I.D. Mission or to the proper regional office of A.I.D., Washington 25, D. C.

Letters of application (there is no special application form) must be in English. Three copies should be sent to the U. S. A.I.D. Mission in the appropriate country or to the proper regional office of A.I.D., Washington 25, D. C.

The letter of application should include the following, where applicable:

1. Applicant's full legal name, address, nature (whether corporation, partnership, etc.), and the country in which organized or incorporated.

2. A brief biographical sketch of the principal owners, directors, officers and managers, including the percentage of United States and other ownership. Indicate the extent of management's experience and qualifications.

3. The amount of the loan requested from A.I.D. and a statement showing the specific uses to be made of the funds to be borrowed. If the

loan is to finance the procurement of fixed assets, break down such procurement by categories—land, buildings, machinery, services and equipment, etc. If it is to provide working capital, divide into general purposes —inventory, installment sales or receivables, refinancing, payrolls, general expenses, etc.

4. The desired repayment period (in the form of a tentative repayment schedule).

5. If the enterprise is already in operation, submit (a) a current balance sheet and balance sheets for the prior three years, including statements of surplus; (b) a profit and loss statement for the past five years; (c) a statement of sources and uses of funds; and (d) a current cash flow statement, together with similar statements for the past three years. All financial statements should be audited if possible. Otherwise, they should be signed by an officer of the applicant.

6. All applicants must submit pro-forma balance sheets, and profit and loss and cash flow statements estimated for future years until operations become fully developed with debt servicing stabilized. Such statements should indicate clearly the assumptions made in the projections and the bases of these assumptions.

7. The name(s) of applicant's bank(s).

8. The total cost of the proposed project (including all equity investment contemplated), and the amount of source of, security for, and repayment terms for all proposed borrowing and other financing.

9. Pertinent economic data, including market studies, indicating the benefits which the proposed activity would yield to the enterprise and to the country.

10. If the activity will produce items for export, an estimate of the value of such exports and the probable markets.

11. If the applicant is not a U. S. firm or affiliate, an account of how the proposed activity will expand markets for U. S. agricultural commodities.

12. The name and address of any proposed guarantor, together with an audited, or signed, current financial statement of the guarantor.

Investment guaranties. As described earlier, A.I.D. will make dollar and local currency loans, and share the cost of conducting investment surveys. The agency will also enter into a contract with a firm that is planning to make a new investment or expand an existing investment in order to guaranty the firm against some of the political risks and, in certain cases, against a portion of the business risks inherent in foreign investment.

The purpose of the guaranty programs is to encourage and facilitate those private U. S. investments abroad which further the development of the economic resources and productive capacities of a less-developed country. Thus, guaranties are generally available only for new investment rather than for existing investments or investments which have been irrevocably committed before an application for a guaranty has been filed. Guaranties are available for additions to existing investments.

The role of the United States government is to encourage desirable investment in those countries in which the investment guaranty program applies and then to act solely as a guarantor.

Under Sections 221 and 224 of the Foreign Assistance Act of 1961, Congress has authorized three investment guaranty programs: (1) the specific political risk guaranties against (a) inconvertibility of foreign currency, (b) expropriation or confiscation, (c) loss due to war, revolution or insurrection; (2) the extended risk guaranties which cover a portion of both political and business risks; and (3) the extended risk guaranties covering losses on pilot or demonstration private housing projects in Latin America.

The specific political risk guaranty program has been in operation almost 15 years. The other two programs are new, and the policies and procedures governing them are, therefore, less refined.

A. *The Specific (Political) Risk Program*

Guaranties are now available in 48 less-developed countries (and a number of overseas dependencies of the developed countries) against one, two, or all three of the following political risks: (1) inability to convert into dollars foreign currency representing earnings on, or return of, capital; (2) loss due to expropriation or confiscation; (3) loss due to war, revolution or insurrection. (A list of the countries in the Specific-Risk Investment Guaranty Program, with the risks currently covered in each, is contained in Exhibit V.)

AGREEMENTS WITH FOREIGN GOVERNMENTS. Before guaranties can be issued for investments in a particular country or area, an agreement between the United States and the foreign government is signed to institute the guaranty program.

Primarily, this agreement provides the understandings between the two governments as to procedures, the status of local currency, and other claims which may be acquired by the United States when contracts of guaranty are invoked. This agreement also provides, in advance, orderly procedures for the handling of such currencies and claims.

Negotiations with countries not now in the guaranty program are currently underway, and it is therefore anticipated that additional countries will enter the program. Discussions are also being held with those countries which have so far only agreed to cover one or two of the specific risks described above, in the hope that they may agree to authorize additional coverage.

The agreement with the foreign government does not provide for special treatment by the host government of guarantied investments. Guaranties, however, provide the investor with the United States government's assurance that he will be protected up to the amount specified in the guaranty from inconvertibility or from loss due to expropriation, confiscation, war, revolution, or insurrection.

THE CONTRACT. After an agreement has been signed with the government, and the investment guaranty program is put into effect, guaranties are issued to the investor in the form of a contract between the investor and A.I.D.

The contract provides that payments due thereunder to investors shall be made from funds provided by the Congress. No obligations are placed on the investor other than those necessary in the administration of the guaranties. There is no interference in the operation of the business of the investor (or in the business of the recipient of the investment). However, the United States government will, in accordance with good business practice—upon paying a claim to the guarantied investor—acquire the currency or claim on which the payment is based. All the agreements between the United States government and the investor are set forth a contract. Each contract is negotiated in the light of the special circumstances of the investment concerned, and this contract governs the relationship between the investor and the United States government.

ELIGIBILITY. To be eligible for guaranties the investment must be made by a citizen of the United States or a corporation, partnership, or other association created under the laws of the United States or of any state or territory, and substantially beneficially owned by citizens of the United States. Ordinarily, a company organized under United States law will be considered an eligible investor if more than one-half of the total value of all classes of its stock is owned by U. S. citizens.

In 1961, Congress also extended eligibility for investment guaranties to the wholly-owned foreign subsidiaries of eligible U. S. corporations.

It should be noted that there is no fixed form which an investment must take to be eligible for coverage.

INVESTMENT CONTRIBUTIONS. Whether in the form of equity, loan, royalty (or leasing agreement), the investment contribution may be any of the following:

Cash: If cash is to be invested, it must be dollars or credits in dollars, or foreign currency (a) purchased with dollars for the purpose of the investment, or (b) otherwise acquired or owned by the investor, and freely transferable into dollars.

Materials or Equipment: Both new and used materials or equipment may be considered to be investment contributions. If new, material or equipment will ordinarily be valued at its cost to the investor. If used, it will ordinarily be valued at the value determined by an independent appraisal.

Patents, Processes or Techniques: Congress has made these intangible assets eligible for guaranty because of the desirability of encouraging the spread of advanced technological methods. However, the licensing of trade names, trade-marks and good will, often closely associated with the licensing of patents, processes and techniques, is not eligible for guaranty. It should also be understood that, to be eligible for guaranty, the patents, processes and techniques included in the investment should represent predominantly a body of information and experience already in existence.

Services: Contributions of engineering and management services will usually be considered investments only when performed for the purpose of transmitting other eligible investments, such as processes and techniques, and provided, of course, that the services are not to be currently and separately paid for. The cost of engineering surveys in advance of construction, and before the commitment for the investment is made, can be included as a part of the total investment if essential to the project for which the guaranty is sought—if such costs have been incurred for the express purpose of making construction of the project possible.

Loan Guaranties: In addition to the above types of investment contributions, guaranties of repayment given by investors on loans made by financial institutions may be considered to be eligible investments. This type of investment raises special problems. So, at the earliest opportunity, investors should write to: Investment Guaranties Division, A.I.D., Washington 25, D. C., outlining the proposed transaction.

TERMS AND CONDITIONS. In general, guaranties must be approved by A.I.D. as furthering the economic development and productive capacities of a needy friendly country. This includes most projects which promote trade, increase production, raise standards of living, improve technical efficiency, etc.

At this time, there is no restriction as to size of the investments which may be guaranteed. Guaranty contracts have been written for as little as $1,000 and for as much as $60 million. Guaranty contracts may be written for a maximum term of 20 years from the date of issuance.

Before any investment guaranty contract is issued, A.I.D. requires the investor to secure approval from the foreign government for the inclusion of his project under the investment guaranty agreement between the foreign government and the United States. This is done to (1) assure that the project is within the scope of the inter-governmental agreement, and (2) protect the interests of the Unied Staes, should a claim arise.

It must be emphasized that it is the responsibility of the investor to present to the foreign government the plan and details of the investment, to fulfill the foreign government's requirements regarding the investment, and to request the foreign government's written expression to the A.I.D. Mission or American Embassy of the approval of the project for investment guaranty purposes.

When the investor has obtained approval from the foreign government for inclusion of his project under the investment guaranty program, and when the terms of the proposal are clearly understood and found by A.I.D. to meet the criteria determining the availability of investment guaranties, a draft of a guaranty contract will be sent to the applicant for his approval. Each contract is drafted to meet the particular circumstances of the investment and the needs of the investor. After agreement is reached with the investor on the terms of the contract, the proposed contract and the application are submitted to the administrator of A.I.D. or his delegate for final approval. If approved, the guaranty contract is then executed on behalf of the United States government by A.I.D.

FEES. A fee is charged of ½ per cent of the amount of each coverage in force in any given contract year. There is also an annual fee of ¼ per cent of the amount of standby coverage—that is, the difference between the amount in force and the maximum amount which the investor may elect to have put in force. For the purpose of measuring fees there are three types of specific risk coverage: (1) inconvertibility; (2) expropriation and confiscation; and (3) war, revolution, and insurrection.

How TO APPLY. When a prospective investor's plans have been sufficiently developed to make it possible for him to do so, but before he has made the investment or committed himself to make it, he may file an application for an investment guaranty. Such an application need not be complete and final in every detail but should contain the essential facts about the proposed investment.

Where it is desirable for an investor to make an investment, or to enter into a firm commitment to make an investment, before an investment guaranty contract is issued, the investor may request that A.I.D. issue an assurance against prejudice on his application.

Such an assurance, sometimes called a "waiver" (or "no prejudice") letter, provides that the investor may proceed with his investment plans or enter into contracts without prejudicing his application for a guaranty. This assurance is usually valid for six months and may be extended.

This assurance, of course, does not commit A.I.D. to issue a guaranty contract, nor indicate that the foreign government will approve the project, nor assure the investor that further information about the proposed investment may not make it ineligible for guaranty. It merely avoids any subsequent objection that the application is untimely.

Inquiries regarding the specific-risk investment guaranty program should be sent directly to: Investment Guaranties Division, A.I.D., Washington 25, D. C.

Details on "How to Apply" are given in the A.I.D. *Investment Guaranty Handbook* which may be obtained without charge from the Investment Guaranties Division. U. S. Department of Commerce Field Offices are also generally familiar with the Investment Guaranty Program and can usually provide information and copies of this book.

B. *The Extended-Risk Programs*

In addition to the specific-risk guaranties described on preceding pages, Congress has authorized A.I.D. to issue guaranties which cover commercial risks as well as political risks. These guaranties are issued in special and specific cases which occupy high-priority positions in the host country's development.

Two extended-risk guaranties are now offered. One type—General —may be applied in less-developed friendly countries to cover certain losses of private investment in priority projects, including housing. The other type—Latin American Housing Guaranties—is specifically limited to guarantying private investment in self-liquidating pilot or demonstration housing projects in Latin America.

EXTENDED-RISK GENERAL GUARANTEES ELIGIBILITY. The rules governing eligibility for specific-risk guaranties also apply to the extended-risk "general" guaranties.

TERMS AND CONDITIONS. (1) Extended-risk guaranties will be considered only for projects where it can be clearly demonstrated that the private investment would not otherwise be made. (2) This type of guaranty will be issued only to investments in industries, or other areas of economic activity, which have been identified by A.I.D. as being of sufficient importance to qualify for a development loan. Emphasis shall be placed upon projects which further social progress and the development of small independent business enterprises. The Foreign Assistance Act of 1962 expressly provides that extended-risk guaranties may be issued for loan investments in housing projects located in any of the developing countries. (3) Guaranties are available for loans as well as for equity investment. (4) Ordinarily, a fee of 2 per cent per annum of the face value will be charged for an extended-risk guaranty. (5) No individual guaranty shall exceed $25 million for a loan, $10 million otherwise. (6) The guaranty coverage will not extend to loss resulting from fraud or misconduct for which the investor is responsible or from normally insurable risks.

HOW TO APPLY. Inquiries regarding this program should be directed to: Office of Development Finance and Private Enterprise, A.I.D., Washington 25, D. C. This office will then advise prospective applicants of the procedure to be followed.

EXTENDED-RISK LATIN AMERICAN HOUSING GUARANTIES. The Foreign Assistance Act of 1961 also authorized A.I.D. to guaranty private United States investment in self-liquidating pilot or demonstration private housing projects in Latin America.

This program is intended to stimulate private home ownership for middle and lower-middle income families by means of guaranties of long-term mortgage-type financing of housing projects, suitable for conditions in Latin America, and similar to those provided in the United States by the Federal Housing Administration. Guaranties may not be granted for investment in rental housing projects.

Since the housing guaranty program is designed to stimulate the development of demonstration housing projects which would not have been undertaken without a guaranty, only applications for new housing projects will be considered.

ELIGIBILITY. Guaranties for Latin American housing projects are limited to U. S. capital investments made by U. S. citizens or U. S. business entities which are substantially beneficially owned by U. S. citizens.

TERMS AND CONDITIONS. While A.I.D. may not fully guaranty an investment, it is permissible for an investor to obtain security from other sources for all or any part of the portion of the investment not guarantied by A.I.D.

Mortgages may not be held directly by U. S. investors under the guaranty program. An appropriate fiduciary in the host country should hold and service the individual mortgages for the benefit of the U. S. investor.

A fee, based upon the amount of the investment guaranteed, will be charged by A.I.D. for the guaranty. Such fee would not exceed 2 per cent of the amount of that portion of the investment guarantied. No individual guaranty shall exceed $10 million.

HOW TO APPLY. Inquiries regarding this program should be directed to: Housing Guaranties Division, Office of Capital Development Bureau for Latin America, A.I.D., Washington 25, D. C.

Types of Credit Granted

The term "development credit" has been applied loosely to numerous types of financial assistance, running the gamut from outright grants-in-aid to various "soft" and "hard" loans. When properly used, however, grants-in-aid do not qualify as development credit since they include only financial assistance for which no repayment is expected. Soft loans are similar to aid and are, in fact, contingent part-grants. There are many varieties of soft loans, but usually such financial assistance is very long-term (often carrying a maturity of 99 years) and has a low rate of interest. Moreover, soft loans are often repayable in local currency regardless of the currency in which the credit is initially extended. This latter provision is a particularly desirable feature to an underdeveloped country, which often finds it difficult to acquire other currencies.

Hard loans, are made on commercial terms, i.e., with a maturity of 10 or more years (but with a maximum between 20 and 30 years) and at a market rate of interest. Moreover, these loans must be repaid in the currency lent.

As defined in this analysis, the development credit of the lending institutions is *long-term,* with a maturity of 10 years and over. Other characteristics of credit, however, vary among the institutions. These characteristics include the purpose and size of loans, the repayment schedule and currency of repayment, and costs of borrowing.

Purpose of Loans

Most of the development credit extended by the World Bank has been in relatively large loans (with many in the $50- to $100-million range), and has been used primarily for electric power facilities and transportation. The World Bank finances only the foreign exchange portion of the credit. Industrial and agricultural credit, which in general is of smaller average size, has played a comparatively minor role in World Bank lending activity.

The IDA also extends credit for "social overhead" purposes such as road construction and improvement of harbor facilities, but the amount of credit extended by IDA is smaller in size.

The IFC, in contrast, specializes in *lending to or investing in private industrial enterprises, often through local development institutions in participation with private banks.* The IFC participation is usually the smallest component of the total credit and is directed to a wide variety of industries.

The lending activities of the IADB are broad, encompassing most of the principal features of the World Bank and its affiliates. IADB generally seeks to participate with other lending institutions, in that it is willing to finance up to a maximum of one-half of a particular program. Loan commitments have been somewhat smaller in size that those of the World Bank, depending primarily on the type of project financed.

The Ex-Im Bank and AID establish a revolving fund for a borrower to purchase specific capital equipment and machinery produced in the United States. Since emphasis is placed on having the proceeds spent in the country which grants the credit—in this case the United States— such credit has often been termed "tied loans."

A common procedure of the Ex-Im Bank, for example, is to *guarantee payment of letters of credit issued by the commercial bank in favor of the supplier of goods in the United States.* The borrower is then notified of the transaction and that repayment is to be made to the Ex-Im Bank as prearranged. In contrast, credit extended by the World Bank and other multilateral institutions is granted to the borrower in the currency with which the borrower purchases the goods. Tied loans are not an uncommon feature of bilateral credit, since many countries lend on this basis.

Repayment Terms

World Bank credit, which usually carries a maturity of 15 to 25 years, is repayable in installments after a short-duration grace period. Credit of the IFC often carries various stock option features upon maturity. An important development during 1962 was an amendment to the Articles of Agreement of the IFC which removed the restriction on equity investment, thereby enabling IFC to make first investments in equity form as well as to participate for the first time in an underwriting of common shares. Previously, the complex investment formulas that IFC had to employ in order to obtain some equity features in extending credit were a serious barrier to the expansion of operations.

All IDA credit is on identical terms, which are considerably more liberal than those of either the parent body or IFC. IDA credit not only carries a maturity of 50 years, which is much longer than was previously available to underdeveloped nations, but also defers amortization until after a ten-year grace period. All credit of the multilateral institutions, however, is repayable in the currency in which equipment and services are originally purchased.

The credit terms offered by the regional institution, IADB, vary. Private undertakings usually can obtain credit with maturities of 12 years, while public or social overhead ventures may obtain credit with maturities up to 20 years.

While the maturities of the Ex-Im Bank are similar to those of the World Bank, the maturities of AID are often longer. AID's predecessor permitted repayment in the currency of the borrower even though the goods or services were originally purchased in the United States. (In some cases the loans of AID carry maturities up to 50 years and thus verge on being "soft" loans.)

Although most of Ex-Im's credit to finance the movement of goods is intermediate-length credit, a substantial amount of total credit is long-term. For example, of the $942,000,000 credit extended in the fiscal year 1962, about $235,000,000, or one-fourth, carried a maturity of 10 years and over.

Lending Rates

All of the development institutions except IDA lend on commercial terms. The World Bank, for example, bases the interest rate on development credit on the rate it would have to pay on a bond issue of similar maturity. (All countries which borrow at a particular time are charged the same rate of interest.) To this rate is added 1.25 percentage points to cover administrative costs. The rate charged by the World Bank has been historically between four and six per cent. The current rate in mid-1963, is 5.75 per cent. The IADB, the Ex-Im Bank, and AID in their hard loans are currently charging similar rates.

In contrast, the rate charged by IFC has almost always been higher than that of the other institutions (the current rate is 7 per cent). A principal reason for the relatively high rate charged by IFC is the amount of risk usually involved in its loans. Unlike the other development institutions, the credit or investments of IFC in private enterprise carry no government guarantee of repayment. Conversely, the second affiliate of the World Bank, IDA, charges no interest except a service charge of ¾ per cent. Whereas the types of investments made by IFC are expected to provide a reasonable return, the credit of IDA is for social overhead purposes which usually are accepted as nonprofit making.

The easier terms of IDA are undoubtedly a major factor in the relative attractiveness of IDA loans. Another important aspect of the appeal of IDA credit is related to the stage of economic development of the particular borrower. Since the type of credit extended by IDA usually precedes that of the IFC in terms of what a country needs for its growth, loans from the former have performed a vital preliminary function, and have thus been vigorously sought.

With the exception of IDA, and some credit extended by AID, the terms of credit of the other development institutions, although not identical, are similar and can be grouped under the "hard" loan definition. Thus, the principal differences of the development institutions lie along the lines of whether credit is multilateral or bilateral, and whether such credit is "tied."

When tied loans are employed in strictly bilateral agreements, trade among several nations geared to the grounds of comparative advantage is rendered difficult. The tying of loans favors the creditor rather than the borrower; thus it is potentially a hindrance to the growth of underdeveloped areas. This is so especially as compared with credit which can be utilized in a variety of ways in different countries thus promoting wider channels of trade.

Significant "Breakthrough" in Foreign Trade Financing

Certain highly significant developments in 1962 and 1963 have made new channels of financing and credit for foreign trade interests accessible on a scale which had not previously existed. These revolutionary results were accomplished through the expanded activities of the Export-Import Bank of Washington, whereby the Ex-Im Bank now functions in an effective partnership with the entire commercial banking system of the nation. Consequently, virtually every commercial bank in the land—including even the small institutions—can now provide foreign trade financing, whereas, in the past, only the larger banks were in a position to provide such facilities.

The programs and services of the Ex-Im Bank are addressed primarily to financing United States exports. To supplement its own dollar loans, the Bank is dedicated to the task of making financial assistance from private sources more readily available to the American exporter. Ex-Im Bank now places the weight of its resources behind private overseas sales efforts *by underwriting foreign credit insurance, by issuing guarantees to commercial banks, and by considering direct guarantees and financing for exporters when either insurance or commercial bank assistance cannot be obtained.*

In providing these facilities, the Bank considers: the ability of the obligor to make payment; the appropriateness of the credit terms involved; and the ability of the importer's country to service dollar debt.

To give U. S. sellers an export credit insurance system comparable to or better than insurance plans available to their competitors in other countries, the Bank in 1961 arranged for the formation of the Foreign Credit Insurance Association (FCIA). Policies issued by the FCIA enable shippers to insure against political and credit risks on sales whose terms call for payment within five years.

The exporter who has his sale insured should be in position to extend more credit to customers and thus better meet competition. Moreover, he should find it easier to obtain financing for his foreign business at U. S. commercial banks.

The Foreign Credit Insurance Association (FCIA) is comprised of more than 70 major American casualty, marine, and property insurance companies. Policies issued by the FCIA cover both political and credit risks; *political* risks are met by Ex-Im Bank and *credit* risks are shared by the Bank and the FCIA. Proceeds of FCIA policies are assignable to those financing the transaction. *Political risks* are governmental actions which prevent consummation of or payment for the overseas sale: war, civil strife, expropriation, import or export restrictions, or foreign exchange restrictions. *Credit risks* are insolvency of the buyer or protracted default of payment after acceptance of the goods.

The FCIA issues two types of policies. In both the premium rates vary according to terms of payment and the country of the buyer. Under each type, payment is insured from the time the goods are shipped—alternately from the date the order is received—until final payment date: (1) Policies for *short-term transactions* (terms up to 180 days, exceptionally one year, after arrival at destination): the exporter is required to insure all exports to all countries, Canada optional, during a period of one year; cover is for 85 per cent of losses due to credit risks and 95 per cent for political risks. (3) Policies for *medium-term transactions* (six months to five years): the exporter may insure a single sale, or repetitive sales to one buyer during one year, with insurance cover of 85 per cent of losses due to either credit or political risks.

Foreign Credit Insurance and the Commercial Bank

Any bank in the country may now be asked by an exporter to finance an overseas sale covered by export credit insurance issued by the Foreign Credit Insurance Association. Since both political and credit risks are insured, the bank can finance the exporter at small risk to itself.

Alternatively, on medium-term sales exporters may seek *non-recourse financing* from their banks instead of obtaining export credit insurance. Normally, up to 85 per cent of the credit may be financed *without recourse,* meaning that if payment is not received from abroad after the goods have been accepted, the loss, except for the 15 per cent assumed by the exporter, does not fall upon him.

To help provide such financing, export credit guarantees from Ex-Im Bank are available to commercial banks and other financial institutions if the obligations of the foreign buyer are financed without recourse on the U. S. exporter, and if the commercial bank assumes the credit risk on the early maturities of the notes. The guarantee to the lending bank covers political risks on all maturities of the export paper and credit risks on the later maturities. Fees for the guarantees vary by groupings of countries ranked by soundness of the market and by the term of the credit.

The private bank financing an export transaction with Ex-Im Bank guarantees, or the private bank financing an export sale insured by the FCIA immediately pays the exporter 85 per cent of the financed portion and holds the promissory notes of the foreign buyer.

Medium-Term Credit Criteria

In a normal medium-term export transaction: (1) The term of the credit may be from six months to five years after shipment, but not longer than is customary for the goods in international trade. (2) The foreign buyer makes a cash payment of at least 20 per cent (as little as 10 per cent if buyer and market are good risks). (3) The balance (financed portion) is payable in equal installments (semiannually or oftener) in U. S. dollars at a bank in the United States. (4) The exporter carries without Ex-Im Bank guarantee or insurance at least 15 per cent of the financed portion of the credit spread over all installments. (5) The exporter presents evidence that the buyer is fully credit-worthy for the financed portion of the transaction, or that the support of a guarantor is offered.

Responsibilities of the Exporter

It is the intent of Ex-Im Bank to promote export financing with minimum recourse upon the exporter but, as is the case in all other exporting countries, it is felt that the exporter cannot be absolved of all responsibility in his own transactions. Accordingly, the exporter is asked to carry for his own account at least 15 per cent of the financial portion in medium-term sales, regardless of the form of Ex-Im Bank's assistance. Further, the Bank will show a continuing interest in the financial responsibility of the exporter, his experience as an exporter, and his ability satisfactorily to fulfill the terms of his sales contract.

Other Ex-Im Bank Programs

A. *For Exporters*

Export consignment insurance. Ex-Im Bank provides export consignment insurance covering export shipments of U. S. commodities awaiting sale in foreign countries. Coverage is against loss or damage due to war, civil commotion, or from orders emanating from any government or public authority confiscating, expropriating, or requisitioning the goods. The insurance is utilized by U. S. exporters shipping stocks of cotton, tobacco and similar commodities prior to sale. The policies are issued by commercial underwriters, with the American War Risk Agency of New York being authorized by the Bank to act as clearing agent in coordinating, controlling, and recording consignment insurance transactions.

Direct Credits and Guarantees to Exporters—Should an exporter be unable to finance his medium-term transaction through a commercial bank or to insure it with the FCIA, he may apply directly to Ex-Im Bank either for a guarantee or for non-recourse financing. It should be pointed out, however, that Ex-Im Bank will provide direct guarantees or financing only if the reasons for the unwillingness of commercial banks or of FCIA to grant assistance do not also preclude the Bank from engaging in the transactions.

B. For Exporters' Foreign Customer

Long-term project loans. The bulk of the Bank's traditional dollar lending has been through the "project credit" for sizeable purchases of U.S. industrial equipment, materials, and services usually associated with a specific development project abroad; for example power projects, basic manufacturing facilities, road building programs, etc. The application in these cases is made to the Bank by the prospective borrower overseas, who may be either a private or government entity. Terms of repayment are those appropriate for the project and range upwards from five years.

Loans for Agricultural Commodities—Ex-Im Bank makes loans on terms of 12 to 15 months for the overseas sale of U. S. agricultural commodities where circumstances justify these unusual terms. Commodity exports financed by the Bank have included shipments of cotton, wheat, barley, tobacco, and other agricultural products. Borrowers generally are commercial or central banks abroad.

Part 2

CLASSIFIED FINANCING GUIDE

The following section presents a quick reference guide to capital sources for various financing purposes.

ACCOUNTS RECEIVABLE FINANCING
See:
> Commercial Banks
> Finance Companies

AGRICULTURAL FINANCING & LOANS
See:
> Commercial Banks
> U.S. Government Sources (Dept. of Agriculture, Farmers Home Adm.; Commodity Credit Adm.; Farm Credit Adm.; Production Credit Adm.)

AGRICULTURAL PRODUCTION CREDIT
See:
> Commercial Banks
> U.S. Government Sources (Farm Credit Adm.; Production Credit Associations)

AGRICULTURAL RESEARCH PROJECTS, FINANCING FOR
See:
> Foundations
> U.S. Government Sources (Dept. of Agriculture)

AREA REDEVELOPMENT LOANS
See:
> Chambers of Commerce and Industrial Foundations
> U.S. Government Sources (Area Redevelopment Adm.)

AUTO-DEALER FINANCING
See:
> Commercial Banks
> Finance Companies

AUTOMOBILE FINANCING
See:
> Commercial Banks
> Finance Companies

BANK STOCKS, INVESTORS IN
See:
> College and University Endowment Funds
> Investment Companies
> Labor Unions

> Life Insurance Companies
> Pension Funds
> Savings Banks

BANKERS' ACCEPTANCES
See:
> Capital Sources of Special Interest
> Commercial Banks

BANKS
See:
> Commercial Banks
> "Edge Act" Corporations
> Foreign Commercial Banks
> Savings Banks
> Savings & Loan Associations
> Quasi-Government International Finance Agencies

"BEST EFFORTS" UNDERWRITINGS
See:
> Investment Bankers & Underwriters

BOAT (SMALL) FINANCING
See:
> Commercial Banks
> Finance Companies

BOND FINANCING
See:
> Investment Bankers and Underwriters
> Life Insurance Companies
> Small Business Investment Companies

BROKERS' LOANS
See:
> Capital Sources of Special Interest
> Commercial Banks

BUILDING LOANS
See:
> Construction Loans

CALIFORNIA-BASED CHARITIES
See:
> Foundations (California)

"CALL" LOANS
See:
> Capital Sources of Special Interest
> Commercial Banks

CANADIAN PROJECTS, FINANCING FOR
See:
Foreign Commercial Banks (Canadian Section)

CANCER RESEARCH PROJECTS, FINANCING FOR
See:
Foundations

CHATTEL-MORTGAGE FINANCING
See:
Commercial Banks
Finance Companies
Life Insurance Companies

CHEMICAL PROJECTS, FINANCING FOR
See:
Capital Sources of Special Interest (particularly Empire Trust Co.)
Small Business Investment Companies

CHEMICAL SECURITIES, INVESTORS IN
See:
Investment Companies (particularly Chemical Fund)

CHILD WELFARE PROJECTS, FINANCING FOR
See:
Foundations

CHURCH FINANCING
See:
Capital Sources of Special Interest (particularly B.C. Ziegler & Co.)
Foundations
Life Insurance Companies

CIVIL DEFENSE LOANS
See:
Commercial Banks
U.S. Government Sources (Office of Emergency Planning)

COLLATERAL LOANS
See:
Capital Sources of Special Interest (particularly D. H. Blair & Co.; Garvin, Bantel & Co.)
Commercial Banks
Finance Companies

COLLEGE-AID PROJECTS
See:
Foundations

COLLEGE FUNDS FOR INVESTMENT
See:
College & University Endowment Funds

COLLEGE-HOUSING LOANS
See:
U.S. Government Sources (Housing & Home Financing Agency)

COLORADO-BASED CHARITIES
See:
Foundations (Colorado)

COMMERCIAL LOANS
See:
Commercial Banks
Finance Companies

COMMERCIAL PAPER
See:
Capital Sources of Special Interest (particularly First Boston Corp.; Goldman, Sachs & Co.; Salomon Bros. & Hutzler Co.)

COMMODITY LOANS
See:
Commercial Banks
Finance Companies
U.S. Government Sources (particularly Commodity Credit Corp.)

COMMON STOCK FINANCING`
See:
Investment Bankers and Underwriters
Small Business Investment Companies

COMMUNITY AID AND ASSISTANCE LOANS
See:
U.S. Government Sources (particularly Housing & Home Finance Agency)

CONSERVATION LOANS
See:
U.S. Government Sources (particularly Farmers Home Adm.)

CONSTRUCTION LOANS
See:
Life Insurance Companies
Savings Banks
Savings & Loan Associations

"COOLEY LOANS"
See:
Quasi-Government International Finance Agencies (Agency for International Development)

COOPERATIVE (FARM) FINANCING
See:
U.S. Government Sources (Farm Credit Adm.)

CORPORATE-FINANCING (LONG-TERM)
See:
    College & University Endowment Funds
    Investment Bankers & Underwriters
    Labor Union Funds
    Life Insurance Companies
    Pension Funds
    Small Business Investment Companies

CORPORATE FINANCING (SHORT-TERM)
See:
    Capital Sources of Special Interest
    Commercial Banks
    Finance Companies

CORRESPONDENT BANK FACILITIES
See:
    Commercial Banks

CROP STORAGE FACILITY LOANS
See:
    U.S. Government Sources (Commodity
    Credit Corp.)

DEBENTURES (CONVERTIBLE) FINANCING
See:
    Investment Bankers and Underwriters
    Labor Unions
    Life Insurance Companies
    Pension Funds
    Small Business Investment Companies

DEFENSE PRODUCTION LOANS
See:
    Commercial Banks
    U.S. Government Sources (Federal
    Reserve Banks)

DEVELOPMENT FINANCING (DOMESTIC)
See:
    Chambers of Commerce and Industrial
    Foundations
    Small Business Investment Companies
    U.S. Government Sources (Small
    Business Adm.)

DEVELOPMENT FINANCING (INTERNATIONAL)
See:
    "Edge Act" Corporations
    Quasi-Government International
    Finance Agencies

DISASTER LOANS
See:
    U.S. Government Sources (Farmers
    Home Adm.; Small Business Adm.)

DISCOUNTING (OF ACCOUNTS RECEIVABLE)
See:
    Commercial Banks
    Finance Companies

DISCOUNTING (OF COMMERCIAL PAPER AND OTHER FINANCE INSTRUMENTS)
See:
    Capital Sources of Special Interest
    (particularly Discount Corp.; First
    Boston Corp.; Goldman Sachs & Co.;
    Salomon Bros. & Hutzler Co.)
    Finance Companies

DISPLACED BUSINESSES, LOANS FOR
See:
    U.S. Government Sources (Small
    Business Adm.)

ECONOMIC RESEARCH PROJECTS, FINANCING FOR
See:
    Foundations

"EDGE ACT" FINANCING
See:
    "Edge Act" Corporations

EDUCATIONAL AND RESEARCH PROJECTS, FINANCING FOR
See:
    Foundations

ELECTRONICS PROJECTS, FINANCING FOR
See:
    Capital Sources of Special Interest
    (American Research & Development
    Co.; Empire Trust Co.)
    Small Business Investment Companies

ELECTRONICS SECURITIES, INVESTORS IN
See:
    Investment Companies (particularly
    Television Electronics Fund, Inc.;
    United Science Fund)

ENDOWMENT FUNDS
See:
    College & University Endowment Funds

EQUIPMENT & MACHINERY FINANCING
See:
    Commercial Banks
    Finance Companies

EQUITY FINANCING
See:
  Investment Bankers and Underwriters
  Small Business Investment Companies

"EURO-DOLLAR" FUNDS
See:
  Commercial Banks (particularly the large
  "international" banks: Bank of
  America; Chase-Manhattan Bank;
  First National Bank of Boston; First
  National City Bank of N.Y.;
  Morgan-Guaranty Trust Co.)
  Foreign Commercial Banks (see banks
  listed for various European countries)

EUROPEAN SECURITIES, INVESTORS IN
See:
  Capital Sources of Special Interest
  Foreign Commercial Banks
  Investment Companies

EXPORT FINANCING
See:
  Commercial Banks
  Finance Companies
  Foreign Commercial Banks
  Quasi-Government International
  Finance Agencies

EXPORT INSURANCE
See:
  Quasi-Government International
  Finance Agencies (particularly
  Export-Import Bank)

FACTORING
See:
  Commercial Banks
  Finance Companies

FARM EQUIPMENT FINANCING
See:
  U.S. Government Sources (Farm Credit
  Adm. Federal Land Bank Adm.)

FARM LOANS
  (See: Agricultural Loans)

FHA LOANS
See:
  Commercial Banks
  Insurance Companies
  Savings & Loan Associations
  Saving Banks
  U.S. Government Sources (Federal
  Housing Adm.)

FINE ARTS PROJECTS, FINANCING FOR
See:
  Foundations

"FIRM UNDERWRITING" FINANCING
See:
  Investment Bankers and Underwriters

FISHERY PROJECT FINANCING
See:
  U.S. Government Sources (Bur. of
  Commercial Fisheries)

FOREIGN CREDIT INSURANCE
See:
  U.S. Government Sources (Export
  Import Bank)

FOREIGN CURRENCY LOANS
See:
  Commercial Banks
  Foreign Commercial Banks
  Quasi-Government International
  Finance Agencies

FOREIGN EXCHANGE FUNDS
See:
  Capital Sources of Special Interest
  (particularly American Express Co.;
  Deak & Co.)
  Commercial Banks
  Foreign Commercial Banks

FOREIGN SECURITIES, INVESTORS AND UNDERWRITERS
See:
  Capital Sources of Special Interest
  Foreign Commercial Banks
  Investment Bankers and Underwriters
  Investment Companies

FOREIGN TRADE FINANCING
See:
  Capital Sources of Special Interest
  Commercial Banks
  Finance Companies
  Quasi-Government International
  Finance Agencies

FORESTRY LOANS
See:
  Commercial Banks
  U.S. Government Sources (Farmers
  Home Adm.)

GEORGIA-BASED CHARITIES
See:
  Foundations (Georgia)

HANDICAPPED CHILDREN PROJECTS, FINANCING FOR
See:
  Foundations

HEALTH PROJECTS, FINANCING FOR
See:
  Foundations

HOME IMPROVEMENT FINANCING
See:
  Commercial Banks
  Finance Companies
  Life Insurance Companies
  Savings Banks
  Savings & Loan Associations

HORTICULTURAL PROJECTS, FINANCING FOR
See:
  Foundations
  U.S. Government Sources (Farm Credit Adm.)

HOSPITAL PROJECTS, FINANCING FOR
See:
  Foundations

HOTEL INDUSTRY RESEARCH PROJECTS
See:
  Foundations

HOUSING LOANS
See:
  Commercial Banks
  Life Insurance Companies
  Savings Banks
  Savings & Loan Associations
  U.S. Government Sources of Capital (Federal Housing Adm.)

ILLINOIS-BASED CHARITIES
See:
  Foundations (Illinois)

IMPORT FINANCING
See:
  Commercial Banks
  Finance Companies

INDIANS, LOANS TO
See:
  U.S. Government Sources (Bur. of Indian Affairs)

INDUSTRIAL EQUIPMENT, FINANCING FOR
See:
  Commercial Banks

Finance Companies
Industrial Foundations

INDUSTRIAL LOANS
See:
  Commercial Banks
  Finance Companies
  Industrial Foundations

INDUSTRIAL PLANTS, FINANCING FOR
See:
  Industrial Foundations
  Investment Bankers and Underwriters

INSTALLMENT LOANS
See:
  Commercial Banks
  Finance Companies
  U.S. Government Sources (Small Business Adm.)

INSURANCE POLICIES, LOANS SECURED BY
See:
  Commercial Banks
  Finance Companies
  Life Insurance Companies

INSURANCE STOCKS, INVESTORS IN
See:
  College and University Endowment Funds
  Investment Companies (particularly Insurance Securities Trust Funds)
  Labor Unions
  Pension Funds

INTER-AMERICAN DEVELOPMENT FINANCING
See:
  Capital Sources of Special Interest (particularly Deltec Panamericana, S.A.; Frederick B. Hatch & Co.; New York Hanseatic Corp.; Truman & Co.)
  Quasi-Government International Finance Agencies

INTERMEDIATE CREDIT (AGRICULTURAL)
See:
  U.S. Government Sources (Farm Credit Adm.; Federal Intermediate Credit Banks)

INTERNATIONAL FINANCE CORPORATION
See:
  Quasi-Government International Finance Agencies

INTERNATIONAL TRADE FINANCING
See:
   Capital Sources of Special Interest
   Commercial Banks
   Finance Companies
   Foreign Commercial Banks
   Quasi-Government International
   Finance Agencies

INVENTORY LOANS
See:
   Commercial Banks
   Finance Companies

INVESTORS IN CORPORATE SECURITIES (STOCKS, BONDS, ETC.)
See:
   College and University Endowment
   Funds
   Foundations
   Investment Companies
   Labor Unions
   Life Insurance Companies
   Pension Funds
   Savings Banks
   Small Business Investment Companies

JAPANESE FINANCING
See:
   Foreign Commercial Banks (Japan)

JEWISH CHARITIES
See:
   Foundations

LAND-BANK LOANS
See:
   U.S. Government Sources (Farm Credit
   Adm., Federal Land Banks)

LAND DEVELOPMENT PROJECTS
See:
   Small Business Investment Companies

LATIN-AMERICAN FINANCING
See:
   Capital Sources of Special Interest
   (particularly Deltec Panamericana,
   S.A.; Frederick B. Hatch & Co.;
   New York Hanseatic Corp.; Truman
   & Co.)
   "Edge Act" Corporations
   Foreign Commercial Banks (see Banks
   in Latin-American Nations)
   Quasi-Government International
   Finance Agencies

LEASEBACK FINANCING (see
   Sale-Leaseback Financing)

LEASING AND EQUIPMENT — LEASE FINANCING
See:
   Commercial Banks
   Finance Companies

LETTERS OF CREDIT
See:
   Capital Sources of Special Interest
   (particularly American Express Co.)
   Commercial Banks
   Foreign Commercial Banks

LIBRARY AID PROJECTS
See:
   Foundations

LIVESTOCK FINANCING
See:
   Commercial Banks
   U.S. Government Sources (Farm Credit
   Adm.; Farmers Home Adm.)

MICHIGAN-BASED CHARITIES
See:
   Foundations (Michigan)

MOBILE-DRYER EQUIPMENT LOANS
See:
   U.S. Government Sources

MONEY-ORDERS, INTERNATIONAL
See:
   Capital Sources of Special Interest
   (American Express Co.)
   Commercial Banks
   Foreign Commercial Banks

MORTGAGE FINANCING, SOURCES OF
See:
   College & University Endowment Funds
   Commercial Banks
   Foundations
   Labor Unions
   Life Insurance Companies
   Pension Funds
   Savings Banks
   Savings & Loan Associations

MUNICIPAL FINANCING
See:
   Investment Bankers and Underwriters
   Life Insurance Companies
   U.S. Government Sources (Housing and
   Home Financing Agency; Community
   Facilities Adm.)

MUTUAL FUNDS
See:
Investment Companies

NATURAL GAS PROJECTS, FINANCING FOR
See:
Capital Sources of Special Interest (Empire Trust Co.)
Commercial Banks (particularly Bank of America; Chase-Manhattan Bank; First National City Bank of N.Y.; Republic National Bank, Dallas)
Investment (Bankers and Underwriters) (particularly Bache & Co.; Eastman-Dillon-Union Securities Co.; Kuhn, Loeb & Co.)
Small Business Investment Companies

NATURAL RESOURCES PROJECTS, FINANCING FOR
See:
Capital Sources of Special Interest (Empire Trust Co.)
Small Business Investment Companies
U.S. Government Sources (Dept. of Interior)

NEW YORK STATE-BASED CHARITIES
See:
Foundations (New York)

NORTH CAROLINA-BASED CHARITIES
See:
Foundations (North Carolina)

"NOTIFICATION" FINANCING AND "NON-NOTIFICATION" FINANCING
See:
Finance Companies

NUCLEAR ENERGY PROJECTS, FINANCING FOR
See:
Small Business Investment Companies

OHIO-BASED CHARITIES
See:
Foundations (Ohio)

OIL PROJECTS, FINANCING FOR
See:
Capital Sources of Special Interest (Empire Trust Co.)
Commercial Banks (particularly Bank of America; Chase-Manhattan Bank; First National City Bank of N.Y.; Republic National Bank of Dallas)

Investment Bankers and Underwriters (particularly Bache & Co.; Eastman-Dillon-Union Securities Corp.; Kuhn, Loeb & Co.)
Life Insurance Companies (particularly Metropolitan Life Insurance Co.)
Small Business Investment Companies

OIL SECURITIES, INVESTORS IN
See:
College and University Endowment Funds
Investment Companies
Labor Unions
Life Insurance Companies
Pension Funds
Small Business Investment Companies

OKLAHOMA-BASED CHARITIES
See:
Foundations (Oklahoma)

PENNSYLVANIA-BASED CHARITIES
See:
Foundations (Pennsylvania)

PERSONAL LOANS
See:
Commercial Banks
Finance Companies

PRESBYTERIAN CHURCH PROJECTS, FINANCING FOR
See:
Foundations

PRICE-SUPPORT LOANS (Agricultural)
See:
U.S. Government Sources (Commodity Credit Corp.)

PRIVATE-PLACEMENT FINANCING
See:
Investment Bankers and Underwriters

PROTESTANT CHURCH PROJECTS, FINANCING FOR
See:
Foundations

PUBLIC FACILITY LOANS
See:
U.S. Government Sources (Housing and Home Financing Agency; Community Facilities Adm.)

PUBLIC HOUSING FINANCING
See:
U.S. Government Sources (Housing and Home Financing Agency; Community Facilities Adm.)

PUBLIC UNDERWRITING
See:
    Investment Bankers and Underwriters

PUBLIC WORKS FINANCING
See:
    U.S. Government Sources (Housing and
    Home Financing Agency; Community
    Facilities Adm.)

RAILROAD SECURITIES, INVESTORS IN
See:
    College and University Endowment
    Funds
    Investment Companies
    Labor Unions
    Life Insurance Companies
    Pension Funds

REAL ESTATE FINANCING
See:
    Commercial Banks
    Finance Companies
    Life Insurance Companies
    Savings Banks
    Savings & Loan Associations
    Small Business Investment Companies
    U.S. Government Sources (Farmers
    House Adm.; Federal Housing Adm.;
    Veterans Adm.)

RECLAMATION PROJECT LOANS
See:
    U.S. Government Sources (Dept. of
    Interior, Bur. of Reclamation)

RECREATIONAL FACILITIES, FINANCING FOR
See:
    U.S. Government Sources (Farmers
    Home Adm.)

REDISCOUNTING (OF LOANS)
See:
    Commercial Banks
    Finance Companies
    U.S. Government Sources (Federal
    Reserve)

REGULATION A UNDERWRITING

REGULATION A-R UNDERWRITING

REGULATION A-M UNDERWRITING

REGULATION B UNDERWRITING

REGULATION B-T UNDERWRITING
See:
    Investment Bankers and Underwriters

ROMAN CATHOLIC CHURCH PROJECTS, FINANCING FOR
See:
    Foundations

ROTHSCHILD BANKING INTERESTS
See:
    Capital Sources of Special Interest

RURAL ELECTRIFICATION LOANS
See:
    U.S. Government Sources (Rural
    Electrification Adm.)

RURAL HOUSING LOANS
See:
    U.S. Government Sources (Farmers
    Home Adm.)

RURAL TELEPHONE PROJECTS, FINANCING FOR
See:
    U.S. Government Sources (Rural
    Electrification Adm.)

SALE-LEASEBACK FINANCING
See:
    Finance Companies
    Life Insurance Companies

SCHOLARSHIP FUNDS
See:
    Foundations

SCIENTIFIC PROJECTS, FINANCING FOR
See:
    Foundations
    Small Business Investment Companies

SECURED LOANS
See:
    Capital Sources of Special Interest
    Commercial Banks
    Finance Companies
    Life Insurance Companies
    Small Business Investment Companies

"SENIOR CITIZENS" HOUSING LOANS
See:
    U.S. Government Sources (Housing and
    Home Financing Agency)

SHIP FINANCING
See:
    U.S. Government Sources (Dept. of
    Interior, Bur. of Commercial
    Fisheries, Maritime Adm.)

SMALL BUSINESS FINANCING
See:
    Commercial Banks
    Finance Companies
    Life Insurance Companies
    Small Business Investment Companies
    U.S. Government Sources (Small
    Business Adm.)

SOCIAL PROGRESS TRUST FUND
See:
    Quasi-Government International
    Finance Agencies (Inter-American
    Development Bank)

"STANDBY" FINANCING
See:
    Finance Companies

STATE DEVELOPMENT FINANCING
See:
    Chambers of Commerce and Industrial
    Foundations
    U.S. Government Sources (Small
    Business Adm.)

STEEL SECURITIES, INVESTORS IN
See:
    College and University Endowment
    Funds
    Investment Companies
    Labor Unions
    Life Insurance Companies
    Pension Funds

STOCKMEN'S LOANS
See:
    Commercial Banks
    U.S. Government Sources (Farm Credit
    Adm., Federal Land Bank Assns.)

SWISS BANK ACCOUNTS

SWISS BANK FINANCING
See:
    Foreign Commercial Banks (Switzerland)

TECHNOLOGICAL PROJECTS,
FINANCING FOR
See:
    Capital Sources of Special Interest
    (American Research & Development
    Corp.)
    Small Business Investment Companies

TENNESSEE-BASED CHARITIES
See:
    Foundations (Tennessee)

TERM LOANS
See:
    Commercial Banks
    Finance Companies
    Life Insurance Companies
    Small Business Investment Companies

TEXAS-BASED CHARITIES
See:
    Foundations (Texas)

TIME DEPOSITS AND CERTIFICATE
OF DEPOSIT FINANCING
See:
    Capital Sources of Special Interest
    Commercial Banks

"UNDERDEVELOPED NATIONS,"
FINANCING FOR
See:
    Quasi-Government International
    Finance Agencies

U.S. GOVERNMENT SECURITIES AND
SECURITIES OF GOVERNMENT
AGENCIES, INVESTORS IN
See:
    Capital Sources of Special Interest
    College and University Endowment
    Funds
    Commercial Banks
    Investment Companies
    Labor Unions
    Life Insurance Companies
    Pension Funds
    Savings Banks
    Savings & Loan Associations

URBAN RENEWAL PROJECTS,
FINANCING FOR
See:
    U.S. Government Sources (Housing and
    Home Financing Agency, Urban
    Renewal Adm.)

UTILITY (ELECTRIC) SECURITIES,
INVESTORS IN
See:
    Capital Sources of Special Interest
    College and University Endowment
    Funds
    Investment Companies
    Labor Unions
    Life Insurance Companies
    Savings Banks

V-LOANS
See:
Commercial Banks
U.S. Government Sources (Federal Reserve)

VENTURE CAPITAL
See:
Capital Sources of Special Interest
Small Business Investment Companies

VETERANS' LOANS
See:
Commercial Banks
U.S. Government Sources (Veterans Adm.)

WAREHOUSE RECEIPTS, LOANS SECURED BY
See:
Commercial Banks
Finance Companies

WATERSHED LOANS
See:
U.S. Government Sources (Farmers Home Adm.)

WELFARE PROJECTS, FINANCING FOR
See:
Foundations

WORKING CAPITAL LOANS
See:
Commercial Banks
Finance Companies
Life Insurance Companies

"WORLD BANK" FINANCING
See:
Quasi-Government International Finance Agencies (International Bank for Reconstruction and Development)

YOUTH PROJECTS, FINANCING FOR
See:
Foundations

Part 3

DIRECTORY OF CAPITAL SOURCES AND MAJOR INVESTING INSTITUTIONS

COMMERCIAL BANKS

The following is a list of principal commercial banks of the United States arranged in order of deposits.

Bank of America, NT and SA
300 Montgomery St.
San Francisco 20, Cal.
Financial Officer: Nolan Browning, V. P.
Deposits: $12,095,965,000

Chase Manhattan Bank
1 Chase Manhattan Plaza
New York 15, N. Y.
Financial Officer: Clement A. Bramley Jr.,
V. P. and Treas.
Deposits: $9,631,947,000

First National City Bank
55 Wall St.
New York 15, N. Y.
Financial Officer: A. H. Cook, Exec. V. P.
Deposits: $9,141,539,000

Manufacturers-Hanover Trust Co.
40 Wall St.
New York 5, N. Y.
Financial Officer: B. C. Deering, Exec. V. P.
Deposits: $5,674,454,000

Chemical Bank—New York Trust Co.
165 Broadway
New York 15, N. Y.
Financial Officer: John L. Gibbons,
Exec. V. P.
Deposits: $4,562,502,000

Morgan Guaranty Trust Co.
140 Broadway
New York 15, N. Y.
Financial Officer: H. F. Anderson, Sr., V. P.
Deposits: $4,381,189,000

Security First National Bank
Sixth and Spring Sts.
Los Angeles 54, Cal.
Financial Officer: W. E. Siegel, Exec. V. P.
Deposits: $3,949,766,000

Continental Illinois National Bank & Trust Co.
231 So. La Salle St.
Chicago 90, Ill.
Financial Officer: J. F. Mannion, Sr., V. P.
Deposits: $3,542,054,000

Bankers Trust Co.
16 Wall St.
New York 5, N. Y.
Fin. Officer: John M. Budinger, Sr. V. P.
Deposits: $3,476,441,000

First National Bank of Chicago
38 So. Dearborn St.
Chicago 90, Ill.
Financial Officer: R. H. Becker, Exec. V. P.
Deposits: $3,314,590,000

Wells Fargo Bank
464 California St.
San Francisco 20, Cal.
Fin. Officer: D. W. Chapman, Exec. V. P.
Deposits: $2,941,295,000

United California Bank
600 So. Spring St.
Los Angeles 14, Cal.
Financial Officer: Hal Mendon, Exec. V. P.
Deposits: $2,389,192,000

Irving Trust Co.
1 Wall St.
New York 1, N. Y.
Fin. Officer: Wm. E. Peterson, Exec. V. P.
Deposits: $2,354,058,000

National Bank of Detroit
Woodward Ave. and Fort St.
Detroit 32, Mich.
Financial Officer: H. T. Bodman, Exec. V.P.
Deposits: $2,178,777,000

Mellon National Bank and Trust Co.
Mellon Square
Pittsburgh 30, Pa.
Financial Officer: John A. Mayer, Sr., V. P.
Deposits: 2,172,849,000

Crocker-Angelo National Bank
1 Montgomery St.
San Francisco 20, Cal.
Financial Officer: J. J. Hogan, First V. P.
Deposits: $2,134,493,000

First National Bank
67 Milk St.
Boston 6, Mass.
Financial Officer: H. M. Chadsey, Sr., V. P.
Deposits: $1,692,445,000

Cleveland Trust Co.
Euclid and East 9th St.
Cleveland 1, Ohio
Financial Officer: R. M. Bourne, V. P.
Deposits: $1,505,004,000

First Pennsylvania Banking and Trust Co.
15th and Chestnut Sts.
Philadelphia 1, Pa.
Financial Officer: W. B. Walker, Exec. V. P.
Deposits: $1,268,679,000

Republic National Bank
Republic Bank Bldg.
Dallas 22, Tex.
Financial Officer: L. S. Dupree, Exec. V. P.
Deposits: $1,201,330,000

Philadelphia National Bank
Broad and Chestnut Sts.
Philadelphia, Pa.
Fin. Officer: John McDowell, Exec. V. P.
Deposits: $1,145.994,000

Seattle First National Bank
Second Ave. and Columbia St.
Seattle 24, Wash.
Fin. Officer: R. S. Beaupre, Exec. V. P.
Deposits: $1,089,500,000

Harris Trust and Savings Bank
111 West Monroe St.
Chicago 90, Ill.
Financial Officer: B. A. Brannin, Exec. V. P.
Deposits: $1,089,500,000

First National Bank
Dallas, Tex.
Fin. Officer: R. H. Stewart, III, Sr., V. P.
Deposits: $1,054,850,000

Franklin National Bank
199 Second St.
Mineola, N. Y.
Fin. Officer: P. E. Prosswimmer, Exec. V. P.
Deposits: $1,043,906,000

Union Bank (Los Angeles)
  Eighth and Hill Sts.
Los Angeles 54, Cal.
Financial Officer: Hal W. Cross, Exec. V. P.
Deposits: $1,016,113,000

First National Bank of Oregon
400 S. W. Sixth Ave.
Portland, Ore.
Financial Officer: R. M. Colwell Sr., V. P.
Deposits: $1,002,158,000

Detroit Bank and Trust Co.
State and Griswold Sts.
Detroit 31, Mich.
Financial Officer: C. H. Hewitt, Exec. V. P.
Deposits: $983,743,000

United States National Bank
Sixth and Broadway
Portland, Ore.
Financial Officer: D. E. Abram, Sr. V. P.
Deposits: $983,473,000

Manufacturers National Bank
151 West Fort St.
Detroit 31, Mich.
Fin. Officer: R. A. Newhart, Exec. V. P.
Deposits: $981,166,000

Pittsburgh National Bank
Fifth Ave. and Wood St.
Pittsburgh 30, Pa.
Fin. Officer: M. E. Lambling, Exec. V. P.
Deposits: $972,921,000

National City Bank of Cleveland
623 Euclid Ave.
Cleveland 1, Ohio
Fin. Officer: J. S. Fangboner, First V. P.
Deposits: $904,262,000

Northern Trust Co.
La Salle and Monroe Sts.
Chicago 90, Ill.
Financial Officer: D. R. Fuller Sr., V. P.
Deposits: $855,369,000

Marine Trust Co. of Western N. Y.
237 Main St.
Buffalo 5, N. Y.
Financial Officer: A. L. Sanderson Sr., V. P.
Deposits: $819,582,000

Wachovia Bank and Trust Co.
Winston-Salem, N. C.
Financial Officer: R. M. Davis, Sr. V. P.
Deposits: $817,215,000

First City National Bank
931 Main St.
Houston 1, Tex.
Financial Officer: T. W. Gregory, Exec. V. P.
Deposits: $816,979,000

First Wisconsin National Bank
743 No. Water St.
Milwaukee, Wis.
Fin. Officer: J. W. Simpson, Jr., Exec. V. P.
Deposits: $808, 461, 000

Marine-Midland Trust Co.
120 Broadway
New York 15, N. Y.
Financial Officer: D. P. Adams, Adm., V. P.
Deposits: $801,040,000

Central National Bank
123 W. Prospect Ave.
Cleveland 15, Ohio
Financial Officer: E. L. Carpenter Sr., V. P.
Deposits: $747,556,000

Valley National Bank
141 No. Central Ave.
Phoenix, Ariz.
Financial Officer: James Dismuke, V. P.
   and cashier
Deposits: $743,791,000

Citizens National Bank
457 So. Spring St.
Los Angeles 54, Cal.
Financial Officer: E. G. Rider, V. P. and
   cashier
Deposits: $736,081,000

Bank of California
400 California St.
San Francisco 20, Cal.
Financial Officer: A. J. Mayman Sr., V. P.
Deposits: $732,284,000

Mercantile Trust Co.
Eighth and Locust Sts.
St. Louis 1, Mo.
Financial Officer: H. F. Coerver Sr., V. P.
Deposits: $707,298,000

Meadow Brook National Bank
91-16 168th St.
Jamaica, N. Y.
Financial Officer: J. R. Mc Lees, Exec. V. P.
Deposits: $704,298,000

Bank of New York
48 Wall St.
New York 15, N. Y.
Financial Officer: C. M. Bliss, Exec. V. P.
Deposits: $676,162,000

First National Bank in St. Louis
510 Locust St.
St. Louis 1, Mo.
Financial Officer: J. B. Mitchell, Exec. V. P.
Deposits: $675,735,000

Northwestern National Bank of
   Minneapolis
620 Marquette Ave
Minneapolis 2, Minn.
Fin. Officer: H. T. Rutledge, Exec. V. P.
Deposits: $646,428,000

National Bank of Commerce
Second Ave. and Spring St.
Seattle 11, Wash.
Financial Officer: R. J. Stonwell Sr., V. P.
Deposits: $619,097,000

County Trust Co.
White Plains, N. Y.
Financial Officer: W. W. Post, Exec. V. P.
Deposits: $616,083,000

EDGE ACT CORPORATIONS

The Edge Act and applicable regulations provide for two kinds of U.S. financial institutions authorized to do business outside the United States. Broadly defined: one, a banking corporation, may engage in commercial banking activities but may not make equity investments; the other, a financing corporation, may not receive deposits but may make equity investments.

FINANCING CORPORATION	OWNED BY
Bamercial International Financial Corp.	Bank of America National Trust & Savings Assn., San Francisco, Cal.
Bankers International Financing Co., Inc.	Bankers Trust Company New York, N. Y.
Boston Overseas Financial Corp.	First National Bank of Boston Boston, Mass.
Chase International Investment Corp.	Chase Manhattan Bank New York, N.Y.
Chemical International Finance, Ltd.	Chemical Bank New York Trust Co. New York, N.Y.
Continental International Finance Corp.	Continental Illinois National Bank and Trust Co. of Chicago, Chicago, Ill.
First National City Overseas Investment Corp.	First National City Bank New York, N.Y.
First Pennsylvania Overseas Finance Corp.	First Pennsylvania Banking & Trust Co., Philadelphia, Pa.
Manufacturers Hanover International Finance Corp.	Manufacturers Hanover Trust Co. New York, N. Y.
Morgan Guaranty International Finance Corp.	Morgan Guaranty Trust Company New York, N.Y.
Philadelphia International Investment Corp.	Philadelphia National Bank Philadelphia, Pa.

BANKING CORPORATION	OWNED BY
Bank of America (International)	Bank of America National Trust & Savings Assn., San Francisco, Cal.
Bankers International Corporation	Bankers Trust Company New York, N.Y.
Chase Manhattan Overseas Banking Corp.	Chase Manhattan Bank New York, N.Y.
Chemical International Banking Corp.	Chemical Bank New York Trust Co. New York, N.Y.
Continental Bank International	Continental Illinois National Bank and Trust Co., Chicago, Ill.
The First Bank of Boston International	The First National Bank of Boston Boston, Mass.
Manufacturers Hanover International Banking Corp.	Manufacturers Hanover Trust Co. New York, N.Y.
Morgan Guaranty International Banking Corp.	Morgan Guaranty Trust Co. New York, N.Y.
Western Bancorporation International Bank	Western Bancorporation Los Angeles, Cal.

IMPORTANT FOREIGN COMMERCIAL BANKS

ARGENTINA
Banco De La Nacion
Bartolome Mitre 326
Buenos Aires, Argentina
Financial Officer: Dr. Modesto A.
　Sagastume, Gen. Mgr.
Resources: $637,039,000

AUSTRALIA
Bank of New South Wales
341 George St.
Sydney, Australia
Financial Officer: H. C. C. Marshall,
　Gen. Mgr.
Resources: $1,212,649,000

**Commonwealth Trading Bank of
Australia**
Pitt St. and Martin Pl.
Sydney, Australia
Financial Officer: L. A. McWatters,
　Gen. Mgr.
Resources: $779,794,000

AUSTRIA
Creditanstalt Bankverein
6 Schottengasse
Vienna, Austria
Financial Officer: Dr. Josef Joham,
　Man. Dir.
Resources: $366,566,000

BELGIUM
Banque "Societe Generale" de Belgique
3 Montagne Sur Parc
Brussels, Belgium
Financial Officer: Gaston Verbuyt,
　Man. Dir.
Resources: $1,025,874,000

BRAZIL
Banco Do Brasil, S.A.
Rua Primeiro De Marco 66
Rio De Janeiro, Brazil
Financial Officer: Joao B. L. Figuerido,
　Chief Gen. Mgr.
Resources: $1,064,792,000

CANADA
Royal Bank of Canada
360 St. James St. West
Montreal 1, Quebec
Financial Officer: C. B. Neapole,
　Gen. Mgr.
Resources: $4,310,756,000

Canadian Bank of Commerce
25 King St. West
Toronto 1, Ontario
Financial Officer: J. P. R. Wadsworth,
　V.P. & Gen. Mgr.
Resources: $4,185,973,000

Bank of Montreal
129 St. James St., West
Montreal, Quebec
Financial Officer: R. D. Mulholland,
　V.P. & Gen. Mgr.
Resources: $3,532,346,000

Bank of Nova Scotia
44 King St., West
Toronto 1, Ontario
Financial Officer: J. D. Gibson, Gen. Mgr.
Resources: $2,049,706,000

Toronto-Dominion Bank
King and Bay Sts.
Toronto 1, Ontario
Financial Officer: A. E. Hall, Gen. Mgr.
Resources: $1,903,568,000

CHILE
Banco del Estado de Chile
Alemeda Bernaro O'Higgins 1111
Santiago, Chile
Financial Officer: Augustin P. Duran,
　Gen. Mgr.
Resources: $252,517,000

DENMARK
Kjobenshavns Handelsbank, AS
2 Holmens Kanal
Copenhagen, Denmark
Financial Officer: E. Glashof, Gen. Mgr.
Resources: $402,664,000

EGYPT
Banque Misr, SAE
Rue Mohamed Bey Farid
Cairo, Egypt
Financial Officer: Mohamed Rouchdy,
　Chm. & Man. Dir.
Resources: $367,906,000

ENGLAND
Barclays Bank, Ltd.
54 Lombard St.
London, E.C. 3, England
Financial Officer: R. G. Thornton,
　Gen. Mgr.
Resources: $5,104,261,000

Midland Bank Ltd.
Poultry
London, E.C. 2, England
Financial Officer: O. E. Wood
  Chf. Gen. Mgr.
Resources: $4,777,688,000

Lloyds Bank, Ltd.
71 Lombard St.
London, E.C. 3, England
Financial Officer: E. J. N. Warburton,
  Chf. Gen. Mgr.
Resources: $3,944,355,000

Westminster Bank, Ltd.
41 Lothbury St.
London, E.C. 2, England
Financial Officer: A. D. Chesterfield,
  Chf. Gen. Mgr.
Resources: $3,172,754,000

Martins Bank, Ltd.
4 Water St.
Liverpool 2, England
Financial Officer: M. Conacher
  Chf. Gen. Mgr.
Resources: $1,052,924,000

FINLAND
Kansallis-Osaki Pankki
Aleksanteriwkatu, 42
Helsinki, Finland
Financial Officer: Matti Virkkunen
  Chf. Gen. Mgr.
Resources: $441,723,000

FRANCE
Credit Lyonnais, S.A.
19 Boulevard Des Italiens
Paris, France
Financial Officer: Marcel Wiriath,
  Chf. Gen. Mgr.
Resources: $2,853,958,000

Societe Generale
29 Boulevard Haussmann
Paris, France
Financial Officer: J. Ferronniere,
  Gen. Mgr.
Resources: $2,509,506,000

Banque National Pour le Commerce et
  L'Industrie, SA
16 Boulevard des Italiens
Paris, France
Financial Officer: M. P. Chevreer,
  Man. Dir.
Resources: $2,110,740,000

Comptoir Nationale d'Escompte de Paris
14 Rue Bergere
Paris, France
Financial Officer: C. Farnier, Pres.
Resources: $1,240,177,000

GERMANY
Deutsche Bank, A.G.
5-11 Junghofstrasse
Frankfurt, A.M., Germany
Financial Officer: Hermann J. Abs,
  Gen. Mgr.
Resources: $2,784,576,000

Dresdner Bank, A.G.
7 Gallus Anlage
Frankfurt, A.M., Germany
Financial Officer: Fritz Andre, Gen. Mgr.
Resources: $2,063,473,000

Commerzbank, A.G.
Breitstrasse 25
Duesseldorf, Germany
Financial Officer: Dr. Hanns Deuss,
  Dept. Chmn.
Resources: $1,663,355,000

Rheinische Girozentrale und
  Provinziebank
56-60 Friedrichstrasse
Duesseldorf, Germany
Financial Officer: Fritz Butschkau,
  Gen. Mgr.
Resources: $1,570,222,000

GREECE
National Bank of Greece, SA
Cotzia Square
Athens, Greece
Financial Officer: Dimitri Helmas, Gov.
Resources: $425,671,000

HONG KONG
Hong Kong & Shanghai Banking Corp.
1 Queens Rd. Central
Honk Kong, Hong Kong
Financial Officer: M. W. Turner, Chf. Mgr.
Resources: $1,136,341,000

INDIA
State Bank of India
P.O. Box 12
Bombay, India
Financial Officer: B. P. Patez, Man. Dir.
Resources: $1,178,815

Central Bank of India, Ltd.
Mahatma Gandhi Rd.
Bombay, India
Financial Officer: Dharamsey M. Khatau,
    Gen. Mgr.
Resources: $464,163,000

IRISH FREE STATE
Munster and Leinster Bank, Ltd.
66 South Mall
Cork, Irish Free State
Financial Officer: T. H. Donovan, Chf.
    Gen. Mgr.
Resources: $268,178,000

ISRAEL
Bank Leumi le-Israel
26-28 Yehuda Halevi St.
Tel Aviv, Israel
Financial Officer: E. Lehmann, Gen. Mgr.
Resources: $550,396,000

ITALY
Banca Nazionale del Lavora
119 Via Vittoria Veneto
Rome, Italy
Financial Officer: Imbriani Longo,
    Gen. Mgr.
Resources: $2,785,538,000

Banca Commerciale Italiana
6 Piazza Scala
Milan, Italy
Financial Officer: Filippo Migliorisi,
    Man. Dir.
Resources: $2,295,228,000

Banca di Roma
Via Del Corso, 307
Rome, Italy
Financial Officer: Raffaele Mancinelli,
    Man. Dir.
Resources: $1,700,162,000

Credito Italiano
Piazza Cordusio
Milan, Italy
Financial Officer: Mario Schiavi,
    Man. Dir.
Resources: $1,694,186,000

Banca di Napoli
Via Roma, 478
Naples, Italy
Financial Officer: Dr. Stanislao Fusco,
    Gen. Mgr.
Resources: $1,402,795,000

Banca di Sicilia
Via Roma, 185
Palermo, Italy
Financial Officer: Dr. Giuseppe La
    Barbera, Gen. Mgr.
Resources: $1,095,850,000

JAPAN
Fuji Bank, Ltd.
1 Chome Otzmachi
Tokyo, Japan
Financial Officer: Kunihiko Sasaki,
    Gen. Mgr.
Resources: $2,255,809,000

Mitsubishi Bank, Ltd.
2 Chome Marunouchi
Tokyo, Japan
Financial Officer: Ichiro Machida,
    Man. Dir.
Resources: $2,157,481,000

Sanna Bank, Ltd.
Fushimimachi 4 Chome
Osaka, Japan
Financial Officer: Tatsoo Sumi, Sr.
    Man. Dir.
Resources: $2,067,172,000

Sumitomo Bank, Ltd.
5 Chome Kitahama
Osaka, Japan
Financial Officer: Eiya Furuhata,
    Chief Man. Dir.
Resources: $2,061,434,000

MEXICO
Banco Nacional de Mexico, S.A.
Avenida Isabel La Catolica 44
Mexico City, D.F., Mexico
Financial Officer: Javier Bustos, Jr.,
    Dep. Pres.
Resources: $329,447,000

Banco de Comercio, S.A.
Gante 20
Mexico City, D. F., Mexico
Financial Officer: J. A. Velasco, Sr. V. P.
Resources: $133,834,000

NETHERLANDS
Cooperative Centrale Raiffeisen-Bank
St. Jacobsstraat, 30
Utrecht, Netherlands
Financial Officer: L. De Bruyn, Mgr.
Resources: $988,742,000

Amsterdamsche Bank, N.V.
Herengracht, 595
Amsterdam, Netherlands
Financial Officer: C. A. Klaasse,
  Man. Dir.
Resources: $681,006,000

Nederlandsche Handel-Maatschappij, N.V.
Vijzelstraat, 32
Amsterdam, Netherlands
Financial Officer: K. F. Zeeman, Man. Dir.
Resources: $660,654,000

Cooperative Centrale Boerenleenbank
Dommelstraat, 9
Eindhoven, Netherlands
Financial Officer: Dr. P. C. M. Van
  Campen, Man. Dir.
Resources: $587,351,000

NEW ZEALAND
Bank of New Zealand
239-247 Lambton Quay
Wellington, New Zealand
Financial Officer: R. D. Moore, Gen. Mgr.
Deposits: $393,324,000

NORTHERN IRELAND
Ulster Bank, Ltd.
Waring St.
Belfast, Northern Ireland
Financial Officer: Hugh Clark, Man. Dir.
Resources: $179,863,000

NORWAY
Den Norske Creditbank
Kirkgaten, 21
Oslo, Norway
Financial Officer: Johan Melander,
  Man. Dir.
Resources: $236,233,000

PAKISTAN
National Bank of Pakistan
Victoria Road
Karachi, Pakistan
Financial Officer: A. Mushajir, Man. Dir.
Resources: $220,815,000

PHILIPPINES
Philippine National Bank
296-302 Escolta St.
Manila, Philippines
Financial Officer: Conrado P. Sevilla,
  Exec. V. P.
Resources: $397,261,000

PORTUGAL
**Banco Espirito Santo e Comercial de
  Lisboa**
Rua do Comercio
Lisbon, Portugal
Financial Officer: Alvaro P. De Souza,
  Vice Gov.
Resources: $171,549,000

REPUBLIC OF SOUTH AFRICA
Volkskas, Ltd.
229 Van Der Walt St.
Pretoria (Transvaal), Republic of South
  Africa
Financial Officer: Johannes A. Hurten,
  Gen. Mgr.
Resources: $234,914,000

SCOTLAND
**National Commercial Bank of Scotland,
  Ltd.**
42 St. Andrew St.
Edinburgh, Scotland
Financial Officer: David Alexander,
  Gen. Mgr.
Resources: $642,298,000

Bank of Scotland
The Mound
Edinburgh, Scotland
Financial Officer: The Rt. Hon. Lord
  Polwarth, Dep. Gov.
Resources: $539,374,000

SPAIN
Banco Espanol de Credito
Alcala, 14
Madrid, Spain
Financial Officer: Epifanio R. Botija,
  Man. Dir.
Resources: $986,979,000

Banco Hispanio-Americano
Plaza de Canalejas
Madrid, Spain
Financial Officer: Luis de Usera y
  Lopez-Gonzales, Man. Dir.
Resources: $944,976,000

SWEDEN
Svenska Handelsbanken
Arsnalsgatan, 11
Stockholm, Sweden
Financial Officer: T. Browaldh, Gen. Mgr.
Resources: $1,203,715,000

Skandinaviska Banken
Vastra Hamangatan, 6
Goteborg, Sweden
Financial Officer: F. Ahren, Man. Dir.
Resources: $994,049,000

SWITZERLAND
Swiss Credit Bank
Paradeplatz
Zurich, Switzerland
Financial Officer: Dr. E. Reinhardt,
Gen. Mgr.
Resources: $1,272,330,000
Swiss Bank Corporation
Aeschenvorstadt, 1
Basle, Switzerland
Financial Officer: C.Tuerler, Gen. Mgr.
Resources: $1,259,000,000
Union Bank of Switzerland
Bahnhofstrasse, 45
Zurich, Switzerland

Financial Officer: Dr. A. Schaefer
Chief Gen. Mgr.
Deposits: $1,232,240,000

TURKEY
Turkiye Cumhuriyeti Ziraat Bankasi
Bankalar Cadessi
Ankara, Turkey
Financial Officer: Munir Mostar,
Gen. Mgr.
Resources: $294,711,000

VENEZUELA
Banco De Venezuela, S.A.
Sociedad A Traposos
Caracas, Venezuela
Financial Officer: Eduard S. Fernandez,
V.P.
Resources: $250,570,000

MUTUAL SAVINGS BANKS
Arranged in order of deposits, herein referred to as "resources."

The Bowery Savings Bank
110 East 42nd St.
New York 7, N. Y.
Financial Officer: J. W. Larsen, Exec. V.P.
Resources: $1,726,034,000

The Dime Savings Bank of Brooklyn
De Kalb Ave. and Fulton St.
Brooklyn 1, N. Y.
Financial Officer: A. R. Marcks, Sr. V. P.
Resources: $1,323,247,000

Philadelphia Saving Fund Society
1212 Market St.
Philadelphia 7, Pa.
Financial Officer: Donaldson Cresswell,
Sr. V. P.
Resources: $1,275,640,000

Emigrant Industrial Savings Bank
51 Chambers St.
New York 8, N. Y.
Financial Officer: R. A. Gay, Adm. V. P.
Resources: $1,082,963,000

**Dollar Savings Bank of the City of
New York**
2530 Grand Concourse
New York 58, N. Y.
Financial Officer: T. W. Christy, Sr. V. P.
Resources: $871,747,000

Williamsburgh Savings Bank
1 Hanson Place
Brooklyn 1, N. Y.
Financial Officer: W. J. Buehler,
Exec. V. P.
Resources: $853,700,000

Bank for Savings in the City of New York
280 Park Ave. So.
New York 10, N. Y.
Financial Officer: R. F. Marchant,
Exec. V. P.
Resources: $688,545,000

Greenwich Savings Bank
Broadway & 36th St.
New York 18, N. Y.
Financial Officer: H. G. Berdolt, Sr. V. P.
Resources: $661,507,000

Lincoln Savings Bank
531 Broadway
Brooklyn 6, N.Y.
Financial Officer: E. G. Murphy, V. P.
Resources: $636,211,000

Dry Dock Savings Bank
742 Lexington Ave.
New York 17, N. Y.
Financial Officer: D. C. Welton, Sr. V.P.
Resources: $635,832,000

East New York Savings Bank
Atlantic and Pennsylvania Aves.
Brooklyn 7, N. Y.
Financial Officer: J. P. McGrath,
    Chm. Exec. Comm.
Resources: $599,020,000

East River Savings Bank
26 Cortlandt St.
New York 7, N. Y.
Financial Officer: C. C. Joyce, Sr. V. P.
Resources: $579,182,000

Seamen's Bank for Savings
30 Wall St.
New York 5, N. Y.
Financial Officer: E. C. Egerton,
    Sr. V. P.
Resources: $569,905,000

Buffalo Savings Bank
545 Main St.
Buffalo 1, N. Y.
Financial Officer: R. F. Eisenhardt,
    Sr. V. P.
Resources: $521,563,000

Union Dime Savings Bank
1065 Ave. of the Americas
New York 18, N. Y.
Financial Officer: F. H. Ecker, Sr. V. P.
Resources: $510,476,000

Jamaica Savings Bank
161-02 Jamaica Ave.
Jamaica 32, N. Y.
Financial Officer: H. G. Ficken, Sr. V. P.
Resources: $492,195,000

Central Savings Bank
2100 Broadway
New York 42, N. Y.
Financial Officer: J. O. Dornbusch, V. P.
Resources: $479,816,000

Howard Savings Institution
768 Broad St.
Newark 1, N. J.
Financial Officer: N. P. McGrory, Sr. V. P.
Resources: $478,881,000

Western Saving Fund Society
Broad and Chestnut Sts.
Philadelphia 7, Pa.
Financial Officer: G. H. Jones, V. P.
Resources: $473,820,000

Boston Five Cents Savings Bank
30 School St.
Boston 8, Mass.
Financial Officer: D. L. Brown, V. P.
Resources: $469,231,000

Manhattan Savings Bank
385 Madison Ave.
New York 17, N. Y.
Financial Officer: F. J. Ludemann, V. P.
Resources: $429,863,000

New York Savings Bank
8th Ave. and 14th St.
New York 11, N. Y.
Financial Officer: A. J. Quinn, V.P.
Resources: $414,416,000

Provident Institution for Savings
36 Temple Place
Boston 5, Mass.
Financial Officer: J. S. Howe, Sr. V. P.
Resources: $413,629,000

Harlem Savings Bank
125th and Lexington Ave.
New York 35, N. Y.
Financial Officer: G. B. Somerville, V. P.
Resources: $409,937,000

Erie County Savings Bank
16 Niagara St.
Buffalo 2, N. Y.
Financial Officer: Maurice Austin, V. P.
Resources: $407,512,000

Farmers and Mechanics Savings Bank
90 So. Sixth St.
Minneapolis 2, Minn.
Financial Officer: H. J. Arnott, Exec. V. P.
Resources: $374,607,000

Brooklyn Savings Bank
Pierrepont and Clinton Sts.
Brooklyn 1, N. Y.
Financial Officer: P. L. Greenawalt,
    Exec. V. P.
Resources: $360,705,000

Long Island City Savings Bank
Bridge Plaza North
Long Island City 1, N. Y.
Financial Officer: J. S. Hicks, Jr., V. P.
Resources: $356,029,000

Washington Mutual Savings Bank
1101 Second Ave.
Seattle, Wash.
Financial Officer: J. M. Ryder, Sr. V. P.
Resources: $351,185,000

Bronx Savings Bank
Tremont and Park Aves.
Bronx 57, N. Y.
Financial Officer: F. J. Freeze, Sr. V. P.
Resources: $350,054,000

Society for Savings
31 Pratt St.
Hartford, Conn.
Financial Officer: E. H. Burkle, Sr. V. P.
Resources: $304,934,000

Franklin Savings Bank
8th Ave. and 42nd St.
New York 36, N. Y.
Financial Officer: J. H. Roach, Sr. V. P.
Resources: $302,508,000

Greater New York Savings Bank
5th Ave. and 9th St.
Brooklyn 15, N. Y.
Financial Officer: F. Lipinski, Sr. V. P.
Resources: $296,071,000

People's Savings Bank
Main and State Sts.
Bridgeport 1, Conn.
Financial Officer: G. B. Longstreth,
   Exec. V. P.
Resources: $293,966,000

Greenpoint Savings Bank
807 Manhattan Ave.
Brooklyn 22, N. Y.
Financial Officer: W. L. Linton,
   Exec. V. P.
Resources: $290,934,000

Ridgewood Savings Bank
Myrtle and Forest Aves.
Ridgewood 27, N. Y.
Financial Officer: Herman Dippold,
   Sr. V. P.
Resources: $289,604,000

Beneficial Mutual Savings Bank
1200 Chestnut St.
Philadelphia 7, Pa.
Financial Officer: F. J. McKee, V. P.
Resources: $262,563,000

Suffolk Franklin Savings
45 Franklin St.
Boston 10, Mass.
Financial Officer: J. H. Bacheller,
   Exec. V. P.
Resources: $256,381,000

Savings Bank of Baltimore
Charles and Baltimore Sts.
Baltimore 3, Maryland
Financial Officer: Leonard Eagan,
   Sr. V. P.
Resources: $253,827,000

Queens County Savings Bank
38-25 Main St.
Flushing, N. Y.
Financial Officer: W. C. Rollauer, V. P.
Resources: $237,791,000

South Brooklyn Savings Bank
Court St. and Atlantic Ave.
Brooklyn 1, N. Y.
Financial Officer: D. C Dalziel, Sr. V. P.
Resources: $235,256,000

Providence Institution for Savings
86 S. Main St.
Providence 1, Rhode Island
Financial Officer: B. H. Ineson,
   V. P. & Treas.
Resources: $234,095,000

Onondaga County Savings Bank
101 N. Salina St.
Syracuse 1, N. Y.
Financial Officer: F. A. Balitz, V. P.
Resources: $229,834,000

Rochester Savings Bank
40 Franklin St.
Rochester, N. Y.
Financial Officer: J. W. Gray, V. P.
Resources: $217,868,000

Bay Ridge Savings Bank
5th Ave. and 54th St.
Brooklyn 20, N. Y.
Financial Officer: S. J. Arnessen,
   First V. P.
Resources: $213,461,000

Kings Highway Savings Bank
Kings Highway and E. 16th St.
Brooklyn 29, N. Y.
Financial Officer: J. A. Seidman, V. P.
Resources: $207,032

Hamburg Savings Bank
1456 Myrtle Ave.
Brooklyn 37, N. Y.
Financial Officer: Louis Meyer, V. P.
Resources: $201,927,000

Western Savings Bank
438 Main St.
Buffalo 2, N. Y.
Financial Officer: F. H. Richard, V. P.
Resources: $201,026,000

Dollar Savings Bank
4th Ave. and Smithfield St.
Pittsburgh 30, Pa.
Financial Officer: G. B. Oates, V. P.
Resources: $200,539,000

SAVINGS AND LOAN ASSOCIATIONS

Arranged in order of deposits, herein referred to as "resources."

Home Savings & Loan Association
761 S. Broadway
Los Angeles 14, Cal.
Financial Officer: Leonard R. Lockhart,
  Exec. V. P.
Resources: $1,102,725,000

California Federal Savings & Loan Association
601 Wilshire Blvd.
Los Angeles 14, California
Financial Officer: Oliver M. Chatborn,
  Sr. V. P.
Resources: $679,981,000

Twin City Federal Savings & Loan Association
801 Marquette Ave.
Minneapolis 2, Minn.
Financial Officer: Burch N. Bell, Sr. V. P.
Resources: $446,045,000

Great Western Savings & Loan Association
4401 Crenshaw Blvd.
Los Angeles 43, Cal.
Financial Officer: J. C. Greene,
  V. P. & Sec.
Resources: $407,065,000

Perpetual Building Association
11th & E Sts., N. W.
Washington, D. C.
Financial Officer: William H. Dyer,
  Exec. V. P.
Resources: $395,730,000

First Federal Savings & Loan Association
1 S. Dearborn St.
Chicago 3, Ill.
Financial Officer: Raymond J. Graham,
  Sr. V. P.
Resources: $372,597,000

Pioneer Investors Savings & Loan Association
55 W. Santa Clara St.
San Jose 6, Cal.
Financial Officer: Sherman Miller,
  Exec. V. P.
Resources: $334,922,000

American Savings & Loan Association
210 E. Philadelphia St.
Whittier, Cal.
Financial Officer: Lowell Peterson,
  Exec. V. P.
Resources: $316,099,000

Talman Federal Savings & Loan Association
5501 S. Kedzie Ave.
Chicago 29, Ill.
Financial Officer: John J. Seps, Sr. V. P.
Resources: $312,159,000

Bell Savings & Loan Association
Monroe and Clark Sts.
Chicago 3, Ill.
Financial Officer: Bide M. Ransom,
  Sr. V. P.
Resources: $307,919,000

First Federal Savings & Loan Association
100 N. E. First Ave.
Miami 32, Fla.
Financial Officer: Robert V. Walker,
  Exec. V. P.
Resources: $306,151,000

Pacific First Federal Savings & Loan
204 S. 11th St.
Tacoma 1, Wash.
Financial Officer: Elmer M. Erickson,
  Sr. V. P.
Resources: $288,885,000

**Farm and Home Savings & Loan
  Association**
221 W. Cherry St.
Nevada, Mo.
Financial Officer: Audy M. Byram,
  First V. P.
Resources: $285,448,000

First Federal Savings & Loan Association
First Federal Bldg.
St. Petersburg 1, Fla.
Financial Officer: John W. Wahlman,
  Sr. V. P.
Resources: $256,772,000

Minneapolis Savings & Loan Association
8th & Marquette Sts.
Minneapolis 2, Minn.
Financial Officer: Albert C. Price,
  Sr. V. P.
Resources: $254,807,000

West Side Savings & Loan Association
1790 Broadway
New York 19, N. Y.
Financial Officer: Austin H. Mehrhof,
  Exec. V. P.
Resources: $252,496,000

**Fidelity Federal Savings & Loan
  Association**
225 E. Broadway
Glendale 5, Cal.
Financial Officer: Robert L. Rand,
  Sr. V. P.
Resources: $215,332,000

**Baltimore Federal Savings & Loan
  Association**
Fayette and St. Paul
Baltimore 2, Md.
Financial Officer: Eugene K. Reilly,
  Sr. V. P.
Resources: $208,121,000

Carteret Savings & Loan Association
866 Broad St.
Newark 2, N.J.
Financial Officer: Marcy C. Wilkinson, Sr.
  V.P.
Resources: $204,700,000

**Minnesota Federal Savings & Loan
  Association**
355 Minnesota St.
St. Paul 1, Minn.
Financial Officer: Gerald P. Uttley, Sr.
  V.P.
Resources: $199,885,000

Lytton Savings & Loan Association
8151 Sunset Blvd.
Hollywood 46, Cal.
Financial Officer: Maurice Starrels, Sr.
  V.P.
Resources: $192,511,000

**Worcester Federal Savings & Loan
  Association**
2 Elm St.
Worcester, Mass.
Financial Officer: Frank L. Farr, Sr. V.P.
Resources: $187,566,000

Gibraltar Savings & Loan Association
9111 Wilshire Blvd.
Beverly Hills, Cal.
Financial Officer: Harold J. Shields,
  Sr. V.P.
Resources: $182,056,000

**Dade Federal Savings & Loan
  Association**
101 E. Flagler St.
Miami 32, Fla.
Financial Officer: Charles Beatty
Resources: $169,727,000

**Miami Beach Federal Savings & Loan
  Association**
401 Lincoln Rd.
Miami Beach 38, Fla.
Financial Officer: Carl Weinkle, Sr. V.P.
Resources: $167,028,000

Gem City Savings Association
6 N. Main St.
Dayton 2, Ohio
Financial Officer: Fred M. Stockstill
Resources: $164,388,000

**First Federal Savings and Loan
  Association**
1274 Avenue of the Americas
New York 20, N.Y.
Financial Officer: Wesley H. Bahr, Sr.
  V.P.
Resources: $158,313,000

COMMERCIAL FINANCE AND SPECIAL FINANCING COMPANIES

Arranged in order of resources.

CIT Financial Corp.
650 Madison Ave.
New York 22, N. Y.
Financial Officer: A. D. Dietz,
 Chmn. Exec. Comm.
Resources: $2,444,132,000
Main Purposes: Various types of commercial financing, factoring, auto loans, equipment leasing

Commercial Credit Corp.
300 St. Paul Place
Baltimore 2, Md.
Financial Officer: P. S. Grimes, Treas.
Resources: $2,190,842,000
Main Purposes: Various types of commercial financing, factoring, personal loans, equipment leasing, lease financing

Associates Investment Co.
320 Associates Bldg.
South Bend, Ind.
Financial Officer: G. C. Coquillard, Treas.
Resources: $1,399,428,000
Main Purposes: Financing of auto dealers, commercial-industrial loans, personal loans

Pacific Finance Corp.
621 So. Hope St.
Los Angeles, 17, Cal.
Financial Officer: R. W. Borden,
 V. P. & Treas.
Resources: $727,888,000
Main Purposes: Finances auto dealers, commercial financing, personal loans

James Talcott, Inc.
225 Fourth Ave.
New York 3, N. Y.
Financial Officer: H. M. Kelsey, Jr.,
 V. P. & Treas.
Resources: $460,709,000
Main Purposes: Various types of commercial financing, factoring, installment receivables financing.

General Acceptance Corp.
1105 Hamilton St.
Allentown, Pa.
Financial Officer: R E. Kemmerer, Treas.
Resources: $387,474,000
Main Purposes: Auto financing, rediscounting, installment loans

Walter E. Heller & Co.
105 West Adams St.
Chicago 90, Ill.
Financial Officer: L. A. Petersen,
 V. P. & Treas.
Resources: $352,729,000
Main Purposes: Various forms of commercial financing, purchasing of installment paper, factoring

American Investment Co. of Illinois
8251 Maryland Ave.
St. Louis 5, Mo.
Financial Officer: H. W. Hartley,
 Sr., V. P. & Treas.
Resources: $310,897,000
Main Purposes: Finances auto dealers, personal loans

General Finance Corp.
1301 Central St.
Evanston, Ill.
Financial Officer: W.S. Litawa, Treas.
Resources: $251, 945,000
Main Purposes: Auto financing, small loans

SFC Corp. (formerly Standard Financial Corp.)
530 Fifth Ave.
New York 36, N. Y.
Financial Officer: E. B. Meredith,
 Exec. V. P.
Resources: $133,895,000
Main Purposes: Various forms of commercial financing, auto loans, equipment loans

Pioneer Finance Co.
1400 First Natl. Bank Bldg.
Detroit 26, Mich.
Financial Officer: J. E. Boyle, Jr., Treas.
Resources: $121,274,000
Main Purposes: Discounting receivables, chattel mortgages, financing of homes, equipment financing

Southwestern Investment Co.
205 E. 10th St.
Amarillo, Tex.
Financial Officer: L. L. Cummings, Treas.
Resources: $118,353,000
Main Purposes: Discounts receivables, secured loans

A.J. Armstrong, Inc.
850 Third Ave.
New York, N. Y.
Financial Officer: Jacob Seiler, Exec. V. P.
Resources: $117,617,000
Main Purposes: Various forms of commercial financing, complete import-export financing and service, secured loans, real estate loans

General Contract Finance Corp.
901 Washington Ave.
St. Louis 1, Mo.
Financial Officer: S. H. Smith, Treas.
Resources: $95,082,000
Main Purposes: Consumer credit, home improvement financing, personal loans

Aetna Finance
120 So. Central Ave.
St. Louis 5, Mo.
Financial Officer: R. L. Yalem, V. P. & Treas.
Resources: $76,079,000
Main Purpose: Consumer financing

Thorp Finance Corp.
Thorp, Wis.
Financial Officer: F. D. Dreger, Treas.
Resources: $72,159,000
Main Purposes: Auto loans; chattel mortgage loans, installment loans

Securities Investment Co. of St. Louis
901 Washington Ave.
St. Louis, 1, Mo.
Financial Officer: W. C. Avis, Treas.
Resources: $69,848,000
Main Purposes: Financing—discounting receivables, secured loans

Kirkeby-Natus Corp.
40 Wall St.
New York 5, N. Y.
Financial Officer: Joseph Lesser, V. P.
Resources: $51,082,000
Main Purposes: Loans secured by real estate and other assets; stand-by financing for business firms; rediscounting. Interim financing

Inland Credit Corp.
200 Park Ave.
New York, N. Y.
Financial Officer: I. H. Lutzker, Exec. V. P.
Resources: $42,988,000
Main Purposes: Various types of commercial financing; import-export financing; short-term loans on plants, equipment and real estate

LIFE INSURANCE COMPANIES

Arranged in order of assets, herein referred to as "resources."

Metropolitan Life Insurance Co.
1 Madison Ave.
New York 10, N.Y.
Financial Officer: G. P. Jenkins, V.P.
Resources: $19,596,085,000

The Prudential Insurance Co.
Prudential Plaza
Newark 1, N. J.
Financial Officer: Monroe Chappelear, V.P.
Resources: $18,621,928,000

Equitable Life Assurance Society of The U. S.
373 Seventh Ave.
New York 1, N.Y.
Financial Officer: J. Henry Smith, V.P.
Resources: $10,823,551,000

New York Life Insurance Co.
51 Madison Ave.
New York 10, N.Y.
Financial Officer: E. W. McPherson, V.P.
Resources: $7,732,901,000

John Hancock Mutual Life Insurance Co.
200 Berkeley St.
Boston 17, Mass.
Financial Officer: H. S. P. Rowe Sr., V.P.
Resources: $6,794,588,000

Aetna Life Insurance Co.
151 Farmington Ave.
Hartford 15, Conn.
Financial Officer: H. A. Moreen, V.P.
  & Cashier
Resources: $4,578,316,000

Northwestern Mutual Life Insurance Co.
720 E. Wisconsin Ave.
Milwaukee 2, Wis.
Financial Officer: C. W. Adamson, Treas.
Resources: $4,494,455,000

Travelers Insurance Co.
700 Main St.
Hartford 15, Conn.
Financial Officer: G. W. Baker, Chm. of
  Fin. Comm.
Resources: $3,556,520,000

Mutual Life Insurance Co. of New York
1740 Broadway
New York 19, N.Y.
Financial Officer: J. M. Hughes, Exec. V.P.
Resources: $2,917,572,000

Massachusetts Mutual Life Insurance Co.
1295 State St.
Springfield, Mass.
Financial Officer: R. M. Colton, V.P. &
  Fin. Sec.
Resources: $2,739,636,000

Connecticut General Life Insurance Co.
900 Cottage Grove Rd.
Bloomfield, Conn.
Financial Officer: Al Joyce, V.P.
Resources: $2,592,687,000

New England Mutual Life Insurance Co.
501 Boylston St.
Boston 17, Mass.
Financial Officer: S. C. Badger, Fin. V.P.
Resources: $2,418,565,000

Mutual Benefit Life Insurance Co.
520 Broad St.
Newark 1, N.J.
Financial Officer: W. L. Phillips, V.P.
Resources: $1,989,802,000

Penn Mutual Life Insurance Co.
Independence Square
Philadelphia 5, Pa.
Financial Officer: F. T. Starr, Fin. Sec.
  & V.P.
Resources: $1,931,714,000

Connecticut Mutual Life Insurance Co.
140 Garden St.
Hartford 15, Conn.
Financial Officer: H. M. Tenney, V.P.
Resources: $1,796,160,000

Lincoln National Life Insurance Co.
1301 So. Harrison St.
Fort Wayne, Ind.
Financial Officer: M. C. Ledden, V.P. &
  Treas.
Resources: $1,665,694,000

Bankers Life Co.
711 High St.
Des Moines 7, Iowa
Financial Officer: H. F. Dean, V.P. &
  Treas.
Resources: $1,226,535,000

Western and Southern Life Insurance Co.
400 Broadway
Cincinnati 1, Ohio
Financial Officer: R. G. Ward, Treas.
Resources: $1,200,773,000

National Life and Accident Insurance Co.
National Bldg.
Nashville 3, Tenn.
Financial Officer: E. T. Wilson, Treas.
Resources: $1,025,635,000

Phoenix Mutual Life Insurance Co.
79 Elm St.
Hartford 15, Conn.
Financial Officer: S. K. Sullivan, Sec. &
  Treas.
Resources: $990,898,000

American National Insurance Co.
Moody Ave. and Market St.
Galveston, Texas
Financial Officer: L. Mosell, V.P. & Treas.
Resources: $971,884,000

**Occidental Life Insurance Co. of
  California**
1511 So. Broadway
Los Angeles, Cal.
Financial Officer: E. V. Hoff, Treas.
Resources: $958,860,000

National Life Insurance Co.
National Life Drive
Montpelier, Vt.
Financial Officer: L. D. Meredith,
    Exec. V.P. & Chm. Fin. Comm.
Resources: $941,971,000

Provident Mutual Life Insurance Co.
    of Philadelphia
Market and 46th Sts.
Philadelphia 39, Pa.
Financial Officer: D. L. Monahan,
    Fin. V.P.
Resources: $923,714,000

Continental Assurance Co.
310 So. Michigan Ave.
Chicago 4, Ill.
Financial Officer: B. N. Everett, V.P.
    & Treas.
Resources: $886,010,000

Teachers' Insurance and Annuity
    Association of America
730 Third Ave.
New York 17, N.Y.
Financial Officer: F. A. McConnell, V.P.
Resources: $867,465,000

Union Central Life Insurance Co.
3-5 West Fourth St.
Cincinnati 2, Ohio
Financial Officer: E. R. Best, Treas.
Resources: $825,160,000

State Mutual Life Assurance Co. of
    America
440 Lincoln St.
Worcester 5, Mass.
Financial Officer: R. H. Wilson, V.P. Fin.
Resources: $806,931,000

Equitable Life Insurance Co. of Iowa
604 Locust St.
Des Moines 6, Iowa
Financial Officer: R. H. Richards,
    V.P. Fin.
Resources: $735,066,000

Franklin Life Insurance Co.
812 So. Sixth St.
Springfield, Ill.
Financial Officer: L. E. Striebeck, Treas.
Resources: $709,462,000

Jefferson Standard Life Insurance Co.
Jefferson Square
Greensboro, S.C.
Financial Officer: G. K. Cavenaugh, Sr.
    V.P. Fin.
Resources: $695,513,000

Pacific Mutual Life Insurance Co.
523 West Sixth St.
Los Angeles 54, Cal.
Financial Officer: T. L. Lowe, Fin. V.P.
Resources: $665,987,000

Southwestern Life Insurance
Southwestern Life Bldg.
Dallas 1, Texas
Financial Officer: A. D. Harder,
    Exec. V.P. & Treas.
Resources: $662,187,000

Life Insurance Co. of Virginia
Capitol and 10th Sts.
Richmond 9, Va.
Financial Officer: C. A. Taylor, Chm.
    Inv. Comm.
Resources: $581,694,000

Guardian Life Insurance Co.
201 Park Ave. So.
New York 3, N.Y.
Financial Officer: G. T. Conklin, Jr.,
    V.P.
Resources: $576,360,000

Home Life Insurance Co.
253 Broadway
New York 8, N.Y.
Financial Officer: R. D. Guibord, V.P.
Resources: $475,531,000

Acacia Mutual Life Insurance Co.
51 Louisiana Ave. N.W.
Washington 1, D.C.
Financial Officer: D. F. Roberts, Fin. V.P.
Resources: $441,969,000

Kansas City Life Insurance Co.
3520 Broadway
Kansas City 41, Mo.
Financial Officer: H. R. Carpenter, Treas.
Resources: $436,299,000

United Benefit Life Insurance Co.
3316 Farnam St.
Omaha 31, Neb.
Financial Officer: G. P. Milne, Treas.
Resources: $424,405,000

Northwestern National Life Insurance Co.
430 Oak Grove St.
Minneapolis 3, Minn.
Financial Officer: D. E. Jondahl, V.P. Fin.
Resources: $416,584,000

Fidelity Mutual Life Insurance Co.
The Parkway at Fairmount Ave.
Philadelphia 1, Pa.
Financial Officer: W. C. Keesey, Sr.
  V.P. Inv.
Resources: $407,406,000

Liberty National Life Insurance Co.
Liberty National Life Bldg.
Birmingham 2, Ala.
Financial Officer: E. A. Camp Jr., V.P.
  & Treas.
Resources: $393,581,000

**Life and Casualty Insurance Co. of
  Tennessee**
Life and Casualty Tower
Nashville, Tenn.
Financial Officer: G. S. Parrish, Treas.
Resources: $350,903,000

Washington National Insurance Co.
1630 Chicago Ave.
Evanston, Ill.
Financial Officer: E. G. Graff, Treas.
Resources: $342,678,000

Minnesota Mutual Life Insurance Co.
Victory Square
St. Paul 1, Minn.

Financial Officer: E. A. Johnson, Treas.
Resources: $340,702,000

Mutual of Omaha Insurance Co.
3316 Farnam St.
Omaha 1, Neb.
Financial Officer: N. L. Criss, V.P. &
  Treas.
Resources: $314,536,000

General American Life Insurance Co.
15th and Locust Sts.
St. Louis 66, Mo.
Financial Officer: J. G. Driscoll, Fin. V.P.
Resources: $311,805,000

California-West States Life Insurance Co.
2020 L St.
Sacramento 14, Cal.
Financial Officer: M. H. Evans, V.P. &
  Treas.
Resources: $280,228,000

Monumental Life Insurance Co.
Charles and Chase Sts.
Baltimore 2, Md.
Financial Officer: J. T. Lehane, Treas.
Resources: $271,065,000

Provident Life & Accident Insurance Co.
Provident Bldg., Fountain Square
Chattanooga, Tenn.
Financial Officer: L. N. Webb, Exec. V.P.
Resources: $269,196,000

MAJOR INVESTMENT COMPANIES

The following is a list of selected investment companies arranged in order of total assets.

Type I — Mutual Funds

Investors Mutual
800 Investors Bldg.
Minneapolis 2, Minn.
Financial Officer: W. G. Clark, Sr., V. P.
Resources: $1,726,380,000

Massachusetts Investors Trust
200 Berkeley Street
Boston 16, Mass.
Financial Officer: R. H. Ladd, Treas. & Sec.
Resources: $1,630,811,000

Wellington Fund, Inc.
1630 Locust Street
Philadelphia 3, Pa.
Financial Officer: J. E. Welch, Exec. V. P.
Resources: $1,415,459,000

Investors Stock Fund, Inc.
Investors Bldg.
Minneapolis 2, Minn.
Financial Officer: W. G. Clark, Sr., V. P.
Resources: $885,842,000

Insurance Securities Trust Fund
100 California Street
San Francisco 11, Cal.
Financial Officer: E. R. Foley, Sr., V. P.
Resources: $883,431,000

Affiliated Fund, Inc.
63 Wall Street
New York 5, N. Y.
Financial Officer: R. S. Driscoll, Exec. V. P.
Resources: $690,141,000

Fundamental Investors, Inc.
Westminster and Parker Streets
Elizabeth 3, N. J.
Financial Officer: C. J. Vollhardt,
    V. P. & Treas.
Resources: $649,425,000

United Accumulative Fund
20 West 9th Street
Kansas City, Mo.
Financial Officer: C. L. Waddell, V. P.
Resources: $609,286,000

**Massachusetts Investors Growth Stock
    Fund, Inc.**
200 Berkeley Street
Boston 16, Mass.
Financial Officer: R. W. Ladd, Treas. & Sec.
Resources: $553,077,000

National Securities-Stock Series
120 Broadway
New York 6, N. Y.
Financial Officer: H. K. Meyer, Exec. V. P.
Resources: $448,188,000

Fidelity Fund, Inc.
35 Congress Street
Boston 9, Mass.
Financial Officer: D. G. Sullivan, Exec. V. P.
Resources: $409,568,000

Dreyfus Fund, Inc.
2 Broadway
New York 4, N. Y.
Financial Officer: H. M. Stein, Adm. V. P.
Resources: $364,460,000

United Income Fund
20 West 9th Street
Kansas City, Mo.
Financial Officer: C. L. Waddell, V. P.
Resources: $342,941,000

Television-Electronics Fund, Inc.
120 South LaSalle Street
Chicago 3, Ill.
Financial Officer: W. H. Cooley, V. P.
Resources: $331,874,000

National Investors Corp.
65 Broadway
New York 6, N. Y.
Financial Officer: T. P. Blodgett, V. P.
Resources: $304,147,000

George Putnam Fund of Boston
60 Congress Street
Boston, Mass.
Financial Officer: C. E. Werly,
    Chmn. of Trustees
Resources: $287,181,000

Boston Fund, Inc.
111 Devonshire Street
Boston 9, Mass.
Financial Officer: R. L. Osgood, V. P.
Resources: $278,980,000

Investors Variable Payment Fund, Inc.
Investors Bldg.
Minneapolis 2, Minn.
Financial Officer: W. G. Clark, Sr., V. P.
Resources: $274,340,000

Dividend Shares, Inc.
1 Wall Street
New York 5, N. Y.
Financial Officer: Francis Goodhue III,
    V. P.
Resources: $269,266,000

Incorporated Investors
200 Berkeley Street
Boston 16, Mass.
Financial Officer: G. D. Aldrich,
    Vice Chmn. & Treas.
Resources: $259,458,000

Chemical Fund, Inc.
65 Broadway
New York 6, N. Y.
Financial Officer: P. B. Cannell, Exec. V. P.
Resources: $257,331,000

Broad Street Investing Corp.
65 Broadway
New York 6, N. Y.
Financial Officer: T. P. Blodgett, V. P.
Resources: $249,639,000

One William Street Fund, Inc.
1 William Street
New York 4, N. Y.
Financial Officer: E. B. Burr, Exec. V. P.
Resources: $248,618,000

Investment Company of America
900 Wilshire Blvd.
Los Angeles 17, Cal.
Financial Officer: C. W. Morton, Exec. V. P.
Resources: $246,912,000

Financial Industrial Fund, Inc.
950 Broadway
Denver 3, Colo.
Financial Officer: J. W. Tempest,
　Exec. V. P.
Resources: $229,447,000

Eaton & Howard Balanced Fund
24 Federal Street
Boston 10, Mass.
Financial Officer: C. F. Eaton,
　Chmn. of Trustees
Resources: $208,787,000

State Street Investment Corp.
140 Federal Street
Boston 10, Mass.
Financial Officer: R. C. Paine, Treas.
Resources: $207,180,000

Eaton & Howard Stock Fund
24 Federal Street
Boston 10, Mass.
Financial Officer: C. F. Eaton, Jr.,
　Chmn. of Trustees
Resources: $184,192,000

United Science Fund
20 West 9th Street
Kansas City, Mo.
Financial Officer: C. L. Waddell, V. P.
Resources: $182,337,061

Axe-Houghton Fund "B , Inc.
730 Fifth Avenue
New York, N. Y.
Financial Officer: Ruth H. Axe, Exec. V. P.
Resources: $163,857,000

American Mutual Fund, Inc.
900 Wilshire Blvd.
Los Angeles 17, Cal.
Financial Officer: J. B. Lovelace, Jr.,
　Exec. V. P.
Resources: $163,380,000

Commonwealth Investment Co.
615 Russ Bldg.
San Francisco 4, Cal.
Financial Officer: L. V. Coleman, Sr. V. P.
Resources: $156,119,000

Keystone Custodian Funds—Series S-4
50 Congress Street
Boston 9, Mass.
Financial Officer: G. N. Lempereur,
　Exec. V. P.
Resources: $149,729,000

Incorporated Income Fund
200 Berkeley Street
Boston 16, Mass.
Financial Officer: G. D. Aldrich,
　Vice-Chmn. & Treas.
Resources: $124,947,000

Institutional Growth Fund
85 Broad Street
New York 4, N. Y.
Financial Officer: G. S. Newell,
　V. P. & Treas.
Resources: $116,813,000

Selected American Shares, Inc.
135 South LaSalle Street
Chicago 3, Ill.
Financial Officer: R. S. Cutler, V. P.
Resources: $111,603,000

Diversified Growth Stock Fund, Inc.
Parker and Westminster Streets
Elizabeth 2, N. J.
Financial Officer: C. J. Vollhardt,
　V. P. & Treas.
Resources: $110,087,000

Lazard Fund, Inc.
44 Wall Street
New York 5, N. Y.
Financial Officer: F. W. Wilson, V. P.
Resources: $100,810,000

Type II — Closed-End Funds

M. A. Hanna Co.
1300 Leader Bldg.
Cleveland, Ohio
Financial Officer: W. A. Hobbs,
   Pres. & Treas.
Resources: $459,878,000

Lehman Corp.
1 South William Street
New York 4, N. Y.
Financial Officer: A. W. Pearson, Exec. V. P.
Resources: $314,252,000

Tri-Continental Corp.
65 Broadway
New York 6, N. Y.
Financial Officer: T. P. Blodgett, V. P.
Resources: $239,981,000

Madison Fund, Inc.
660 Madison Avenue
New York 21, N. Y.
Financial Officer: B. G. Davis, V. P.
Resources: $141,616,000

Electric Bond & Share Co.
2 Rector Street
New York 6, N. Y.
Financial Officer: B. M. Betsch, Treas.
Resources: $138,173,000

U. S. & Foreign Securities Corp.
1 Headley Road
Morristown, N. J.
Financial Officer: August Belmont, V. P.
Resources: $108,805,000

Adams Express Co.
48 Wall Street
New York 5, N. Y.
Financial Officer: D. G. McCormack, V. P.
Resources: $92,080,000

United Corporation
522 Fifth Avenue
New York 36, N. Y.
Financial Officer: W. E. Boyland,
   V. P. & Treas.
Resources: $81,306,000

General Public Service Corp.
90 Broad Street
New York 4, N. Y.
Financial Officer: C. E. Miller, V. P. & Treas.
Resources: $77,857,000

INVESTMENT BANKERS AND UNDERWRITERS

Abbott, Proctor & Paine
911 E. Main St.
Richmond 19, Va.
Hugh E. Paine
Robert B. Rawles

Allen & Co.
30 Broad St.
New York 4, N.Y.
Charles Allen
Merritt Coleman

A. C. Allyn & Co.
122 S. LaSalle St.
Chicago 3, Ill.
John W. Allyn
James E. Snyder

Amott, Baker & Co., Inc.
150 Broadway
New York 38, N.Y.
Harry R. Amott
Allan H. Levian

Auchincloss, Parker & Redpath
1705 H. St. N.W.
Washington, D.C.
Hugh D. Auchincloss
Millard F. West, Jr.

Bache & Co.
36 Wall St.
New York 5, N.Y.
Alfred B. Averell
Edward B. Conway

Baker, Weeks & Co.
1 Wall St.
New York 5, N.Y.
Hugh B. Baker
James F. Keresey

Ball, Burge & Kraus
1414 Union Commerce Bldg.
Cleveland 14, Ohio
Peter Ball
Fred W. Hudson

J. Barth & Co.
404 Montgomery St.
San Francisco, Cal.
Marco F. Hellman
Robert E. Sinton

Bear, Sterns & Co.
1 Wall St.
New York 5, N.Y.
Salim L. Lewis
Vincent P. Coakley, Jr.

A. G. Becker & Co.
120 S. LaSalle St.
Chicago, Ill.
Joseph J. Levin
Arthur W. Curtis

Blair & Co.
20 Broad St.
New York 5, N.Y.
Emmons Bryant
Homer J. O'Connell

D. H. Blair & Co.
66 Beaver St.
New York 4, N.Y.
Robert W. Miller
Charles J. Miller

Blyth & Co., Inc.
14 Wall St.
New York 5, N.Y.
Sydney Duffy

Burnham & Co.
15 Broad St.
New York, N.Y.
I. W. Burnham, II

Willis S. Burnside & Co., Inc.
55 Broadway
New York 6, N.Y.
Robert Burnside
Willis E. Burnside

H. M. Byllesby & Co.
135 S. LaSalle St.
Chicago 3, Ill.
Burton M. Eagan

Clark, Dodge & Co.
61 Wall St.
New York 5, N.Y.
Eugene M. Geddes
William M. Rex

Courts & Co.
11 Marietta St.
Atlanta 1, Ga.
R. W. Courts
Hugh D. Carter, Jr.

Dempsey-Tegeler & Co.
1000 Locust St.
St. Louis 1, Mo.
Jerome F. Tegeler
Bert H. Horning

Dillon, Read & Co.
46 William St.
New York 5, N.Y.
Joseph Ludin

Dominick & Dominick
14 Wall St.
New York 5, N.Y.
Bayard Dominick
Avery Rockefeller, Jr.

Dominion Securities Corp.
40 Exchange Pl.
New York 5, N.Y.
James R. Clarke
George P. Rutherford

Drexel & Co.
1500 Walnut St.
Philadelphia 1, Pa.
Edward Hopkinson, Jr.
Raymond L. Talcott
Clarence W. Bartow

Dreyfus & Co.
2 Broadway
New York 4, N.Y.
George W. Fox
Jack J. Dreyfus, Jr.

Francis I. Dupont & Co.
1 Wall St.
New York 5, N.Y.
Alfred R. Dupont
Neil T. Carr

Eastman Dillon, Union Securities & Co.
1 Wall St.
New York 5, N.Y.
Lloyd S. Gilmour
H. Lawrence Bogert, Jr.

F. Eberstadt & Co.
65 Broadway
New York 6, N.Y.
Andrew W. Eberstadt

A. G. Edwards & Sons
409 N. 8th St.
St. Louis 1, Mo.
Benjamin F. Edwards, III
Richard Broome (New York)

Eisele & King, Libaire, Stout & Co.
50 Broadway
New York 4, N.Y.
Horace I. Poole

Equitable Securities Corp.
322 Union St.
Nashville 3, Tenn.
G. G. Halliburton

Estabrook & Co.
40 Wall St.
New York 5, N.Y.
Robert J. Lewis
John Mattison

Evans & Co., Inc.
300 Park Ave.
New York 22, N.Y.
George C. Bradley
Daniels C. Brasted

First Boston Corp.
20 Exchange Pl.
New York 5, N.Y.
William B. Chappell
Austin H. Patterson

Geore, Forgan & Co.
45 Wall St.
New York 5, N.Y.
J. Russell Forgan
T. Scott Russell

Goldman, Sachs & Co.
20 Broad St.
New York 5, N.Y.
Gustave L. Levy
John W. Callaghan

Goodbody & Co.
2 Broadway
New York 4, N.Y.
Harold P. Goodbody
Thomas E. Feeley

Granbery, Marache & Co.
67 Wall St.
New York 5, N.Y.
William L. Lendman
Robert A. Don

Hallgarten & Co.
44 Wall St.
New York 5, N.Y.
Calvin M. Cross
Leonard D. Newborg

Halsey, Stuart & Co.
123 S. LaSalle St.
Chicago 90, Ill.
T. E. Hough

Hardy & Co.
25 Broad St.
New York 4, N.Y.
Raymond A. McMann
James Hodes

Harriman Ripley & Co., Inc.
63 Wall St.
New York 5, N.Y.
Philip W. Carao, Jr.

Hayden, Stone & Co.
25 Broad St.
New York 4, N.Y.
Richard E. Boesel, Jr.

Hemphill, Noyes & Co.
8 Hanover St.
New York 4, N.Y.
Blancke Noyes
Stephen C. Reynolds, Jr.

H. Hentz & Co.
72 Wall St.
New York 5, N.Y.
Robert P. Baruch
Frank J. McCormack

Hirsch & Co.
25 Broad St.
New York 4, N.Y.
Maurice Meyer, Jr.

J. A. Hogle & Co.
132 S. Main St.
Salt Lake City 1, Utah
James E. Hogle
Herbert Dewitz

Hornblower & Weeks
1 Chase Manhattan Plaza
New York 5, N.Y.
Joseph T. Walker, Sr.
George T. Flynn

E. F. Hutton & Co.
1 Chase Manhattan Plaza
New York 5, N.Y.
W. Allen Taylor
James F. Burns

W. E. Hutton & Co.
14 Wall St.
New York 5, N.Y.
William C. Miller, Jr.
Earl K. Bassett
Capton M. Paul
R. J. Yunker

Kidder, Peabody & Co.
20 Exchange Pl.
New York 5, N.Y.
Albert H. Gordon
Bruce G. Coe

Kuhn, Loeb & Co.
30 Wall St.
New York 5, N.Y.
J. Emerson Thors
Hugh Knowlton

Ladenburg, Thalmann & Co.
25 Broad St.
New York 4, N.Y.
Carl K. Erpf
Leo G. Shaw

Laird, Bissell & Meeds
120 Broadway
New York 5, N.Y.
George F. Hackl, Jr.
Middleton Rose

W. C. Langley & Co.
115 Broadway
New York 6, N.Y.
Edwin W. Laffey
Maitland T. Ijams

Lazard Freres & Co.
44 Wall St.
New York 5, N.Y.
Edwin H. Herzog
W. Bruce McConnel, Jr.

Lee Higginson Corp.
20 Broad St.
New York 5, N.Y.
Richard De La Chappelle

Lehman Brothers
1 Williams St.
New York 4, N.Y.
Monroe C. Gutman
Thomas F. Joyce, III

Carl M. Loeb, Rhoades & Co.
42 Wall St.
New York 5, N.Y.
Armand G. Erpf
Richard N. Beaty

D. A. Lomasney & Co.
39 Broadway
New York 6, N.Y.
David A. Lomasney

Myron A. Lomasney & Co.
67 Broad St.
New York 5, N.Y.
Myron A. Lomasney

McDonald & Co.
1250 Union Commerce Bldg.
Cleveland 14, Ohio
Herman J. Sheedy
H. Leonard Flynn

McDonnell & Co., Inc.
120 Broadway
New York 5, N.Y.
T. Murray McDonnell
Robert A. W. Brauns

Merrill Lynch, Pierce, Fenner & Smith, Inc.
70 Pine St.
New York 5, N.Y.
George J. Leness
Norman Smith

Mitchum, Jones & Templeton, Inc.
650 S. Spring St.
Los Angeles 14, Cal.
Carl G. Gebhart
G. W. Gowan

Model, Roland & Co.
120 Broadway
New York 5, N.Y.
Walter A. Everitt

Morgan Stanley & Co.
2 Wall St.
New York 5, N.Y.
Hudson B. Lemkau
Charles F. Morgan

F. S. Moseley & Co.
120 Broadway
New York 5, N.Y.
Frederick C. Brawn, Jr.

New York Hanseatic Corp.
60 Broad St.
New York 4, N.Y.
Kurt H. Grunebaum
Paul Hirshland

Paine, Webber, Jackson & Curtis
25 Broad St.
New York 4, N.Y.
John Brick
Robert D. Thorson

Paribas Corp.
40 Wall St.
New York 5, N.Y.
Charles R. Treuhold

Carl H. Pforzheimer & Co.
25 Broad St.
New York 4, N.Y.
Theodore H. Ball

Piper, Jaffray & Hopwood
115 S. Seventh St.
Minneapolis 2, Minn.
C. Palmer Jaffray

W. C. Pitfield & Co.
30 Broad St.
New York 4, N.Y.
Archie F. MacAllaster

R. W. Pressprich & Co.
80 Pine St.
New York 5, N.Y.
Barrett Brown
Charles L. Bergmann

Reynolds & Co.
120 Broadway
New York 5, N.Y.
Thomas F. Staley
John F. Bryan

L. F. Rothschild & Co.
120 Broadway
New York 5, N.Y.
Henry L. Heming
Walter W. Hess, Jr.

Salomon Brothers & Hutzler
60 Wall St.
New York 5, N.Y.
Benjamin J. Levy
John H. Gutfreund

Scott & Stringfellow
P.O. Box 1575
Richmond 13, Va.
James Scott
S. Buford Scott

Shields & Co.
44 Wall St.
New York 5, N.Y.
Macrae Sykes
Thomas McGlade

Smith, Barney & Co.
20 Broad St.
New York 4, N.Y.
Robert A. Powers
Robert F. Seebeck

F. S. Smithers & Co.
45 Wall St.
New York 5, N.Y.
C. Francis Smithers
Walter W. Cooper

Stifel, Nicolaus & Co., Inc.
314 N. Broadway
St. Louis 2, Mo.
John W. Bunn

Stone & Webster Securities Corp.
90 Broad St.
New York 4, N.Y.
Peter J. Murphy, Jr.
Edgar D. Beacham

Stroud & Co.
123 S. Broad St.
Philadelphia 9, Pa.
Robert G. Rowe

Sutro & Co.
460 Montgomery St.
San Francisco 4, Cal.
Paul N. Duggan

Sutro Bros. & Co.
80 Pine St.
New York 5, N.Y.
Morton Grayson
Stephen H. Floersheimer

Spencer Trask & Co.
25 Broad St.
New York 4, N.Y.
C. Everett Bacon
Harold H. Cook

Tucker, Anthony & R. L. Day
120 Broadway
New York 5, N.Y.
Robert Haydock
Ernest W. Borkland, Jr.

Van Alstyne, Noel & Co.
40 Wall St.
New York 5, N.Y.
David Van Alstyne, Jr.
William H. McElnea, Jr.

G. H. Walker & Co.
45 Wall St.
New York 5, N.Y.
John M. Walker
Frederick S. Wonham

Walston & Co., Inc.
74 Wall St.
New York 5, N.Y.
Alberta C. Purkiss
Gustave A. Alexisson

Watling, Lerchen & Co.
Ford Bldg.
Detroit 26, Mich.
J. Gordon Hill
Herbert D. Hunter

Wertheim & Co.
1 Chase Manhattan Plaza
New York 5, N.Y.
Allen C. DeBois
William D. Kerr

White, Weld & Co.
20 Broad St.
New York 5, N.Y.
Philip D. Baker
Raymond D. Stitzer

Arthur Wiesenberger & Co.
61 Broadway
New York 6, N.Y.
Edson B. Gould, Jr.
Arthur V. Tomaselli

J. R. Williston & Beane
2 Broadway
New York 4, N.Y.
Alpheus C. Beane
Stanley L. Bartels

Winslow, Cohu & Stetson, Inc.
26 Broadway
New York 4, N.Y.
Samuel R. Winslow
Karl Pierce Herzer

J. A. Winston & Co.
11 Broadway
New York 4, N.Y.
Joel A. Winston

Dean Witter & Co.
45 Montgomery St.
San Francisco 6, Cal.
Dean Witter
Guy Witter

Wood, Struthers & Co.
30 Wall St.
New York 5, N.Y.
Rowland H. George
Russell A. Lowe

SMALL BUSINESS INVESTMENT COMPANIES
LICENSED BY THE SMALL BUSINESS ADMINISTRATION

(AO* Signifies "Area of Operation")

ALABAMA

Business Investors, Inc.
2233 Fourth Avenue, North
Birmingham 3, Ala.
AO* Alabama

**Morhand Small Business
Investment Company**
27 South 20th Street
Birmingham 2, Ala.
AO* Alabama

**Nor-Ala Small Business
Investment Company**
1901 Mulberry Avenue
Anniston, Alabama
AO* Alabama

ALASKA

Alaska-Pacific Capital Corporation
210 Glover Building
Fifth Avenue and E. Street
Anchorage, Alaska
AO* Alaska, Washington and California

Trans-America Equity, Inc.
2207 McRae Road
Anchorage, Alaska
AO* Alaska, Washington and Oregon

ARIZONA

Arizona Business Equities
44 West Monroe Street
Phoenix 3, Ariz.
BRANCH OFFICE:
160 North Stone Avenue
Tucson, Ariz.
AO* Arizona

Arizona Capital Corporation
Arizona Land Title Building
Tucson, Ariz.
Branch Office:
800 North Central Avenue
Phoenix, Ariz.
AO* Arizona

**First Southwest Small Business
Investment Company**
1611 East Camelback
Phoenix 16, Ariz.
AO* Arizona

**Reliance Small Business Investment
Corporation**
Suite 208
4533 North Scottsdale Road
Scottsdale, Ariz.
AO* Arizona

Small Business Capital Arizona Ltd.
705 Guaranty Bank Building
3550 North Central Avenue
Phoenix 12, Ariz.
AO* Arizona

ARKANSAS

AGE Capital Corporation
410 West Third Street
Little Rock, Ark.
AO* Arkansas

CALIFORNIA

Acme Capital Corp.
4100 Ardmore Avenue
South Gate, Cal.
AO* California

Agri-Supply Finance Company
Howland Road
Post Office Box 198
Lathrop, Cal.
AO* California

Alameda Investment Corporation
8400 MacArthur Boulevard
Oakland 5, Cal.
AO* California

Alexander Hamilton Equities, Inc.
255 California Street
San Francisco 11, Cal.
AO* California

All State Capital Company
405 Montgomery Street
San Francisco 4, Cal.
AO* California

Amco Capital Corporation
681 Market Street
San Francisco 5, Cal.
AO* California

American Business Capital Corporation
727 West 7th Street
Los Angeles 17, Cal.
AO* California

ANA Small Business Investments, Inc.
2122 Market Street
San Francisco 14, Cal.
AO* California

Argo Investment Corporation
202 University Avenue
Palo Alto, Cal.
AO* California

Berkeley Science Capital Corp.
260 California St., Room 1200
San Francisco 11, Cal.
Branch Office:
2015 Center Street
Berkeley, Cal.
AO* California
Special Interests: Scientific and
technological companies

Betatron Corporation
12th Floor, Bank of America Building
12th & Broadway
Oakland 12, Cal.
AO* California

Beverly Hills Capital Corp.
435 North Bedford Drive
Beverly Hills, Cal.
AO* California

Bryan Capital, Inc.
155 Montgomery Street
San Francisco, Cal.
AO* California

California Equity Corporation
2 Pine Street, Room 624
San Francisco, Cal.
AO* California

California Growth Capital, Inc.
111 Sutter Street
San Francisco 4, Cal.
AO* California

California-Northwest Capital Company
513 Sixth Street
Eureka, Cal.
AO* California

Cal-West Capital Corp.
465 California Street, Room 703
San Francisco 4, Cal.
AO* California

Capital Assistance Corporation
301 Broadway
San Francisco 11, Cal.
AO* California

Capital City Equity Co.
3450 El Camino Avenue
Sacramento 21, Cal.
AO* California

Capital Dynamics
4250 Wilshire Boulevard
Los Angeles, Cal.
AO* California

Capital for Advanced Technology, Inc.
435 North Bedford Drive
Beverly Hills, Cal.
AO* California
Special Interests: Technological companies

Capital For Small Business, Inc.
1314 Westwood Boulevard
Los Angeles 24, Cal.
AO* California

Capital Infusion, Inc.
5065 Weeks Avenue
San Diego 10, Cal.
AO* California

Capital For Technical Industries, Inc.
1281 Westwood Boulevard
Los Angeles 24, Cal.
AO* California
Special Interests: Technical and
   technological companies

**Central California Small Business
   Investment Co.**
369 Pine Street, Room 521
San Francisco 4, Cal.
Branch Office:
Rt. 6, Box 2437
East Orangeburg Avenue
Modesto, Cal.
AO* California

City Capital Corporation
9229 Sunset Boulevard
Los Angeles 69, Cal.
AO* California

Coast Small Business Investment Co.
706 Forest Avenue
Pacific Grove, Cal.
AO* California

Columbia Capital Corporation
2201 Park Towne Circle
Sacramento 21, Cal.
AO* California

Comstock Small Business Investment Co.
235 Montgomery Street
San Francisco 4, Cal.
AO* California

Continental Capital Corporation
Equitable Building—23rd Fl.
120 Montgomery Street
San Francisco 4, Cal.
AO* California

Contra Costa Commerce Corporation
158 Santa Clara Avenue
Oakland 10, Cal.
AO* California

Diversified Equities Corporation
155 Montgomery Street
San Francisco 4, Cal.
AO* California

Drake Capital Corporation
2359 Warren Road
Walnut Creek, Cal.
AO* California

Draper & Johnson Investment Company
780 Welch Road
Palo Alto, Cal.
AO* California

Dynatech Capital Corporation
9465 Wilshire Boulevard
Beverly Hills, Cal.
AO* California
Special Interests: Technical and
   technological companies

East Bay Small Business Investment Co.
2909 Telegraph Avenue
Berkeley 5, Cal.
AO* California

Edvestco, Inc.
150 Isabella Avenue
Atherton, Cal.
AO* California

Electronics Capital Corporation
1400 Fifth Avenue
San Diego 1, Cal.
Br.: 10 Post Office Square
Boston, Mass.
Br.: 44 Wall Street
New York, N. Y.
AO* California, New York, Massachusetts
Special Interests: Electronics

Equity Capital Corporation
485 Ramona Street
Post Office Box 209
Palo Alto, Cal.
Br.: Suite 511
233 Sansome Street
San Francisco, Cal.
AO* California

First Financial Corporation of
   the West Capital Corporation
2650 Zoe Avenue
Huntington Park, Cal.
AO* California

First Preferred Capital Investment Corp.
1306 Wilshire Boulevard
Los Angeles, Cal.
AO* California

First Small Business Investment
   Company of California
215 West Sixth Street
Los Angeles 14, Cal.
AO* California

First Small Business Investment
   Company of Los Angeles
Suite 442
9171 Wilshire Blvd.
Beverly Hills, Cal.
AO* California; Counties of Los Angeles,
   Orange and San Bernardino

Fresno Small Business Investment Co.
5300 North Fresno Street
Fresno, Cal.
AO* California

Gibraltar Capital Corporation
155 Montgomery St., Suite 1005
San Francisco 4, Cal.
AO* California

Goodwin Small Business Investment Co.
First National Building
San Diego 1, Cal.
AO* California; Counties of San Diego,
    Imperial, Riverside and Orange

Greater California Capital Corporation
8693 Wilshire Boulevard
Beverly Hills, Cal.
AO* California

Growth Assistance Co.
721 Central Building
Oakland 12, Cal.
AO* California

H & R Investment Capital Co.
100 El Camino Real
San Carlos, Cal.
AO* California

Harvard Small Business Investment Co.
33 East Huntington Drive
Arcadia, Cal.
AO* California

Interstate Capital Corporation
2958 West Seventh Street
Los Angeles 5, Cal.
AO* California

Judson-Murphy Capital Corporation
420 Market Street
San Francisco 11, Cal.
AO* California

Krasne Fund for Small Business, Inc.
Suite 404
9350 Wilshire Boulevard
Beverly Hills, Cal.
AO* California

Lyon Capital Corporation
800 Welch Road
Palo Alto, Cal.
AO* California

Lytton Small Business Investment Co., Inc.
8150 Sunset Blvd.
Los Angeles, Cal.
AO* California

Maryland Capital Corporation
157 Sutter Street
San Francisco 4, Cal.
AO* California

Merchants' Equity Co.
2849 Fulton Avenue
Sacramento 21, Cal.
AO* California

Milton Equity Corporation
6535 Wilshire Boulevard
Los Angeles 48, Cal.
Branch Office:
500 Seventh Avenue
New York, N. Y.
AO* New York, Nevada and California

New Capital For Small Businesses, Inc.
961 Mills Building
220 Montgomery Street
San Francisco, Cal.
AO* California

New Capital Investments, Inc.
Suite 600
126 Post Street
San Francisco 8, Cal.
AO* California

North American Capital Corporation
315 Montgomery Street
San Francisco 4, Cal.
AO* California

Northern California Capital Corporation
2 Pine Street—Room 214
San Francisco 11, Cal.
AO* California

**Northern California Small Business
Investment Company**
2500 El Camino Real
Palo Alto, Cal.
AO* California; Counties North of
    San Bernardino, Kern and San Luis
    Obispo

North Coast Capital Corporation
25 Washington Street
Petaluma, Cal.
AO* California

Pacific Capital Fund
607 South Hobart Boulevard
Los Angeles 5, Cal.
AO* California

Pacific Delta Investment Corp.
3101 Monterey Road
San Jose 12, Cal.
AO* California

Palomar Capital Corporation
500 University Avenue
San Diego 3, Cal.
AO* California

Pan Pacific Investment Capital Co.
11 Tillman Place
San Francisco 8, Cal.
AO* California

**Professional Small Business
    Investment Co.**
5979 West Third Street
Los Angeles, Cal.
AO* California

San Francisco Capital Corporation
400 Montgomery Street
San Francisco, Cal.
Branch Office:
232 North Canon Drive
Beverly Hills, Cal.
AO* California

**San Francisco Small Business
    Investment Company**
235 Montgomery Street
San Francisco 4, Cal.
AO* California

**San Joaquin Small Business
    Investment Corporation**
1012 Chester Avenue
Bakersfield, Cal.
AO* California

Santa Cruz Small Business Investment Co.
Room 1112
200 Bush Street
San Francisco 4, Cal.

Science Investment Company
351 California Street
San Francisco, Cal.
Branch Office:
Room 408
417 South Hill Street
Los Angeles 13, Cal.
AO* California
Special Interests: Science and technology

Security Capital Corporation
200 Bush Street, Suite 1400
San Francisco 4, Cal.
AO* California

Sierra Capital Company
351 California Street
San Francisco 4, Cal.
AO* California

Small Business Enterprises
300 Montgomery Street
San Francisco 4, Cal.
AO* California

Southwestern Capital Corporation
233 A Street
San Diego 9, Cal.
Branch Office:
8665 Wilshire Boulevard
Beverly Hills, Cal.
AO* California

Space Age Small Business Investment Co.
819 A Street
San Rafael, Cal.
AO* California

Space Ventures, Inc.
1129 Torrey Pines Road
La Jolla, Cal.
AO* California & Nevada

Sutter Capital Company
58 Sutter Street
San Francisco, Cal.
AO* California

Sutter Hill Capital Company
Room 190
2390 El Camino Real
Palo Alto, Cal.
AO* California

Stanford Capital Corporation
1212 Columbus Avenue
San Francisco 11, Cal.
AO* California

Technology Investors, Inc.
Suite 830, 523 West Sixth St.
Los Angeles 14, Cal.
AO* California
Special Interests: Science and technology

Transnational Capital Corporation
6434 Wilshire Boulevard
Los Angeles 48, Cal.
AO* California

Unlimited Small Business Investment Corporation
1200 Yalupa Avenue
Santa Rosa, Cal.
AO* California

Valley Capital Company
1411 Lee Tower Building
5455 Wilshire Boulevard
Los Angeles 36, Cal.
Branch Office:
111 Sutter Street
San Francisco, Cal.
AO* California

C. R. Warde Equity Capital Corporation
Room 1014
3440 Wilshire Boulevard
Los Angeles 5, Cal.
AO* California

West Coast Capital Company
Shepard Square Building
1240 High Street
Auburn, Cal.
AO* California

Westamco Investment Company
7805 Sunset Boulevard
Los Angeles 46, Cal.
AO* California

Western Business Assistance Corporation
601 California Street
San Francisco, Cal.
AO* California

Western Equity Capital Corporation
9460 Wilshire Boulevard
Beverly Hills, Cal.
AO* California

Western Small Business Investment Co.
1534 Fifth Avenue
San Rafael, Cal.
Branch Office:
2065 Chestnut Street
San Francisco, Cal.
AO* California

Western States Small Business Investment Co.
1330 Broadway—Suite 1314
Oakland 12, Cal.
AO* California and Nevada

Western Urban Redevelopment Investment Corporation
1472 Russ Building
235 Montgomery Street
San Francisco 4, Cal.
AO* California
Special Interests: Real estate and construction

Westland Capital Corporation
9229 Sunset Boulevard
Los Angeles 69, Cal.
AO* California, Arizona, New Mexico, Oregon, Washington, New York, Massachusetts, New Jersey, Connecticut, Illinois and Pennsylvania

Westwood Capital Company
Suite 201
14328 Victory Boulevard
Van Nuys, Cal.
Branch Office:
1129 Westwood Boulevard
West Los Angeles 24, Cal.
AO* California

Wilshire Capital Corporation
215 So. La Cienega Blvd.
Beverly Hills, Cal.
AO* California

COLORADO

Applied Science Capital Corporation
Suite 2308 Tower Building
Denver U. S. National Center
1700 Broadway
Denver 17, Colo.
AO* Colorado
Special Interests: Science and technology

Central Investment Corporation of Denver
15th and Arapahoe Streets
Denver 2, Colo.
AO* Colorado, Idaho, Kansas, Montana, Nebraska, New Mexico, S. Dakota, ' Wyoming
Special Interests: Oil and natural resources; farm and land situations

Colorado Capital Corporation
1554 Broadway
Denver 2, Colo.
AO* Colorado, Missouri, Kansas

Colorado Equity Capital Investment Corp.
1536 Welton Street
Denver 2, Colo.
AO* Colorado

Grocers Capital Corporation
5151 Bannock Street
Denver, Colo.
AO* Colorado

CONNECTICUT

All State Venture Capital Corporation
955 Main Street
Bridgeport 3, Conn.
AO* Connecticut
Special Interests: Venture capital

American Investors Corporation
25 Bank Street
Stamford, Conn.
AO* Connecticut

Business Ventures, Incorporated
983 Main Street
Hartford, Conn.
AO* Connecticut
Special Interests: Venture capital

Chartered Capital Corporation
174 Bridge Street
Groton, Conn.
Branch Office:
821 Main Street
Manchester, Conn.
AO* Connecticut

The Connecticut Business Investment Co.
Colonial Green
256 East State Street
Westport, Conn.
AO* Connecticut

Connecticut Capital Corp.
354 Whalley Avenue
New Haven, Conn.
AO* Connecticut

Connecticut Growth Capital, Inc.
267 Main Street
Ansonia, Conn.
AO* Connecticut

Connecticut Venture Capital Corporation
984 Silas Deane Highway
Wethersfield, Conn.
AO* Connecticut
Special Interests: Venture capital

Dewey Investment Corporation
11 Donald Street
Hartford 5, Conn.
AO* Connecticut

Fairfield Equity Corporation
550 Summer Street
Stamford, Conn.
AO* Connecticut

The First Connecticut Small Business Investment Company
955 Main Street, Suite 303
Bridgeport, Conn.
Branch Office:
120 East 56th Street
New York 22, N. Y.
AO* Connecticut
Special Interests: Realty financing

The First Hartford Fund, Inc.
254 Prospect Avenue
Hartford, Conn.
AO* Connecticut

General Investment Company of Connecticut, Inc.
348 Orange Street
New Haven, Conn.
AO* Connecticut

General Venture Capital Corporation
155 Church Street
New Haven 10, Conn.
AO* Connecticut
Special Interests: Venture capital

Hartford Small Business Capital Corp.
Pine Meadows, Town of Hartford
Litchfield County, Conn.
AO* Connecticut

Investors Capital Corporation
217 Kossuth Street
Bridgeport, Conn.
AO* Connecticut

Manufacturers Small Business Investment Company of Connecticut, Incorporated
1488 Chapel Street
New Haven 11, Conn.
AO* Connecticut

Nationwide Funding Corporation
685 Parker Street
Manchester, Conn.
AO* Connecticut

Nutmeg Capital Corporation
130 Haven Street
New Haven, Conn.
AO* Connecticut

Pequot Capital Corporation
325 State Street
New London, Conn.
AO* Connecticut

Putnam Investors, Inc.
10 East State Street
Westport, Conn.
Br.: 75 East Putnam Avenue
Greenwich, Conn.
AO* Connecticut

**The Small Business Investment
Company of Connecticut, Inc.**
1188 Main Street
Bridgeport 3, Conn.
AO* Connecticut
Special Interests: Electronics

DELAWARE

Delaware Investment Company
200 West Ninth Street
Wilmington 1, Del.
AO* Delaware

DISTRICT OF COLUMBIA

Allied Capital Corporation
1625 Eye Street, Northwest
Washington, D. C.
Branch Office:
7720 Wisconsin Avenue
Bethesda, Md.
AO* District of Columbia & Maryland

American Growth Investment Company
325 Woodward Building
15th & H Streets, N. W.
Washington 5, D. C.
AO* District of Columbia

Avionics Investing Corporation
406 Commerce Building
1700 K Street, N. W.
Washington 6, D. C.
Branch Office:
1271 Avenue of the Americas
New York 20, N. Y.
AO* District of Columbia,
Massachusetts, New York, California
Special Interests: Aviation, electronics

Capital Corporation of America
1000 Vermont Avenue, N. W.
Washington 5, D. C.
AO* Florida & D. C.

**Capital Investment Company of
Washington**
Suite 941
1001 Connecticut Avenue, N. W.
Washington 6, D. C.
AO** District of Columbia

**Citizens Small Business Investment
Corporation**
808 Seventeenth St., N. W.
Washington 6, D. C.
AO* District of Columbia

Farragut Square Investment Corporation
Suite 423
1028 Connecticut Avenue
Washington 6, D. C.
AO* District of Columbia, Delaware

General Business Investment Corporation
830 Bowen Building
821 - 15th Street, N. W.
Washington 5, D. C.
Branch Office:
Potomac National Bank Building
River and Falls Road
Potomac, Md.
AO* District of Columbia, Maryland

General Capital Investment Corporation
11th Floor
1000 Vermont Avenue, N. W.
Washington 5, D. C.
AO* District of Columbia

**Greater Washington Industrial
Investments, Inc.**
1725 K Street, N. W.
Washington 6, D. C.
AO* District of Columbia, Maryland,
Virginia
Special Interests: Electronics, nuclear
technological projects

Prudential Business Funds, Inc.
729 15th Street, N. W.
Washington 5, D. C.
AO* District of Columbia

FLORIDA

American Equity Capital Corporation
7660 Gainesville Avenue
Jacksonville, Fla.
AO* Florida

**American Small Business Investment
Company**
1018 First National Bank Bldg.
Tampa 2, Fla.
AO* Florida

Atlantic Investment Fund, Inc.
501 N. Grandview Avenue
Daytona Beach, Fla.
AO* Florida

Boca Raton Capital Corporation
110 East Palmetto Park Road
Boca Raton, Fla.
AO* Florida

Caladesi Capital Corporation
1002 Broadway
Dunedin, Fla.
AO* Florida

Canaveral Capital Corporation
1900 S.W. 3rd Avenue
Miami, Fla.
AO* Florida

Capital Resources Corporation
Suite 200, 600 Brickell Ave.
Miami 32, Fla.
AO* Florida

Central Florida Investment, Inc.
56 East Pine Street
Orlando, Fla.
AO* Florida

Creative Equities Corporation
9200 Northwest 27th Avenue
Miami, Fla.
Branch Office:
105-20 Queens Boulevard
Forest Hills, N. Y.
AO* Florida and New York

First Financial Corporation
716 North Federal Highway
Fort Lauderdale, Fla.
AO* Florida

First Florida Funding Corporation
Citizens Bank and Trust Company Building
110 South Orange Avenue
Sarasota, Fla.
AO* Florida

**First Miami Small Business
Investment Company**
420 Lincoln Road, Rm. 235
Miami Beach 39, Fla.
Branch Office:
293 Post Road, Orange, Conn.
AO* Florida and Connecticut

**First North Florida Small Business
Investment Company**
107 North Madison Street
Quincy, Fla.
AO* Florida

**First Small Business Investment
Company of Tampa, Inc.**
608 Tampa Street
Tampa 2, Fla.
AO* Florida

First Southern Investment Company, Inc.
1335 Lincoln Road
Miami Beach 39, Fla.
AO* Florida

Florida Capital Corporation
396 Royal Palm Way
Palm Beach, Fla.
Branch: 1610 Congress Building
Miami, Fla.
AO* Florida
Special Interests: Realty and
land development

Florida Equity Investments, Inc.
110 Fifth Street South
St. Petersburg 1, Fla.
AO* Florida

Florida Small Business Corporation
Town & Country Plaza
The Mall
Pensacola, Fla.
AO* Florida

Gold Coast Capital Corp.
2650 Biscayne Boulevard
Miami 37, Fla.
AO* Florida

Gulf States Capital Corporation
3605 North Davis Street
Pensacola, Fla.
AO* Florida

Kavanaugh Equity Capital, Inc.
Suite 4-B Richardson Building
33 South Hogan Street
Jacksonville 2, Fla.
AO* Florida

**Lincoln Small Business
    Investment Co., Inc.**
Suite 510
1451 N. Bayshore Drive
Miami Beach 32, Fla.
AO* Florida

Magna Investments, Inc.
Carolina Insurance Group Building
Corner Osceola & Expressway
Jacksonville, Fla.
AO* Florida

Maritime Investment Corporation
7541 N. E. Third Place
Miami, Fla.
Branch Office:
8641 Colesville Road
Silver Spring, Md.
AO* Florida & Maryland

Mutual Capital Corporation
5711 South Dixie Highway
South Miami 43, Fla.
Branch Office:
730 Fifth Avenue
New York, N. Y.
AO* New York & Florida

Research Capital Corporation
2909 Bay to Bay
Tampa, Fla.
AO* Florida

Small Business Funds, Inc.
1258 South Highland Avenue
Clearwater, Fla.
AO* Florida

Southern Capital Corporation
407 Lincoln Road
Miami Beach, Fla.
AO* Florida

Space Capital Corporation
1036 First Federal Building
St. Petersburg, Fla.
AO* Florida

United Capital Corporation
305 South County Road
Palm Beach, Fla.
AO* Florida

GEORGIA

CSRA Capital Corporation
c/o Village Enterprises, Inc.
Daniel Village Shopping Center
Post Office Box 927
Augusta, Ga.
AO* Georgia

**The Citizens and Southern
    Capital Corporation**
Marietta & Broad Streets
Post Office Box 4899
Atlanta 3, Ga.
AO* Georgia

Continental Equity Corporation
Atlanta Merchandise Mart
240 Peachtree Street, N. W.
Atlanta, Ga.
AO* Georgia

First American Investment Corporation
914 New Walton Building
Atlanta 3, Ga.
AO* Georgia

First Atlanta Investment Corporation
2637 Peachtree Road, N. E.
Atlanta 5, Ga.
AO* Georgia

Georgia Capital Corporation
2603 Bank of Georgia Building
34 Peachtree Street, Northwest
Atlanta 3, Ga.
AO* Georgia

Georgia Southern Business Equities, Inc.
Shurlington Plaza Shopping Center
Macon, Ga.
AO* Georgia

Growth Fund, Incorporated
1280 W. Peachtree St., N. W.
Atlanta 8, Ga.
AO* Georgia

Investors' Equity, Inc.
26 Pryor Street, N.E.
Atlanta, Ga.
AO* Georgia

Peachtree Capital Corporation
2358 Bank of Georgia Building
Atlanta 3, Ga.
AO* Georgia

**Small Business Investment
   Corporation of Georgia**
22 Marietta Street, N. W.
Atlanta 3, Ga.
AO* Georgia

Southern Equities, Incorporated
615 Forsyth Building
Atlanta 3, Ga.
AO* Georgia

Transamerica Capital Corporation
1 South Oakwood Drive
Savannah, Ga.
AO* Georgia

HAWAII

Hawaiian Business Investments, Inc.
c/o Bank of Hawaii
King & Bishop Streets
Post Office Box 2900
Honolulu 2, H. I.
AO* Hawaii

**Small Business Investment Co.
   of Hawaii, Inc.**
1575 South Beretania Street
Honolulu, H. I.
AO* Hawaii

IDAHO

   None

ILLINOIS

Adams Street Capital Incorporated
120 South La Salle Street
Chicago 3, Ill.
AO* Illinois

Advance Growth Capital Corporation
Suite 730
30 North La Salle Street
Chicago, Ill.
AO* Illinois

Albany Capital Corporation
105 W. Adams St., Suite 2118
Chicago 3, Ill.
AO* Illinois

AMCAP Investments, Inc.
105 South La Salle St.
Chicago 3, Ill.
AO* Illinois

**Bloomington Small Business
   Investment Company**
403 West Washington Street
Bloomington, Ill.
AO* Illinois

Business Capital Corporation
208 South La Salle Street
Chicago 4, Ill.
AO* Illinois

**Businessmen's Small Business
   Investment Company**
188 West Randolph, (Room 1615)
Chicago 1, Ill.
AO* Illinois

Capital Opportunities, Inc.
Box 392
903 Seventh Street
Rochelle, Ill.
AO* Illinois

Capital Service Corporation
121 East Livingston
Monticello, Ill.
AO* Illinois

Central Capital Corporation
7254 West Touhy Avenue
Chicago 48, Ill.
AO* Illinois

Century Capital Corporation
250 North Water
Decatur, Ill.
AO* Illinois

Chicago Capital Corporation
135 South LaSalle Street
Chicago 3, Ill.
AO* Illinois

Coleman Financial Corporation
Suite 1022
208 South LaSalle Street
Chicago 4, Ill.
AO* Illinois

Enterprise Funds, Inc.
79 West Monroe Street
Chicago 3, Ill.
AO* Illinois

Exchange Capital Corporation
134 S. LaSalle Street
Chicago 3, Ill.
AO* Illinois

First Capital Corporation of Chicago
The First National Bank of Chicago
38 S. Dearborn Street
Chicago 3, Ill.
AO* Illinois

Geriatrics Capital Corporation
Route 4, 614 North Ale
Peoria, Ill.
AO* Illinois

Illinois Capital Investment Corporation
135 South LaSalle Street
Chicago, Ill.
AO* Illinois

Illinois Medical Capital Corporation
P. O. Box 81
1024 East Ogden Avenue
Naperville, Ill.
AO* Illinois
Special Interests: Medical projects

Industry Capital Corporation
Room 1070
208 South LaSalle Street
Chicago 4, Ill.
AO* Illinois

LaSalle Street Capital Corporation
134 South LaSalle Street
Chicago 3, Ill.
AO* Illinois
Special Interests: Electronics, scientific
    industrial projects

Manufacturers Capital Corporation
Suite 2820
105 West Adams Street
Chicago 3, Ill.
AO* Illinois

Mid-America Capital Corporation
100 North LaSalle Street
Chicago, Ill.
AO* Illinois

Mid-North Capital Corporation
Suite 1239
First National Bank Bldg.
38 South Dearborn St.
Chicago 3, Ill.
AO* Illinois

Midwest Capital Corporation
201 First Avenue
Rock Falls, Ill.
AO* Illinois

Republic Capital Corporation
33 N. LaSalle Street
Chicago 2, Ill.
AO* Illinois

Small Business Management Investors, Inc.
33 N. LaSalle Street
Chicago, Ill.
AO* Illinois

Vanguard Venture Capital Corporation
120 South LaSalle Street
Chicago 3, Ill.
AO* Illinois, Indiana, Iowa, Missouri,
    Wisconsin, New York and California
Special Interests: Venture capital

INDIANA

American Fidelity Corporation
425 East Market Street
Indianapolis, Ind.
AO* Indiana

Central States Small Business Corporation
2021 Cedar Crest Drive, Room 100
Kokomo, Ind.
AO* Indiana

**Evansville Small Business
  Investment Corporation**
416 Main Street
Evansville 2, Ind.
AO* Indiana, Illinois, Kentucky

General Equity Investment Corp.
3033 Wayne Trace
Fort Wayne 1, Ind.
AO* Indiana

**Great Lakes Small Business
  Investment Corporation**
Citizens National Bank Bldg.
Room 1
Tipton, Ind.
AO* Indiana

Incentive Capital Corporation
569 Broadway
Gary, Ind.
AO* Indiana

Industrial Growth Capital Corporation
Merchants Bank Building
111 South Meridian Street
Indianapolis 4, Ind.
AO* Indiana

**Kiefer-Stewart Small Business
  Investment Corp.**
141 West Georgia Street
Indianapolis 25, Ind.
AO* Indiana

**Small Business Investment Corporation
  of Indiana**
1428 Circle Tower
5 East Market Street
Indianapolis 4, Ind.
AO* Indiana

IOWA

Business Capital, Inc. of Iowa
109 First Avenue Building
411 First Avenue, Southeast
Cedar Rapids, Iowa
AO* Iowa

Iowa Growth Investment Company
128 First Avenue, N. E.
Cedar Rapids, Iowa
AO* Iowa

KANSAS

The Kansas Investment Corporation, Inc.
309 East 3rd Street
Wichita 2, Kan.
AO* Kansas

**Midland Business Investment
  Corporation, Inc.**
122 West Myrtle Street
Independence, Kan.
AO* Kansas, Oklahoma, Missouri, and
  Arkansas

KENTUCKY

None

LOUISIANA

Business Loan and Investment Corporation
1428 National Bank of Commerce
  Building
New Orleans 12, La.
AO* Louisiana

Citizens Investment Corporation
200 West Thomas Street
Hammond, La.
AO* Louisiana

Delta Capital Corporation
Room 620, 210 Baronne Street
New Orleans 12, La.
AO* Louisiana

First Commercial Investment Corporation
Boles Building
P. O. Box 210
Rayville, La.
AO* Louisiana

First Louisiana Investment Corporation
226 South Grand Street
Monroe, La.
AO* Louisiana

**First Small Business Investment
Company of La Fourche, Inc.**
1614 South Bayou Drive
Golden Meadow, La.
AO* Louisiana

**The First Small Business Investment
Co. of Louisiana, Inc.**
637 Common Street
New Orleans 12, La.
AO* Louisiana

**First Small Business Investment
Company of New Orleans, Inc.**
1568 Pleasure Street
New Orleans, La.
AO* Louisiana & Mississippi

L. P. Gas Capital, Inc.
324 North Florida Street
Covington, La.
AO* Louisiana, Mississippi, Alabama,
Georgia and Florida

**Louisiana Capital Investment
Company, Inc.**
901, Henry C. Beck Building
Shreveport, La.
AO* Louisiana

Mid-South Capital Corporation
312 Polk Street
Mansfield, La.
AO* Louisiana

Royal Street Investment Corporation
521 Royal Street
New Orleans 16, La.
AO* Louisiana

**Shreveport Business Investment
Company, Inc.**
3503 Madison Park Boulevard
Shreveport, La.
AO* Louisiana

**Small Busines Capital Corporation
of Louisiana**
1202 Petroleum Tower
Shreveport, La.
AO* Louisiana

**Southern Small Business Investment
Company, Inc.**
8137 Oleander Street
New Orleans, La.
AO* Louisiana

MAINE

None

MARYLAND

Aviation Growth Investments, Inc.
8645 Colesville Road
Silver Spring, Md.
AO* Maryland

Baltimore Business Investment Company
1104 Mercantile Trust Bldg.
Baltimore 2, Md.
Branch: 7801 Woodmont Avenue
Bethesda, Md.
Branch: 1520 K Street, N. W.
Washington 5, D. C.
AO* Maryland, District of Columbia,
Delaware, Pennsylvania

Beverage Capital Corporation
1601 Guilford Avenue
Baltimore 2, Md.
AO* Maryland

**Charles Small Business Investment
Corporation**
Suite 204
101 North Charles Street
Baltimore 1, Md.
AO* Maryland

Inter-State Business Investment Company
233 Equitable Building
Calvert & Fayette Streets
Baltimore 2, Md.
AO* Maryland

**Maryland Small Business Investment
Company**
Beacon Building
Leonardtown, Md.
AO* Maryland

MASSACHUSETTS

American Capital Corporation
1330 Beacon Street
Brookline 46, Mass.
AO* Massachusetts

Anderson New England Capital Corporation
150 Causeway Street
Boston 14, Mass.
Branch Offices:
11 Asylum Street
Hartford, Conn.
230 Park Avenue
New York 17, N. Y.
AO* Massachusetts, New York,
    Connecticut and Maine

Andover Capital Corporation
11 Pemberton Square
Rooms 312-319
Boston 8, Mass.
AO* Massachusetts

Atlas Capital Corporation
38 Park Square Building
31 St. James Avenue
Boston 16, Mass.
AO* Massachusetts

Bay State Capital Corporation
255 Atlantic Avenue—6th Floor
Boston 10, Mass.
AO* Massachusetts

Beacon Capital Corporation
471 Commonwealth Avenue
Boston 15, Mass.
AO* Massachusetts

Beaconsfield Investment Corporation
209 Washington Street
Boston 8, Mass.
AO* Massachusetts

Boston Capital Corporation
31 Milk Street
Boston 9, Mass.
Branch Office:
9171 Wilshire Blvd.
Suite 536
Beverly Hills, Cal.
AO* Massachusetts and California

Boylston Investment Corporation
81 Boylston Street
Brookline, Mass.
AO* Massachusetts

Business Assistance Corporation
11 Pemberton Square
Boston 8, Mass.
AO* Massachusetts

Cambridge Capital Corporation
92 State Street
Boston 9, Mass.
AO* Massachusetts

Cambridge Science Advancement Corporation
1 State Street
Boston 9, Mass.
AO* Massachusetts
Special Interests: Science and technology

Chestnut Hill Capital Corporation
1287 Commonwealth Avenue
Boston, Mass.
AO* Massachusetts and New York

Colony Capital Corporation
80 Federal Street
Boston, Mass.
AO* Massachusetts

Dynamic Capital Corp.
960 Massachusetts Ave.
Boston, Mass.
AO* Massachusetts

Essex Capital Corporation
209 Washington Street
Boston 8, Mass.
AO* Massachusetts

Financial Investors of Boston, Inc.
185 Devonshire Street
Boston 8, Mass.
AO* Massachusetts

First Capital Corporation of Massachusetts
33 State Street
Boston 9, Mass.
AO* Massachusetts

First Realty Small Business Investment Company, Inc.
7 Pemberton Square
Boston 8, Mass.
AO* Massachusetts
Special Interests: Real estate

First Small Business Investment Corporation of New England
1 Federal Street
Boston 10, Mass.
AO* Massachusetts, Vermont,
    New Hampshire, Connecticut, and
    Rhode Island

Great American Capital Corporation
Suite 310
220 Boylston Street
Newton 67, Mass.
AO* Massachusetts

Hancock Capital Corporation
3 St. Ann Street
Jamaica Plain 30, Mass.
AO* Massachusetts

**Industrial Small Business Investment
   Corporation**
141 Milk Street
Boston 8, Mass.
AO* Massachusetts

Massachusetts Capital Corporation
520 Boylston Street
Boston 16, Mass.
Branch Offices:
922 Elm Street
Manchester, N. H.
142 High Street
Portland, Me.
AO* Massachusetts, New Hampshire
   & Maine

**Massachusetts Small Business
   Investment Company, Inc.**
45 Milk Street
Boston 9, Mass.
AO* Massachusetts

Massapoag Investment Corporation
235 Harvard Street
Brookline 46, Mass.
AO* Massachusetts

**Mutual Small Business Investment
   Corporation**
357 Park Square Building
31 St. James Avenue
Boston, Mass.
AO* Massachusetts

New England Capital Corporation
1 Court Street
Boston 8, Mass.
AO* Massachusetts

**New England Enterprise Capital
   Corporation**
28 State Street
Boston 9, Mass.
AO* Massachusetts

Pilgrim Capital Corporation
10 Pleasant Street
Brookline, Mass.
AO* Massachusetts

Pioneer Capital Corporation
725 Providence Pike
Dedham, Mass.
AO* Massachusetts

Polytechnic Capital Corporation
50 Congress Street
Boston 9, Mass.
AO* Massachusetts
Special Interests: Technology

**Prudential Small Business Investment
   Co., Inc.**
26 New Street
Cambridge 38, Mass.
AO* Massachusetts, Vermont, Connecticut,
   New York, New Hampshire

**The Small Business Investment
   Corporation of Western Massachusetts**
29 Pearl Street
Worcester 8, Mass.
AO* Massachusetts, Rhode Island

Technological Investment Corporation
75 Federal Street, 8th Floor
Boston 10, Mass.
AO* Massachusetts
Special Interests: Technology

Union Capital Corporation
85 State Street
Boston 9, Mass.
AO* Massachusetts

**Western Electronics Investment
   Corporation**
607 Boylston Street
Boston, Mass.
Branch Office:
428 Boston Post Road
Weston 93, Mass.
AO* Massachusetts
Special Interests: Electronics

Yankee Capital Corporation
77 Franklin Street
Boston 10, Mass.
AO* Massachusetts

MICHIGAN

Creative Capital of Michigan, Inc.
1100 N. Woodward Avenue
Birmingham, Mich.
AO* Michigan

Greater Michigan Investment Company
1200 Penobscot Building
Griswold at Fort Streets
Detroit, Mich.
AO* Michigan

Michigan Equity Corporation
609 South Burdick Street
Kalamazoo, Mich.
AO* Michigan

**Midwest Small Business
  Investment Company**
2951 Guardian Building
Detroit 26, Mich.
AO* Michigan

Regional Investment Corporation
#9 Bloomfield Center
P. O. Box 305
1565 Woodward Avenue
Bloomfield Hills, Mich.
AO* Michigan

Tectronics Capital Corporation
David Stott Building
1150 Griswold Street
Detroit 26, Mich.
AO* Michigan
Special Interests: Electronics

MINNESOTA

**Arrowhead Small Business Investment
  Company**
402 Minnesota Building
St. Paul 1, Minn.
Branch Office:
Suite 24
Denver 6, Colo.
AO* Minnesota & Colorado

Bonzer Investment Co.
8212 Highway No. 7
Minneapolis 26, Minn.
AO* Minnesota

Community Investment Enterprises, Inc.
126 South Main Street
Le Sueur, Minn.

AO* Minnesota, Wisconsin, Iowa,
  North Dakota, South Dakota

Equity Capital Company
430 First Avenue N.
Minneapolis 1, Minn.
AO* All United States
Special Interests: Secondary Financing
  of real estate

First Bancstock Equity Corporation
1315 First National Bank Bldg.
Minneapolis 2, Minn.
AO* Minnesota, North Dakota,
  South Dakota, Wisconsin and Montana

First Continental Capital Corporation
2511 First National Bank Building
120 S. Sixth Street
Minneapolis 2, Minn.
AO* Minnesota, North Dakota,
  South Dakota and Wisconsin

First Heartland Investment Company
209 Third Avenue, N. W.
Austin, Minn.
AO* Minnesota, Wisconsin, Illinois, Iowa,
  Kansas, Missouri, Nebraska, Arkansas,
  Louisiana

First Midwest Capital Corporation
703 Northstar Center
10 South 7th Street
Minneapolis 2, Minn.
Branch Office:
1411 Fourth Avenue Bldg.
Seattle 1, Wash.
AO* Minnesota, South Dakota, North
  Dakota, Wisconsin, Iowa, Michigan,
  Illinois, Indiana, Montana, Nebraska,
  Arizona and Washington

Minnesota Capital Corporation
712 First National Bank Bldg.
120 South Sixth Street
Minneapolis 2, Minn.
AO* Minnesota

**Minnesota Small Business Investment
  Company**
2338 Central Avenue, Northeast
Minneapolis 18, Minn.
AO* Minnesota

Northwest Growth Fund, Inc.
953 Northwestern Bank Bldg.
Minneapolis 40, Minn.
AO* Minnesota, North Dakota, South
  Dakota, Montana, Iowa, Nebraska,
  Wisconsin

Retailers Growth Fund, Inc.
15 North Eighth Street
Minneapolis 3, Minn.
AO* Minnesota, Iowa, North Dakota,
    South Dakota and Wisconsin
Special Interests: Retailing

MISSISSIPPI

Magnolia Capital Corporation
Highway 61, South
P. O. Box 1044
Vicksburg, Miss.
AO* Mississippi

Sunflower Investment Corporation
Intersection of U. S. Hwy.
49 W. with Second Street Extended
Indianola, Miss.
AO* Mississippi

**Vicksburg Small Business Investment
    Company**
204-205 First National Bank Building
Vicksburg, Miss.
AO* Mississippi

MISSOURI

**Atlas Small Business Investment
    Corporation**
1808 Main Street
Kansas City 8, Mo.
AO* Missouri, Kansas, Nebraska

Commercial Capital Corporation
408 Lathrop Building
1005 Grand Avenue
Kansas City, Mo.
AO* Missouri

ComTrusCo Investment Company
318 Commerce Trust Building
922 Walnut Street
Kansas City 6, Mo.
AO* Kansas, Missouri

Hogan Investment Company
117 West 4th Street
P. O. Box 1192
Joplin, Mo.
AO* Missouri

Mid-State Business Capital Corporation
411 North Seventh Street
St. Louis 1, Mo.
AO* Missouri, Illinois

**The Missouri Fund For Business
    Capital, Inc.**
1000 Broadway
Kansas City, Mo.
AO* Missouri

St. Louis Capital, Inc.
1506 Railway Exchange Building
611 Olive Street
St. Louis 1, Mo.
AO* Missouri

MONTANA

Capital Investors Corporation of Montana
1130 West Broadway
Missoula, Mont.
AO* Montana

Intermountain Capital, Inc.
Suite 33, Professional Building
North 28th Street and Poly Drive
Billings, Mont.
AO* Montana and Wyoming

Small Business Improvement Company
7 North 33rd Street
Post Office Box 1175
Billings, Mont.
AO* Montana and Wyoming

NEBRASKA

Nebraska Capital Corporation
1309 L Street
Lincoln 8, Nebr.
AO* Nebraska, Iowa & Wyoming
Special Interests: Electronics

Omaha Industrial Capital, Inc.
510 Service Life Building
1904 Farnam Street
Omaha 2, Nebr.
AO* Nebraska

NEVADA

None

NEW HAMPSHIRE

Sci-Tronics Fund, Inc.
6 Manchester Street
Nashua, N. H.
AO* New Hampshire
Special Interests: Electronics and
technology

NEW JERSEY

Atlantic Capital Corporation
744 Broad Street
Newark, N. J.
AO* New Jersey

**Atlantic Small Business Investment
Corporation**
1 South South Carolina Street
Atlantic City, N. J.
AO* New Jersey

Brunswick Investment Corp.
1460 Morris Avenue
Union, N. J.
AO* New Jersey

**Coastal Small Business Investment
Company, Inc.**
1143 East Jersey Street
Elizabeth, N. J.
Branch Office:
100 West 42nd Street
New York, N. Y.
AO* New Jersey & New York

**Developers Small Business Investment
Corporation**
214 Engle Street
Englewood, N. J.
AO* New Jersey and New York
Special Interests: Realty

**Eastern States Small Business
Investment Corporation**
No. 1 Kinderkarmack Rd.
Hackensack, N. J.
AO* New Jersey

Electro-Space Capital Corporation
23 Fulton Street
Newark 2, N. J.
AO* New Jersey
Special Interests: Electronics and
technology

**Essex Small Business Investment
Company**
744 Broad Street
Newark 2, N. J.
AO* New Jersey

First Equity Capital Corporation
Office Bldg., Menlo Park Shopping Center
Metuchen, N. J.
AO* New Jersey

**First Small Business Investment
Corporation of New Jersey**
810 Broad Street
Newark 2, N. J.
AO* New Jersey
Special Interests: Realty and land
development

**Garden State Small Business Investment
Company**
1180 Raymond Blvd.
Suite 2212
Newark, N. J.
AO* New Jersey

Growth Ventures, Inc.
127 Washington Street
Newark, N. J.
Branch Office:
27 William Street
New York, N. Y.
AO* New Jersey & New York
Special Interests: Venture capital

Investor Enterprises, Inc.
3 East Main Street
Denville, N. J.
Branch Office:
51 East 42nd Street
New York 17, N. Y.
AO* New York, New Jersey

Monmouth Capital Corp.
First National Bank Building
Main Street
Freehold, N. J.
AO* New Jersey

New Jersey Business Investment Corp.
162 West State Street
Trenton 8, N. J.
AO* New Jersey, Pennsylvania: Counties
of Bucks, Berks, Philadelphia, Delaware,
Monroe, Montgomery, Northampton,
Pike, Wayne and Lehigh

SBIC of the Eastern States, Inc.
1438 U. S. Route 130
Cinnaminson, N. J.
AO* New Jersey and Pennsylvania

**Small Business Investment Company
of South Jersey**
Suite 500, 519 Federal Street
Camden, N. J.
AO* New Jersey and Pennsylvania

Space Age Capital Corporation
2839 Route #4
Fort Lee, N. J.
AO* New Jersey

Utility Capital Corp.
526 North Avenue East
P. O. Box 133
Westfield, N. J.
AO* New Jersey

NEW MEXICO

**First New Mexico Small Business
Investment Company**
Bank of N. M. Building
Albuquerque, N. M.
Branch Offices:
Kruger Building
227 E. Palace Ave.
Sante Fe, N. M.
77 Third Avenue, Room 101
West Scottsdale, Ariz..
AO* New Mexico and Arizona

Ranchers Investment Corporation
4204 Coal Avenue, Southeast
Albuquerque, N. M.
AO* New Mexico

**Roswell Small Business Investment
Company**
124 East 4th Street
Roswell, N. M.
AO* New Mexico

NEW YORK

**Alar Small Business Investment
Corporation**
150 Broadway
New York 38, N. Y.
AO* New York
Special Interests: Electronics,
land development

American Business Resources Corp.
261 Broadway
New York 7, N. Y.
AO* New York

The Amsterdam Fund, Inc.
42 Broadway
New York 4, N. Y.
AO* New York

Basic Capital Corp.
460 Park Avenue, South
New York 11, N. Y.
AO* New York

Battery Small Business Investment Corp.
26 Broadway
New York 4, N. Y.
AO* New York

Beneficial Capital Corp.
733 Third Avenue
New York 17, N. Y.
AO* New York

Bonan Equity Corp.
420 Lexington Avenue
New York 1, N. Y.
AO* New York

Broad Street Capital Corp.
67 Broad Street
New York 4, N. Y.
AO* New York

Broadway Capital Corporation
80 Pine Street
New York, N. Y.
AO* New York

**Buffalo Small Business Investment
Corporation**
Room 610
120 Delaware Avenue
Buffalo 2, N. Y.
AO* New York

CMNY Capital Company, Inc.
20 Broad Street
New York 5, N. Y.
AO* New York

Capital for Future, Inc. (SBIC)
405 Park Avenue
New York 21, N. Y.
AO* New York

Capital for Progress Fund, Inc.
71 Fifth Avenue
New York, N. Y.
AO* New York

Central Equities Corporation
58 Park Avenue
New York 16, N. Y.
AO* New York

**The Central New York Small Business
   Investment Co., Inc.**
736 Erie Boulevard East
Syracuse 3, N. Y.
AO* New York

Chase Manhattan Capital Corporation
1 Chase Manhattan Plaza
New York 15, N. Y.
AO* New York

**Chevron Capital Corporation
244 Madison Avenue**
New York 16, N. Y.
AO* New York

Commonwealth Capital Corp.
Suite 510
295 Madison Avenue
New York 17, N. Y.
AO* New York

Communications Fund, Inc.
1271 Avenue of the Americas
New York 20, N. Y.
AO* New York

Consolidated Capital Corporation
303 West 42nd Street
New York 36, N. Y.
AO* New York
Special Interests: Real estate

Country Capital Corp.
560 South Broadway
Hicksville, N. Y.
AO* New York

Criterion Capital Corp.
10 Fiske Place, Room 517
Mount Vernon, N. Y.
AO* New York

Directors Capital Corporation
339 Fifth Avenue
New York 16, N. Y.
AO* New York

Donner Capital Corp.
125-10 Queens Boulevard
Jamaica, N. Y.
AO* New York

Donner Equities Corp.
10 East 40th Street
New York 16, N. Y.
AO* New York

**Eastern Small Business Investment
   Corporation**
122 East 42nd Street
New York 17, N. Y.
AO* New York

Economy Growth Corp. of N. Y.
370 Lexington Avenue
New York, N. Y.
Branch Office:
1604 Walnut Street
Philadelphia 3, Pa.
AO* New York and Pennsylvania

Equi-Tronics Capital Corp.
122 East 42nd Street
New York 17, N. Y.
AO* New York
Special Interests: Electronics

Equitable Capital Corp.
55 Liberty Street
New York 5, N. Y.
AO* New York

**Equitable Small Business Investment
   Corporation**
350 Fifth Avenue, Suite 5820
New York 1, N. Y.
AO* New York
Special Interests: Real estate

F-A-J Small Business Investment Corp.
366 Broadway
New York 13, N. Y.
AO* New York

Federated Capital Corporation
122 East 42nd Street
New York 17, N. Y.
AO* New York

First Brooklyn Capital Corp.
530 Morgan Avenue
Brooklyn 22, N. Y.
AO* New York

First City Small Business Investment Corporation
60-10 Roosevelt Avenue
Woodside 77, N. Y.
AO* New York

First Manhattan Small Business Investment Corporation
11 West 42nd Street
New York 36, N. Y.
AO* New York
Special Interests: Real estate

First Realty Capital Funds Corporation
770 Lexington Avenue
New York 21, N. Y.
AO* New York
Special Interests: Real estate

First Rochester Capital Corp.
25 Exchange Street
Rochester 14, N. Y.
AO* New York

The First Westchester Corporation
491 Main Street
New Rochelle, N. Y.
AO* New York

Fortuna Capital Corporation
341 Madison Avenue
New York 17, N. Y.
AO* New York

The Franklin Corporation
3 West 57th Street
New York 19, N. Y.
Branch: 37 Branches on Long Island
AO* New York

Frontiers Capital Corporation
50 Rockefeller Plaza
New York 20, N. Y.
AO* New York

Globe Capital Corporation
221 West 57th Street
New York 19, N. Y.
AO* New York

Grand Central Capital Corporation
60 East 42nd Street
New York 17, N. Y.
AO* New York

Great American Investors, Inc.
Room 201
114 North Tiega Street
Ithaca, N. Y.
AO* New York

Great Eastern Small Business Investment Corporation
20 East 41st Street
New York 17, N. Y.
Branch Office:
266 Pearl Street
Hartford, Connecticut
AO* New York & Connecticut

Greater New York Capital Corporation
12 East 41st Street
New York 17, N. Y.
AO* New York

The Hamilton Capital Fund, Inc.
660 Madison Avenue
New York 21, N. Y.
AO* New York

The Hanover Capital Corporation
30 East 42nd Street
New York 17, N. Y.
AO* New York
Special Interests: Real estate

Health Capital Corporation
1228 Wantagh Avenue
Wantagh, N. Y.
AO* New York
Special Interests: Health and
    pharmaceutical projects

Hudgins & Associates Small Business Investment Corporation
501 West 145th Street
New York 31, N. Y.
AO* New York

Intercoastal Capital Corp.
25 West 43rd Street
New York 36, N. Y.
AO* New York

Island Small Business Investment Corporation
3900 Sunrise Highway
Seaford, N. Y.
AO* New York

Kohler Capital Corporation
325 Broadway
New York 4, N. Y.
AO* New York

Lake Success Capital Corp.
200 Shames Drive
Westbury, N. Y.
AO* New York
Special Interests: Real estate

Lexington Capital Corp.
275 Madison Avenue
New York 16, N. Y.
AO* New York

Long Island Capital Corp.
220 Old Country Road
Mineola, N. Y.
AO* New York

Maiden Lane Capital Corporation
1 Liberty Street
New York 38, N. Y.
AO* New York

Marwit Capital Corp.
420 Lexington Avenue
New York 1, N. Y.
AO* New York

Master Capital Corporation
65 East 55th Street
New York 22, N. Y.
AO* New York
Special Interests: Real estate

The Medical and General Capital Fund, Inc.
178-01 90th Avenue
Jamaica, N. Y.
AO* New York
Special Interests: Medical and pharmaceutical

Mercantile Investors Corp.
132 Madison Avenue
New York 1, N. Y.
AO* New York

Mercury Capital Corp.
70 Pine Street
New York 5, N. Y.
AO* New York

Metropolitan Small Business Investment Corporation
570 Seventh Avenue
New York 18, N. Y.
AO* New York

Midland Capital Corporation
110 William Street
New York, N. Y.
Branch Office:
241 Main Street
Buffalo 3, N. Y.
AO* New York

Monticello Capital Corporation
217 Broadway
Monticello, N. Y.
AO* New York

New Amsterdam Capital Corp.
535 Fifth Avenue
New York, N. Y.
AO* New York
Special Interests: Real estate

New Horizons Capital Corp.
Muttontown Road, RFD #1
Syosset, N. Y.
AO* New York

Newton Capital Corporation
733 Third Avenue
New York 17, N. Y.
AO* New York

New York Business Assistance Corp.
Suite 806
79 Wall Street
New York 5, N. Y.
AO* New York

New York Capital For Industry, Inc.
The-Sherry-Netherlands
781 Fifth Avenue
New York 22, N. Y.
AO* New York

N. Y. Enterprise Capital Corp.
Room 2005
30 East 42nd Street
New York, N. Y.
AO* New York

New York Monetary Fund, Inc.
9 East 35th Street
New York 16, N. Y.
AO* New York
Special Interests: Real estate

North American Small Business Investment Corporation
280 Madison Avenue
New York 16, N. Y.
AO* New York

Pioneer Venture Corporation
22 East 40th Street
New York, N. Y.
AO* New York
Special Interests: Venture capital

Prestige Capital Corporation
485 Fifth Avenue
New York 17, N. Y.
AO* New York

Progress Capital Inc.
150 East 49th Street
New York 17, N. Y.
AO* New York

R & R Financial Corp.
1451 Broadway
New York 36, N. Y.
AO* New York

Real Estate Capital Corp.
20 South Broadway
Yonkers, N. Y.
AO* New York
Special Interests: Real estate

Roosevelt Capital Corp.
600 Old Country Road
Garden City, N. Y.
AO* New York

Royal Business Funds Corporation
60 East 42nd Street
New York, N. Y.
AO* New York

Schuster, Mather Capital Corp.
37 Wall Street
New York 5, N. Y.
AO* New York

Slayton Equities Corp.
105 Madison Avenue
New York 16, N. Y.
AO* New York

Small Business Assistance Corp.
335 Broadway
New York 13, N. Y.
AO* New York

Small Business Capital Corporation
22 East 40th Street
New York 16, N. Y.
AO* New York

Small Business Electronics Investment Corporation
122 East 42nd Street
New York, N. Y.
AO* New York
Special Interests: Electronics

Small Business Investment Company of New York, Inc.
64 Wall Street
New York 5, N. Y.
AO* New York

Small Business Ventures, Inc.
Room 2904
515 Madison Avenue
New York 22, N. Y.
AO* New York
Special Interests: Venture capital

Southern-Tier Small Business Investment Corporation
114 Highland Avenue
Woodridge, N. Y.
AO* New York

Sterling Capital Corp.
49 West 37th Street
New York 18, N. Y.
AO* New York

The Stuyvesant Capital Corp.
116-55 Queens Boulevard
Forest Hills 75, N. Y.
AO* New York
Special Interests: Electronics, real estate

Summit Capital Corporation
5 Hanover Square
New York 4, N. Y.
AO* New York

Talco Capital Corporation
350 5th Avenue
New York 1, N. Y.
AO* New York
Special Interests: Electronics

Technical Capital Corporation
235 East 42nd St.
New York 17, N. Y.
AO* New York
Special Interests: Electronics, industrial,
  technological projects

Tower Capital Corporation
Sixty Wall Tower Building
70 Pine Street
New York 5, N. Y.
AO* New York

Transcapital Corporation
80 Broad Street (Room 904)
New York, N. Y.
AO* New York

**Transcontinental Small Business
  Investment Corporation**
375 Park Avenue
New York 22, N. Y.
AO* New York

**Union Small Business Investment
  Company, Inc.**
160 Broadway
New York 38, N. Y.
AO* New York & New Jersey

**Upstate Small Business Investment
  Company, Inc.**
202 E. State Street (Room 512)
Ithaca, N. Y.
AO* New York

Venture Capital Corporation of America
26 Broadway
New York 4, N. Y.
AO* New York
Special Interests: Venture capital

Water Industries Capital Corp.
122 East 42nd Street
New York 17, N. Y.
AO* New York

Westchester Capital Corporation
698 Saw Mill River Road
Ardsley, N. Y.
AO* New York

Westchester Financial Corp.
279 Halstead Avenue
Harrison, N. Y.
AO* New York

Woodrock Business Capital Corporation
100 Park Avenue
New York 17, N. Y.
AO* New York

NORTH CAROLINA

Cameron-Brown Capital Corporation
900 Wade Avenue
Raleigh, N. C.
AO* North Carolina

Cape Fear Capital Corporation
1309 South 9th Street
Wilmington, N. C.
AO* North Carolina

Capitronics Investment Corporation
1028 South Boulevard
Charlotte, N. C.
AO* North Carolina
Special Interests: Electronics

Carolinas Capital Corporation
1200 North Carolina National
  Bank Building
202 South Tryon Street
Charlotte 2, N. C.
AO* North Carolina and South Carolina

Catawba Capital Corporation
806 Liberty Life Building
Charlotte, N. C.
Branch Office:
4 North Front Street
Wilmington, N. C.
AO* North Carolina

Eastern Capital Corporation
12 Oak Avenue
Spruce Pine, N. C.
AO* North Carolina

First Carolina Capital Corporation
128 South Tryon Street
Charlotte, N. C.
AO* North Carolina

Goodyear Capital Corporation
500 East Morehead Street
Charlotte, N. C.
AO* North Carolina

Granite Capital Corporation
Highland & 23rd Street
Hickory, N. C.
AO* North Carolina, Florida, Texas &
　Georgia

Hanover Small Business Investment
　Company
411 South College Street
Post Office Box 747
Charlotte 1, N. C.
AO* North Carolina, Virginia, South
　Carolina

Northwestern Capital Corporation
924 B Street
North Wilkesboro, N. C.
AO* North Carolina

Pinnacle Investment Corporation
806 Liberty Life Building
Charlotte, N. C.
AO* North Carolina

Plaza Investment Corp.
U. S. Highway 70A, P. O. Box 398
Haw River, N. C.
AO* North Carolina

NORTH DAKOTA

　None

OHIO

Capital Funds Corporation
127 Public Square
Cleveland 14, Ohio
AO* Ohio

Capitol Investors, Inc.
8 East Long Street
Columbus 15, Ohio
AO* Ohio

Cleveland Capital, Inc.
701 The Superior Building
815 Superior Avenue
Cleveland 14, Ohio
AO* Ohio

Cleveland Small Business Investment Co.
55 Public Square
1663 Illuminating Building
Cleveland 13, Ohio
AO* Ohio

Columbus Capital Corporation
20 East Broad Street
Columbus 16, Ohio
AO* Ohio

Corporate Resources, Inc.
National City Bank Building
Room 1007
623 Euclid Avenue
Cleveland 1, Ohio
AO* Ohio

Cosmopolitan Small Business
　Investment Company, Inc.
340 Engineers Building
Cleveland 14, Ohio
AO* Ohio

Dycap, Inc.
50 West Broad Street
Columbus 15, Ohio
AO* Ohio

Enterprise Capital, Inc.
2000 Lee Road
Cleveland Heights, Ohio
AO* Ohio

First Toledo Small Business
　Investment Company, Inc.
625 Security Building
245 Huron Street
Toledo 4, Ohio
AO* Ohio & Michigan

Growth Capital, Inc.
Bulkley Building
1501 Euclid Avenue
Cleveland 15, Ohio
AO* Ohio

Karr Investment Corporation
923 East Broad Street
Columbus 5, Ohio
AO* Ohio

Ohio Capital, Inc.
331 Leader Bldg.
Cleveland 14, Ohio
AO* Ohio

Ohio Security and Small Business
　Investment Company, Inc.
6218 St. Clair Avenue
Cleveland 3, Ohio
AO* Ohio

Ohio Valley Capital Corporation
827 Union Central Building
Cincinnati 2, Ohio
AO* Ohio

Realty & Industrial Capital Corp.
1220 Huron Road
Cleveland 14, Ohio
AO* Ohio
Special Interests: Real estate

Techno-Fund, Inc.
50 West Gay Street
Columbus 15, Ohio
AO* Ohio
Special Interests: Science and technology

OKLAHOMA

Alliance Business Investment Company
510 McFarlin Building
11 East Fifth Street
Tulsa 3, Okla.
AO* Okla.

American United Capital Corporation
16 South Pennsylvania
Oklahoma City 7, Okla.
AO* Oklahoma and Puerto Rico

Business Growth Investment Corp.
525 South Troost Street
Post Office Box 1087
Tulsa 1, Okla.
AO* Oklahoma

Capital, Inc.
207 Penn Square
National Bank Building
Oklahoma City, Okla.
AO* Oklahoma

First American Capital Corporation
2511 Liberty Bank Building
Oklahoma City 2, Okla.
AO* Oklahoma and Puerto Rico

First Growth Capital, Inc.
819 S. W. 30th Street
Oklahoma City, Okla.
AO* Okla.

First Industries Capital Corporation
726 West Sheridan Avenue
Oklahoma City, Okla.
AO* Oklahoma

First Oklahoma Capital Corporation
120 North Robinson
Oklahoma City 2, Okla.
AO* Oklahoma

Henderson Funding Corporation
3120 North May Avenue
Oklahoma City, Okla.
AO* Oklahoma

New Frontier Investment Company, Inc.
312 North Independence
Enid, Okla.
AO* Oklahoma

**Oklahoma Small Business
   Investments, Inc.**
4416 North Western Avenue
Oklahoma City 18, Okla.
AO* Oklahoma

Retailers Capital Corporation
311 West Main Street
Oklahoma City 2, Okla.
AO* Oklahoma

United Midwestern Capital Corporation
4408 North Western
Oklahoma City, Okla.
AO* Oklahoma

OREGON

Continental Investment Corporation
811 S. W. Sixth Avenue
910 Executive Building
Portland 4, Ore.
AO* Oregon, Washington, Idaho, Alaska
   and Hawaii

Northern Pacific Capital Corporation
210 Oregon Bank Building
Portland 4, Ore.
AO* Oregon

Northwest Science Investment Corp.
609 American Bank Building
621 Southwest Morrison
Portland 5, Ore.
AO* Oregon

Oregon Small Business Investment Co.
661 High Street, N. E.
Salem, Ore.
AO* Oregon

Preferred Growth Capital, Inc.
Sylvan Building
2035 S. W. 58th Avenue
Portland 1, Ore.
AO* Oregon and Washington

Trans-Pacific Capital Corporation
715 U. S. Nat'l. Bank Building
309 S. W. 6th Avenue
Portland 4, Ore.
AO* Oregon

United Supermarket Investment Co.
6433 SE Lake Road
P. O. Box 5807
Portland, Ore.
AO* Oregon

Western Growth Fund, Inc.
610 Board of Trade Building
Portland 4, Ore.
AO* Oregon

PENNSYLVANIA

ABI Investment Corporation
12 South 12th Street
Philadelphia 7, Pa.
AO* Pennsylvania

Adelphia Capital Investment Corporation
1518 Walnut Street
Philadelphia 3, Pa.
AO* Pennsylvania

American Commercial Finance Corp.
Suite 507—Lewis Tower Bldg.
15th and Locust Street
Philadelphia 3, Pa.
Branch Office:
Parkade Building, Lower Level
5th and Market Streets
Camden, N. J.
AO* Pennsylvania and New Jersey

Apollo Investment Company
Frick Building
437 Grant Street
Pittsburgh 19, Pa.
AO* Pennsylvania

Business Investment Capital Fund, Inc.
Penn Square Building
Juniper & Filbert Street
Philadelphia, Pa.
AO* Pennsylvania, New Jersey

Capital Interests Corporation
133 South 36th Street
Philadelphia 4, Pa.
AO* Pennsylvania

**Consolidated Small Business
Investment Corporation**
2233 North Broad Street
Philadelphia 32, Pa.
AO* Pennsylvania

Consolidated Technical Capital Corp.
Suite 620
121 South Broad Street
Philadelphia 7, Pa.
AO* Pennsylvania

Corporate Capital Corporation
15th & Chestnut Streets
Philadelphia 2, Pa.
AO* Pennsylvania

Corporate Investment Company
2304-09 Grant Building
330 Grant Street
Pittsburgh 19, Pa.
AO* Pennsylvania

**Delaware Valley Small Business
Investment Company**
Wolf Building
Market Square
Chester, Pa.
Branch Office:
Fidelity Phila. Trust Bldg.
Broad & Sansom Streets
Philadelphia, Pa.
AO* Pennsylvania

Eastern Pennsylvania Investment Co.
3 Penn Center Plaza
Philadelphia 2, Pa.
AO* Third Federal Reserve District
in Pennsylvania

First Central Penn Investment Corp.
102 Village Green Lane
Lancaster, Pa.
AO* Pennsylvania

**First Pittsburgh Small Business
Investment Company**
1218 Frick Building
Pittsburgh 19, Pa.
AO* Pennsylvania

**Frankford Grocery Small Business
Investment Company, Inc.**
G Street & Erie Avenue
Philadelphia 24, Pa.
AO* Pennsylvania; Counties of Bucks,
Chester, Delaware, Montgomery and
Philadelphia

Funds for Business Growth, Inc.
1609 E. Wadsworth Avenue
Philadelphia 50, Pa.
AO* Pennsylvania

Great Eastern Capital Corporation
Three Penn Center Plaza,
Philadelphia 2, Pa.
AO* Pennsylvania

Greater Pittsburgh Capital Corporation
952 Union Trust Building
Pittsburgh, Pa.
AO* Pennsylvania

Independence Capital Corporation
Suite 1010
1518 Walnut Street
Philadelphia, Pa.
AO* Pennsylvania

Keystone Small Business Investment Co.
400 Penna. Power & Light Bldg.
Scranton 3, Pa.
AO* Pennsylvania; Counties Lackawanna,
Luzerne, Monroe, Pike, Susquehanna,
Wayne and Wyoming

Penn Capital Corporation
43 Main Street
Bradford, Pa.
AO* Pennsylvania

Pennsylvania Capital Growth Corp.
220 South 16th Street
Philadelphia, Pa.
AO* Pennsylvania

Pennsylvania Growth Investment Corp.
Room 454
#2 Gateway Center
Pittsburgh 22, Pa.
AO* Pennsylvania

Recreation Capital, Inc.
1900 Architects Building
Philadelphia, Pa.
AO* Pennsylvania

Science Capital Corporation
123 South Broad Street
Philadelphia, Pa.
AO* Pennsylvania and New Jersey
Special Interests: Science and technology

Sharon Small Business Investment Co.
385 Shenango Avenue
Sharon, Pa.
AO* Pennsylvania

**The Small Business Investment
Company of Pennsylvania**
42 South 15th Street
Philadelphia 2, Pa.
AO* Pennsylvania

U.A.G. Investment Corporation
430-450 North Third Street
Reading, Pa.
AO* Pennsylvania

Universal Investment Company
12th Floor Packard Building
Philadelphia 2, Pa.
Branch Office:
12 Haddon Avenue
Camden, N. J.
AO* Pennsylvania, New Jersey

Watkins Investment Company
1313 Robinson Building
42 South 15th Street
Philadelphia 3, Pa.
AO* Pennsylvania

PUERTO RICO

First Caribbean Mainland Capital Company
405 Condominium San Alberta
San Juan, Puerto Rico
AO* Puerto Rico, New York and
Virgin Islands

Puerto Rico Capital Corporation
First Federal Savings Bldg.
Stop 23, Ponce de Leon Avenue
Santurce, San Juan, Puerto Rico
AO* Puerto Rico

RHODE ISLAND

Assistance Investment Corporation
1128 Industrial Bank Building
Providence 3, R. I.
AO* Rhode Island

**Eastern Capital Corporation of
　Rhode Island**
118 Bellevue Avenue
Newport, R. I.
AO* Rhode Island

Narragansett Capital Corporation
10 Dorrance Street
Providence 3, R. I.
AO* Rhode Island

Northeast Capital Corporation
428 Smith Street
Providence 8, R. I.
AO* Rhode Island

SOUTH CAROLINA

Charleston Capital Corporation
19 Broad Street
Charleston, S. C.
AO* South Carolina

Confederate Capital Corporation
Post Office Box 2057
Federal Station
314 East Coffee Street
Greenville, S. C.
AO* South Carolina

Empire Capital Corporation
109 Oak Street
Greenwood, S. C.
AO* South Carolina

First Capital Corp. of South Carolina
1208 Washington Street
Columbia, S. C.
AO* South Carolina

First Carolina Fund
Main Street
Hodges, S. C.
AO* South Carolina

First Investment Capital Corporation
General Trust Building
Aiken, S. C.
AO* South Carolina and Georgia

The Floco Investment Company, Inc.
Lake City, S. C.
AO* South Carolina and North Carolina

Lowcountry Investment Corporation
c/o Piggly Wiggly Wholesale, Inc.
4444 Bennett Street
P. O. Box 4957
Seven Mile Viaduct
Charleston Heights, S. C.
AO* South Carolina

Merchants Investment Corporation
4531 Bennett Street
Post Office Box 4934
Charleston Heights, S. C.
AO* South Carolina

Norwood Capital Corporation
109 Stokes Building
E. Coffee Street
Greenville, S. C.
AO* South Carolina

Southern Growth Industries, Inc.
P. O. Box 3217, Sta. A.
1930 Augusta Road
Greenville, S. C.
AO* South Carolina, North Carolina,
　Florida, Georgia, Virginia, Tennessee,
　Mississippi, Louisiana, Alabama,
　Commonwealth of Puerto Rico

Webster Capital Corporation
Drawer 5427, Station B
Rickenbacker Road
Greenville, S. C.
AO* South Carolina

SOUTH DAKOTA

None

TENNESSEE

Financial Resources, Inc.
1909 Sterick Building
Memphis 3, Tenn.
AO* Tennessee

Southeastern Capital Corporation
Life & Casualty Tower
23rd Floor
Church Street & Fourth Avenue
Nashville 3, Tenn.
AO* Tennessee, Alabama, Florida,
　Kentucky, Mississippi, North Carolina,
　South Carolina and Georgia

**Standard Small Business
Investment Company, Inc.**
1101 Lebanon Road
c/o Mt. Olivet Cemetery Co.
Nashville, Tenn.
AO* Tennessee

**The Third's Small Business
Investment Company**
Third National Bank Building
P. O. Box 2523, Arcade Station
Nashville 3, Tenn.
AO* Tennessee

TEXAS

Admiral Investment Co., Inc.
Stewart Building
22nd Avenue & C
Galveston, Tex.
Branch Office:
Guaranty Building
1302 Rusk Avenue
Houston 2, Tex.
AO* Texas

Arlington Small Business Loans, Inc.
601 West Abram Street
Arlington, Tex.
AO* Texas

**Associated Small Business
Investment Co., Inc.**
319 Davis Building
Dallas 2, Tex.
AO* Texas

Business Funds, Inc.
824 Bettes Building
201 Main Street
Houston 2, Tex.
Branch Offices:
Maryland Trust Building
Baltimore, Md.
155 East 44th Street
New York, N. Y.
AO* Texas, California, Florida, New York,
    Maryland, Delaware, Pennsylvania and
    New Jersey

Capital Southwest Corporation
940 Hartford Building
Dallas, Tex.
Branch Office:
Equitable Life Assurance
Society Building
Los Angeles, Cal.
AO* Texas, Arizona and California
Special Interests: Oil and Gas

Central Business Investments, Inc.
249 Lake Air Center
Waco, Tex.
AO* Texas

**Central Texas Small Business
Investment Corporation**
514 Austin Avenue
Waco, Tex.
AO* Texas

Citizens Funding Corporation of Texas
2066 Butternut Street
Abilene, Tex.
AO* Texas

**Clif-Tex Small Business
Investment Company, Inc.**
1514 Commerce Street
Dallas 1, Tex.
AO* Texas

Construction Capital Corporation
715 Avenue H East
Arlington, Tex.
AO* Texas
Special Interests: Building and
    construction projects

Construction Funds, Inc.
101 North First Street
Diboll, Tex.
AO* Texas
Special Interests: Building and
    construction projects

Corpus Small Business Investment Co.
307 Jones Building
Corpus Christi, Tex.
AO* Texas

Dallas Small Business Investment Co., Inc.
1323 Davis Building
1300 Main Street
Dallas 2, Tex.
AO* Texas

Diversified Capital Funding Corp.
601 North Lincoln Street
Odessa, Tex.
AO* Texas

Electrical Equities, Inc.
1502 Good-Latimer Expressway
Dallas 10, Tex.
AO* Texas

Fidelity Capital Corporation
1705 Avondale Street
Amarillo, Tex.
AO* Texas

First Business Investment Corporation
2515 Irving Boulevard
Dallas 7, Tex.
AO* Texas

First Capital Corporation
2205 Austin Avenue
Waco, Tex.
AO* Texas

First Dallas Capital Corporation
1401 Main Street
Dallas 2, Tex.
AO* Texas

First Texas Investment Company
120 Jefferson Street
Sulphur Springs, Tex.
AO* Texas

First United Capital Corporation
1320 Americana Building
811 Dallas Street
Houston 2, Tex.
Branch Office:
1235 Shadowdale Road
Houston 24, Tex.
AO* Texas

First West Texas Capital Corporation
305 First Nat'l. Bank Building
Odessa, Tex.
AO* Texas & New Mexico

Fort Worth Capital Corporation
Fort Worth Title Bldg.
1200 West Freeway
Fort Worth, Tex.
AO* Texas

Foster Capital Corporation
6209 Alameda
El Paso, Tex.
AO* Texas

Frankfurt's Texas Investment Corporation
4217 Loma Alto Street
Dallas, Tex.
AO* Texas

General Southwest Investment Corp.
721 Fort Worth National Bank Building
7th and Main Streets
Fort Worth, Tex.
AO* Texas

Grocers Investment Corporation
5800 Armour Drive
Houston, Tex.
AO* Texas

Growth-Industry Corp.
505 Caples Building
El Paso, Tex.
AO* Texas and New Mexico

Gulf Investors, Inc.
11329 Todd Road
Houston 24, Tex.
AO* Texas

Gulf-Southwest Capital Corporation
1320 Niels Esperson Bldg.
Houston 2, Tex.
AO* Texas

Investment Capital Corporation of Dallas
Fidelity Union Tower
1501 Pacific Ave.
Dallas, Tex.
AO* Texas

Lone Star Capital Corporation
Suite 324 Rose Building
Pampa, Tex.
AO* Texas

Mid-Tex Capital Corporation
104 North Avenue E
Clifton, Tex.
AO* Texas

M. E. Moore Investment Company, Inc.
1404 Hartford Building
Dallas 1, Tex.
AO* Texas

New Funds, Inc.
7808 Carpenter Freeway
Dallas 7, Tex.
AO* Texas

North Texas Capital Corporation
2444 West Main Street
Grand Prairie, Tex.
AO* Texas

Northwestern Investment Company
906 College Avenue
Levelland, Tex.
AO* Texas

Parker, Ford Capital Corporation
2000 Vaughn Building
Dallas 1, Tex.
AO* Texas

Petro-Capital Corporation
6130 Sherry Lane
Dallas 25, Tex.
AO* Texas
Special Interests: Oil and gas

Petroleum Finance Corporation
5738 North Central Expressway
Dallas, Tex.
AO* Texas
Special Interests: Oil and gas

**Republic Small Business
   Investment Company**
Republic National Bank Building
Corner Ervay Street & Pacific Ave.
Dallas 1, Tex.
AO* Texas

Rice Investment Co.
3200 Produce Row
Houston, Tex.
AO* Texas

San Antonio Capital Corporation
720 North St. Marys Street
San Antonio, Tex.
AO* Texas

**The Small Business Investment
   Company of Houston**
Central Nat'l Bank of Houston
640 West Building
Houston 2, Tex.

So-Tex Investment Corporation
103 North Aransas Street
Box 771
Alice, Tex.
AO* Texas

**South Texas Small Business
   Investment Company**
204 North Brownson
Victoria, Tex.
AO* Texas

Tarrant Capital Corporation
Fort Worth Nat'l Bank Building
800 Main Street
Fort Worth 2, Tex.
AO* Texas

Techno-Growth Capital Corporation
4703 Ross Avenue
Dallas 21, Tex.
AO* Texas
Special Interests: Science and technology

Texas Business Investments Co.
540 Bettes Building
204 Fannin Street
Houston, Tex.
Branch Office:
202 Austin Savings and Loan Building
Austin, Tex.
AO* Texas

Texas Capital Corporation
104 East 8th Street
Georgetown, Tex.
AO* Texas
Special Interests: Oil and gas situations;
   realty and land development

Texas Continental Investment Co., Inc.
1416 Commerce Street
(8th Floor)
Dallas 1, Tex.
AO* Texas

Texas Equity Corporation
215 Cotton Exchange Bldg.
Dallas, Tex.
AO* Texas

Texas Small Business Investment Corp.
3131 E. Holcombe Blvd.
Houston 21, Tex.
AO* Texas

Trammell Crow Investment Company
1401 Hartford Building
Dallas 1, Tex.
AO* Texas

Trinity Capital Funds, Inc.
Suite 108
2133 McKinney Avenue
Dallas 1, Tex.
AO* Texas

West Central Capital Corporation
P. O. Box 1400
1548 North First Street
Abilene, Tex.
AO* Texas

Western Capital Corporation
704 Adolphus Tower
Dallas 2, Tex.
AO* Texas

UTAH

Creative Capital Corporation
51 West 3rd South
Salt Lake City, Utah
AO* Utah

First Capital Corporation of Utah
903 Deseret Building
Salt Lake City, Utah
AO* Utah

First Western Capital Corporation
10 Exchange Place
Salt Lake City 1, Utah
AO* Utah

Utah Capital Corporation
2510 South State Street
Salt Lake City 15, Utah
AO* Utah

VERMONT

None

VIRGIN ISLANDS

Caribbean Capital Corporation
23 Dronningens Gale
St. Thomas, U. S., Virgin Islands
AO* Virgin Islands

VIRGINIA

Capitol Area Investors, Inc.
Potomac Bank & Trust Building
106 North Payne Street
Fairfax, Va.
AO* Virginia, Maryland and
    District of Columbia

Chesapeake Capital Corporation
120 North St. Asaph Street
Alexandria, Va.
Branch Office:
1633 Connecticut Avenue, N. W.
Washington, D. C.
AO* Virginia, Maryland &
    District of Columbia

Colonial Capital Corporation
500 Helena Building
Granby and Plume Streets
Norfolk, Va.
AO* Virginia

Dominion Capital Corporation
1031 Kennedy Lane
Falls Church, Va.
AO* Virginia

Investment Funds, Incorporated
6665 New Kempsville Drive
Norfolk 2, Va.
AO* Virginia

Old Dominion Capital Corporation
3333 Virginia Beach Boulevard
Virginia Beach, Va.
AO* Virginia

Potomac Small Business Funds, Inc.
7251 Maple Street
Annandale, Va.
AO* Virginia, Maryland,
    District of Columbia

Riverdan Investment Corp.
2321 Riverside Drive
Danville, Va.
AO* Virginia

**Security Small Business Investment
Company**
474 Leesburg Pike
Falls Church, Va.
AO* Virginia, Maryland and
District of Columbia

**Small Business Investment Corporation
of Norfolk**
1216 Granby Street
Norfolk 10, Va.
AO* Virginia

Southside Capital Corporation
2020 Riverside Drive
Danville, Va.
AO* Virginia and North Carolina

Tidewater Industrial Capital Corporation
308 Lonsdale Building
207 Granby Street
Norfolk 10, Va.
AO* Virginia

Virginia Capital Corporation
908 State Planters Bank Building
Richmond 19, Va.
AO* Virginia, West Virginia, North Carolina

Webb Investment Corp.
110 North Payne Street
Fairfax, Va.
AO* Virginia

WASHINGTON

Cascade Capital Corporation
The Old National Bank Building
Spokane 1, Wash.
AO* Washington, Idaho, Oregon,
Alaska, Nevada and Hawaii

Farwest Capital Corporation
202 Logan Building
Seattle 1, Wash.
AO* Washington, Oregon and Alaska

**Northwest Business Investment
Corporation**
Farmers & Merchants Bank Bldg.
Rockford, Wash.
AO* Washington and Idaho

**Pacific Small Business Investment
Company**
1600 Norton Building
801 Second Avenue
Seattle 4, Wash.
AO* Washington

Small Business Investment Co. of America
1208 Norton Building
2nd Avenue & Columbia
Seattle, Wash.
AO* Washington

Washington Capital Corporation
106 North Second Ave.
P. O. Box 1020
Walla Walla, Wash.
AO* Washington

WEST VIRGINIA

**West Virginia First Small Business
Investment Corporation**
Post Office Box 967
215 Ninth Street
Huntington 13, W. Va.
AO* West Virginia

WISCONSIN

Badger Capital Corporation
612 North Water Street
Milwaukee 2, Wisc.
AO* Wisconsin

Capital Investments, Inc.
238 West Wisconsin Avenue
Milwaukee, Wisc.
AO* Wisconsin

First Wisconsin Investment Corporation
735 North Water Street
Milwaukee 2, Wisc.
AO* Wisconsin, Iowa, Minnesota,
Michigan, Illinois

Industrial Capital of Wisconsin, Inc.
122 S. Pickney Street
Madison, Wisc.
AO* Wisconsin

Inland Capital Corp.
759 N. Milwaukee Street
Milwaukee 2, Wisc.
AO* Wisconsin

Marine Capital Corporation
622 North Water Street
Milwaukee 2, Wisc.

Branch Office:
Room 2116
First National Bank Building
Minneapolis, Minn.
AO* Wisconsin and Minnesota

Northern States Capital Corporation
330 East Wilson Street
Madison 3, Wisc.
AO* Wisconsin

PENSION FUNDS

The following is a selected list of pension funds which includes a number of the largest corporations in the United States. The address indicated is that specified for administration of each company's pension fund, which is not always that of the corporation's executive headquarters.

Allegheny Ludlum Steel Corp. (P.T.)*
Oliver Building
Pittsburgh 22, Pa.
Administrators: S. A. McCaskey, Jr., and
    John E. Groves
Total Assets:** $25,103,000

Allis Chalmers Co. (P.T.)
56 N. Queen St.
York, Pa.
Administrators: Earl H. Hilker and
    William W. Mussmann
Total Assets: $4,840,000

Alpha Portland Cement Co. (P.T.)
15 S. Third St.
Easton, Pa.
Administrator: H. F. Stepanke, Sec.
Total Assets: $3,542,000

Aluminum Co. of America (P.T.)
1501 Alcoa Bldg.
Pittsburgh 19, Pa.
Administrators: S. M. Harrison, V.P., and
    M. M. Anderson, V.P.
Total Assets: $107,887,000

* Pension Trust
** Indicates the aggregate holdings committed to the pension fund and may consist of stocks, bonds, cash, real estate or other assets.

Amerada Petroleum Corp. (P.T.)
120 Broadway
New York 5, N. Y.
Administrator: E. P. Potter, Treas.
Total Assets: $7,358,000

Amalgamated Clothing Workers (P.T.)
15 Union Square West
New York 3, N. Y.
Administrators: H. Blumberg and F. Bergen
Total Assets: $33,713,000

**Amalgamated Lithographers
    Local No. 1 (P.T.)**
113 University Pl.
New York 3, N. Y
Administrators: S. E. Swayduck and
    E. Hanson
Total Assets: $23,894,000

American Airlines Inc. (P.T.)
100 Park Ave.
New York 17, N. Y.
Administrator: P. G. Larie
Total Assets: $6,443,000

American Brake Shoe Co. (P.T.)
530 Fifth Ave.
New York 36, N. Y.
Administrator: A. H. Munkenbeck, Jr.,
    Sec. & Treas.
Total Assets: $36,100,000 (2 plans)

American Can Co. (P.T.)
100 Park Ave.
New York 17, N. Y.
Administrator: R. W. Edison, Asst. Gen. Mgr.
Total Assets: $32,800,000 (4 plans)

American Cyanamid Co. (P.T.)
Employees Ret. Plan
30 Rockefeller Plaza
New York 20, N. Y.
Administrator: G. C. Walker
Total Assets: $78,253,000

American Electric Power Co. (P.T.)
2 Broadway
New York 8, N. Y.
Administrator: Donald C. Cook, Pres.,
    AEP Service Co.
Total Assets: $52,470,000

American Enka Corp. (P.T.)
350 Fifth Ave.
New York 1, N. Y.
Administrators: L. M. Rievers and
    H. J. Berry
Total Assets: $8,498,000 (2 plans)

American Express Co. (P.T.)
65 Broadway
New York 6, N. Y.
Administrator: Norman F. Page
Total Assets: $5,480,000

American Insurance Co. (P.T.)
15 Washington St.
Newark 1, N. J.
Administrators: George T. Westwood, V.P.
    & Compt. and R. G. Guthrie, V.P. & Treas.
Total Assets: $12,251,000

American Oil Co. (P.T.)
555 Fifth Ave.
New York 17, N. Y.
Administrator: F. X. Mannix
Total Assets: $183,160,000

American Steel Foundries, Inc. (P.T.)
Prudential Plaza
Chicago 1, Ill.
Administrator: R. E. Larsen, Compt.
Total Assets: $7,613,000

American Telephone & Telegraph Co. (P.T.)
195 Broadway
New York 7, N. Y.
Administrator: E. J. McNeely
Total Assets: $159,919,000

American Tobacco Co. (P.T.)
150 E. 42nd St.
New York 17, N. Y.
Administrator: A. L. Janson, V.P. & Compt.
Total Assets: $7,501,000

American Viscose Corp. (P.T.)
1617 Pennsylvania Blvd.
Philadelphia 3, Pa.
Administrator: William H. Brown, V.P. &
    Treas.
Total Assets: $14,852,000

Arkansas Louisiana Gas Co. (P.T.)
P. O. Box 1734
Shreveport, La.
Adminstrator: Frank L. Halleman, Chm.
    Ret. Comm.
Total Assets: $7,648,000

Armour & Co. (P.T.)
401 N. Wabash Ave.
Chicago 90, Ill.
Administrators: E. J. McAdams, Chm. Pens.
    Bd. and Harold E. Brooks, V.P.
Total Assets: $116,984,000

Atchison, Topeka & Sante Fe Railway Co. (P.T.)
80 E. Jackson Blvd.
Chicago 4, Ill.
Administrator: E. S. Marsh, Pres.
Total Assets: $52,828,000

Atlas Powder Co.
Concord Pike
Wilmington, Del.
Administrators: C. C. Gammons and
    N. E. Miller
Total Assets: $8,092,000

Baldwin-Lima-Hamilton (P.T.)
Philadelphia National Bank Building
Philadelphia, Pa.
Administrator: Charles E. Acker, V.P.
Total Assets: $15,800,000 (2 plans)

Bank of America (P.T.)
300 Montgomery St.
San Francisco 1, Cal.
Administrators: Samuel B. Stewart,
    Exec. V.P. and Roland Pierotti
Total Assets: $4,731,000

Batten, Barton, Durstine & Osborne Inc. (P.S.)*
383 Madison Ave.
New York 17, N. Y.
Administrator: Tom Dillon, Chm. of Prof.-
　Sharing Comm.
Total Assets: $9,151,000

Beech Nut Life Savers (P.T.)
Canajoharie, N. Y.
Administrator: F. L. Fero
Total Assets: $10,481,000

Bell Aircraft Corp. & Bell Helicopter Corp. (P.T.)
P. O. Box 1
Buffalo 5, N. Y.
Administrator: W. G. Gisel, V.P. & Treas.
Total Assets: $4,361,000

Bell Telephone Laboratories Inc. (P.T.)
463 West St.
New York 14, N. Y.
Administrator: G. B. Small, Compt.
Total Assets: $81,741,000

Bell Telephone Co. of Pennsylvania (P.T.)
1835 Arch St.
Philadelphia 3, Pa.
Administrator: John Markle, II, V.P.
Total Assets: $141,357,000

Beneficial Finance Co. (P.T.)
1300 Market St.
Wilmington 99, Del.
Administrators: E. T. Felter and
　T. A. McGrath
Total Assets: $16,572,000

Berwind-White Coal Mining Co. (P.T.)
One Broadway
New York 4, N. Y.
Administrators: C. E. Dunlap and
　G. C. Berwind
Total Assets: $7,966,000

Bethlehem Steel Corp. (P.T.)
701 E. Third St.
Bethlehem, Pa.
Administrator: B. D. Broeker
Total Assets: $272,393,000

* Profit-sharing Trust.

Boston Edison Co. (P.T.)
182 Tremont St.
Boston 12, Mass.
Administrator: Albert C. McMenimen,
　Fin. V.P. & Treas.
Total Assets: $4,019,000

Bristol Myers Co. (P.T.)
630 Fifth Ave.
New York 20, N. Y.
Administrator: Lee H. Bristol, Chm. of Bd.
Total Assets: $7,775,000

Brooklyn Union Gas Co. (P.T.)
176 Remsen St.
Brooklyn 1, N. Y.
Administrators: J. Nokelty and W. E.
　Hinsworth
Total Assets: $10,094,000

Bulova Watch Co. (P.T.)
Bulova Park
Flushing 70, N. Y.
Administrator: Robert De Louise
Total Assets: $21,014,000

California Electric Power Co. (P.T.)
2885 Foothill Blvd.
San Bernardino, Cal.
Administrator: John A. Talley, V.P. &
　Gen. Mgr.
Total Assets: $4,976,000

Callaway Mills Co. (P.T.)
1 Dallas St.
La Grange, Ga.
Administrators: Lewis Price and George
　E. Sims, Jr.
Total Assets: $6,028,000

Capital Airlines, Inc.
c/o United Airlines
P.O. Box 880
Chicago 66, Ill.
Administrators: Clark E. Luther and
　Robert J. Wilson
Total Assets: $8,686,000

Carborundum Company (P.T.)
Niagara Falls, N. Y.
Administrator: G. J. Stewart, Treas.
Total Assets: $8,108,000

Chase Manhattan Bank (P.T.)
One Chase Manhattan Plaza
New York 15, N. Y.
Administrator: Harold F. Moeller, Exec. V.P.
Total Assets: $127,233,000 (2 plans)

Chesapeake & Potomac Telephone Co.
(P.T.)
930 H St. N.W.
Washington, D. C.
Administrator: A. P. Clow, V.P.
Total Assets: $36,505,000

Chesapeake & Potomac Telephone Co.
of Maryland (P.T.)
320 St. Paul Pl.
Baltimore, Md.
Administrator: L. Mercer Smith, V.P.
Total Assets: $44,176,000

Chesebrough-Ponds, Inc. (P.T.)
485 Lexington Ave.
New York 17, N. Y.
Administrators: J. H. Calvert and Frank
J. McGroarty
Total Assets: $5,650,000 (2 plans)

Chrysler Corp. (P.T.)
341 Massachusetts Ave.
Detroit 3, Mich.
Administrators: W. J. Simms, Treas. and
E. H. Graham, Compt.
Total Assets: $170,446,000

Cleveland Electric Illuminating Co. (P.T.)
55 Public Square
Cleveland 1, Ohio
Administrators: Robert E. Walker, V.P. and
F. Warren Brooks, V.P., Fin.
Total Assets: $32,155,000

Coca Cola Co. (P.T.)
P. O. Drawer 1734
Atlanta, Ga.
Administrators: D. A. Turner, Chm., Ret.
Plan Comm., and C. H. Candler, Jr.
Total Assets: $22,814,000

Colorado Fuel & Iron Corp. (P.T.)
361 Delaware Ave.
Buffalo, N. Y.
Administrator: H. J. Jones
Total Assets: $6,447,000

Columbia Broadcasting System, Inc. (P.T.)
485 Madison Ave.
New York 17, N. Y.
Administrator: Samuel R. Deon, Treas.
Total Assets: $10,989,000

Commerce Clearing House, Inc. (P.T.)
4025 West Peterson Ave.
Chicago 46, Ill.
Administrators: James T. Aspbury and
Robert C Bartlett
Total Assets: $7,387,000

Commercial Credit Co. (P.T.)
300 St. Paul St.
Baltimore 2, Md.
Administrators: James T. Flynn and
J. S. Grimes, Treas.
Total Assets: $16,720,000

Consolidated Edison Co. of N. Y. (P.T.)
Four Irving Pl.
New York 3, N. Y.
Administrator: B. E. Gallagher, V.P.
Total Assets: $52,127,000

Consolidation Coal Co. (P.T.)
1924 Koppers Bldg.
Pittsburgh 19, Pa.
Administrator: Holly W. Spahr
Total Assets: $5,667,000

Continental Baking Co. (P.T.)
P. O. Box 731
Rye, N. Y.
Adminstrator: Ellis C. Baum
Total Assets: $16,804,000

Continental Can Co. (P.T.)
100 E. 42nd St.
New York 17, N. Y.
Administrator: L. Wilkinson, Exec. V.P.
Total Assets: $45,250,000 (3 plans)

Corning Glass Works (P.T.)
Corning, N. Y.
Administrator: T. Waaland, Treas.
Total Assets: $29,468,000

Creole Petroleum Corp.
1230 Ave. of the Americas
New York 20, N. Y.
Administrator: J. C. Anderson, V.P.
Total Assets: $128,887,000

Crocker-Anglo National Bank (P.T.)
1 Montgomery St.
San Francisco 20, Cal.
Administrators: Joseph F. Hogan, First V.P.
  and R. M. Pike, Sec.
Total Assets: $13,657,000

Crouse & Hinds Co. (P.T.)
Wolf & 7th North Sts.
Syracuse, N. Y.
Administrator: R. W. Cummings, Treas.
Total Assets: $5,155,000

Crown Zellerbach Co. (P.T.)
Rincon Annex, Box 3475
San Francisco 17, Cal.
Administrator: C. S. Cullenbine, Sec.
Total Assets: $61,205,000

Crucible Steel Co. of America (P.T.)
Box 2518
Pittsburgh 30, Pa.
Administrator: R. I. Kingsley
Total Assets: $13,178,000

Curtis Publishing Co. (P.T.)
Independence Square
Philadelphia, Pa.
Administrator: Robert W. Edwards, Sec.
Total Assets: $46,458,000

Curtiss-Wright Corp. (P.T.)
304 Valley Blvd.
Wood-Ridge, N. J.
Administrator: Frank H. Miller, Treas.
Total Assets: $53,860,000 (2 plans)

Dayton Power & Light Co. (P.T.)
25 North Main St.
Dayton 1, Ohio
Administrators: K. C. Long, Chm., Ret. Bd.
  and J. V. Colley, Sec., Ret. Bd.
Total Assets: $6,918,000

DeLuxe Check Printers, Inc. (P.T.)
2199 N. Pascal St.
St. Paul 13, Minn.
Administrators: Mitchell W. Shearer and
  William B. Gerry
Total Assets: $10,425,000

Detroit Edison Co. (P.T.)
2000 Second Ave.
Detroit 26, Mich.
Administrator: E. M. Spencer, Treas.
Total Assets: $84,243,000

Detroit Steel Corp. (P.T.)
1025 South Oakwood Blvd.
Detroit 17, Mich.
Administrator: Nathan H. Siegel, Sec.
Total Assets: $9,004,000

Diamond National Co. (P.T.)
122 E. 42nd St.
New York 17, N. Y.
Administrator: P. S. Woodbury, Treas.
Total Assets: $7,492,000

Diamond State Telephone Co. (P.T.)
1835 Arch St.
Philadelphia, Pa.
Administrator: L. B. McClain
Total Assets: $4,823,000

E. I. DuPont de Nemours & Co. (P.T.)
Wilmington 98, Del.
Administrator: R. R. Pippin, Treas.
Total Assets: $497,560,000

**Duquesne Light & Allegheny County
  Steam Heating Co. (P.T.)**
435 Sixth Ave.
Pittsburgh 9, Pa.
Administrator: S. G. Page
Total Assets: $20,856,000

Eastern Air Lines Inc. (P.T.)
45 Wall St.
New York 5, N. Y.
Administrator: T. E. Creighton, Treas.
Total Assets: $3,847,000

Eastman Kodak Co. (P.T.)
343 State St.
Rochester 4, N. Y.
Administrator: M. V.. Dill, Dir. of Ind.
  Relations
Total Assets: $29,409,000

Ebasco Services (P.T.)
Two Rector St.
New York 6, N. Y.
Administrators: E. P. Noppel and K. W.
  Reese
Total Assets: $11,803,000

Electric Storage Battery Co.
2 Penn Center Plaza
Philadelphia 2, Pa.
Administrator: W. P. Cairo, Sec.
Total Assets: $6,595,000

Elliott Company (P.T.)
Carrier Parkway
Syracuse 1, N. Y.
Administrator: G. V. Wright
Total Assets: $5,488,000

El Paso Natural Gas Co. (P.T.)
P. O. Box 1492
El Paso, Tex.
Administrator: Virgil Rittmann, Sec. &
　Treas.
Total Assets: $21,006,000

Endicott-Johnson Corp. (P.T.)
Endicott, N. Y.
Administrator: L. Stanford, Sec. Emp. Ret.
　Fund
Total Assets: $49,794,000

Equitable Gas Company (P.T.)
420 Boulevard of the Allies
Pittsburgh, Pa.
Administrator: C. J. Mulholland, Sr., V.P.
　& Treas.
Total Assets: $9,168,000

Fidelity-Philadelphia Trust Co. (P.T.)
Broad & Walnut Sts.
Philadelphia 1, Pa.
Administrators: B. Lewis Clarke, Jr., Sec.
　and L. Saunders
Total Assets: $6,643,000

**First National Bank of Boston and
Old Colony Trust Co. (P.T.)**
67 Milk St.
Boston 6, Mass.
Administrators: Roger C. Damon, Chm.,
　Ret. Comm. and Horace M. Chadsey
Total Assets: $25,640,000

First National Bank of Chicago (P.T.)
38 South Dearborn St.
Chicago 90, Ill.
Administrators: Richard B. Keck, Compt.
　and Robert V. Guapp, Asst. Auditor
Total Assets: $79,080,000

**First National City Bank of N. Y. (P.T. &
P.S.)**
55 Wall St.
New York 5, N. Y.
Administrator: J. Mac N. Thompson, V.P.
Total Assets: $59,595,000 (P.T.) and
$9,700,000 (P.S.)

**The First Pennsylvania Banking & Trust
Co. (P.S.)**
15th & Chestnut Sts.
Philadelphia 1, Pa.
Administrators: W. L. Day and W. F. Kelly
Total Assets: $3,883,000

**The First Pennsylvania Banking & Trust
Company (P.T.)**
15th & Chestnut Sts.
Philadelphia 1, Pa.
Administrators: J. W. Thorn and A. C. Graff
Total Assets: $8,378,000

Florida Power Corp. (P.T.)
101 Fifth St. South
St. Petersburg, Fla.
Administrators: J. S. Gracy, Chm., Ret. Bd.
　and G. F. Foley
Total Assets: $15,921,000

Florida Power & Light Co. (P.T.)
Ingraham Bldg.
Miami 32, Fla.
Administrators: H. G. Simpson and B. W.
　Powell
Total Assets: $24,330,000

Ford Motor Co. (P.T.)
The American Rd.
Dearborn, Mich.
Administrator: Richard L. Johnson, Treas.
Total Assets: $352,008,000

Friden, Inc. (P.T.)
2350 Washington Ave.
San Leandro, Cal.
Administrators: P. R. Samwell and
H. M. Billings
Total Assets: $8,832,000

**General Accident Fire & Life Assurance,
Ltd. (P.T.)**
444 Walnut St.
Philadelphia, Pa.
Administrators: Dudley M. Pruitt and
Robert C. Hall
Total Assets: $5,870,000

General Aniline & Film Corp. (P.T.)
111 W. 50th St.
New York 20, N. Y.
Administrator: F. A. Gibbons
Total Assets: $27,458,000

General Dynamics Corp. (P.T.)
445 Park Ave.
New York 22, N. Y.
Administrator: A. D. Marshall, V.P.
Total Assets: $46,807,000

General Electric Co. (P.T.)
570 Lexington Ave.
New York 22, N. Y.
Administrators: Philip D. Reed and
    J. D. Lockton
Total Assets: $1,051,258,000

General Mills, Inc. (P.T.)
9200 Wayzata Blvd.
Minneapolis 26, Minn.
Administrators: D. E. Balch, Chm., Employ.
    Benefit Bd. and H. S. Kingman
Total Assets: $77,362,000

General Motors Corp. (P.T)
c/o Insurance & Pension Section
3044 West Grand Blvd.
Detroit 2, Mich.
Administrators: A. O. Lundin, Treas. and
    R. C. Mark, Compt.
Total Assets: $602,255,000

General Precision Equip. Corp. (P.T.)
92 Gold St.
New York 36, N. Y.
Administrator: B. H. Richardson, Treas.
Total Assets: $5,740,000

General Railway Signal Co. (P.T.)
801 West Ave.
Rochester, N. Y.
Administrator: Paul Renshaw, Chm. of
    Comm.
Total Assets: $5,463,000

Girard Trust Corn Exchange Bank (P.T.)
Broad & Chestnut Sts.
Philadelphia 1, Pa.
Administrator: J. M. Davie, Asst. Sec.
Total Assets: $6,103,000 (2 plans)

Glens Falls Ins. Co. (P.T.)
291 Glen St.
Glens Falls, N. Y.
Administrators: L. A. Beeman and
    L. P. Brown
Total Assets: $8,426,000

W. R. Grace & Co. (P.T.)
7 Hanover Square
New York 5, N. Y.
Administrator: R. E. Marks, Asst. V.P.
Total Assets: $12,119,000

Grand Union Co. (P.T.)
100 Broadway
East Paterson, N. J.
Administrator: John H. Milbank, Compt.
Total Assets: $9,179,000

W. T. Grant Co.
1441 Broadway
New York, N. Y.
Administrator: W. G. Finnan
Total Assets: $34,989,000

Graybar Electric Co. Inc. (P.S.)
420 Lexington Ave.
New York 17, N. Y.
Administrator: R. D. Paine, Sec.
Total Assets: $34,418,000

Great American Group of Ins. Cos. (P.T.)
99 John St.
New York 36, N. Y.
Administrator: J. G. Niederlitz, Sec. of
    Ret. Comm.
Total Assets: $9,361,000

Great Lakes Carbon Corp. (P.T.)
18 East 48th St.
New York 17, N. Y.
Administrators: G. S. Jubiler, Compt., Ret.
    Comm. and B. J. Flemming
Total Assets: $8,009,000

H. L. Green Co. Inc. (P.T.)
902 Broadway
New York, N. Y.
Administrators: M. E. Olen and
    J. M. Nicely
Total Assets: $8,398,000

Grumman Aircraft Engineering Corp. (P.T.)
Bethpage, L. I.
Administrators: E. Clinton Towle and
    L. Willing
Total Assets: $48,695,000

Gulf, Mobile & Ohio Railroad Co. (P.T.)
104 & Francis Sts.
Mobile, Ala.
Administrators: T. T. Martin and
   J. N. Ogden
Total Assets: $6,478,000

Gulf Oil Company (P.T. & P.S.)
P. O. Box 1166
Pittsburgh 30, Pa.
Administrators: David Proctor, Chm. and
   W. L. Naylor
Total Assets: $293,593,000 (2 plans)

Hanover Bank (P.T.)
70 Broadway
New York 4, N. Y.
Administrator: C. H. Bush, V.P.
Total Assets: $8,447,000

Harris Trust & Savings Bank (P.T.)
111 West Monroe St.
Chicago 90, Ill.
Administrators: Henry L. Parker and
   George S. Allen
Total Assets: $18,705,000

H. J. Heinz Co. (P.T.)
1062 Progress St.
Pittsburgh 30, Pa.
Administrators: Charles Heinz and
   C. A. Brinkman
Total Assets: $26,853,000

Hewlett-Packard Co. (P.T.)
1501 Page Mill Rd.
Palo Alto, Cal.
Administrators: William R. Hewlett and
   Luis Alvarez
Total Assets: $5,705,000

Hooker Chemical Corp. (P.T.)
Buffalo Ave. & 47th St.
Niagara Falls, N. Y.
Administrator: Ansley Wilcox II, Sec. of
   Ret. Pgm. Comm.
Total Assets: $6,164,000

**Pension Fund of N. Y. City Trucking
Industry Local No. 807**
325 Spring St.
New York 13, N. Y.
Administrators: J. E. Strong and
   J. F. Morgan
Total Assets: $8,680,000

Ingersoll-Rand (P.T.)
11 Broadway
New York 4, N. Y.
Administrator: E. R. D. Sheerin, Treas.
Total Assets: $37,347,000

Interchemical Corp. (P.T.)
67 W. 44th St.
New York 36, N. Y.
Administrator: Claud Brown, V.P. & Treas.
Total Assets: $6,903,000

**International Brotherhood of Electric
Workers (P.T.)**
1200 15th St. N.W.
Washington, D. C.
Administrators: J. D. Keenan and
   J. P. Sullivan
Total Assets: $85,010,000

International Harvester Co. (P.T.)
180 North Michigan Ave.
Chicago 1, Ill.
Administrators: Roscoe W. Batts, Dir. of
   Ind. Rel. and Ivan L. Willis, V.P.
Total Assets: $131,961,000

International Paper Co. (P.T.)
220 East 42nd St.
New York 17, N. Y.
Administrators: J. P. Monge, Chm., Ret.
   Bd. and George J. Adams
Total Assets: $108,750,000

**International Telephone & Telegraph Co.,
ITT Federal Laboratories (P.T.)**
500 Washington Ave.
Nutley, N. J.
Administrators: C. A. McNeill, Dir. of Ind.
   Rel. and W. T. Rapp, V.P. & Compt.
Total Assets: $2,488,000

Irving Trust Co. (P.T.)
One Wall St.
New York 5, New York
Administrator: A. V. Doherty, V.P.
Total Assets: $9,987,000

Jersey Central Power & Light Co. (P.T.)
501 Grand Ave.
Asbury Park, N. J.
Administrator: H. B. Allen, V.P.
Total Assets: $20,705,000 (2 plans)

Jewel Tea Co. (P.T.)
1955 West North Ave.
Melrose Park, Ill.
Administrators: J. M. Friedlander and
   W. W. Tongue
Total Assets: $55,023,000

Johns Manville Corp. (P.T.)
22 E. 40th St.
New York 16, N. Y.
Administrator: J. M. Shackleford, Treas.
Total Assets: $78,022,000

Jones & Laughlin Steel Corp. (P.T.)
Three Gateway Center
Pittsburgh 30, Pa.
Administrator: Herbert Johnson, V.P.
Total Assets: $75,585,000 (3 plans)

Koppers Co. Inc. (P.T.)
Koppers Bldg.
Pittsburgh 19, Pa.
Administrator: R. R. Montgomery, Sec.
   of Pens. Comm.
Total Assets: $28,792,000

S. H. Kress & Co. (P.T.)
114 Fifth Ave.
New York 12, N. Y.
Administrator: L. K. Guiler, Treas.
Total Assets: $10,627,000

**Ladies Garment Workers Eastern
   Region (P.T.)**
1710 Broadway
New York 19, N. Y.
Administrators: A. Bambace and J. Brodsky
Total Assets: $17,310,000

Lane Bryant, Inc. (P.T.)
465 Fifth Ave.
New York 16, N. Y.
Administrators: R. Malsin and T. R. Malsin
Total Assets: $5,545,000

Leeds & Northrup Co. (P.T.)
4901 Stanton Ave.
Philadelphia, Pa.
Administrators: D. H. Schultz and
   C. W. Hall
Total Assets: $14,155,000

Lever Brothers Co. (P.T.)
390 Park Ave.
New York 22, N. Y.
Administrator: J. Warren Moore, Treas.
Total Assets: $19,781,000

Liggett & Myers Tobacco Co. (P.T.)
630 Fifth Ave.
New York 20, N. Y.
Administrator: J. B. Anderson, V.P.
Total Assets: $9,780,000

Long Island Railroad Co. (P.T.)
15 North 32nd St.
Philadelphia, Pa.
Administrators: J. P. Newell and
   D. C. Bevan
Total Assets: $5,024,000

Longshoremen's N.Y. Shipping Assn. (P.T.)
80 Broad St.
New York 4, N. Y.
Administrators: P. Lynch and E. S. May
Total Assets: $19,542,000

P. Lorillard Company (P.T.)
200 E. 42nd St.
New York 17, N. Y.
Administrator: George O. Davies, V.P.
Total Assets: $5,323,000

M. Lowenstein & Sons Inc. (P.T.)
1430 Broadway
New York 19, N. Y.
Administrator: Bernard R. Rapaport, Asst.
   Treas.
Total Assets: $7,641,000

Mack Trucks, Inc.
1000 S. 2nd St.
Plainfield, N. J.
Administrator: C. A. Slifer, Asst. Compt.
Total Assets: $7,051,000 (2 plans)

R. H. Macy & Co. Inc. (P.T. & P.S.)
34th St. & Herald Square
New York, N. Y.
Administrator: Marvin Fenster, Sec.
Total Assets: $15,210,000 (P.T.) and
   $21,075,000 (P.S.)

Manufacturers Trust Co. (P.T. & P.S.)
55 Broad St.
New York 4, N. Y.
Administrator: Gilbert T. Davison, Asst. Sec.
Total Assets: $26,078,000

Marine Midland Corp. (P.T.)
241 Main St.
Buffalo 5, N. Y.
Administrators: George F. Phillips, Chm.
   and Charles E. Rhodes
Total Assets: $26,594,000

The Martin Company (P.T.)
Middle River
Baltimore 3, Md.
Administrator: W. L. Lucas, Treas.
Total Assets: $6,547,000

Maryland Casualty Co. (P.T.)
701 W. 40th St.
Baltimore 3, Md.
Administrators: W. T. Harper and P. H. May
Total Assets: $9,596,000

McCrory-McLennan Stores Corp. (P.T.)
1107 Broadway
New York 16, N. Y.
Administrators: F. W. Paul and C. R. Purdon
Total Assets: $16,381,000

McKesson & Robbins Inc. (P.T.)
155 E. 44th St.
New York 17, N. Y.
Administrator: J. A. Mitchell, Jr., Sec. of
   the Ret. Comm.
Total Assets: $28,608,000

Melville Shoe Corp. (P.T.)
25 W. 43rd St.
New York 36, N. Y.
Administrator: J. Frederick Rossell, V.P.
Total Assets: $4,889,000

I. W. Means & Co.
2516 Wabash Ave.
Chicago 16, Ill.
Administrators: F. J. Brady and George
   L. Carstens
Total Assets: $8,608,000

Merck & Co. Inc. (P.T.)
Rahway, N. J.
Administrator: R. H. Lander, Sec.
Total Assets: $13,537,000

Merganthaler Linotype Co. (P.T.)
29 Ryerson St.
Brooklyn 5, N. Y.
Administrators: C. L. Daniels and
   James Roth
Total Assets: $7,017,000

Merrill Lynch, Pierce, Fenner & Smith Inc.
   (P.T.)
70 Pine St.
New York 5, N. Y.
Administrators: T. J. Cassidy and
   R. E. Harris
Total Assets: $27,792,000 (2 plans)

Mesta Machine Co. (P.T.)
Seventh Ave.
West Homestead, Pa.
Administrator: V. F. Koerner, Asst. Sec.
Total Assets: $17,388,000

Minneapolis-Honeywell Regulator Co. (P.T.)
2753 Fourth Avenue S.
Minneapolis 8, Minn.
Administrator: R. W. Laxson, Sec. & Treas.
Total Assets: $18,033,000

Monsanto Chemical Co. (P.T.)
800 N. Lindbergh Blvd.
St. Louis 66, Mo.
Administrators: E. M. Queeny, Chm. Fin.
   Comm. and P. J. Dowd, Treas.
Total Assets: $23,828,000

Montgomery Ward & Co. (P.T.)
619 West Chicago Ave.
Chicago 7, Ill.
Administrators: C. J. Barnhill, Sec., and
   L. R. Butzen, Records Mgr.
Total Assets: $31,138,000

Mountain States Telephone & Telegraph
   Co. (P.T.)
931 14th St.
Denver 2, Colo.
Administrators: A. S. Alston, V.P., Personnel,
   and E. E. Wyland, Asst. V.P., Personnel
Total Assets: $89,161,000

G. C. Murphy Co. (P.T.)
531 Fifth Ave.
McKeesport, Pa.
Administrator: W. S. Thompson, Sec.
Total Assets: $13,470,000

National Biscuit Co. (P.T.)
425 Park Ave.
New York 22, N. Y.
Administrator: H. T. Eggert
Total Assets: $44,155,000

National Distillers & Chemical Corp. (P.T.)
99 Park Ave.
New York 16, N. Y.
Administrator: Paul C. Jameson
Total Assets: $34,896,000 (2 plans)

National Maritime Union (P.T.)
346 W. 17th St.
New York, N. Y.
Administrators: J. Curran and R. E. Casey
Total Assets: $25,800,000

The National Sugar Refining Co. (P.T.)
100 Wall St.
New York 5, N. Y.
Administrator: H. Letzler, Asst. Treas.
Total Assets: $7,286,000 (2 plans)

Nekoosa-Edwards Paper Co. (P.T.)
Port Edwards, Wis.
Administrators: Charles H. Reese, Chm.,
    Adm. Comm., and Samuel A. Casey, Sec.,
    Adm. Comm.
Total Assets: $9,037,000

The Nestle Co. Inc. (P.T.)
100 Bloomingdale Rd.
White Plains, N. Y.
Administrators: L. A. Wilkins and
    R. H. Cronk
Total Assets: $15,071,000 (2 plans)

**New England Telephone & Telegraph Co.
    (P.T.)**
185 Franklin St.
Boston 7, Mass.
Administrators: Robert V. Jones, V.P. &
    Compt., and Joseph T. Crowley, Asst.
    Sec.
Total Assets: $183,239,000

New York Central System (P.T.)
466 Lexington Ave.
New York 17, N. Y.
Administrators: W. R. Grant, V.P. Fin. and
    L. B. Fee, V.P. Empl. Rel.
Total Assets: $72,070,000

New York & Pennsylvania Co. Inc. (P.T.)
425 Park Ave.
New York 22, N. Y.
Administrator: J. B. Bryerton, Asst. Treas.
Total Assets: $9,096,000

New York Telephone Co. (P.T.)
140 West St.
New York 6, N. Y.
Administrator: B. R. Young, V.P. Fin. &
    Compt.
Total Assets: $399,184,000

Niagara Mohawk Corp. (P.T.)
300 Erie Blvd.
Syracuse 2, N. Y.
Administrators: James H. Morrell, Treas.,
    and F. M. Osta, V.P.
Total Assets: $35,806,000

Northern States Power Co. (P.T.)
100 North Barstow St.
Eau Claire, Wisc.
Administrator: N. F. Naybert, V.P. & Treas.
Total Assets: $42,547,000

Ohio Edison Co. (P.T.)
47 N. Main St.
Akron 8, Ohio
Administrators: Otto Brunenmeister, Jr.,
    V.P., and R. L. Wagner, Asst. Treas.
Total Assets: $35,715,000

**Oklahoma Tire & Supply Co. (a division of
    McCrory Corp.)**
6901 E. Pine St.
Tulsa, Okla.
Administrators: Samuel H. Minsky and
    Maurice Sanditen

Olin Mathieson Chemical Corp. (P.T.)
460 Park Ave.
New York 22, N. Y.
Administrator: Everett H. Bellows, Dir. of
    Personnel
Total Assets: $82,486,000

Otis Elevator Co. (P.T.)
260 Eleventh Ave.
New York 1, N. Y.
Administrators: J. B. Donohue, Asst. Sec.,
    and J. B. Forsyth, Asst. Treas.
Total Assets: $6,117,000

Pacific National Bank of Seattle (P.S.)
900 Second Ave.
Seattle, Wash.
Administrator: G. H. Anderson, Auditor
Total Assets: $1,384,000

Pacific Telephone & Telegraph Co. (P.T.)
140 New Montgomery St.
San Francisco 5, Cal.
Administrators: J. O. Einerman, V.P. and
Dean Anderson, Treas.
Total Assets: $362,243,000

Pan American International Oil Co. (P.T.)
555 Fifth Ave.
New York 17, N. Y.
Administrators: N. L. Watson, Compt., and
R. M. McGowen, Asst. Compt.
Total Assets: $227,298,000

Pan-Am Southern Corp. (P.T.)
555 Fifth Ave.
New York 17, N. Y.
Administrator: F. X. Mannix
Total Assets: $12,012,000

Pan American World Airways Inc. (P.T.)
28-19 Bridge Plaza North
Long Island City 1, N. Y.
Administrators: John S. Woodbridge,
Compt., and John C. Leslie
Total Assets: $2,363,000

Pennsylvania Railroad System (P.T.)
Room 607
15 N. 32nd St.
Philadelphia, Pa.
Administrator: David Bevan, Mgr. of Pens.
Total Assets: $101,106,000

Charles Pfizer & Co. Inc. (P.T.)
11 Bartlett St.
Brooklyn 6, N. Y.
Administrator: J. William Stuart, V.P.
Total Assets: $25,044,000

Philadelphia National Bank (P.T.)
Ninth & Chestnut Sts.
Philadelphia 1, Pa.
Administrator: Francis L. Pell, Jr., V.P.
Total Assets: $13,479,000

Phillips Petroleum Co. (P.T.)
Room 254—Adams Bldg.
Bartlesville, Okla.
Administrators: B. F. Stradley and William
J. Zeman
Total Assets: $17,553,000

Prentice-Hall Inc. (P.S.)
Sylvan Ave.
Englewood Cliffs, N. J.
Administrator: Frank J. Dunnigan, Treas.
Total Assets: $17,470,000

Provident Tradesmen Bank & Trust Co. (P.T.)
17th & Chestnut Sts.
Philadelphia 1, Pa.
Administrator: Frank G. Howard, V.P.
Total Assets: $8,895,000

Pullman-Standard Corp. (P.T.)
200 S. Michigan Ave.
Chicago 4, Ill.
Administrator: O. J. Engle, V.P.
Total Assets: $6,674,000

Quaker Oats Co. (P.T.)
345 Merchandise Mart Bldg.
Chicago 54, Ill.
Administrator: Thomas V. Bartel, V.P.
Total Assets: $4,819,000

Radio Corp. of America (P.T.)
30 Rockefeller Plaza
New York 20, N. Y.
Administrator: J. J. Brant, Dir. of Pers.
Total Assets: $114,407,000

Rayonier, Inc. (P.T.)
161 E. 42nd St.
New York 17, N. Y.
Administrator: J. B. Talbird, Asst. Treas.
Total Assets: $10,925,000

Reeves Bros. Inc. (P.S.)
1071 Ave. of the Americas
New York 20, N. Y.
Administrators: J. M. Reeves and Charles
D. Green
Total Assets: $8,096,000

Remington Division of Sperry-Rand Corp. (P.T.)
315 Park Ave. S.
New York 10, N. Y.
Administrator: G. Thomas, Treas.
Total Assets: $37,063,000

Republic Aviation Corp. (P.T.)
Farmingdale, N. Y.
Administrator: T. Davis, V.P.
Total Assets: $20,353,000 (2 plans)

Republic National Bank of Dallas (P.S.)
P.O. Box 241
Dallas 21, Tex.
Administrators: Karl Hoblitzelle and James
   W. Aston
Total Assets: $11,624,000

**Retail, Wholesale & Department Store
   Union (P.T.)**
13 Astor Pl.
New York 3, N. Y.
Administrators: J. Paley and D. Arvan
Total Assets: $26,449,000

Reynolds Metals Co. (P.T.)
Reynolds Metals Bldg.
Richmond 18, Va.
Administrators: J. D. Reynolds, V.P., and
   M. W. Smither, Mgr., Employ. Sec. Div.
Total Assets: $7,257,000

Rochester Telephone Co. (P.T.)
10 Franklin St.
Rochester, N. Y.
Administrator: G. A. Henner, Compt.
Total Assets: $10,144,000

Rockwell-Standard Corp. (P.T.)
Coraopolis, Pa.
Administrator: L. R. Lawton, V.P., Ind. Rel.
Total Assets: $10, 191,000

Royal McBee Corp. (P.T.)
Westchester Ave.
Port Chester, N. Y.
Administrator: D. H. Collins, Asst. Treas.
Total Assets: $7,297,000

Schenley Industries Inc. (P.T.)
Empire State Bldg.
New York 1, N. Y.
Administrator: Gunter Bethke, V.P. &
   Compt.
Total Assets: $24,689,000

Scott Paper Co. (P.T.)
Front & Market Sts.
Chester, Pa.
Administrator: W. M. Carney, Chm. of
   Ret. Bd.
Total Assets: $24,492,000

Joseph E. Seagram & Sons (P.T.)
375 Park Ave.
New York 22, N. Y.
Administrator: Joseph G. Friel, Sec. Ret. Bd.
Total Assets: $36,184,000

Sharon Steel Corp. (P.T.)
Sharon, Pa.
Administrators: Kenneth Swanson and
   William Blair
Total Assets: $15,907,000 (2 plans)

Shell Oil Company (P.T.)
111 W. 50th St.
New York 20, N. Y.
Administrators: H. S. M. Burns and R. C.
   McCurdy
Total Assets: $679,749,000 (2 plans)

Simmons Company (P.T.)
300 Park Ave.
New York 22, N. Y.
Administrators: G. G. Simmons, Jr. and
   J. V. Quarles
Total Assets: $9,679,000

Smith-Corona Company (P.T.)
701 E. Washington St.
Syracuse 1, N. Y.
Administrator: C. D. Boysen, Asst. Treas.
Total Assets: $8,925,000

Socony Mobil Oil Company (P.T.)
150 E. 42nd St.
New York 17, N. Y.
Administrator: A. M. Sherwood
Total Assets: $33,401,000

Southern California Edison Co. (P.T.)
601 West Fifth St.
Los Angeles 53, Cal.
Administrators: T. M. McDaniel, Jr., Chm.
   Pens. Comm. and R. G. Holden
Total Assets: $9,535,000

Southern Railway Co. (P.T.)
Box 1808
Washington 13, D.C.
Administrator: Charles M. Davison, Jr.,
   Chm. of Ret. Comm.
Total Assets: $19,062,000

St. Regis Paper Co. (P.T.)
150 E. 42nd St.
New York 17, N. Y.
Administrator: J. E. Cowles, Treas.
Total Assets: $28,182,000

Standard Oil Co. of California (P.T.)
225 Bush St.
San Francisco 20, Cal.
Administrator: E. A. Hansen, Asst. Sec.
Total Assets: $256,529,000

Standard Oil Co. of New Jersey (P.T.)
1230 Avenue of the Americas
New York 20, N. Y.
Administrator: T. C. Anderson, V.P.
Total Assets: $4,572,000

Standard Oil Co. of Ohio (P.T.)
Midland Bldg.
Cleveland 15, Ohio
Administrators: O. A. Ohmann, Dir. Employ.
 Rel., and T. R. Cadwell, Asst. Sec.
Total Assets: $8,494,000

The Stanley Works (P.T.)
Bridgeport, Conn.
Administrators: E. H. Burr, Treas. and
 D. R. Anderson, Compt.
Total Assets: $16,129,000 (3 plans)

J. P. Stevens Company (P.T.)
1460 Broadway
New York 36, N. Y.
Administrator: H. H. Foster, Jr.
Total Assets: $11,402,000

Superior Oil Co. (P.T.)
P.O. Box 3015, Terminal Annex
Los Angeles 54, Cal.
Administrators: S. H. Durkee, V.P. and
 T. O. Bunch, Ins. Mgr.
Total Assets: $6,380,000

Tennessee Corporation (P.T.)
61 Broadway
New York 6, N. Y.
Administrator: James H. Davidson, Asst.
 Treas.
Total Assets: $13,384,000

Todd Shipyards Corp. (P.T.)
One Broadway
New York 4, N. Y.
Administrator: E. Costello, Sec.
Total Assets: $19,278,000

Trans World Airlines Inc. (P.T.)
380 Madison Ave.
New York 17, N. Y.
Administrator: W. H. Rooker, Asst. Treas.
Total Assets: $8,027,000

Twentieth Century Fox Film Corp. (P.T.)
444 W. 56th St.
New York, N. Y.
Administrator: E. E. McCartney, Asst. Treas.
Total Assets: $25,119,000

Union Bag-Camp Paper Corp. (P.T.)
233 Broadway
New York 7, N. Y.
Administrator: Stanley G. Calder, Treas.
Total Assets: $11,742,000

Union Carbide Corp. (P.T.)
30 E. 42nd St.
New York 17, N. Y.
Administrator: J. E. Tobin, Plan Adm.
Total Assets: $55,834,000

Union Electric Co. (P.T.)
315 North Twelfth Blvd.
St. Louis 66, Mo.
Administrator: E. J. Shapiro, Sec. & Treas.
Total Assets: $26,638,000

United Engineering & Foundry Co. (P.T.)
948 Fort Duquesne Blvd.
Pittsburgh 22, Pa.
Administrator: W. S. McKay, Sec.
Total Assets: $21,485,000 (2 plans)

United Gas Corp.
P.O. Box 1407
Shreveport, La.
Administrators: E. Parkes, Pres. and
 J. H. Mirade, V.P.
Total Assets: $45,009,000

United Gas Improvement Co. (P.T.)
1401 Arch St.
Philadelphia 5, Pa.
Administrators: J. H. MacKenzie and
W. E. McElroy
Total Assets: $7,858,000

**United Merchants & Manufacturers, Inc.
(P.T.)**
1407 Broadway
New York 18, N. Y.
Administrator: P. H. Kirshen, V.P.
Total Assets: $8,262,000

United States Lines Co. (P.T.)
One Broadway
New York 4, N. Y.
Administrator: Q.Joseph M.Quinn, V.P. &
Treas.
Total Assets: $9,858,000

United States Steel Corp. (P.T.)
525 William Penn Pl.
Pittsburgh 30, Pa.
Administrator: A. R. Mathieson, Pres.
Total Assets: $1,241,887,000

United States Tobacco Company (P.T.)
630 Fifth Ave.
New York 20, N. Y.
Administrator: R. J. Kohberger, Sec. &
Treas.
Total Assets: $3,926,000

United Steel Workers of America (P.T.)
1500 Commonwealth Bldg.
Pittsburgh 22, Pa.
Administrators: D. J. McDonald and
I. W. Abel
Total Assets: $7,647,000

Utah Power & Light Co. (P.T.)
1407 West North Temple
Salt Lake City 1, Utah
Administrator: T. C. Woodside, V.P. & Treas.
Total Assets: $10,164,000

Vick Chemical Company (P.T.)
122 E. 42nd St.
New York 17, N. Y.
Administrator: Bruce Thurston, Sec.
Ret. Comm.
Total Assets: $5,597,000

Wagner Electric Corp. (P.T.)
6400 Plymouth Ave.
St. Louis 33, Mo.
Administrator: Joseph P. Harbucek, Asst.
Sec. & Treas.
Total Assets: $6,225,000

Walworth Company (P.T.)
750 Third Ave.
New York 17, N. Y.
Administrator: A. W. Mack, V.P.
Total Assets: $5,557,000

Washington Gas Light Co. (P.T.)
1100 H St. N.W.
Washington, D.C.
Administrators: Everett J. Boothby and
Edward T. Stafford
Total Assets: $22,037,000

Wells Fargo Bank (P.T.)
464 California St.
San Francisco 20, Cal.
Administrators: Harris C. Kirk, Chm., Ret.
Comm. and Carl J. Benson
Total Assets: $27,393,000

West Virginia Pulp & Paper Co. (P.T.)
230 Park Ave.
New York 17, N. Y.
Administrator: Joseph M. Water, V.P.
Total Assets: $14,031,000

Western Electric Company (P.T.)
195 Broadway
New York 7, N. Y.
Administrator: A. P. Clow, V.P.
Total Assets: $561,687,000

Western Printing & Lithographing Co. (P.T.)
1220 Mound Ave.
Racine, Wisc.
Administrators: H. M. Benstead, Chm.,
Pens. Comm. and F. J. Leyerle
Total Assets: $6,433,000

Western Union Telegraph Co. (P.T.)
60 Hudson St.
New York 14, N. Y.
Administrators: R. D. Slocum and
P. F. Oates
Total Assets: $24,480,000

Wilson & Co., Inc. (P.T.)
Prudential Plaza
Chicago 1, Ill.
Administrators: Vern P. Messer, Sec., Ret.
   Bd. and James D. Cooney
Total Assets: $26,787,000

F. W. Woolworth Co. (P.T.)
233 Broadway
New York, N. Y.
Administrators: R. C. Kirkwood and
   H. J. Cook
Total Assets: $32,993,000

Worthington Corporation (P.T.)
401 Worthington Ave.
Harrison, N. J.
Administrator: W. A. Meiter, V.P.
Total Assets: $5,870,000

Yale & Towne Manufacturing Co. (P.T.)
405 Lexington Ave.
New York 17, N. Y.
Administrator: D. W. Morrow, Asst. Treas.
Total Assets: $9,856,000

Young & Rubicam (P.S.)
285 Madison Ave.
New York 17, N. Y.
Administrators: George N. Farrand and
   W. Washburn
Total Assets: $19,528,000

SPECIAL PENSION FUNDS AND RETIREMENT SYSTEMS

Address communications to Office of the Treasurer for each organization.

**Board of Education Retirement System of
   the City of N. Y.**
131 Livingston St.
Brooklyn 1, N. Y.

**Board of Pensions of the Reformed
   Church in America**
475 Riverside Dr.
New York 27, N. Y.

Church Pension Fund
20 Exchange Pl.
New York 5, N. Y.

College Retirement Equities Fund
730 Third Ave.
New York 17, N. Y.

**National Health and Welfare Retirement
   Assn., Inc.**
800 Second Ave.
New York 17, N. Y.

N. Y. City Employees' Retirement System
2 Lafayette St.
New York, N. Y.

**N. Y. Fire Department Pension Fund,
   Article 1-A**
Municipal Bldg.
New York 7, N. Y.

**N. Y. Fire Department Pension Fund,
   Article 1-B**
Municipal Bldg.
New York 7, N. Y.

N. Y. State Bankers Retirement System
16 Wall St.
New York 5, N. Y.

N. Y. State Employees' Retirement System
90 South Swan St.
Albany, N. Y.

N. Y. State Hospital Retirement System
State Compt. Office
Albany, N. Y.

N. Y. State Teachers Retirement System
143 Washington Ave.
Albany 10, N. Y.

Police Pension Fund, Article 2
240 Centre St.
New York 13, N. Y.

Savings Banks Retirement System
70 Sunrise Highway
Freeport, N. Y.

Savings and Security Plan for Non-
Secretarial Employees of the Y. W. C. A.
600 Lexington Ave.
New York 22, N. Y.

Teachers' Retirement System of the City
of New York
154 Nassau St.
New York 38, N. Y.

Y.M.C.A. Retirement Fund, Inc., Savings &
Security Plan
291 Broadway
New York 7, N. Y.

Y.M.C.A. Retirement Fund, Inc., Secretarial
Plan
291 Broadway
New York 7, N. Y.

Y.W.C.A. Retirement Fund, Inc.
600 Lexington Ave.
New York 22, N. Y.

MAJOR FRATERNAL BENEFIT SOCIETIES

Address communications to Office of the Treasurer for each organization.

Aid Association for Lutherans
222 W. College Ave.
Appleton, Wis.

Artisans Order of Mutual Protection
3318 Lancaster Ave.
Philadelphia 4, Pa.

Association of Lithuanian Workers
104-07 102d St.
Ozone Park 17, N. Y.

Association of Sons of Poland
665 Newark Ave.
Jersey City 6, N. J.

Baptist Life Assn.
1321 Kensington Ave.
Buffalo 15, N. Y.

Bnai Zion
225 W. 57th St.
New York 19, N. Y.

Brith Abraham (Fraternal Order)
37 E. 7th St.
New York 3, N. Y.

Catholic Benevolent Legion
1 Hanson Place
Brooklyn 17, N. Y.

Catholic Women's Benevolent Legion
353 W. 57th St.
New York 19, N. Y.

Croatian Catholic Union of U.S.A.
125 W. 5th Ave.
Gary 3, Ind.

Czechoslovak Society of America
2138 South 61st Court
Cicero 50, Ill.

Danish Brotherhood in America
908 W. O. W. Bldg.
Omaha 2, Neb.

Evangelical Slovak Women's Union of
America
3842 Oswego St.
Pittsburgh 12, Pa.

Farband-Labor Zionist Order
575 Avenue of Americas
New York 11, N. Y.

First Catholic Slovak Ladies Union of
U.S.A.
3756 Lee Rd.
Cleveland 28, Ohio

First Catholic Slovak Union, U.S.A.
3829 E. 55th St.
Cleveland, Ohio

First Slovak Wreath of the Free Eagle
650 Arctic St.
Bridgeport 8, Conn.

Foresters, Independent Order
590 Jarvis St.
Toronto, Can.

Free Sons of Israel
257 W. 93rd St.
New York 25, N. Y.

Golden Cross, United Order of
Box 297
Knoxville, Tenn.

Golden Eagle Life Insurance Corp.
105 Court St.
Brooklyn 1, N. Y.

Grand Carniolian Slovenian Catholic Union of the U.S.A.
351 N. Chicago St.
Joliet, Ill.

Greater Beneficial Union of Pittsburgh
4254 Clairton Blvd.
Pittsburgh 27, Pa.

Greek Catholic Union of the U.S.A.
3528 Forbes Ave.
Pittsburgh 13, Pa.

Hungarian Reformed Federation of America
1346 Connecticut Ave., N.W.
Washington 6, D.C.

Junior Order United American Mechanics of U.S. of N.A.
3025 N. Broad St.
Philadelphia 32, Pa.

Knights of Columbus
Drawer 1670
New Haven 7, Conn.

Ladies' Catholic Benevolent Assn.
305 W. Sixth St.
Erie, Pa.

Lithuanian Alliance of America
307 W. 30th St.
New York 1, N. Y.

Lithuanian Roman Catholic Alliance of America
71-73 So. Washington St.
Wilkes-Barre, Pa.

Lutheran Brotherhood
701 Second Ave. So.
Minneapolis 2, Minn.

Modern Woodmen of America
1504 Third Ave.
Rock Island, Ill.

Mutual Beneficial Assn. of Penna. R. R. Employees, Inc.
15 No. 32nd St.
Philadelphia 4, Pa.

National Fraternal Society of the Deaf
6701 W. North Ave.
Oak Park, Ill.

National Slovak Society of the U.S.A.
516 Court Pl.
Pittsburgh 19, Pa.

(Penna.) Polish Union of the U.S. of N.A.
53 N. Main St.
Wilkes-Barre, Pa.

Polish National Alliance of Brooklyn, U.S.A.
155 Noble St.
Brooklyn 22, N. Y.

Polish National Alliance of the U.S. of N.A.
1514 W. Division St.
Chicago 22, Ill.

Polish National Union of America
1002 Pittston Ave.
Scranton 5, Pa.

Polish Roman Catholic Union of America
984 N. Milwaukee Ave.
Chicago 22, Ill.

Polish Union of America
761 Fillmore Ave.
Buffalo 12, N. Y.

Polish Women's Alliance of America
1309 N. Ashland Ave.
Chicago 22, Ill.

Protected Home Circle
30 E. State St.
Sharon, Pa.

Royal Arcanum
Box 392
Boston 1, Mass.

Royal Clan, Order of Scottish Clans
38 Chauncey St.
Boston 11, Mass.

Royal Neighbors of America
230 16th St.
Rock Island, Ill.

Russian Brotherhood Organization of U.S.A.
1733 Spring Garden St.
Philadelphia 30, Pa.

**Russian Consolidated Mutual Aid Society
of Am.**
853 Broadway
New York 3, N. Y.

Serb National Federation
3414 Fifth Ave.
Pittsburgh 13, Pa.

Slovak Catholic Sokol
205 Madison St.
Passaic, N. J.

**Slovak Evangelical Union, Augsburg
Confession of America**
1701 Banksville Rd.
Pittsburgh 16, Pa.

**Slovak Gymnastic Union "Sokol" of the
U.S.A.**
285 Oak St.
Perth Amboy, N. J.

Slovene National Benefit Society
2657 S. Lawndale Ave.
Chicago 23, Ill.

Sons of Norway
1455 W. Lake St.
Minneapolis 8, Minn.

Travelers Protective Assn. of America
3755 Lindell Blvd.
St. Louis 8, Mo.

Ukrainian National Assn., Inc.
81 Grand St.
Jersey City 3, N. J.

Ukrainian Workingmen's Assn.
440 Wyoming Ave.
Scranton, Pa.

Union St. Jean-Baptiste d'Amerique
1 Social St.
Woonsocket, R. I.

United Commercial Travelers of America
632 North Park St.
Columbus 15, Ohio

**United Russian Orthodox Brotherhood
of America**
333 Blvd. of Allies
Pittsburgh 22, Pa.

Unity of Czech Ladies and Men
2130 S. 61st Ave.
Cicero 50, Ill.

Vikings, Independent Order
157 East Ohio St.
Chicago 11, Ill.

William Penn Fraternal Assn.
436 Fourth Ave.
Pittsburgh 19, Pa.

Woman's Benefit Assn.
W. B. A. Bldg.
Port Huron, Mich.

Woodmen Circle, Supreme Forest
3303 Farnam St.
Omaha 31, Neb.

**Woodmen of the World Life Insurance
Society**
17th and Farnam Sts.
Omaha 2, Neb.

Workmen's Benefit Fund of the U.S.A.
714 Seneca Ave.
Brooklyn 27, N. Y.

Workmen's Circle
175 E. Broadway
New York 2, N. Y.

World Fraternal Benefit Society
11 Sumner Ave.
Brooklyn 6, N. Y.

Zivena Beneficial Society
1235 Woodland Ave.
Pittsburgh 12, Pa.

MAJOR CHARITABLE ANNUITY SOCIETIES

Address communications to Office of the Treasurer for each organization.

American Baptist Foreign Mission Society
475 Riverside Drive
New York 27, N. Y.

American Baptist Home Mission Society
164 Fifth Ave.
New York 10, N. Y.

American Bible Society
450 Park Ave.
New York 22, N. Y.

American Leprosy Missions, Inc.
297 Park Ave. S.
New York 10, N. Y.

American Tract Society
513 West 166th St.
New York 32, N. Y.

Board of Christian Education of the United Presbyterian Church in the U.S.A.
Witherspoon Bldg.
Philadelphia 7, Pa.

Board of National Missions of the United Presbyterian Church in the U.S.A.
475 Riverside Dr.
New York 27, N. Y.

Catholic Foreign Mission Society of America, Inc.
Maryknoll, N. Y.

Christian and Missionary Alliance
260 West 44th St.
New York 36, N. Y.

Commission on Ecumenical Mission and Relations of United Presbyterian Church in the U.S.A.
475 Riverside Dr.
New York 27, N. Y.

Division of National Missions of the Board of Missions of the Methodist Church
1701 Arch St.
Philadelphia 3, Pa.

Division of World Missions of the Board of Missions of the Methodist Church
475 Riverside Dr.
New York 27, N. Y.

Friars of the Atonement, Inc.
Graymoor
Garrison, N. Y.

Methodist Hospital of Brooklyn
506 Sixth St.
Brooklyn 15, N. Y.

Ministers and Missionaries Benefit Board of the American Baptist Convention
475 Riverside Dr.
New York 27, N. Y.

New York Bible Society
5 East 48th St.
New York 17, N. Y.

North American Baptists, Inc.
7308 Madison St.
Forest Park, Ill.

Salvation Army
120 West 14th St.
New York 11, N. Y.

Society for the Propagation of the Faith
366 Fifth Ave.
New York 1, N. Y.

Sudan Interior Mission, Inc.
164 West 74th St.
New York 23, N. Y.

United Church Board for Homeland Ministries
287 Park Ave. So.
New York 10, N. Y.

United Lutheran Church in America
231 Madison Ave.
New York 16, N. Y.

United Presbyterian Foundation
123 So. Broad St.
Philadelphia 9, Pa.

Vassar College
Raymond Ave.
Poughkeepsie, N. Y.

Woman's American Baptist Foreign Mission
Society
475 Riverside Dr.
New York 27, N. Y.

Woman's American Baptist Home Mission
Society
164 Fifth Ave.
New York 10, N. Y.

Woman's Division of Christian Service of
the Board of Missions of the
Methodist Church
475 Riverside Dr.
New York 27, N. Y.

LABOR UNIONS AND ORGANIZATIONS

Actors and Artists of America;
Associated (AFL-CIO),
226 West 47th St.,
New York 36, N. Y.
Treasurer: Hyman R. Faine
Membership: 55,000

Actors' Equity Association
226 West 47th St.,
New York 36, N. Y.
Treasurer: Royal Beal
Social insurance: Albert G. Waters
(Administrator)
Membership: 12,000

American Federation of Television and
Radio Artists
15 West 44th St.,
New York 36, N. Y.
Treasurer: Vicki Vola
Social insurance: Archie Siegel
(Director, AFTRA Pension and
Welfare Fund)
Membership: 15,000

American Guild of Musical Artists, Inc.
1841 Broadway,
New York 23, N. Y.
Secretary-treasurer: Hyman R. Faine
Social insurance: DeLloyd Tibbs
(Assistant executive secretary)
Membership: 2,160

American Guild of Variety Artists
110 West 57th St.,
New York 19, N. Y.
Social insurance: Miss Margie Coate
(Director, Sick and Relief)
Membership: 13,500; branches, 27

Screen Actors Guild Inc.
7750 Sunset Blvd.,
Hollywood 46, Cal.
Social insurance: (National executive
secretary)
Membership: 13,800

Screen Extras Guild, Inc.
723 North Western Ave.,
Hollywood 29, Cal.
Treasurer: Kenner G. Kemp
Social insurance: Byron Ellerbrock
(Administrator, SAG—Producers
Welfare Fund)
Membership: 3,200

Air Line Dispatchers Association
(AFL-CIO)
4620 Lee Highway,
Arlington 7, Va.
Secretary-treasurer: Ernest A. Bressin
Social insurance: (Secretary-treasurer)
Membership: 630

Air Line Pilots Association; International
(AFL-CIO)
55th St. and Cicero Ave.,
Chicago 38, Ill.
Treasurer: Don J. Smith
Social insurance: (Treasurer)
Membership: 13,516

Aluminum Workers International Union
(AFL-CIO)
818 Olive St.,
St. Louis 1, Mo.
Secretary-treasurer: Patrick Reilly, Sr.
Social insurance: (Research and education
director)
Membership: 22,000

**Asbestos Workers; International
Association of Heat and Frost
Insulators and** (AFL-CIO)
1300 Connecticut Ave. NW.,
Washington 6, D. C.
Secretary-treasurer: Albert E. Hutchinson
Social insurance: (Secretary-treasurer)
Membership: 10,000

Associated Unions of America (Ind)
161 West Wisconsin Ave.,
Milwaukee 3, Wisc.
Secretary-treasurer: Donald F. Cameron
Social insurance: (Secretary-treasurer)
Membership: 5,470

**Automobile, Aircraft and Agricultural
Implement Workers of America;
International Union, United** (AFL-CIO)
8000 East Jefferson Ave.,
Detroit 14, Mich.
Secretary-treasurer: Emil Mazey
Social insurance: James Brindle
(Director, Social Security Department)
Membership: 1,136,140

**Bakery and Confectionery Workers'
International Union; American**
(AFL-CIO)
1120 Connecticut Ave. NW.,
Washington 6, D. C.
Secretary-treasurer: Curtis R. Sims
Social insurance: Irving Rachlis
(Temporary Director)
Membership: 85,000

**Barbers, Hairdressers, Cosmetologists
and Proprietors' International Union
of America; Journeymen** (AFL-CIO)
1141 North Delaware St.,
Indianapolis 7, Ind.
President and secretary-treasurer:
William C. Birthright
Membership: 75,000; local unions, 844

**Bill Posters, Billers and Distributors of
the United States and Canada;
International Alliance of** (AFL-CIO)
2940 16th St.,
San Francisco 3, Calif.
Secretary-treasurer: John J. Grady
Membership: 1,600

**Boilermakers, Iron Shipbuilders,
Blacksmiths, Forgers and Helpers;
International Brotherhood of** (AFL-CIO)
8th at State Ave.,
Kansas City 11, Kan.
Secretary-treasurer: Homer E. Patton
Social insurance: Thomas L. Wands, Sr.
(Assistant to the president)
Membership: 140,000

**Bookbinders; International Brotherhood
of** (AFL-CIO)
815 16th St. NW.,
Washington 6, D. C.
Secretary-treasurer: Wesley A. Taylor
Social insurance: (Research director)
Membership: 64,039

**Brewery, Flour, Cereal, Soft Drink and
Distillery Workers of America;
International Union of United** (AFL-CIO)
2347 Vine St.,
Cincinnati 19, Ohio
Secretary-treasurer: Arthur P. Gildea
Social insurance: (Secretary-treasurer)
Membership 60,000; local unions, 260

**Brick and Clay Workers of America;
United** (AFL-CIO)
1550 West 95th St.,
Chicago 43, Ill.
Secretary-treasurer: Harold R. Flegal
Social insurance: (Secretary-treasurer)
Membership: 23,994

**Bricklayers, Masons and Plasterers'
International Union of America**
(AFL-CIO)
815 15th St. NW.,
Washington 5, D. C.
Treasurer: George King
Membership: 155,000

**Broadcast Employees and Technicians;
National Association of** (AFL-CIO)
80 East Jackson Blvd.,
Chicago 4, Ill.
Secretary-treasurer: Arthur Hjorth
Membership: 5,862

**Building Service Employees' International
Union** (AFL-CIO)
312 West Randolph St.,
Chicago 6, Ill.
Secretary-treasurer: George E. Fairchild
Membership: 272,000 local unions, 381

**Carpenters and Joiners of America;
United Brotherhood of** (AFL-CIO)
101 Constitution Ave. NW.,
Washington 1, D. C.
Treasurer: Peter E. Terzick
Convention: Every 4 years; 1962
Publication: The Carpenter (monthly)
Editor: James A. Eldridge
Membership: 800,000

**Cement, Lime and Gypsum Workers
International Union; United** (AFL-CIO)
7830 West Lawrence Ave.,
Chicago 31, Ill.
Secretary-treasurer: Toney Gallo
Social insurance: (Research and education
director)
Membership: 39,351; local unions, 276

Chemical Workers Union; International
(AFL-CIO)
1659 West Market St.,
Akron 13, Ohio
Secretary-treasurer: Marshall Shafer
Social insurance: (Research and education
director)
Membership: 79,000; local unions, 403

**Cigar Makers' International Union of
America** (AFL-CIO)
1003 K St. N.W.,
Washington 1, D. C.
Secretary-treasurer: Otto C. Dehn
Social insurance: (Secretary-treasurer)
Membership: 5,800

**Clothing Workers of America;
Amalgamated** (AFL-CIO)
15 Union Sq.,
New York 3, N. Y.
Secretary-treasurer: Frank Rosenblum
Social insurance: Hyman Blumberg
(Executive vice president)
Membership: 377,000

Communications Association; American
(Ind)
5 Beekman St.,
New York 38, N. Y.
Secretary-treasurer: William Bender
Membership: 8,000; local unions, 6

Communications Workers of America
(AFL-CIO)
1925 K St. NW.,
Washington 6, D. C.
Secretary-treasurer: William A. Smallwood
Social insurance: (Research director)
Membership: 259,917

**Coopers' International Union of North
America** (AFL-CIO)
120 Boylston St.,
Boston 16, Mass.
President and secretary-treasurer:
James J. Doyle
Membership: 3,457; local unions, 34

Die Sinkers' Conference; International
(Ind)
7039 Superior Ave.,
Cleveland 3, Ohio
Secretary-treasurer: Richard G. Arnold
Membership: 4,000

Directors Guild of America, Inc. (Ind)
7950 Sunset Blvd.,
Hollywood 46, Calif.
Treasurer: Howard W. Koch
Social insurance: Joseph C. Youngerman
(National executive secretary)
Membership: 2,150

**Distillery, Rectifying and Wine Workers'
International Union of America**
(AFL-CIO)
707 Summit Ave.,
Union City, N. J.
Secretary-treasurer: George J. Oneto
Social-insurance: (President)
Membership: 34,400

**Electrical, Radio and Machine Workers;
International Union of** (AFL-CIO)
1126 16th St. NW.,
Washington 6, D. C.
Secretary-treasurer: Al Hartnett
Social insurance: Joseph Swire (Director,
Pension, Health and Welfare
Department)
Membership: 287,937; local unions, 525

**Electrical, Radio and Machine Workers of
America; United** (Ind)
11 East 51st St.,
New York 22, N. Y.
Secretary-treasurer: Julius Emspak
Social insurance: (Research director)
Membership: 160,000

**Electrical Workers; International
Brotherhood of** (AFL-CIO)
1200 15th St. N.W.,
Washington 5, D. C.
Treasurer: Jeremiah P. Sullivan
Social insurance: (Research and education
director)
Membership: 771,000

**Elevator Constructors; International
Union of** (AFL-CIO)
12 South 12th St.,
Philadelphia 7, Pa.
Secretary-treasurer: Edwin C. Magee
Social insurance: (Secretary-treasurer)
Membership: 11,400

**Engineers; American Federation of
Technical** (AFL-CIO)
900 F St. NW.,
Washington 4, D. C.
Secretary-treasurer: Edward J. Coughlin
Membership: 13,000

**Engineers; International Union of
Operating** (AFL-CIO)
1125 17th St. NW.,
Washington 6, D.C.
Secretary-treasurer: Hunter P. Wharton
Membership: 291,000

**Federal Employees; National Federation
of** (Ind)
1729 G St. NW.,
Washington 6, D. C.
Secretary-treasurer: Miss Florence I.
Broadwell
Membership: 53,000

Fire Fighters; International Association of
(AFL-CIO)
815 16th St. NW.,
Washington 6, D. C.
Secretary-treasurer: John C. Kabachus
Membership: 95,000

**Firemen and Oilers; International
Brotherhood of** (AFL-CIO)
100 Indiana Ave. NW.,
Washington 1, D. C.
Secretary-treasurer: William E.
Fredenberger
Membership: 53,000

**Flight Engineers' International
Association** (AFL-CIO)
100 Indiana Ave. NW.,
Washington 1, D. C.
Secretary-treasurer: Henry J. Breen
Social insurance: (Secretary-treasurer)
Membership: 3,250

Furniture Workers of America; United
(AFL-CIO)
700 Broadway,
New York 3, N. Y.
Secretary-treasurer: Fred Fulford
Membership: 50,000

Garment Workers of America; United
(AFL-CIO)
31 Union Sq. West,
New York 3, N. Y.
Secretary-treasurer: Miss E. M. Hogan
Membership: 35,000

**Garment Workers' Union; International
Ladies'** (AFL-CIO)
1710 Broadway,
New York 19, N. Y.
Secretary-treasurer: Louis Stulberg
Social insurance: Adolph Held (Director,
Health and Welfare Department)
Membership: 446,554

**Glass Bottle Blowers Association of the
United States and Canada** (AFL-CIO)
226 South 16th St.,
Philadelphia 2, Pa.
Secretary-treasurer: Newton W. Black
Social insurance: Charles Purnell
(Insurance consultant)
Membership: 54,255

**Glass and Ceramic Workers of North
America; United** (AFL-CIO)
556 East Town St., Columbus 15, Ohio
Secretary-treasurer: Lewis McCracken
Social insurance: (Secretary-treasurer)
Membership: 40,000

**Glass Cutters League of America;
Window** (AFL-CIO)
1078 South High St.,
Columbus 6, Ohio
Secretary-treasurer: R. A. Lorant, Sr.
Social Insurance: (President) Howard P.
Chester
Membership: 1,450

Glass Workers Union of North America;
American Flint (AFL-CIO)
204 Huron St.,
Secretary-treasurer: James W. Mitchell
Social insurance: (Secretary-treasurer)
Membership: 30,706
Toledo 4, Ohio

Glove Workers' Union of America;
International (AFL-CIO)
430 Bridge St.,
Marinette, Wisc.
Secretary-treasurer: James Van Der Wall
Membership: 2,212

Government Employees; American
Federation of (AFL-CIO)
900 F St. N.W.,
Washington 4, D. C.
Membership: 70, 322; local unions, 781

Grain Millers; American Federation of
(AFL-CIO)
4949 Olson Memorial Highway,
Minneapolis 22, Minn.
Secretary-treasurer: H. A. Schneider
Social insurance: (Secretary-treasurer)
Membership: 42,000

Guard Workers of America; United Plant
(Ind.)
14214 East Jefferson Ave.,
Detroit 15, Mich.
Secretary-treasurer: Roy I. Haines
Social insurance: (Secretary-treasurer)
Membership: 8,500

Guards Union of America; International
(Ind.)
932 Upper Midwest Bldg.,
Minneapolis 1, Minn.
Secretary-treasurer: C. J. Junglen
Membership: 1,682

Hatters, Cap and Millinery Workers
International Union; United (AFL-CIO)
245 5th Ave.,
New York 16, N. Y.
Social insurance: Harold Malin
(Comptroller)
Membership: 40,000

Hod Carriers', Building and Common
Laborers' Union of America;
International (AFL-CIO)
905 16th St. NW.,
Washington 6, D.C.
Secretary-treasurer: Peter Fosco
Membership: 442,473

Hosiery Workers; American Federation of
(AFL-CIO)
2319 North Broad St.,
Philadelphia 32, Pa.
Secretary-treasurer: Major Banachowicz
Social insurance: (Secretary-treasurer)
Membership: 5,333; local unions, 32

Hotel & Restaurant Employees and
Bartenders International Union
(AFL-CIO)
525 Walnut St.,
Cincinnati 2, Ohio
Secretary-treasurer: Jack Weinberger
Social insurance: O. L. Diefenbach
(Administrative assistant to the
president)
Membership: 443,000

Industrial Workers of America;
International Union, Allied (AFL-CIO)
3520 West Oklahoma Ave.,
Milwaukee 15, Wisc.
Secretary-treasurer: Gilbert Jewell
Social insurance: (President) Carl W.
Griepentrog
Membership: 68,000

Insurance Agents: International Union
of Life (Ind.)
161 West Wisconsin Ave.,
Milwaukee 3, Wisc.
Secretary-treasurer: William Luedke
Membership: 2,000

Insurance Workers International Union
(AFL-CIO)
1017 12th St. N.W.,
Washington 5, D. C.
Secretary-treasurer: William A. Gillen
Membership: 22,000

Iron Workers; International Association of Bridge, Structural and Ornamental (AFL-CIO)
3615 Olive St.,
St. Louis 8, Mo.
Treasurer: James V. Cole
Membership: 147,982

Jewelry Workers' Union; International (AFL-CIO)
152 West 42nd St.,
New York 36, N. Y.
President and secretary-treasurer: Harry Spodick
Membership: 12,732

Lathers International Union; The Wood, Wire and Metal (AFL-CIO)
6530 New Hampshire Ave.,
Takoma Park 12, Md.
Secretary-treasurer: Harold Mills
Membership: 16,800

Laundry and Dry Cleaning International Union (AFL-CIO)
212 Wood St.,
Pittsburgh 22, Pa.
Secretary-treasurer: Sam H. Begler
Social insurance: (President)) Winfield S. Cherner
Membership: 22,000

Laundry, Dry Cleaning and Dye House Workers International Union (Ind.)
360 North Michigan Ave.,
Chicago 1, Ill.
Secretary-treasurer: Mrs. Mildred Gianini
Membership: 65,700; local unions, 102

Leather Goods, Plastic and Novelty Workers' Union; International (AFL-CIO)
265 West 14th St.,
New York 11, N. Y.
Secretary-treasurer: Jack Wieselberg
Social insurance: Charles Feinstein (Director, Health and Welfare Fund)
Membership: 32,000

Leather Workers International Union of America (AFL-CIO)
10 Lowell St.,
Peabody, Mass.
Secretary-treasurer: Joseph A. Duffy
Social insurance: (Secretary-treasurer)
Membership, 9,500

Letter Carriers of the United States of America; National Association of (AFL-CIO)
100 Indiana Ave. N. W.,
Washington 1, D. C.
Secretary-treasurer: R. B. Kremers
Membership: 138,000; local unions, 4,900

Letter Carriers' Association; National Rural (Ind.)
1040 Warner Bldg.,
Washington 4, D. C.
Membership: 38,321

Lithographers of America; Amalgamated (Ind)
233 West 49th St.,
New York 19, N. Y.
Secretary-treasurer: Donald W. Stone
Social insurance: (Secretary-treasurer)
Membership: 37,099

Locomotive Engineers; Brotherhood of (Ind.)
1112 Brotherhood of Locomotive Engineers Bldg.,
Cleveland 14, Ohio
Secretary-treasurer: H. F. Hempy
Social insurance: (Secretary-treasurer)
Membership: 43,165

Locomotive Firemen and Enginemen; Brotherhood of (AFL-CIO)
318 Keith Bldg.,
Cleveland 15, Ohio
Secretary-treasurer: Ray Scott
Social insurance: (President), H. E. Gilbert
Membership: 81,107

Longshoremen's Association; International (AFL-CIO)
265 West 14th St.,
New York 11, N. Y.
Secertary-treasurer: Harry R. Hasselgren
Membership: 50,000

Longshoremen's and Warehousemen's Union; International (Ind.)
150 Golden Gate Ave.,
San Francisco 2, Calif.
Secretary-treasurer: Louis Goldblatt
Social insurance: (Secretary-treasurer)
Membership: 60,000; local unions, 81

Machine Printers' Beneficial Association of the United States (Ind.)
3 Riverview Dr.,
Barrington, R. I.
President: Eric W. Lindberg
Secretary-treasurer: John T. Patton
Social insurance: (President and secretary-treasurer)
Membership: 1,400; local unions,——.

Machinists; International Association of (AFL-CIO)
1300 Connecticut Ave. NW.,
Washington 1, D. C.
Secretary-treasurer: Elmer E. Walker
Social insurance: (Research director),
V. Jirikowic
Membership: 898,139

Mailers Union; International (Ind)
2240 Bell Ct.,
Denver 15, Colo.
Secretary-treasurer: Gene Johnson
Social insurance: (Secretary-treasurer)
Membership: 3,800

Maintenance of Way Employees; Brotherhood of (AFL-CIO)
12050 Woodward Ave.,
Detroit 3, Mich.
Secretary-treasurer: Frank L. Noakes
Social insurance: (President), H. C. Crotty
Membership: 164, 447

Marble, Slate and Stone Polishers, Rubbers and Sawyers, Tile and Marble Setters' Helpers and Marble Mosaic and Terrazzo Workers' Helpers International Association of (AFL-CIO)
821 15th St. NW.,
Washington 5, D. C.
President and secretary-treasurer:
William Peitler
Membership: 9,856

Marine Engineers' Beneficial Association; National (AFL-CIO)
400 First S. NW.,
Washington 1, D. C.
President: Edward N. Altman
Secretary-treasurer: Jesse Calhoon
47 Battery Pl.,
New York 4, N. Y.
Social insurance: (President and secretary-treasurer)
Membership: 11,000

Marine and Shipbuilding Workers of America; Industrial Union of (AFL-CIO)
534 Cooper St.,
Camden 2, N. J.
Secretary-treasurer: Ross D. Blood
Social insurance: (Secretary-treasurer)
Membership: 30,000

Maritime Union of America; National (AFL-CIO)
346 West 17th St.,
New York 11, N. Y.
Secretary-treasurer: Steve Federoff
Social insurance: Robert Nesbitt
(National representative)
Membership: 40,000

Masters, Mates and Pilots; International Organization of (AFL-CIO)
17 Battery Pl.,
New York 4, N. Y.
Secretary-treasurer: Captain John M.
Bishop
Social insurance: Robert Creasey
(Administrator)
11 Broadway,
New York, N. Y.
Membership: 10,000

Meat Cutters and Butcher Workmen of North America; Amalgamated (AFL-CIO)
2800 North Sheridan Rd.,
Chicago 14, Ill.
Secretary-treasurer: Patrick E. Gorman
Social insurance: Joseph S. Sullivan
(Resident counsel)
Membership: 333,482

Mechanics Educational Society of America (AFL-CIO)
1974 National Bank Bldg.,
Detroit 26, Mich.
Secretary: Miss Elizabeth McCracken
Membership: 38,058

Messengers; The National Association of Special Delivery (AFL-CIO)
112 C St. NW.,
Washington 1, D. C.
Secretary-treasurer: William E. Peacock
Membership: 2,000

Metal Polishers, Buffers, Platers and Helpers International Union (AFL-CIO)
5578 Montgomery Rd.,
Cincinnati 12, Ohio
President and secretary-treasurer: Ray Muehlhoffer
Social insurance: Robert A. Wilson (Attorney)
1104 Fifth Third Bank Bldg.,
Cincinnati 2, Ohio
Membership: 18,000

Mine, Mill and Smelter Workers; International Union of (Ind.)
941 East 17th Ave.,
Denver 18, Colo.
Secretary-treasurer: Irving Dichter
Social insurance: (Research director), Bernard W. Stern
Membership: 100,000; local unions, 200

Mine Workers of America; United (Ind.)
900 15th St. NW.,
Washington 5, D. C.
Secertary-treasurer: John Owens
Social insurance: (Secretary-treasurer)
Membership: 600,000

Molders' and Allied Workers' Union of North America; International (AFL-CIO)
1225 East McMillan St.,
Cincinnati 6, Ohio
Treasurer: Roland Belanger
Social insurance: (Secretary), Walter Griffiths
Membership: 53,833

Musicians; American Federation of (AFL-CIO)
425 Park Ave.,
New York 22, N. Y.
Treasurer: George Clancy
Social insurance: (President), Herman D. Kenin
Membership: 266,618

Newspaper Guild; American (AFL-CIO)
1126 16th St. NW.,
Washington 6, D. C.
Secretary-treasurer: Charles A. Perlik, Jr.
Social insurance: Stephen Ripley (Executive secretary, Contracts Committee)
Membership: 31,411

Newspaper and Mail Delivers' Union of New York and Vicinity (Ind)
25 Ann St.,
New York 38, N. Y.
Secretary-treasurer: Stanley J. Lehman
Membership: 4,000

Office Employees International Union (AFL-CIO)
1012 14th St. NW.,
Washington 5, D. C.
Secretary-treasurer: J. Howard Hicks
Social insurance: (Secretary-treasurer)
Membership: 52,981

Oil, Chemical and Atomic Workers International Union (AFL-CIO)
Secretary-treasurer: T. M. McCormick
Membership: 174,000

Packinghouse, Food and Allied Workers; United (AFL-CIO)
608 South Dearborn St.,
Chicago 5, III.
Secretary-treasurer: G. R. Hathaway
Social insurance: Charles Fischer (Administrative assistant to the president)
Membership: 102,598

Painters, Decorators and Paperhangers of America; Brotherhood of (AFL-CIO)
217-219 North 6th St.,
Lafayette, Ind.
Secretary-treasurer: William H. Rohrberg
Social insurance: (Secretary-treasurer)
Membership: 192,568

Paperhangers and Paperworkers; United (AFL-CIO)
Papermakers Bldg.,
Albany 1, N. Y.
Secretary-treasurer: A. E. Brown
Social insurance: Robert A. Bargeron (Director, Health and Welfare Department)
Membership: 140,000

Pattern Makers' League of North America (AFL-CIO)
1000 Connecticut Ave. NW.,
Washington 6, D. C.
President: Gunnar Hallstrom
Membership: 13,900

Petroleum Workers, Inc.; International Union of (Ind.)
1522 18th St.,
Bakersfield, Calif.
Secretary-treasurer George T. Golden
Membership: 3,500

Photo-Engravers' Union of North America International (AFL-CIO)
3605 Potomac St.,
St. Louis 16, Mo.
Secretary-treasurer: Ben G. Schaller
Social insurance: (Secretary-treasurer)
Membership: 17,090

Plasterers' and Cement Masons' International Association of the United States and Canada; Operative (AFL-CIO)
1125 17th St. N.W.,
Washington 6, D. C.
Secretary-treasurer: John J. Hauck
Social insurance: (Secretary-treasurer)
Membership: 68,000

Plumbing and Pipe Fitting Industry of the United States and Canada; United Association of Journeymen and Apprentices of the (AFL-CIO)
901 Massachusetts Ave. NW.,
Washington 1, D. C.
Secretary-treasurer: William C. O'Neill
Membership: 251,273

Porters; Brotherhood of Sleeping Car
AFL-CIO)
217 West 125th St.,
New York 27, N. Y.
Secretary-treasurer: Ashley L. Totten
Membership: 6,000

Post Office and General Services Maintenance Employees; National Association of (Ind.)
724 9th St. NW.,
Washington 1, D. C.
Secretary-treasurer: James D. Burke
Publication: Maintenance News (bimonthly)

Post Office Motor Vehicle Employees; National Federation of (AFL-CIO)
412 5th St. NW.,
Washington 1, D. C.
Treasurer: Chester W. Parrish
Membership: 5.000

Post Office and Postal Transportation Service Mail Handlers, Watchmen and Messengers: National Association of (AFL-CIO)
900 F St. NW.,
Washington 4, D. C.
Treasurer: Max M. Hirsch
Membership: 4,000

Postal Clerks: United Federation of (AFL-CIO)
817 14th St. NW.,
Washington 5, D. C.
Secretary-treasurer: John F. Bowen
Membership: 135,000

Postal Employees; National Alliance of (Ind.)
1644 11th St. NW.,
Washington 1, D. C.
Treasurer: Phillip W. Holland
Membership: 18,000

Postal Supervisors; National Association of (Ind.)
P. O. Box 2013,
Washington 13, D. C.
Treasurer: Charles J. Turrisi
Membership: 19,250

Postal Union; National (Ind.)
509 14th St. NW.,
Washington 4, D. C.
Secretary-treasurer: David Silvergleid
Membership: 32,000

Postmasters of the United States; National League of (Ind.)
Raleigh Bldg., 12th St. and Pennsylvania Ave. NW.,
Washington 4, D. C.
Secretary-treasurer: Mrs. Aquina Thimmesch
Membership: 12,984

Potters; International Brotherhood of Operative (AFL-CIO)
P. O. Box 752,
East Liverpool, Ohio
President: E. L. Wheatley
Secretary-treasurer: Charles F. Jordan
Social insurance: (President and secretary-treasurer)
Membership: 25,000

**Printing Pressmen and Assistants' Union
of North America; International**
(AFL-CIO)
Pressmen's Home, Tenn.
Secretary-treasurer: Alexander J. Rohan
Social insurance: (Secretary-treasurer)
Membership: 113,903

**Protection Employees; Independent Union
of Plant** (Ind.)
146 Summer St.,
Boston 10, Mass.
Secretary: W. J. Cavanagh
Social insurance: Earle Keans
(Administrator)
Membership: 2,000

**Pulp, Sulphite and Paper Mill Workers;
International Brotherhood of** (AFL-CIO)
Fort Edward, N. Y.
President and secretary: John P. Burke
Treasurer: Henry Segal
Social insurance: (President and secretary)
Membership: 170,544

Radio Association; American (AFL-CIO)
5 Beekman St.,
New York 38, N. Y.
President: William R. Steinberg
Secretary-treasurer: Bernard L. Smith
Social insurance (President)
Membership: 1,500

Railroad Signalmen; Brotherhood of
(AFL-CIO)
2247 Lawrence Ave.,
Chicago 25, Ill.
Secretary-treasurer: C. J. Chamberlain
Social insurance: (President), Jesse Clark
Membership: 14,396

Radio Telegraphers; The Order of
(AFL-CIO)
3860 Lindell Blvd.,
St. Louis 8, Mo.
Secretary-treasurer: E. M. Mosier
Social insurance: (President), G. E. Leighty
Membership: 57,450

Railroad Trainmen; Brotherhood of
(AFL-CIO)
1370 Ontario Street
Cleveland 13, Ohio
Secretary-treasurer: William E. B. Chase
Social insurance: (Secretary-treasurer)
Membership: 159,384

Railroad Yardmasters of America
(AFL-CIO)
537 South Dearborn St.,
Chicago 5, Ill.
Secretary-treasurer: John S. Meyers
Social insurance: (President), Milton G.
Schoch
Membership: 4,500

Railway Carmen of America; Brotherhood
(AFL-CIO)
4929 Main St.,
Kansas City 2, Mo.
Secretary-treasurer: T. S. Howieson
Membership: 125,000

**Railway Conductors and Brakemen;
Order of** (Ind.)
O.R.C.B. Bldg.,
Cedar Rapids, Iowa
Secretary-treasurer: C. H. Anderson
Social insurance: (Secretary-treasurer)
Membership: 25,000; local unions, 501

Railway Patrolmen's International Union
(AFL-CIO)
218 Melon Pl.,
Elizabeth 3, N. J.
Secretary-treasurer: Cecil Smithson
Social insurance: (Secretary-treasurer)
Membership: 3,000

**Railway and Steamship Clerks, Freight
Handlers, Express and Station
Employes; Brotherhood of** (AFL-CIO)
1015 Vine St.,
Cincinnati 2, Ohio
Secretary-treasurer: George M. Gibbons
Social insurance: Edward J. Gubser
(Director of Health and Welfare)
Membership: 300,000

**Railway and Airline Supervisors
Association; The American** (AFL-CIO)
53 West Jackson Blvd.,
Chicago 4, Ill.
Secretary-treasurer: Rudolph Durdik
Social insurance: (Secretary-treasurer)
Membership: 6,311

Retail Clerks International Association
(AFL-CIO)
Connecticut Ave. and DeSales St. NW.,
Washington 6, D. C.
Secretary-treasurer: William W. Maguire
Social insurance: (Secretary-treasurer)
Membership: 342,000

Retail, Wholesale and Department Store Union (AFL-CIO)
132 West 43rd St.,
New York 36, N.Y.
Secretary-treasurer: Alvin E. Heaps
Social insurance: Jack Paley (Executive secretary)
Membership: 143,300

Roofers, Damp and Waterproof Workers Association; United Slate, Tile and Composition (AFL-CIO)
1125 17th St. NW.,
Washington 6, D. C.
Secretary-treasurer: John A. McConaty
Social insurance: (Secretary-treasurer)
Membership: 20,284; local unions, 229

Rubber, Cork, Linoleum and Plastic Workers of America; United (AFL-CIO)
87 South High St.,
Akron 8, Ohio
Secretary-treasurer: I. Gold
Social insurance: Kenneth Oldham (Director, Pension and Insurance Department)
Membership: 170,000

Seafarers' International Union of North America (AFL-CIO)
675 4th Ave.. Brooklyn 32, N. Y.
Secretary-treasurer: John Hawk
Membership: 75,000

Atlantic, Gulf, Lakes and Inland Waters District
675 4th Ave.,
Brooklyn 32, N. Y.
Secretary-treasurer: Al Kerr
Social insurance: Thomas Gould
Membership: 12,000; port branches, 16

Inlandboatmen's Union of the Pacific
Pier 53, Room 117,
Seattle 4, Wash.
Secretary-treasurer: Raoul Vincilione
Social insurance: Mrs. Betty McPhail (Claims Administrator)
Membership: 2,500

Marine Cooks and Stewards' Union
350 Fremont St.,
San Francisco 5, Cal.
Secretary-treasurer: Ed Turner
Social insurance: William H. Clark (Administrator, Stewards Security, Inc.)
Membership: 4,709

Pacific Coast Marine Firemen, Oilers, Watertenders and Wipers Association
240 2d St.,
San Francisco, Cal.
Social insurance: (President), William W. Jordan
Membership: 3,035

Sailors' Union of the Pacific
450 Harrison St.,
San Francisco 5, Cal.
Secretary-treasurer: Morris Weisberger
Social insurance: William H. Clark (Administrator, Sailors' Home of the Pacific)
Membership: 6,585

Sheet Metal Workers' International Association (AFL-CIO)
1000 Connecticut Ave. NW.,
Washington 6, D. C.
President: Edward F. Carlough
Secretary-treasurer: David S. Turner
Membership: 100,000

Shoe and Allied Craftsmen; Brotherhood of (Ind.)
389 Main St.,
Brockton 48, Mass.
Secretary-treasurer: Raymond J. Lynch
Social insurance: (Secretary-treasurer)
Membership: 4,300

Shoe Workers of America; United (AFL-CIO)
1012 14th St. NW.,
Washington 5, D. C.
Secretary-treasurer: Angelo G. Georgian
Social insurance: (Secretary-treasurer)
Membership: 58,000

Shoe Workers' Union; Boot and (AFL-CIO)
246 Summer St.,
Boston 10, Mass.
President and secretary-treasurer: John E. Mara
Membership: 40,000

Stage Employes and Moving Picture
  Machine Operators of the United States
  and Canada; nlternational Alliance
  of Theatrical (AFL-CIO)
1270 Avenue of the Americas,
New York 20, N. Y.
Secretary-treasurer: Harland Holmden
Social insurance: (President) Richard F.
  Walsh
Membership: 61,967; local unions, 975

State, County and Municipal Employees;
  American Federation of (AFL-CIO)
815 Mt. Vernon Pl. NW.,
Washington 1, D. C.
Secretary-treasurer: John L. McCormack
Membership: 210,000

Steelworkers of America; United (AFL-CIO)
1500 Commonwealth Bldg.,
Pittsburgh 22, Pa.
Secretary-treasurer: I. W. Abel
Social insurance: John Tomayko (Director,
  Insurance, Pension and Unemployment
  Benefits Department)
Membership: 1,152,000

Stereotypers' and Electrotypers' Union
  of North America; International
  (AFL-CIO)
205 West Wacker Dr.,
Chicago 6, III.
Secretary-treasurer: Joseph L. O'Neil
752 Old South Bldg.,
Boston 8, Mass.
Social insurance: (Secretary-treasurer)
Membership: 11,000

Stone and Allied Products Workers of
  America; United (AFL-CIO)
289 North Main St.,
Barre, Vt.
Secretary-treasurer: John C. Lawson
Social insurance: (Secretary-treasurer)
Membership: 12,347

Stone Cutters Association of
  North America; Journeymen (AFL-CIO)
46 North Pennsylvania St.
Indianapolis 4, Ind.
President and secretary-treasurer:
  Howard I. Henson
Social insurance: (President and
  secretary-treasurer)
Membership: 1,200

Stove Mounters' International Union of
  North America (AFL-CIO)
2929 South Jefferson Ave.
St. Louis 18, Mo.
Secretary-treasurer: Edward W. Kaiser
Social insurance: (Secretary-treasurer)
Membership: 9,500

Street, Electric Railway and Motor Coach
  Employees of America; Amalgamated
  Association of (AFL-CIO)
5025 Wisconsin Ave. N. W.
Washington 16, D. C.
Secretary-treasurer: O. J. Mischo
Membership: 132,100

Switchmen's Union of North America
  (AFL-CIO)
3 Linwood Ave.
Buffalo 2, N. Y.
Secretary-treasurer: Daniel W. Collins
Social insurance: (Secretary-treasurer)
Membership: 17,200; local unions, 300

Teachers; American Federation of
  (AFL-CIO)
716 North Rush St.
Chicago 11, III.
President: Carl J. Megel
Membership: 56,156

Teamsters, Chauffeurs, Warehousemen
  and Helpers of America; International
  Brotherhood of (Ind.)
25 Louisiana Ave. N. W.
Washington 1, D. C.
Secretary-treasurer: John F. English
Membership: 1,484,433

Telegraphers' Union; The Commercial
  (AFL-CIO)
8605 Cameron St.
Silver Spring, Md.
Secretary-treasurer: John T. Dowling
Membership: 27,345

Telephone Unions; Alliance of
  Independent (Ind)
1422 Chestnut St.
Philadelphia 7, Pa.
Secretary-treasurer: Charles B. Scott
Membership: 90,000

Textile Workers of America; United
(AFL-CIO)
44 East 23rd St.
New York 10, N.Y.
President: George Baldanzi
Secretary-treasurer: Francis Schaufenbil
Social insurance: (President and
secretary-treasurer)
Membership: 40,000

Textile Workers Union of America
(AFL-CIO)
99 University Pl.
New York 3, N.Y.
Secretary-treasurer: John Chupka
Social insurance: (Research Director)
Solomon Barkin
Membership: 192,000

Tobacco Workers International Union
(AFL-CIO)
1003 K St. N.W.
Washington 1, D.C.
Secretary-treasurer: R. J. Petree
Social insurance: (Secretary-treasurer)
Membership: 34,341

Tool Craftsmen; International
Association of (Ind.)
P. O. Box 471
Rock Island, Ill.
Secretary-treasurer: Walter A. Magnuson
Membership: 1,400

Toy Workers of the United States and
Canada; International Union of Doll
and (AFL-CIO)
132 West 43d St.
New York 36, N.Y.
Secretary-treasurer: Milton Gordon
Membership: 19,000

Train Dispatchers Association; American
(AFL-CIO)
10 East Huron St.
Chicago 11, Ill.
Secretary-treasurer: Arthur Covington
Membership: 3,500

Transport Service Employees; United
(AFL-CIO)
444 East 63d St.
Chicago 37, Ill.
Secretary-treasurer: Richard S. Hamme
Social insurance: (Organizing activities)
Walter G. Davis
Membership: 3,000

Transport Workers Union of America
(AFL-CIO)
210 West 50th St.
New York 19, N.Y.
Secretary-treasurer: Matthew Guinan
Social insurance: Ellis Van Riper
(Vice president)
Membership: 135,000

Truck Drivers, Chauffeurs & Helpers
Union of Chicago and Vicinity;
Chicago (Ind.)
809 West Madison St.
Chicago 7, Ill.
Secretary: James Nash
Social insurance: Guy Nave (Fiscal agent)
Membership: 9,776

Typographical Union: International
(AFL-CIO)
2820 North Meridian St.
Indianapolis 6, Ind.
Secretary-treasurer: William R. Cloud
Social insurance: Harry A. Reifin
(Assistant to the president)
Membership: 105,033

Upholsterers' International Union of
North America (AFL-CIO)
1500 North Broad St.
Philadelphia 21, Pa.
Treasurer: R. Alvin Albarino
Social insurance: (President) Sal B.
Hoffmann
Membership: 56,327

Utility Workers of New England Inc.;
Brotherhood of (Ind.)
42 Weybosset St.
Providence, R. I.
Secretary-treasurer: Frank M. Barron
Membership: 4,600

Utility Workers Union of America
(AFL-CIO)
1725 K St. N.W.
Washington 6, D.C.
Secretary-treasurer: Andrew J. McMahon
Membership: 70,000

Watchmen's Association; Independent
(Ind.)
30 East 20th St.
New York 3, N.Y.
Secretary-treasurer: James J. McFaun
Social insurance: (Secretary-treasurer)
Membership: 2,127

Welders; International Union, United (Ind)
780 West El Segundo Blvd.
Hawthorne, Cal.
President and secretary-treasurer:
  James E. Slaughter
Social insurance: (President and
  secretary-treasurer)
Membership: 1,200

Woodworkers of America; International
  (AFL-CIO)
1622 North Lombard St.
Portland 17, Ore.
Secretary-treasurer: William Botkin
Membership: 93,441

Writers Guild of America
  Writers Guild of America, East, Inc.
  (Ind)
22 West 48th St.
New York 36, N. Y.
Treasurer: Richard Graf
Social insurance: Paul Erbach
  (Administrative assistant)
Membership: 1,100

Writers Guild of America
  Writers Guild of America, West, Inc.
  (Ind)
8955 Beverly Blvd.
Los Angeles 48, Cal.
Treasurer: Winston Miller
Social insurance: John Schallert
  (Assistant executive director)
Membership: 1,868

STATE LABOR ORGANIZATIONS

**STATE BODIES AFFILIATED WITH THE
AMERICAN FEDERATION OF LABOR
AND CONGRESS OF INDUSTRIAL
ORGANIZATIONS**

ALABAMA

Alabama Labor Council
604 Lyric Bldg.
Birmingham 3
Secretary-treasurer: Leroy Lindsey

ALASKA

Alaska State Federation of Labor
924 5th Ave.
Anchorage
Secretary-treasurer: Mrs. Lorena Showers

ARIZONA

**Arizona State American Federation of
  Labor and Congress of Industrial
  Organizations**
520 West Adams St.
Phoenix 3
Secretary-treasurer: K. S. Brown

ARKANSAS

Arkansas State Federated Labor Council
316 South Izard St.
Little Rock
Secretary-treasurer: I. Bill Becker

CALIFORNIA

California Labor Federation
95 Market St.
San Francisco 3
Secretary-treasurer: Thomas L. Pitts

COLORADO

Colorado Labor Council
360 Acoma St.
Denver 23, Colo.
Secretary-treasurer: A. Toffoli

CONNECTICUT

Connecticut State Labor Council
100 Willow St.
Waterbury
Secretary-treasurer: Joseph M. Rourke

DELAWARE

Delaware State Labor Council
421 Orange St.
Wilmington 1
Secretary-treasurer: Charles X. Ryan

FLORIDA

Florida State Federated Labor Council
3208 N. W. 17th Ave.
Miami 42
Secretary-treasurer: William E. Allen

GEORGIA

**Georgia State American Federation of
    Labor and Congress of Industrial
    Organizations**
1776 Peachtree St. N. W.
Atlanta 9
Treasurer: Charles C. Mathias

IDAHO

Idaho State AFL-CIO
613 Idaho St.
Boise
Secretary-treasurer: Albert G. Beattie

ILLINOIS

Illinois State AFL-CIO
516 East Monroe St.
Springfield
Secretary-treasurer: Maurice F. McElligott

INDIANA

Indiana State AFL-CIO
910 North Delaware St.
Indianapolis 2
Secretary-treasurer: Max F. Wright

IOWA

Iowa Federation of Labor
1100 Paramount Bldg.
Des Moines 9
Secretary-treasurer: A. Jack Lewis

KANSAS

Kansas State Federation of Labor
503 New England Bldg.
Topeka
Secretary-treasurer: F. E. Black

KENTUCKY

Kentucky State AFL-CIO
312 Armory Pl.
Louisville 2
Secretary-treasurer: Sam Ezelle

LOUISIANA

Louisiana State Labor Council
429 Government St.
Baton Rouge
Secretary-treasurer: E. J. Bourg, Sr.

MAINE

Maine State Federated Labor Council
199 Exchange St.
Bangor
Treasurer: Denis A. Blais

MARYLAND—DISTRICT OF COLUMBIA

**Maryland State and District of Columbia
    AFL-CIO**
309 North Charles St.
Baltimore 1
Secretary-treasurer: Charles A. Della

MASSACHUSETTS

Massachusetts State Labor Council
11 Beacon St.
Boston 8
Secretary-treasurer: Kenneth J. Kelley

MICHIGAN

Michigan State AFL-CIO
716 Lothrop Ave.
Detroit 2
Secretary-treasurer: Barney Hopkins

MINNESOTA

Minnesota AFL-CIO Federation of Labor
47 West 9th St.
St. Paul 2
Secretary-treasurer: Neil C. Sherburne

MISSISSIPPI

Mississippi Labor Council
133 South Lamar St.
Jackson
Secretary-treasurer: Thomas Knight

MISSOURI

Missouri State Labor Council
1401 Hampton Ave.
St. Louis 10
Secretary-treasurer: Frank J. Murphy

MONTANA

Montana State AFL-CIO
Montana Bldg.
Helena
Treasurer: Joe Crosswhite (Vice president)

NEBRASKA

Nebraska State AFL-CIO
1821 California St.
Omaha
Secretary-treasurer: Nels Petersen

NEVADA

Nevada State AFL-CIO
290 North Arlington St.
Reno
Secretary-treasurer: Louis Paley

NEW HAMPSHIRE

New Hampshire Labor Council
58 West St.
Concord
Secretary-treasurer: Robert Hobart

NEW JERSEY

New Jersey State AFL-CIO
790 Broad St.
Newark 2
Secretary-treasurer: Charles H. Marciante

NEW MEXICO

New Mexico State AFL-CIO
216-A Iron Ave. S. W.
Albuquerque
Secretary-treasurer: Tom E. Robles

NEW YORK

New York State AFL-CIO
1 Columbia Pl.
Albany 7
Secretary-treasurer: Harold J. Garno

NORTH CAROLINA

North Carolina State AFL-CIO
608 West Johnson St.
Raleigh
Secretary-treasurer: J. W. Holder

NORTH DAKOTA

North Dakota State AFL-CIO
   Federation of Labor
505 1st Ave. South
Fargo
Secretary-treasurer: Miss Nellie Thompson

OHIO

Ohio AFL-CIO
271 East State St.
Columbus 24
Secretary-treasurer: Elmer F. Cope

OKLAHOMA

Oklahoma State AFL-CIO
531 Commerce Exchange Bldg.
Oklahoma City 2
Secretary-treasurer: J. J. Caldwell

OREGON

Oregon AFL-CIO
1316 S. W. 4th Ave.
Portland 1
Secretary-treasurer: James T. Marr

PENNSYLVANIA

Pennsylvania AFL-CIO
101 Pine St.
Harrisburg
Treasurer: Earl C. Bohr

PUERTO RICO

Puerto Rico AFL-CIO
804 Ponce de Leon Ave.
Santurce
Secretary-treasurer: Alberto E. Sanchez

RHODE ISLAND

Rhode Island State AFL-CIO
357 Westminster St.
Providence 3
Secretary-treasurer: Edwin C. Brown

SOUTH CAROLINA

South Carolina Labor Council
2006 Sumter St.
Columbia
Secretary-treasurer: Bill Kirkland

SOUTH DAKOTA

South Dakota State Federation of Labor
101 South Fairfax Ave.
Sioux Falls
Secretary-treasurer: Francis K. McDonald

TENNESSEE

Tennessee State Labor Council
226 Capitol Blvd.
Nashville 3
Treasurer: Charles M. Houk

TEXAS

Texas State AFL-CIO
402 West 13th St.
Austin 1
Secretary-treasurer: Roy R. Evans

UTAH

Utah State AFL-CIO
161 South 2d East
Salt Lake City 11
Secretary-treasurer: Ormond Konkle

VERMONT

Vermont Labor Council
131 South Main St.
St. Albans 3
Secretary-treasurer: James R. Cross

VIRGINIA

Virginia State AFL-CIO
102 North Belvidere St.
Richmond 20
Secretary-treasurer: Brewster Snow

WASHINGTON

Washington State Labor Council
2800 1st Ave.
Seattle 1
Secretary-treasurer: Marvin L. Williams

WEST VIRGINIA

West Virginia Federation of Labor
1624 Kanawha Blvd., East
Charleston 1
Secretary-treasurer: Benjamin W. Skeen

WISCONSIN

Wisconsin State AFL-CIO
6333 West Bluemound Rd.
Milwaukee 13
Secretary-treasurer: George W. Hall

WYOMING

Wyoming State AFL-CIO
413 West 20th St.
Cheyenne
Secretary-treasurer: Frank M. Perkinson

FOUNDATIONS AND CHARITABLE TRUSTS

CALIFORNIA

Bing Fund, Inc.
9700 West Pico Blvd.
Los Angeles 35, Cal.
Financial Officer: Matthew W. Kanin, V. P.
Resources: $12,437,000
Main Purposes: General charities

S. H. Cowell Foundation
111 Sutter Street
San Francisco 4, Cal.
Financial Officer: Max Thelen, Pres.
Resources: $15,883,000
Main Purposes: California-based general
charities

Crown Zellerbach Foundation
343 Sansome Street
San Francisco 19, Cal.
Financial Officer: R. G. Shepherd, V. P.
Resources: $12,541,000
Main Purposes: Higher education, welfare,
health, rehabilitation

Henry J. Kaiser Family Foundation
Kaiser Bldg.
Oakland 12, Cal.
Financial Officer: W. P. B. Marks, V. P. &
Treas.
Resources: $32,336,000
Main Purposes: Health, religious agencies,
youth projects

Ohio Match Charitable Foundation
3440 Wilshire Blvd.
Los Angeles 5, Cal.
Financial Officer: Address "Executive
Director"
Resources: $10,831,000
Main Purposes: General welfare and
charities

**United Can and Glass Charitable
Foundation**
3440 Wilshire Blvd.
Los Angeles 5, Cal.
Financial Officer: Julia R. Mayer, V. P.
Treas.
Resources: $19,675,000
Main Purposes: Charitable, scientific,
educational

COLORADO

Boettcher Foundation
818 - 17th Street
Denver 2, Colo.
Financial Officer: L. C. Brown, Treas.
Resources: $19,759,000
Main Purposes: Colorado-based hospitals,
welfare, education, scholarship, religious

El Palomar Foundation
Broadman Hotel
Colorado Springs, Colo.
Financial Officer: R. J. Montgomery, Treas.
Resources: $53,834,000
Main Purposes: Colorado-based hospitals,
medical research, fine arts, education

CONNECTICUT

Charles A. Dana Foundation Inc.
Smith Bldg.
Greenwich, Conn.
Financial Officer: Eleanor N. Dana, Treas.
Resources: $17,578,000
Main Purposes: Hospitals, health agencies,
higher education, youth projects, handi-
capped children

DELAWARE

Longwood Foundation, Inc.
2024 Dupont Bldg.
Wilmington 98, Del.
Financial Officer: H. B. Du Pont, Pres.
Resources: $122,712,000
Main Purposes: Horticulture, education,
libraries

Raskob Foundation for Catholic Activities
1205 Hotel Dupont
Wilmington 98, Del.
Financial Officer: Robert P. Raskob, V. P.
Resources: $29,281,000
Main Purposes: Catholic institutions and
charities

Winterthur Corp.
1070 Du Pont Bldg.
Wilmington 98, Del.
Financial Officer: Alfred E. Bissell, Treas.
Resources: $32,271,000
Main Purpose: Operation of Winterthur
Museum

DISTRICT OF COLUMBIA

Brookings Institution
1775 Massachusetts Ave. N. W.
Washington, D. C.
Financial Officer: Robert W. Hartley, V. P.
Resources: $17,282,000
Main Purposes: Research in economics, government, political and social sciences

Carnegie Institution of Washington
1530 P Street, N. W.
Washington 5, D. C.
Financial Officer: Paul A. Scherer, Exec. V. P.
Resources: $92,410,000
Main Purposes: Scientific research, chiefly in astronomy, geophysics, genetics

Alexander and Margaret Stewart Trust
c/o Union Trust Co. of District of Columbia
Washington 5, D. C.
Trustee: Union Trust Co. of D. C.
Resources: $9,604,000
Main Purposes: Cancer research, child welfare

FLORIDA

Howard Hughes Medical Institute
4014 Chase Ave.
Miami Beach 40, Fla.
Financial Officer: Address "Executive Director"
Resources: $22,572,000
Main Purpose: Medical research

GEORGIA

Callaway Community Foundation
209 Broom St.
La Grange, Ga.
Financial Officer: Halton Lovejoy, V. P.
Resources: $35,622,000
Main Purposes: Local educational, student aid, religion, welfare, mostly Protestant

John Bulow Campbell Foundation
315 Trust Co. of Georgia Bldg.
Atlanta 3, Ga.
Financial Officer: Address "Executive Director"
Resources: $19,251,000
Main Purposes: Religious, charitable, educational etc. only in Southeastern States; also Presbyterian Church projects anywhere

Lettie Pate Evans Foundation
205 Whitehead Bldg.
Atlanta 3, Ga.
Financial Officer: Hughes Spalding, Vice Chmn.
Resources: $11,877,000
Main Purposes: Charity, education, religion, mostly Protestant

Emily and Ernest Woodruff Foundation
c/o Trust Co. of Georgia
Atlanta 2, Ga.
Financial Officer: George W. Woodruff, Vice Chairman
Resources: $51,189,000
Main Purposes: Georgia-based orphanages, hospitals, welfare, religious, education

ILLINOIS

Charles F. Kettering Foundation
40 South Clay Street
Hinsdale, Ill.
Financial Officer: Charles E. Cessna, Exec. V. P.
Resources: $55,940,000
Main Purposes: Local medical, research, scientific

William H. Miner Foundation
667 The Rookery
Chicago 4, Ill.
Financial Officer: W. H. Miner, Pres.
Resources: $16,695,000
Main Purposes: Charitable and welfare

Mark Morton Foundation
110 North Wacker Drive
Chicago, Ill.
Financial Officer: Clayton J. A. Davis, V. P.
Resources: $10,855,000
Main Purposes: Broad charitable and welfare

National Merit Scholarship Corp.
1580 Sherman Ave.
Evanston, Ill.
Financial Officer: Edward C. Smith, V. P.
Resources: $11,292,000
Main Purposes: Scholarship awards. Annual awards to winners of competitive examinations

Sears Roebuck Foundation
3333 Arthington St.
Chicago 7, III.
Financial Officer: R. V. Mullen, V. P. and
    Exec. Director
Resources: $20,237,000
Main Purposes: Farm research, medical,
    scholarships, philanthropic

Standard Oil Co. Foundation
910 South Michigan Ave.
Chicago 80, III.
Financial Officer: David Graham, V. P.
Resources: $24,103,000
Main Purposes: Charitable, scientific,
    educational

Wieboldt Foundation
1580 Sherman Ave.
Evanston, III.
Financial Officer: Herbert Sieck, V. P.
Resources: $8,650,000
Main Purposes: Child welfare, health,
    handicapped, higher education

Woods Charitable Fund Inc.
59 East Van Buren Street
Chicago 5, III.
Financial Officer: Frank H. Woods,
    Sec.-Treas.
Resources: $12,758,000
Main Purposes: Illinois-Nebraska health,
    welfare, youth charities

INDIANA

Lilly Endowment, Inc.
914 Merchants Bank Bldg.
Indianapolis 4, Ind.
Financial Officer: Carl F. Eveleigh, V. P.
Resources: $126,935,000
Main Purposes: Educational, religious,
    community services

MASSACHUSETTS

Godfrey M. Hyams Trust
294 Washington Street
Boston 8, Mass.
Financial Officer: Harry L. Sampson,
    Trustee
Resources: $27,996,000
Main Purposes: Massachusetts-based
    hospitals, youth, handicapped, welfare

MICHIGAN

The Cranbrook Foundation
Lone Pine Road
Bloomfield Hills, Mich.
Financial Officer: Arthur B. Wittliff, Sec.
Resources: $9,477,000
Main Purposes: Michigan-based
    educational and cultural projects

Herbert H. and Grace A. Dow Foundation
315 Post Street
Midland, Mich.
Financial Officer: Address "Executive
    Director"
Resources: $48,746,000
Main Purposes: Michigan-based general
    charitable

Ford Motor Co. Fund
The American Road
Dearborn, Mich.
Financial Officer: Ernest R. Breech,
    Exec. V. P.
Resources: $22,529,000
Main Purposes: Health, social welfare,
    education, scientific-research

Josephine E. Gordon Foundation
154 Taylor Ave.
Detroit 2, Mich.
Financial Officer: J. Cooper, V. P.
Resources: $11,448,000
Main Purposes: General charitable

Herrick Foundation
3456 Penobscot Bldg.
Detroit 26, Mich.
Financial Officer: Emmett E. Egan,
    Res. Agent
Resources: $27,202,000
Main Purposes: Educational, Protestant
    church work

W. K. Kellogg Foundation
250 Champion Street
Battle Creek, Mich.
Financial Officer: Emory W. Morris,
    Pres. and Genl. Dir.
Resources: $46,246,000
Main Purposes: Educational and charitable

W. K. Kellogg Foundation
250 Champion Street
Battle Creek, Mich.
Financial Officer: Emory W. Morris,
　Pres. and Genl. Dir.
Resources: $208,014,000
Main Purposes: Educational and charitable

Kresge Foundation
2727 Second Ave.
Detroit 32, Mich.
Financial Officer: Sebastian S. Kresge,
　Treas.
Resources: $89,014,000
Main Purposes: Education, research,
　hospitals, youth projects, aged,
　religious

McGregor Fund
2486 National Bank Bldg.
Detroit 26, Mich.
Financial Officer: Cleveland Thurber, V. P.
Resources: $27,747,000
Main Purposes: Mental health, other
　medical, educational

Charles Stewart Mott Foundation
1401 East Court Street
Flint 2, Mich.
Financial Officer: Charles Stewart Mott,
　Pres. and Treas.
Resources: $76,754,000
Main Purposes: Education, youth work,
　health in local area.

Elsa U. Pardee Foundation
923 West Park Dr.
Midland, Mich.
Financial Officer: Elsa G. Allen, V. P.
Resources: $9,744,900
Main Purposes: Cancer research,
　hospitals, medical

Relm Foundation
902 First National Bldg.
Ann Arbor, Mich.
Financial Officer: William A. Paton, V. P.
Resources: $9,262,000
Main Purposes: Charitable, religious,
　educational.

W. E. Upjohn Unemployment Trustee Corp.
301 Henrietta St.
Kalamazoo, Mich.
Financial Officer: D. S. Gilmore, Vice Chmn.
Resources: $13,106,000
Main Purposes: Projects to relieve
　unemployment

MINNESOTA

Louis W. and Maud Hill Family Foundation
W-500 First National Bank Bldg.
St. Paul, Minn.
Financial Officer: Philip L. Ray, V. P.
Resources: $59,542,000
Main Purposes: Scientific research, mostly
　to Upper Midwest and Northwest

T. B. Walker Foundation, Inc.
1121 Hennepin Ave.
Minneapolis 3, Minn.
Financial Officer: Walter W. Walker, V. P.
Resources: $12,495,000
Main Purposes: Protestant church work,
　educational, charitable

Amherst H. Wilder Foundation
355 Washington St.
St. Paul 2, Minn.
Financial Officer: A. B. Jackson Sr., V. P.
Resources: $41,423,000
Main Purposes: Sick, needy, infirm in
　St. Paul area

MISSOURI

Danforth Foundation
835 South 8th St.
St. Louis 2, Mo.
Financial Officer: Kenneth I. Brown,
　Exec. Dir.
Resources: $98,839,000
Main Purposes: Grants to colleges and
　higher education projects

William Rockhill Nelson Trust
1114 Bryant Bldg.
Kansas City, Mo.
Financial Officer: Milton McGreevy, Trustee
Resources: $12,238,000
Main Purposes: Operates Nelson Gallery
　of Arts

NEBRASKA

Eugene C. Eppley Foundation, Inc.
2635 West 2nd Street
Hastings, Nebr.
Financial Officer: J. R. Reifschneider, V. P.
Resources: $20,886,000
Main Purposes: Charitable and
  educational, mostly local colleges

NEVADA

Max C. Fleischmann Foundation of Nevada
15 East 1st St.
Reno, Nev.
Financial Officer: Julius Bergen,
  Vice Chmn.
Resources: $69,038,000
Main Purposes: Educational and
  scientific research

NEW JERSEY

Helen Fuld Health Foundation
93 Fuld St.
Trenton, N. J.
Financial Officer: Address "Executive
  Director"
Resources: $15,777,000
Main Purposes: Health, projects and
  research

Kate Macy Ladd Fund
744 Broad St.
Newark 2, N. J.
Financial Officer: John S. Bacheller,
  V. P. and Sec.
Resources: $21,222,000
Main Purposes: Operates Kate Ladd
  Convalescent Home

Fannie E. Ripple Foundation
744 Broad Street
Newark 2, N. J.
Financial Officer: John F. Sly, V. P.
Resources: $25,934,000
Main Purposes: Hospitals, aged women,
  research on cancer and heart disease

Turrell Fund
100 North Arlington Ave.
East Orange, N. J.
Financial Officer: Clementine B. Paulsen,
  Exec. Sec.
Resources: $26,374,000
Main Purposes: Needy and
  underprivileged children

Victoria Foundation
253 Ridgewood Ave.
Glen Ridge, N. J.
Financial Officer: Percy Chubb, 2nd, V. P.
Resources: $18,948,000
Main Purposes: Health, social welfare,
  educational

NEW YORK CITY

Altman Foundation
361 Fifth Ave.
New York 16, N. Y.
Financial Officer: Thomas C. Burke, Treas.
Resources: $12,989,000
Main Purposes: New York State charitable,
  benevolent, educational institutions

Vincent Astor Foundation
405 Park Ave.
New York 22, N. Y.
Financial Officer: Allan W. Betts,
  V. P. and Treas.
Resources: $48,582,000
Main Purposes: Hospitals, health services,
  child welfare

Avalon Foundation
713 Park Ave.
New York 21, N. Y.
Financial Officer: R. George White,
  Sec. and Treas.
Resources: $78,766,000
Main Purposes: Health, youth projects,
  artistic, cultural, national heritage

**David, Josephine and Winfield Baird
  Foundation, Inc.**
65 Broadway
New York 6, N. Y.
Financial Officer: David Baird, Trustee
Resources: $10,257,000
Main Purposes: Broad charitable and
  scientific

Winfield Baird Foundation
65 Broadway
New York 6, N. Y.
Financial Officer: David Baird, Trustee
Resources: $17,488,000
Main Purposes: Broad charitable,
  health, and scientific

George Baker Trust
2 Wall Street
New York 5, N. Y.
Financial Officer: Sheridan A. Logan,
  Exec. Sec.
Resources: $15,098,000
Main Purposes: Scholarships and general
  charitable

**Charles Ulrick and Josephine Bay
  Foundation, Inc.**
1 Wall Street
New York 5, N. Y.
Financial Officer: Frederick H. Howell,
  V. P. and Treas.
Resources: $17,197,000
Main Purposes: Medical research

The Bodman Foundation
c/o Morris and McVeith, 60 Wall Street
New York 5, N. Y.
Financial Officer: Morris and McVeith
Resources: $10,654,000
Main Purposes: Church and higher
  education

Booth Ferris Foundation
149 Broadway
New York 6, N. Y.
Financial Officer: Morgan Guaranty
  Trust Co. of N. Y., Trustee
Resources: $30,761,000
Main Purposes: Not reported

Louis Calder Foundation
589 Fifth Avenue
New York 17, N. Y.
Financial Officer: Louis Calder Jr., Trustee
Resources: $30,546,000
Main Purposes: Hospitals, churches,
  schools, libraries

Carnegie Corp. of New York
589 Fifth Avenue
New York 17, N. Y.
Financial Officer: James A. Perkins, V. P.
Resources: $258,933,000
Main Purposes: Training and research on
  higher education and international
  relations

**Carnegie Endowment on International
  Peace**
United Nations Plaza and 46th Street
New York 17, N. Y.
Financial Officer: Lawrence S. Finkelstein,
  V. P.
Resources: $32,622,000
Main Purposes: International peace
  programs

China Medical Board of N. Y.
30 East 30th St.
New York 22, N. Y.
Financial Officer: Oliver R. McCoy, M. D.,
  Director
Resources: $48,030,000
Main Purposes: Projects relating to Far
  East education

Commonwealth Fund
1 East 75th Street
New York 21, N. Y.
Financial Officer: John A. Gifford, V. P.
Resources: $114,571,000
Main Purposes: Health and medical
  projects

The Duke Endowment
30 Rockefeller Plaza
New York 20, N. Y.
Financial Officer: Norman A. Cocke,
  Vice Chmn.
Resources: $463,357,000
Main Purposes: Support of Duke University
  and hospitals in South and North
  Carolinas

Field Foundation
250 Park Ave.
New York 17, N. Y.
Financial Officer: Marshall Field Jr., V. P.
Resources: $50,960,000
Main Purposes: Child Welfare, cultural,
  interracial

The Ford Foundation
477 Madison Avenue
New York 22, N. Y.
Financial Officer: Dyke Brown, V. P.
Resources: $2,196,772,000
Main Purposes: Educational, scientific,
    public affairs, international programs

Charles A. Frueauff Foundation
70 Pine Street
New York 5, N. Y.
Financial Officer: Mrs. Edna S. Evans,
    Sec.-Treas and Exec. Dir.
Resources: $10,796,000
Main Purposes: Hospitals, mental health,
    other health

The Grant Foundation
130 East 59th Street
New York 22, N. Y.
Financial Officer: John G. Byler,
    Exec. Dir. and Treas.
Resources: $20,963,000
Main Purposes: Child and family centered,
    mostly programs on children's
    emotional development

**John Simon Guggenheim Memorial
    Foundation**
551 Fifth Avenue
New York 17, N. Y.
Financial Officer: Henry Allen Moe, V. P.
    and Sec. Gen.
Resources: $49,490,000
Main Purposes: Fellowships to aid in
    advanced studies

Soloman R. Guggenheim Foundation
120 Broadway
New York 5, N. Y.
Financial Officer: Albert E. Thiele, V. P.
Resources: $20,642,000
Main Purposes: Support of Guggenheim
    Museum and cultural-artistic projects

John A. Hartford Foundation, Inc.
420 Lexington Avenue
New York 17, N. Y.
Financial Officer: Ralph W. Burger,
    Pres. and Treas.
Resources: $309,065,000
Main Purposes: Humanities and general
    charitable

Charles Hayden Foundation
25 Broad Street
New York 4, N. Y.
Financial Officer: Edgar A. Doubleday,
    Pres. and Treas.
Resources: $65,861,000
Main Purposes: Boys clubs and similar
    projects

Eugene Higgins Trust
c/o U. S. Trust Co., 45 Wall Street
New York 5, N. Y.
Financial Officer: U. S. Trust Co. Trustee
Resources: $47,988,000
Main Purposes: Selected charities

Lillian Babbit Hyde Foundation
535 Fifth Avenue
New York 17, N. Y.
Financial Officer: Robert W. Parsons,
    Pres. and Treas.
Resources: $15,183,000
Main Purposes: Charitable, scientific,
    literary

International Paper Co. Foundation
220 East 42nd Street
New York 17, N. Y.
Financial Officer: J. L. Tower, V. P.
Resources: $8,672,000
Main Purposes: Educational, social, health

Ittleson Family Foundation
654 Madison Avenue
New York 21, N. Y.
Financial Officer: Nina Ridenour, Sec.
Resources: $10,608,000

James Foundation of New York, Inc.
375 Park Avenue
New York 22, N. Y.
Financial Officer: Robert E. Coulson, Pres.
Resources: $85,361,000
Main Purposes: Charitable, religious,
    educational

W. Alton Jones Foundation, Inc.
70 Pine Street
New York 5, N. Y.
Financial Officer: James P. Farrell,
    Sec.-Treas.
Resources: $15,038,000
Main Purposes: Religious, hospitals,
    charitable, welfare

J. M. Kaplan Fund
55 Fifth Ave.
New York 3, N. Y.
Financial Officer: Jacob M. Kaplan,
    Pres. and Treas.
Resources: $15,038,000
Main Purposes: Benevolent, charitable,
    educational, scientific

Henry Kaufmann Foundation
300 Park Avenue
New York 22, N. Y.
Financial Officer: Norman S. Goetz,
    Exec. V. P.
Resources: $10,901,000
Main Purposes: Community centers and
    camps

Samuel H. Kress Foundation
221 West 59th Street
New York 19, N. Y.
Financial Officer: R. H. Kress, Pres.
Resources: $36,530,000
Main Purposes: Hospitals, education,
    fine arts

Josiah Macy, Jr., Foundation
16 West 46th Street
New York 36, N. Y.
Financial Officer: Frank Fremont-Smith,
    M. D., Exec.-Sec.
Resources: $36,891,000
Main Purposes: Medical research and
    medical education

John and Mary R. Markle Foundation
511 Fifth Avenue
New York 17, N. Y.
Financial Officer: John M. Russell,
    V. P. and Exec. Dir.
Resources: $37,638,000
Main Purposes: Aid to medical students
    and institutions

Charles E. Merrill Trust
70 Pine St.
New York 5, N. Y.
Financial Officer:
Resources: $15,125,000
Main Purposes: Selected charities

Milbank Memorial Fund
41 Wall St.
New York 5, N. Y.
Financial Officer: U. S. Trust Co. of N. Y.,
    Trustee
Resources: $22,386,000
Main Purposes: Public health and
    preventive medicine

William T. Morris Foundation, Inc.
230 Park Ave.
New York 17, N. Y.
Financial Officer: Arthur C. Laske,
    V. P. and Sec.
Resources: $11,529,000
Main Purposes: Broad philanthropic

New World Foundation
475 Riverside Dr.
New York 27, N. Y.
Financial Officer: Vernon A. Eagle,
    Exec. Dir. and Treas.
Resources: $9,964,000
Main Purposes: Child development,
    international relations

Aaron E. Norman Fund, Inc.
380 Madison Avenue
New York 17, N. Y.
Financial Officer: Andrew E. Norman,
    V. P. and Sec.
Resources: $8,657,000
Main Purposes: Broad charitable purposes,
    many fields of interest

Old Dominion Foundation
140 East 62nd Street
New York 21, N. Y.
Financial Officer: John D. Barrett,
    V. P. and Sec.
Resources: $48,465,000
Main Purposes: Conservation, arts,
    mental health

Olin Foundation, Inc.
1 East 44th Street
New York 17, N. Y.
Financial Officer: Charles L. Horn, Pres.
Resources: $45,105,000
Main Purposes: College building programs

Gustavus and Louise Pfeiffer Research Foundation
20 Broad St.
New York 5, N. Y.
Financial Officer: Matthew G. Herold,
    V. P. and Treas.
Resources: $13,225,000
Main Purposes: Public health. Awards to
    tax-exempt organizations only

Research Corporation
405 Lexington Avenue
New York 17, N. Y.
Financial Officer: James M. Knox, V. P.
Resources: $11,429,000
Main Purposes: Research, technical,
    scientific projects

Richardson Foundation, Inc.
122 East 42nd Street
New York 17, N. Y.
Financial Officer: H. S. Richardson,
    Chmn. and Pres.
Resources: $51,624,000
Main Purposes: Youth, farm aid, medical,
    educational, research

Rockefeller Brothers Fund
30 Rockefeller Plaza
New York 20, N. Y.
Financial Officer: Dana S. Creel, Dir.
Resources: $131,221,485
Main Purposes: Grants to agencies doing
    charitable and philanthropic work. Also
    international, cultural, health, scientific

The Rockefeller Institute
York Ave. and East 66th Street
New York 21, N. Y.
Financial Officer: Address "Executive
    Director"
Resources: $198,991,000
Main Purposes: Wide variety of charitable,
    educational and cultural interests

Rockefeller Foundation
11 West 50th Street
New York 20, N. Y.
Financial Officer: Lindsley F. Kimball,
    Exec. V. P.
Resources: $536,022,000
Main Purposes: Grants to universities,
    research institutes and other qualified
    bodies for research in public health,
    agriculture, medical education, etc.

The Rogosin Foundation
261 Fifth Avenue
New York 16, N. Y.
Financial Officer: Israel Rogosin, Pres.
Resources: $8,891,000
Main Purposes: Jewish health and
    welfare projects

Dorothy H. and Lewis Rosenstiel Foundation
350 Fifth Avenue
New York 1, N. Y.
Financial Officer: Estelle S. Frankfurter,
    Exec. Dir.
Resources: $10,594,000
Main Purposes: Selected charities

Samuel H. Rubin Foundation, Inc.
5 West 54th Street
New York 19, N. Y.
Financial Officer: Samuel H. Rubin, Pres.
Resources: $9,340,000
Main Purposes: Scholarships and grants in
    studies of mental health, intercultural
    relations

Russell Sage Foundation
505 Park Ave.
New York 22, N. Y.
Financial Officer: Dave H. Morris Jr., Treas.
Resources: $29,553,000
Main Purposes: Aids selected institutions
    in research on health, welfare, and
    academic projects

Earl C. Sams Foundation, Inc.
375 Park Ave.
New York 22, N. Y.
Financial Officer: Mrs. Gladys C. Porter,
    Pres.
Resources: $14,071,000
Main Purposes: General philanthropic

Scriven Foundation, Inc.
149 Broadway
New York 6, N. Y.
Financial Officer: Charles E. Main, Treas.
Resources: $12,101,000
Main Purposes: Projects in rural areas

Sealantic Fund, Inc.
50 West 50th Street
New York 20, N. Y.
Financial Officer: Dana S. Creel, Dir.
Resources.: $12,427,000
Main Purposes: Protestant theological
    education, limited areas

Alfred P. Sloan Foundation
630 Fifth Avenue
New York 20, N. Y.
Financial Officer: Arnold J. Zurcher,
   V. P. and Exec. Dir.
Resources: $200,149,000
Main Purposes: Scholarships, also grants
   to colleges and universities

**Seth Sprague Educational and
   Charitable Foundation**
c/o U. S. Trust Co., 45 Wall St.
New York 15, N. Y.
Financial Officer: U. S. Trust Co. of N. Y.,
   Trustee
Resources: $19,766,000
Main Purposes: Religious, institutions,
   youth, handicapped, hospitals

Statler Foundation
230 Park Avenue
New York 17, N. Y.
Financial Officer: Harold B. Colles,
   Man. Dir.
Resources: $10,496,000
Main Purposes: Research in hotel industry

Solon E. Summerfield Foundation, Inc.
270 Madison Avenue
New York 16, N. Y.
Financial Officer: William Felstiner, Pres.
Resources: $9,510,000
Main Purposes: Aid to charitable and
   educational institutions

Twentieth Century Fund, Inc.
41 East 70th Street
New York 21, N. Y.
Financial Officer: August Heckscher, Dir.
Resources: $20,240,000
Main Purposes: Finances its own research
   projects

United States Steel Foundation, Inc.
71 Broadway
New York 6, N. Y.
Financial Officer: W. Homer Turner,
   Exec. Dir.
Resources: $12,543,000
Main Purposes: Aid to educational
   institutions, health, public affairs

Whitehall Foundation
20 Exchange Place
New York 5, N. Y.
Financial Officer: James A. Moffett, II,
   Pres. and Treas.
Resources: $13,268,000
Main Purposes: Aid to needy, sick, infirm
   individuals, also educational, health
   and research.

Helen Hay Whitney Foundation
525 East 68th Street
New York, N. Y.
Financial Officer: Dora E. Young, Exec. Sec.
Resources: $11,978,000
Main Purposes: Research in certain
   limited fields of medicine

NEW YORK STATE

Winifred Masterson Burke Relief Fund
White Plains, N. Y.
Financial Officer: Seymour L. Cromwell,
   Pres.
Resources: $13,720,000
Main Purposes: Maintains convalescent
   home and medical clinics.

Fred L. Emerson Foundation Inc.
96 Genesee Street
Auburn, N. Y.
Financial Officer: James F. Ross, Inc.
Resources: $19,761,000
Main Purposes: Grants to charitable,
   benevolent, religious, scientific and
   other organizations

Fund for Adult Education
200 Bloomingdale Rd.
White Plains, N. Y.
Financial Officer: G. H. Griffiths,
   V. P. and Treas.
Resources: $8,214,000
Main Purposes: Adult education programs

General Electric Foundation
Crotonville—P.O. Box 791
Ossining, N. Y.
Financial Officer: G. J. De Koning, Treas.
Resources: $25,324,000
Main Purposes: Scholarships and
   educational grants, also scientific,
   charitable, educational

Sleepy Hollow Restorations, Inc.
42 Main Street
Irvington, N. Y.
Financial Officer: Address "Executive
    Director"
Resources: $14,865,000
Main Purposes: Local cultural projects

Surdna Foundation, Inc.
1156 North Broadway
Yonkers, N. Y.
Financial Officer: Mrs. A. Mewell Benedict,
    Pres.
Resources: $60,774,000
Main Purposes: Child welfare, hospitals,
    medical research

NORTH CAROLINA

Mary Reynolds Babcock Foundation, Inc.
P. O. Box 199—Reynolds Station
Winston Salem, N. C.
Financial Officer: Charles H. Babcock,
    Pres. and Treas.
Resources: $30,547,000
Main Purposes: Educational health,
    handicapped, etc.

Cannon Foundation, Inc.
P. O. Box 1192
Concord, N. C.
Financial Officer: Address "Executive
    Director"
Resources: $18,723,000
Main Purposes: Selected charities

Kate B. Reynolds Charitable Trust
c/o Wachovia Bank and Trust Co.,
P. O. Box 3099
Winston Salem, N. C.
Financial Officer: Wachovia Bank and
    Trust Co., Trustees
Resources: $18,852,000
Main Purposes: North Carolina hospitals
    and charities

Zachary Smith Reynolds Trust
Winston Salem, N. C.
Financial Officer Charles H. Babcock,
    V. P. and Treas.
Resources: $43,829,000
Main Purposes: North Carolina charities
    and benevolences

W. N. Reynolds Trust
c/o Wachovia Bank and Trust Co.
Winston Salem, N. C.
Financial Officer: Wachovia Bank and
    Trust Co., Trustee
Resources: $53,942,000
Main Purposes: Selected charities

OHIO

Louis D. Beaumont Foundation, Inc.
800 National City Bank Bldg.
Cleveland 14, Ohio
Financial Officer.: Nathan L. Danby, **Pres.**
Resources: $32,070,000
Main Purposes: General philanthropic

Leon A. Beeghly Fund
c/o Union National Bank
6 West Federal Street
Youngstown, Ohio
Financial Officer: Union National Bank,
    Trustee
Resources: $8,319,000
Main Purposes: Selected charities

Thomas J. Emery Memorial
414 Walnut Street
Cincinnati 2, Ohio
Financial Officer: Address "Executive
    Director"
Resources: $8,042,000
Main Purposes: Broad aid programs to
    Ohio residents

Firestone Foundation
1200 Firestone Parkway
Financial Officer: Joseph Thomas, Sec.
Resources: $16,482,000
Main Purposes: Broad charitable and
    benevolences

Leenard C. Hanna, Jr. Fund
1300 Leader Bldg.
Cleveland 14, Ohio
Financial Officer: Lewis B. Williams,
    V. P. and Treas.
Resources: $28,878,000
Main Purposes: Cleveland area hospitals,
    youth and other charitable

Edmund Drummond Lilly Trustees
National Bank Bldg.
Toledo 3, Ohio
Financial Officer: Address "Executive
    Director"
Resources: $22,383,000
Main Purposes: Toledo area charitable

Elisabeth Severance Prentiss Foundation
c/o National City Bank, P. O. Box 5756
Cleveland, Ohio
Financial Officer: Lewis B. Williams, Pres.
Resources: $14,419,000
Main Purposes: Cleveland area medical
    programs

Proctor and Gamble Fund
301 East 6th Street
Cincinnati 1, Ohio
Financial Officer: William G. Werner, V. P.
Main Purposes: Charitable, religious,
    scientific, educational

**Republic Steel Corp. Educational and
    Charitable Trust**
c/o Cleveland Trust Co., 916 Euclid Ave.
Cleveland 1, Ohio
Financial Officer: The Trust Committee
Resources: $17,983,000
Main Purposes: Selected educational
    programs

Timken Foundation of Canton
1835 Dueber Ave. S. W.
Canton 6, Ohio
Financial Officer: H. H. Timken Jr., Pres.
Resources: $26,222,000
Main Purposes: Local community projects

OKLAHOMA

J. E. and L. E. Mabee Foundation, Inc.
1916 First National Bank Bldg.
Tulsa 3, Okla.
Financial Officer: E. G. Intelmann, Chmn.
Resources: $10,172,000
Main Purposes: Religious, health,
    charitable

Samuel Roberts Noble Foundation, Inc.
P. O. Box 870
Ardmore, Okla.
Financial Officer: Sam Noble, V. P. and Sec.
Resources: $18,674,000
Main Purposes: Oklahoma medical and
    agricultural programs

Frank Phillips Foundation, Inc.
208 First National Bank Bldg.
Bartlesville, Okla.
Financial Officer: W. C. Smoot, Sec.-Treas.
Resources: $10,760,000
Main Purposes: Aid to organizations in
    religious, charitable, scientific projects

PENNSYLVANIA

The Alcoa Foundation
c/o Mellon National Bank and Trust Co.
Mellon Sq.
Pittsburgh 30, Pa.
Financial Officer: J. A. Cochran, Sec.
Resources: $43,680,000
Main Purposes: Scholarships and
    higher education

American Foundation, Inc.
1718 Philadelphia National Bank Bldg.
Philadelphia 7, Pa.
Financial Officer: Curtis Bok, Sec. and
    Treas.
Resources: $9,196,000
Main Purposes: Certain limited medical
    research programs

Claude Worthington Benedum Foundation
223 Fourth Avenue
Pittsburgh 22, Pa.
Financial Officer: David D. Johnson,
    V. P. and Sec.
Resources: $21,969,000
Main Purposes: Grants to institutions,
    mostly in W. Va. area

Mary Louise Curtis Bok Foundation
1726 Locust Street
Philadelphia 3, Pa.
Financial Officer: Mary Curtis Zimbalist,
    Pres.
Resources: $13,609,000
Main Purposes: Music and fine arts

Buhl Foundation
1 Gateway Center—Suite 373
Pittsburgh 22, Pa.
Financial Officer: Pressly H. McCance, Dir.
Main Purposes: Grants to certain
    institutions in Pittsburgh area

Carnegie Hero Fund Commission
2307 Oliver Bldg.
Pittsburgh 22, Pa.
Financial Officer: David B. Oliver,
    Mgr. and Sec.
Resources: $10,734,000
Main Purposes: Awards for heroism

Donner Foundation, Inc.
2500 Philadelphia National Bank Bldg.
Philadelphia 7, Pa.
Financial Officer: Robert A. Maes, Pres.
Resources: $42,195,000
Main Purposes: Grants and scholarships to
    institutions in medical aid research
    projects

Maurice and Laura Falk Foundation
3315 Grant Bldg.
Pittsburgh 19, Pa.
Financial Officer: J. Steele Gow,
    Exec. Dir.
Resources: $11,291,000
Main Purposes: Grants to certain
    institutions conducting research on
    industry, trade, etc.

Samuel S. Fels Fund
2 Penn Center Plaza
Philadelphia 2, Pa.
Financial Officer: Dale Phalen,
    Sec.-Treas. and Exec. Dir.
Resources: $20,273,000
Main Purposes: Medical, charitable,
    educational

Howard Heinz Endowment
P. O. Box 926
Pittsburgh 30, Pa.
Financial Officer: Jerome P. Corcoran, Sec.
Resources: $43,582,000
Main Purposes: Music, arts, health,
    religion, welfare

**S. W. Mellon Educational and Charitable
    Trust**
525 William Penn Pl.
Pittsburgh 19, Pa.
Financial Officer: Adolph W. Schmidt, Pres.
Resources: $27,802,000
Main Purposes: Selected grants in
    Pittsburgh area.

Richard King Mellon Foundation
525 William Penn Pl.
Pittsburgh 19, Pa.
Financial Officer: Joseph D. Hughes,
    Adm.-Trustee
Resources: $59,879,000
Main Purposes: Health, educational,
    civic projects

The Pew Memorial Trust
c/o Glenmede Trust Co., 1608 Walnut St.
Philadelphia 3, Pa.
Financial Officer: Glenmede Trust Co.,
    Trustee
Resources: $135,309,000
Main Purposes: Educational, social
    welfare, health

Pittsburgh Plate Glass Foundation
1 Gateway Center
Pittsburgh 22, Pa.
Financial Officer: R. P. Bell, Adm. officer
Resources: $16,329,000
Main Purposes: Community funds,
    hospitals, higher educational

Presser Foundation
1717 Samson Street
Pittsburgh 3, Pa.
Financial Officer: John Donald Ott, Pres.
Resources: $10,761,000
Main Purposes: Musical education

Sarah Mellon Scaife Foundation
525 William Penn Pl.
Pittsburgh 30, Pa.
Financial Officer: Charles E. Ford, Sec.
Resources: $21,190,000
Main Purposes: Grants to selected
    institutions in Allegheny county

Trexler Foundation
1227 Hamilton St.
Allentown, Pa.
Financial Officer: Nolan P. Benner,
    Exec. Dir.
Resources: $15,395,000
Main Purposes: Selected public projects
    in Allentown area

Phoebe Waterman Foundation, Inc.
1701 Arch Street, Room 422
Philadelphia 3, Pa.
Financial Officer: F. Otto Haas, V. P.
Resources: $70,668,000
Main Purposes: General philanthropic

SOUTH CAROLINA

Self Foundation
Greenwood, S. C.
Financial Officer: J. C. Self, Jr., Dir.
Resources: $12,613,000
Main Purposes: Hospitals, etc. in
  Greenwood area

TENNESSEE

Benwood Foundation, Inc.
521-23 Chattanooga Bank Bldg.
Chattanooga, Tenn.
Financial Officer: E. H. Lawman, Exec. Dir.
Resources: $8,948,000
Main Purposes: Selected projects in
  Tennessee area

Memorial Welfare Foundation, Inc.
c/o American National Bank and Trust Co.
Financial Officer:
Resources: $8,880,700
Main Purposes: Public welfare

TEXAS

M. D. Anderson Foundation
P. O. Box 2557
Houston 1, Tex.
Financial Officer: John H. Freeman, Pres.
Resources: $39,087,000
Main Purposes: Selected projects in Texas

Amon G. Carter Foundation
P. O. Box 1036
Fort Worth, Tex.
Financial Officer: Amon G. Carter, Jr., Pres.
Resources: $27,967,000
Main Purposes: Educational, religious,
  youth, charitable

Clayton Foundation for Research
706 Bank of the Southwest
Houston 2, Tex.
Financial Officer: Benjamin Clayton, Pres.
Resources: $13,575,000
Main Purposes: Research in agriculture
  and livestock

Gulf Oil Foundation
c/o First National Bank
Houston, Tex.
Financial Officer: Address "Executive
  Director"
Resources: $32,563,000
Main Purposes: Selected charitable
  programs

Hoblitzelle Foundation
501 Majestic Theater Bldg.
Dallas 1, Tex.
Financial Officer: John Q. Adams,
  V. P. and Mgr. Dir.
Resources: $17,075,000
Main Purposes: Selected projects in
  Dallas area

Houston Endowment, Inc.
P. O. Box 1414
Houston 1, Tex.
Financial Officer: John T. Jones Jr., Pres.
Resources: $73,633,000
Main Purposes: Broad charitable,
  philanthropic and religious programs

The Moody Foundation
P. O. Box 904
Galveston, Tex.
Financial Officer: A. T. Whayne, Sec.
Resources: $112,554,000
Main Purposes: Religious and medical
  programs in Texas

Robert A. Welch Foundation
2010 Bank of the Southwest Bldg.
Houston 2, Tex.
Financial Officer: W. O. Milligan,
  Dir. of Res.
Resources: $418,309,000
Main Purposes: Charitable, scientific
  and educational

VIRGINIA

Colonial Williamsburg, Inc.
Williamsburg, Va.
Financial Officer:
Resources: $111,848,000
Main Purposes: Operation of Williamsburg
  colonial restoration

COLLEGES AND UNIVERSITIES WITH ENDOWMENTS
OF $1,000,000 OR MORE

* Book Value

** Market Value

ALABAMA

Auburn University
Auburn, Ala.
Financial Officers: Ralph B. Draughon,
Pres. and W. T. Ingraham, Bus. Mgr.
Endowment: $2,026,000 (B)*
Gifts: $4,836,000

Birmingham Southern College
800 Eighth Ave. W.
Birmingham 4, Ala.
Financial Officers: Henry King Stanford,
Pres. and N. M. Yielding, Treas.
Endowment: $3,604,000 (B)*
                $4,782,000(M)**

Howard College
800 Lakeshore Dr.
Birmingham, Ala.
Financial Officers: Leslie S. Wright, Pres.
and Evan Zeiger, Bus. Mgr.
Endowment: $1,250,000 (M)**

ALASKA

University of Alaska
College, Alaska
Financial Officers: William R. Wood,
Pres. and Harold A. Byrd, Compt.
Endowment: $1,015,000 (B)*
Gifts: $1,446,000 (M)**

ARIZONA

University of Arizona
Tucson, Ariz.
Financial Officers: Richard A. Harvill,
Pres. and Kenneth R. Murphy, Compt.
Endowment: $1,685,000 (B)*
                $1,750,000 (M)**
Gifts: $2,802,000

ARKANSAS

Harding College
Searcy, Ark.
Financial Officers: George S. Benson,
Pres. and Lott Tucker, Bus. Mgr.
Endowment: $5,424,000 (B)*
                $6,000,000 (M)**

Hendrix College
Conway, Ark.
Financial Officers: Marshall T. Steel,
Pres. and J. P. Bumpers, Bus. Mgr.
Endowment: $2,412,000 (B)*
                $3,193,000 (M)**

CALIFORNIA

Fresno State College
Fresno 26, Cal.
Financial Officers: Arnold E. Joval, Pres.
and Carl Levin, Bus. Mgr.
Gifts: $2,607,000

George Pepperdine College
1121 West 79th St.
Los Angeles 44, Cal.
Financial Officers: M. Norvel Young,
Pres. and J. C. Moore, Jr., Bus. Mgr.
Endowment: $1,008,000 (B)*

Humboldt State College
Arcata, Cal.
Financial Officers: Cornelius H. Siemens,
Pres. and Frank E. Devery, Bus. Mgr.
Gifts: $2,770,000

Long Beach State College
6101 East Seventh St.
Long Beach 4, Cal.
Financial Officers: Carl W. McIntosh,
Pres. and Bernard R. Carman, Bus.
Mgr.
Gifts: $6,911,000

**Los Angeles State College
of Applied Arts and Sciences**
5151 State College Dr.
Los Angeles 32, Cal.
Financial Officers: Howard S. McDonald,
Pres. and Jack C. Heppe, Treas.
Gifts: $2,877,000

Loyola University of Los Angeles
7101 West 80th St.
Los Angeles 45, Cal.
Financial Officers: Very Rev. Charles S.
Casassa, Pres. and Clement J.
Schneider, Treas.
Endowment: $4,900,000

Mills College
MacArthur Blvd. and Seminary Ave.
Oakland 13, Cal.
Financial Officers: C. Easton Rothwell,
    Pres. and Robert F. Hitchcock, Treas.
Endowment: $4,442,476 (B)*
        $6,321,019 (M)**

Occidental College
1600 Campus Rd.
Los Angeles 41, Cal.
Financial Officers: Arthur G. Coons, Pres.
    and John A. Brown, Jr., V.P. Fin.
Endowment: $5,137,143 (B)*
        $6,772,173 (M)**

Pomona College
Claremont, Cal.
Financial Officers: E. Wilson Lyon, Pres.
    and William V. Shannon, Treas.
Endowment: $15,169,000 (B)*
        $19,839,000 (M)**
Gifts: $1,801,000

San Diego State College
5402 College Ave.
San Diego 15, Cal.
Financial Officers: Malcolm A. Love,
    Pres. and Selwyn C. Hartigan, Compt.
Gifts: $6,933,000

San Francisco State College
1600 Holloway Ave.
San Francisco 27, Cal.
Financial Officers: Glenn S. Dumke,
    Pres. and Orrin De Land, Bus. Mgr.
Gifts: $2,245,106

Scripps College
Claremont, Cal.
Financial Officers: Fredrick Hard, Pres.
    and William V. Shannon, Treas.
Endowment: $6,248,000 (B)*
        $8,048,000 (M)**

Stanford University
Stanford, Cal.
Financial Officer: J. E. Wallace Sterling,
    Pres. and Kenneth M. Cuthbertson,
    V.P. Fin.
Endowment: $89,937,392 (B)*
        $124,630,817 (M)**
Gifts: $9,569,534

University of California
Berkeley 4, Davis, La Jolla, Los Angeles
    24, Riverside, Santa Barbara
San Francisco 22, Cal.
Financial Officers: Clark Kerr, State-wide
    Pres. and Elmo R. Morgan, V.P. Bus.
Endowment: $97,300,000 (B)*
        $123,800,000 (M)**

University of Redlands
1200 East Colton
Redlands, Cal.
Financial Officers: George H. Armacost,
    Pres. and Charles D. Pierpont, Bus.
    Mgr.
Endowment: $5,818,185 (B)*
        $8,361,513 (M)**

University of San Diego
College for Men
Alcala Park
San Diego 11, Cal.
Financial Officer: John P. Cadden, Pres.
Gifts: $2,000,000

University of San Francisco
San Francisco 17, Cal.
Financial Officers: John F. X. Connoly,
    S.J., Pres. and James M. Corbett,
    Treas.
Endowment: $4,681,268 (B)*
        $4,840,770 (M)**

University of Santa Clara
Santa Clara, Cal.
Financial Officers: Rev. Patrick A.
    Donohoe, S.J., Pres. and Charles F.
    Guenther, Treas.
Endowment: $2,709,941 (B)*
        $3,200,000 (M)**

University of Southern California
University Park
Los Angeles 7, Cal.
Financial Officers: Norman H. Topping,
    Pres. and Carl M. Franklin, V.P. Fin.
Endowment: $7,843,000 (B)*
        $9,255,000 (M)**
Gifts: $1,138,000

Whittier College
Whittier, Cal.
Financial Officer: Paul S. Smith, Pres.
Endowment: $2,321,810 (B)*
$3,000,000 (M)**

COLORADO

Colorado College
Colorado Springs, Colo.
Financial Officers: Louis T. Benezet,
Pres. and Robert W. Broughton, Bus.
Mgr.
Endowment (Total): $5,903,000 (B)*

University of Colorado
Boulder, Colo.
Financial Officers: Ouigg Newton, Pres.
and Leo Hill, Bus. Mgr.
Endowment: $1,417,832 (B)*
Gifts: $2,842,791

University of Denver
Denver 10, Colo.
Financial Officers: Chester M. Alter, Pres.
and Harvey D. Willson, Treas.
Endowment: $4,586,000 (B)*
$5,600,000 (M)**
Gifts: $1,977,000

CONNECTICUT

Connecticut College
New London, Conn.
Financial Officers: Charles E. Shain,
Pres. and Corbin C. Lyman, Bus. Mgr.
Endowment: $3,843,000 (B)*
$5,961,000 (M)**

Southern Connecticut State College
501 Crescent St.
New Haven 15, Conn.
Financial Officers: Hilton C. Buley, Pres.
and Wilson E. Cranford, Jr., Bus. Mgr.
Gifts: $4,410,000

Trinity College
Hartford 6, Conn.
Financial Officers: Albert C. Jacobs, Pres.
and J. Kenneth Robertson, Treas.
Endowment: $10,686,000 (B)*
$17,290,000 (M)**

Wesleyan University
Middletown, Conn.
Financial Officers: Victor L. Butterfield,
Pres. and Howard B. Matthews, Treas.
Endowment: $30,093,000 (B)*
$47,335,000 (M)**
Gifts: $1,438,000

Yale University
New Haven 11, Conn.
Financial Officers: A. Whitney Griswold,
Pres. and Charles S. Gage, Treas.
Endowment: $238,316,000 (B)*
Gifts: $8,050,000

DELAWARE

University of Delaware
Newark, Del.
Financial Officers: John A. Perkins, Pres.
and Bruce J. Partridge, V.P. Bus.
Endowment: $22,800,000 (B)*
$40,520,000 (M)**

DISTRICT OF COLUMBIA

American University
Massachusetts and Nebraska Aves., N.W.
Washington 16, D.C.
Financial Officers: Hurst R. Anderson,
Pres. and William O. Nicholls, Treas.
Endowment: $1,889,000 (B)*
$2,377,000 (M)**

Catholic University of America
630 Michigan Ave., N.E.
Washington 17, D.C.
Financial Officers: Rt. Rev. William J.
MacDonald, Pres. and George D. Rock,
Treas.
Endowment: $5,758,000 (B)*
$8,823,000 (M)**
Gifts: $2,074,000

George Washington University
Washington 6, D.C.
Financial Officers: Thomas H. Carroll,
Pres. and Henry W. Herzog, Treas.
Endowment: $7,200,000 (B)*
$7,800,000 (M)**

Georgetown University
37th and O Sts., N.W.
Washington 7, D.C.
Financial Officers: Very Rev. Edward B.
  Bunn, S.J., Pres. and T. Byron Collins,
  V.P. Bus.
Endowment: $10,995,000 (B)*
          $12,086,000 (M)**
Gifts: $2,044,000

Howard University
2401 Sixth St., N.W.
Washington 1, D.C.
Financial Officers: James M. Nabrit, Jr.,
  Pres. and James B. Clarke, Treas.
Endowment: $3,460,000 (B)*

FLORIDA

Rollins College
Winter Park, Fla.
Financial Officers: Hugh F. McKean,
  Pres. and John M. Tiedtke, Treas.
Endowment: $4,327,000 (B)*

Stetson University
DeLand, Fla.
Financial Officers: J. Ollie Edmunds,
  Pres. and Edward C. Furlong, Bus.
  Mgr.
Endowment: $2,594,004 (B)*
          $2,764,371 (M)**

University of Miami
Coral Gables 46, Fla.
Financial Officers: Henry K. Stanford,
  Pres. and Eugene Cohen, Treas.
Endowment: $6,313,150 (B)*
          $6,813,150 (M)**
Gifts: $1,169,922

GEORGIA

Agnes Scott College
Decatur, Ga.
Financial Officers: Wallace M. Alston,
  Pres. and P. J. Rogers, Jr., Bus. Mgr.
Endowment: $8,746,000 (B)*
          $10,837,000 (M)**

Atlanta University
233 Chestnut St.
Atlanta 14, Ga.
Financial Officers: Rufus E. Clement,
  Pres. and C. Everett Bacon, Treas.
Endowment: $7,840,000 (B)*
          $11,790,000 (M)**

Berry College
Mount Berry, Ga.
Financial Officers: John R. Bertrand,
  Pres. and R. H. McCloskey, Bus. Mgr.
Endowment: $5,350,000 (B)*
          $8,000,000 (M)**

Brenau College
Gainesville, Ga.
Financial Officers: Josiah Crudua, Pres.
  and Erwin C. Merck, Treas.
Endowment: $1,200,000 (M)**

Clark College
240 Chestnut St., S.W.
Atlanta 14, Ga.
Financial Officers: James P. Brawley,
  Pres. and William W. Morrell, Bus.
  Mgr.
Endowment: $1,454,000 (B)*

Emory University
Atlanta 22, Ga.
Financial Officers: S. Walter Martin,
  Pres. and E. E. Bessent, Treas.
Endowment: $42,599,000 (B)*
          $54,300,000 (M)**
Gifts: $1,096,000

Georgia Institute of Technology
225 North Ave., N.W.
Atlanta 13, Ga.
Financial Officers: Edwin D. Harrison,
  Pres. and Jamie R. Anthony, Compt.
Endowment: $1,446,000 (B)*

LaGrange College
LaGrange, Ga.
Financial Officers: Waights G. Henry, Jr.,
  Pres. and Austin P. Cook, Jr., Bus.
  Mgr.
Endowment: $1,473,000 (B)*
          $2,437,000 (M)**

Mercer University
Macon, Ga.
Financial Officers: Rufus C. Harris, Pres.
  and William T. Haywood, Bus. Mgr.
Endowment: $5,050,000 (B)*
  $6,050,000 (M)**

Morehouse College
213 Chestnut St., S.W.
Atlanta, Ga.
Financial Officers: Benjamin E. Mays,
  Pres. and O. Everett Beacon, Treas.
Endowment: $3,293,000 (B)*
  $4,445,000 (M)**

Morris Brown College
643 Hunter St., N.W.
Atlanta 14, Ga.
Financial Officers: Frank Cunningham,
  Pres. and C .W. Moore, Bus. Mgr.
Endowment: $1,069,000 (M)**

Oglethorpe University
Oglethorpe University Station
Atlanta, Ga.
Financial Officers: Donald C. Agnew,
  Pres. and Stanley F. Pitcher, Bus. Mgr.
Endowment: $1,329,720 (B)*

Spelman College
350 Leonard St., S.W.
Atlanta 3, Ga.
Financial Officers: Albert E. Manley, Pres.
  and Lawrence J. MacGregor, Treas.
Endowment: $5,087,000 (B)*
  $8,371,000 (M)**

Tift College
Forsyth, Ga.
Financial Officers: Carey T. Vinzant,
  Pres. and Mrs. L. B. Stabler, Treas.
Endowment: $1,010,000 (B)*

University of Georgia
Athens, Ga.
Financial Officers: O. C. Aderhold, Pres.
  and J. D. Bolton, Treas.
Endowment: $2,738,000 (B)*
  $2,733,000 (M)**

Wesleyan College
4670 Forsyth Rd.
Macon, Ga.
Financial Officers: W. Earl Strickland,
  Pres. and Cameron R. Peden, Jr.,
  Bus. Mgr.
Endowment: $2,570,000 (B)*

IDAHO

College of Idaho
Caldwell, Idaho
Financial Officers: Tom E. Shearer, Pres.
  and Eldon R. Marsh, Bus. Mgr.
Endowment: $1,267,000 (B)*
  $1,395,000 (M)**

University of Idaho
Moscow, Idaho
Financial Officers: D. R. Theophilus,
  Pres. and K. A. Dick, V.P. Fin.
Resources: Total Endowment: $9,953,000

ILLINOIS

Augustana College
Rock Island, Ill.
Financial Officers: Conrad Bergenhoff,
  Pres. and Glen Brolander, Compt.
Endowment: $3,090,000 (B)*
  $3,500,000 (M)**

Blackburn College
Carlinville, Ill.
Financial Officers: Robert P. Ludlum,
  Pres. and Lloyd Costley, Bus. Mgr.
Endowment: $2,680,000 (B)*
  $3,753,000 (M)**

Bradley University
Peoria, Ill.
Financial Officers: Harold P. Rodes, Pres.
  and George R. Beck, Treas.
Endowment: $3,543,000 (B)*
  $3,990,000 (M)**

Carthage College
Carthage, Ill.
Financial Officers: Harold H. Lentz, Pres.
  and L. W. Van Winkle, Bus. Mgr.
Endowment: $1,041,000 (B)*

Chicago Teachers College
6800 S. Stewart Ave.
Chicago 21, Ill.
Financial Officers: Raymond M. Cook,
    Pres. and John M. Beck, Treas.
Gifts: $5,500,000

Eastern Illinois University
Charleston, Ill.
Financial Officers: Quincy Doudna, Pres.
    and Raymond R. Gregg, Bus. Mgr.
Gifts: $2,680,000

Illinois College
Jacksonville, Ill.
Financial Officers: L. Vernon Caine, Pres.
    and Clyde A. McDaniel, Bus. Mgr.
Resources: Endowment: $2,123,000 (B)*

Illinois Institute of Technology
3300 South Federal St.
Chicago 16, Ill.
Financial Officers: John T. Rettaliata,
    Pres. and James J. Ritterskamp,
    Treas.
Endowment: $3,742,000 (B)*
          $4,241,000 (M)**

Illinois Wesleyan University
Bloomington, Ill.
Financial Officers: Lloyd M. Bertholf,
    Pres. and P. W. Kasch, Bus. Mgr.
Endowment: $2,642,000 (B)*

Lake Forest College
Lake Forest, Ill.
Financial Officers: William G. Cole, Pres.
    and John Munshower, Bus. Mgr.
Endowment: $2,700,000 (B)*

Loyola University
820 North Michigan Ave.
Chicago 11, Ill.
Financial Officer: James F. Maguire, S.J.,
    Pres. and Thomas F. Hawkins, Bus.
    Mgr.
Endowment: $6,401,000 (B)*
          $6,901,000 (M)**

MacMurray College
Jacksonville, Ill.
Financial Officer: Louis W. Norris, Pres.
Endowment: $4,971,000 (B)*

Millikin University
Decatur, Ill.
Financial Officers: Gordon E. Michalson,
    Pres. and E. Clarendon Smith, Bus.
    Mgr.
Endowment: $2,402,000 (B)*
          $4,502,000 (M)**

Monmouth College
Monmouth, Ill.
Financial Officers: Robert W. Gibson,
    Pres. and W. Edward Smith, Bus. Mgr.
Endowment: $2,204,000 (B)*

Northern Illinois University
DeKalb, Ill.
Financial Officers: Leslie A. Holmes,
    Pres. and Harold Dorland, Bus. Mgr.
Appropriations: $2,225,000 (B)*

Northwestern University
619 Clark St.
Evanston, Ill.
Financial Officers: J. Roscoe Miller, Pres.
    and William S. Kerr, Bus. Mgr.
Endowment: $118,773,000 (B)*
          $161,488,000 (M)**
Gifts: $1,795,000

Rockford College
Rockford, Ill.
Financial Officers: John A. Howard, Pres.
    and Clyde A. McDaniel, Bus. Mgr.
Endowment: $2,100,000 (B)*
          $2,500,000 (M)**

Southern Illinois University
Carbondale, Ill.
Financial Officers: Delyte W. Morris,
    Pres. and John S. Rendleman, Bus.
    Mgr.
Gifts: $7,732,000

University of Chicago
5801 Ellis Ave.
Chicago 37, Ill.
Financial Officers: Lawrence A. Kimpton,
    Chancellor and William B. Harrell,
    Bus. Mgr.
Endowment: $133,045,000 (B)*
          $210,780,000 (M)**
Gifts: $2,636,000

University of Illinois
Urbana, Ill.
Financial Officers: David Dodds Henry,
  Pres. and Herbert O. Farber, Compt.
Endowment: $5,989,000 (B)*
           $7,292,000 (M)**
Gifts: $1,120,000

Wheaton College
Wheaton, Ill.
Financial Officers: V. Raymond Edman,
  Pres. and Harold G. Faulkner, Bus.
  Mgr.
Endowment: $5,907,000 (B)*

University of Notre Dame
Notre Dame, Ind.
Financial Officers: Rev. Theodore M.
  Hesburgh, C.S.C., Pres. and Jerome
  J. Wilson, Bus. Mgr.
Endowment: $20,500,000 (B)*
           $23,500,000 (M)**

Wabash College
Crawfordsville, Ind.
Financial Officers: Byron K. Trippet,
  Pres. and William B. Degitz, Bus. Mgr.
Endowment: $6,001,000 (B)*
           $7,849,000 (M)**

INDIANA

Butler University
4600 Sunset Ave.
Indianapolis 7, Ind.
Financial Officers: Alexander Jones, Pres.
  and Raymond Gladden, Treas.
Endowment: $7,230,000 (B)*

DePauw University
Greencastle, Ind.
Financial Officers: Russell J. Humbert,
  Pres. and D. W. Smythe, Compt.
Endowment: $10,247,000 (B)*
           $13,041,000 (M)**

Hanover College
Hanover, Ind.
Financial Officers: John E. Horner, Pres.
  and Ralph Burress, Treas.
Endowment: $3,168,000 (B)*
           $4,156,000 (M)**

Indiana University
Bloomington, Ind.
Financial Officers: Herman B. Wells,
  Pres. and J. A. Franklin, Treas.
Endowment: $4,360,000 (B)*
Gifts: $5,890,000 (M)**

Purdue University
Lafayette, Ind.
Financial Officers: Frederick L. Hovde,
  Pres. and L. J. Freehafer, Treas.
Legislative Appropriation: $17,164,000

IOWA

Coe College
1220 First Ave. N.E.
Cedar Rapids, Iowa
Financial Officers: Joseph E. McCabe,
  Pres. and Robert E. Heywood, Bus.
  Mgr.
Endowment: $2,535,000 (B)*
           $4,650,000 (M)**

Cornell College
Mount Vernon, Iowa
Financial Officers: Russell D. Cole, Pres.
  and Charles Cochran, Bus. Mgr.
Endowment: $3,718,000 (B)*
           $4,699,000 (M)**

Grinnell College
Grinnell, Iowa
Financial Officers: Harold R. Bowen,
  Pres. and Charles L. Kaufman, Treas.
Endowment: $8,833,000 (B)*
           $14,170,000 (M)**
Gifts: $1,082,000

State University of Iowa
Iowa City, Iowa
Financial Officers: James W. Maucker,
  Pres. and P. Jennings, Bus. Mgr.
Endowment: $2,118,000 (B)*
           $6,309,000

KANSAS

University of Kansas
Wichita 8, Kan.
Financial Officers: Franklin D. Murphy,
  Chancellor and Keith Nitcher, Compt.
Endowment: $7,730,000 (B)*
              $10,946,000 (M)**
Gifts: $2,000,000

KENTUCKY

Berea College
Berea, Ky.
Financial Officers. Francis S. Hutchins,
  Pres. and L. D. Bibbee, V.P. Bus.
Endowment: $23,658,000 (B)*
              $31,000,000 (M)**

University of Kentucky
University Station
Lexington 29, Ky.
Financial Officers: Frank G. Dickey, Pres.
  and Frank D. Peterson, V.P. Bus.
Appropriations: $19,153,000

University of Louisville
Belknap Campus
Louisville 8, Ky.
Financial Officers: Phillip Davidson,
  Pres. and William J. McGlothin, Bus.
  Mgr.
Endowment: $5,362,000 (B)*
              $7,339,000 (M)**

LOUISIANA

Centenary College of Louisiana
2911 Centenary Blvd.
Shreveport, La.
Financial Officers: J. J. Mickle, Pres.
  and Joel Thomas, Treas.
Endowment: $4,341,000 (B)*
              $6,197,000 (M)**

Dillard University
2601 Gentilly Blvd.
New Orleans 22, La.
Financial Officers: Albert W. Dent, Pres.
  and Roy R. Claytor, Bus. Mgr.
Endowment: $4,770,000

Tulane University
New Orleans 18, La.
Financial Officers: Herbert E. Longnecker,
  Pres. and Clarence Scheps, V.P. &
  Compt.
Endowment: $29,646,000 (B)*
              $49,628,000 (M)**

Louisiana State University
Baton Rouge, La.
Financial Officers: Troy H. Middleton,
  Pres. and Walter B. Calhoun, V.P. Fin.
Appropriations: $19,597,000

MAINE

Bates College
Lewiston, Me.
Financial Officers: Charles F. Phillips,
  Pres. and Norman E. Ross, Bursar
Endowment: $3,458,000 (B)*
              $4,545,000 (M)**

Bowdoin College
Brunswick, Me.
Financial Officers: James Stacy Coles,
  Pres. and Glenn R. McIntyre, Treas.
Endowment: $17,100,000 (B)*
              $21,829,000 (M)**

Colby College
Waterville, Me.
Financial Officer: Robert E. L. Strider,
  Pres.
Endowment: $6,402,000 (B)*
              $9,238,000 (M)**

University of Maine
Orono, Me.
Financial Officer: Prescott Vose, Compt.
Endowment: $2,477,000 (B)*
              $2,946,000 (M)**

MARYLAND

Goucher College
Towson
Baltimore 4, Md.
Financial Officers: Otto F. Kraushaar,
  Pres. and C. Stanley Bosley, Jr.,
  Compt.
Endowment: $4,214,000 (B)*
              $5,394,000 (M)**

Johns Hopkins University
Baltimore 18, Md.
Financial Officers: Milton S. Eisenhower,
  Pres. and Henry S. Baker, V.P. Fin.
Endowment: $69,819,000 (B)*
              $100,751,000 (M)**
Gifts: $3,000,000

Peabody Conservatory of Music
1 E. Mt. Vernon Pl.
Baltimore 2, Md.
Financial Officer: Peter Mennin, Pres.
Endowment: $5,555,000 (B)*
              $6,929,000 (M)**

St. John's College
Annapolis, Md.
Financial Officer: Charles M. Elzey, Treas.
Endowment: $5,666,000 (B)*
              $6,165,000 (M)**
Gifts: $3,641,000

University of Maryland
College Park, Md.
Financial Officers: Wilson H. Elkins,
  Pres. and C. Wilbur Cissel, Dir. Fin.
Endowment: $5,154,000 (B)*
              $6,901,000 (M)**

MASSACHUSETTS

Amherst College
Amherst, Mass.
Financial Officers: Calvin Hastings
  Plimpton, Pres. and Paul D. Weathers,
  Treas.
Endowment: $29,581,000 (B)*
Gifts: $2,799,000

Babson Institute
Babson Park
Wellesly 57, Mass.
Financial Officers: Henry A. Kriebel,
  Pres. and James G. Hawk, Bus. Mgr.
Endowment: $3,243,000 (B)*

Boston College
Chestnut Hill 67, Mass.
Financial Officers: Rev. Michael P.
  Walsh, S.J., Pres. and Thomas
  Fleming, V.P. Fin.
Endowment: $2,108,000 (B)*
              $2,840,000 (M)**

Boston University
755 Commonwealth Ave.
Boston 15, Mass.
Financial Officers: Harold C. Case, Pres.
  and Kurt M. Hertzfeld, V.P. Adm.
Endowment: $12,104,000 (B)*
              $13,761,000 (M)**
Gifts: $1,800,000

Brandeis University
South St.
Waltham 54, Mass.
Financial Officers: Abram L. Sachar,
  Pres. and Lester G. Loomis, Dir. Fin.
Endowment: $3,807,000 (B)*

Clark University
950 Main St.
Worcester 10, Mass.
Financial Officers: Howard B. Jefferson,
  Pres. and Raymond T. Griffith, Treas.
Endowment: $7,721,000 (B)*
              $10,443,000 (M)**

Harvard University
Cambridge 38, Mass.
Financial Officers: Nathan Marsh Pusey,
  Pres. and Paul C. Cabot, Treas.
Endowment: $322,600,000 (B)*
              $530,260,000 (M)**
              $28,516,000

Massachusetts Institute of Technology
77 Massachusetts Ave.
Cambridge 39, Mass.
Financial Officers: Julius A. Stratton,
  Pres. and Joseph J. Snyder, V.P. &
  Treas.
Endowment: $97,865,000 (B)*
              $155,700,000 (M)**
Gifts: $1,000,000

Merrimack College
North Andover, Mass.
Financial Officers: Rev. Vincent A.
  McQuade, O.S.A., Pres. and Patrick
  J. Rice, Bursar
Endowment: $5,650,000 (B)*

Mount Holyoke College
South Hadley, Mass.
Financial Officers: Richard Glenn
  Gettell, Pres. and Otto C. Kohler,
  Bus. Mgr.
Endowment: $15,706,000 (B)*
         $19,800,000 (M)**

Northeastern University
360 Huntington Ave.
Boston 15, Mass.
Financial Officers: Asa S. Knowles, Pres.
  and Lincoln C. Bateson, Fin. Mgr.
Endowment: $12,534,000 (B)*
         $13,779,000 (M)**

Radcliffe College
10 Garden St.
Cambridge 38, Mass.
Financial Officers: Mrs. Mary Bunting,
  Pres. and Robert Maguire, Bus. Mgr.
Endowment: $14,058,000 (B)*
Gifts: $1,780,000 (M)**

Simmons College
300 The Fenway
Boston 15, Mass.
Financial Officers: William E. Park, Pres.
  and Woodrow W. Baldwin, Bus. Mgr.
Endowment: $5,564,000 (B)*
         $8,000,000 (M)**

South College
Northampton, Mass.
Financial Officer: Thomas C. Mendenhall,
  Pres.
Endowment: $22,783,000 (B)*
         $28,900,000 (M)**
Gifts: $2,000,000

Tufts University
Medford 55, Mass.
Financial Officers: Nils Y. Wessell, Pres.
  and C. R. De Burlo, V.P. & Compt.
Endowment: $16,686,000 (B)*
         $20,000,000 (M)**

Wellesley College
Wellesley 81, Mass.
Financial Officers: Margaret Clapp, Pres.
  and Henry A. Wood, Jr., Treas.
Endowment: $3,585,000 (B)*
         $57,453,000 (M)**
Gifts: $2,000,000

Wheaton College
Norton, Mass.
Financial Officer: William C. H. Prentice,
  Pres.
Endowment: $2,100,000 (B)*
         $3,804,000 (M)**

Williams College
Williamstown, Mass.
Financial Officers: James P. Baxter, III,
  Pres. and Charles A. Foehl, Jr., Treas.
Endowment: $23,600,000 (B)*
         $33,980,000 (M)**
Gifts: $1,050,000

Worcester Polytechnic Institute
Worcester 9, Mass.
Financial Officers: Harry P. Storke, Pres.
  and David E. Lloyd, Bus. Mgr.
Endowment: $10,690,000 (B)*

MICHIGAN

Albion College
Albion, Mich.
Financial Officers: William W. White-
  house, Pres. and Paul R. Trautman,
  Bus. Mgr.
Endowment: $6,704,000 (B)*
         $8,900,000 (M)**

Kalamazoo College
Kalamazoo, Mich.
Financial Officer: Weimer K. Hicks, Pres.
Endowment: $4,633,000 (B)*
         $5,000,000 (M)**
Gifts: $2,100,000

**Michigan State University of Agriculture
  & Applied Science**
East Lansing, Mich.
Financial Officers: John A. Hanna, Pres.
  and Philip J. May, V.P. Fin. & Treas.
Endowment: $3,291,000 (B)*
         $3,982,000 (M)**
Gifts: $1,500,000

University of Detroit
4001 W. McNichols Rd.
Detroit 21, Mich.
Financial Officers: Laurence V. Britt,
  Pres. and David E. Meier, Treas.
Endowment: $3,400,000 (B)*

University of Michigan
Ann Arbor, Mich.
Financial Officers: Harlan Hatcher, Pres.
   and Wilbur K. Pierpont, V.P. Bus.
Endowment: $30,567,000 (B)*
                $44,697,000 (M)**
Gifts: $4,800,000

MINNESOTA

Carleton College
Northfield, Minn.
Financial Officers: John W. Nason, Pres.
   and Frank I. Wright, Treas.
Endowment: $9,000,000 (B)*
                $12,000,000 (M)**
Gifts: $1,500,000

Macalester College
St. Paul 1, Minn.
Financial Officers: Harvey M. Rice, Pres.
   and F. N. Budolfson, Bus. Mgr.
Endowment: $5,451,000 (B)*
                $9,240,000 (M)**

University of Minnesota
Minneapolis 14, Minn.
Financial Officers: O. Meredith Wilson,
   Pres. and Laurence R. Lunden, V.P.
   Bus.
Endowment: $52,473,000 (B)*
                $1,100,000

MISSISSIPPI

Mississippi State University
State College, Miss.
Financial Officers: D. W. Colvard, Pres.
   and L. F. Mallory, Compt.
Gifts: $4,878,000

MISSOURI

Lindenwood College
St. Charles, Mo.
Financial Officers: Frank L. McCluer,
   Pres. and Robert C. Colson, Bus. Mgr.
Endowment: $4,017,000 (B)*
                $6,750,000

Park College
Parkville, Mo.
Financial Officers: Paul H. Morrill, Pres.
   and K. R. Houghland, Bus. Mgr.
Endowment: $2,500,000 (B)*
                $3,015,000

St Louis University
St. Louis 3, Mo.
Financial Officers: Very Rev. Paul C.
   Reinert, S.J., Pres. and Bernard T.
   Schuerman, Treas.
Endowment: $10,096,000 (B)*
                $11,435,000 (M)**
Gifts: $2,200,000

University of Missouri
Colombia, Mo.
Financial Officers: Elmer Ellis, Pres.
   and Dale O. Bowling, Bus. Mgr.
Endowment: $3,444,000 (B)*
                $3,600,000 (M)**
Gifts: $5,100,000

Washington University
St. Louis 30, Mo.
Financial Officers: Thomas H. Eliot, Pres.
   and John H. Ernest, Vice-Chanc.,
   Bus. & Fin.
Endowment: $47,294,000 (B)*
                $74,102,000 (M)**

William Jewell College
Liberty, Mo.
Financial Officer: H. Guy Moore, Pres.
Endowment: $3,664,000 (B)*
                $5,370,000 (M)**

MONTANA

Montana State College
Bozeman, Mont.
Financial Officers: Roland R. Renne,
   Pres. and Bernard Copping, Treas.
Endowment: $2,676,000 (B)*

NEBRASKA

Creighton University
2410 California St.
Omaha 31, Neb.
Financial Officers: H. W. Linn, Pres. and
   Edward D. Murphy, Bus. Mgr.
Endowment: $6,258,000 (B)*

University of Nebraska
Lincoln 8, Neb.
Financial Officers: Clifford M. Hardin,
    Chancellor and Joseph Soshnick,
    Compt.
Endowment: $2,181,000 (B)*
        $3,070,000

NEW HAMPSHIRE

Dartmouth College
Hanover, N.H.
Financial Officers: John S. Dickey, Pres.
    and John F. Meck, V.P. & Treas.
Endowment: $55,712,000 (B)*
        $70,800,000 (M)**
Gifts: $5,100,000

University of New Hampshire
Durham, N.H.
Financial Officers: John W. McConnell,
    Pres. and N. W. Myers, Treas.
Endowment: $3,179,000 (B)*
        $3,700,000 (M)**
Gifts: $3,300,000

NEW JERSEY

Drew University
Madison, N.J.
Financial Officers: Robert Fisher Oxnam,
    Pres. and John L. Pepin, Treas.
Endowment: $10,854,000 (B)*
        $17,800,000 (M)**

Fairleigh Dickinson University
207 Montross Ave.
Rutherford, N.J.
Financial Officers: Peter Sammartino,
    Pres. and A. Otto Iwen, Compt.
Endowment: $2,700,000 (B)*
        $3,100,000 (M)**

Princeton University
Princeton, N.J.
Financial Officers: Robert F. Goheen,
    Pres. and Ricardo A. Mestres,
    Fin. V.P. & Treas.
Endowment: $108,000,000 (B)*
        $175,000,000 (M)**
Gifts: $4,000,000

Rutgers-State University
New Brunswick, N.J.
Financial Officers: Mason Gross Welch,
    Pres. and John L. Swink, V.P. & Treas.
Endowment: $13,770,000 (B)*
        $22,400,000 (M)**

Seton Hall University
South Orange, N.J.
Financial Officers: Rt. Rev. Msgr. John J.
    Dougherty, Pres. and John F. Davis,
    V.P. Bus.
Endowment: $6,023,000 (B)*

Stevens Institute of Technology
Castle Point
Hoboken, N.J.
Financial Officers: Jess H. Davis, Pres.
    and Frank Q. Lane, Treas.
Endowment: $7,070,000 (B)*
        $13,990,000 (M)**
Gifts: $1,040,000

NEW MEXICO

University of New Mexico
Albuquerque, N.M.
Financial Officers: Tom L. Popejoy, Pres.
    and John Perovich, Compt.
Endowment: $3,143,000 (B)*

NEW YORK

Barnard College
606 W. 120th St.
New York 27, N.Y.
Financial Officers: Rosemary Park, Pres.
    and Forest L. Abbott, Treas.
Endowment: $9,863,000 (B)*
        $12,545,000 (M)**
Gifts: $1,270,000

Colgate University
Hamilton, N.Y.
Financial Officers: Vincent MacDowell
    Barnett, Pres. and John W. S. Little-
    field, Treas.
Endowment: $8,854,000 (B)*
        $2,930,000

Columbia University
New York 27, N.Y.
Financial Officers: Grayson Kirk, Pres.
  and Robert G. Olmsted, V.P. Fin.
Endowment: $154,371,000 (B)*

Cornell University
Ithaca, N.Y.
Financial Officers: James A. Perkins,
  Pres. and John Burton, V.P. Bus.
Endowment: $70,449,000 (B)*
  $124,258,000 (M)**
Gifts: $11,250,000

Fordham University
Fordham Rd.
Bronx 58, N.Y.
Financial Officers: Rev. Lawrence A.
  Walsh, Pres. and William J. Mulcahy,
  V.P. Fin.
Endowment: $6,220,000 (B)*
Gifts: $4,480,000

Hamilton College
Clinton, N.Y.
Financial Officers: Robert W. McEwen,
  Pres. and Richard W. Cooper,
  Adm. V.P.
Endowment: $8,155,000 (B)*
  $12,140,000 (M)**

Jewish Theological Seminary of America
3080 Broadway
New York 27, N.Y.
Financial Officers: Rabbi Louis Finkel-
  stein, Chancellor and Martin M.
  Grabois, Bus. Mgr.
Endowment: $7,500,000 (B)*
  $8,250,000 (M)**

New York University
Washington Sq.
New York 3, N.Y.
Financial Officers: James M. Hester,
  Pres. and Daniel D. Robinson, V.P.
  & Treas.
Endowment: $48,685,000 (B)*
  $56,098,000 (M)**
Gifts: $1,800,000

Pratt Institute
215 Ryerson St.
Brooklyn 5, N.Y.
Financial Officers: Richard H. Heindel,
  Pres. and Stephen H. Millard, Bus.
  Mgr.
Endowment: $12,759,000 (B)*
  $15,900,000 (M)**

Rensselaer Polytechnic Institute
Troy, N.Y.
Financial Officers: Richard G. Folsom,
  Pres. and Howell A. Jones, V.P. &
  Treas.
Endowment: $23,730,000 (B)*
  $35,143,000 (M)**

Rochester Institute of Technology
65 Plymouth Ave. S.
Rochester 8, N.Y.
Financial Officers: Mark Ellingson, Pres.
  and Frank P. Benz, V.P. Fin.
Endowment: $11,714,000 (B)*
  $21,480,000 (M)**

Syracuse University
Syracuse 10, N.Y.
Financial Officers: William Pearson
  Tolley, Chancellor and Francis A.
  Wingate, V.P. & Treas.
Endowment: $15,710,000 (B)*
  $16,390,000 (M)**

Union College & University
Schenectady 8, N.Y.
Financial Officers: Carter Davidson, Pres.
  and Theodore R. McIlwaine, Bus. Mgr.
Endowment: $18,500,000 (B)*
  $28,000,000 (M)**

University of Buffalo
3435 Main St.
Buffalo 14, N.Y.
Financial Officers: Clifford C. Furnas,
  Chancellor and Claude E. Puffer,
  Vice-Chancellor Bus.
Endowment: $26,000,000 (B)*
  $35,900,000 (M)**
Gifts: $4,300,000

University of Rochester
Rochester, N.Y.
Financial Officers: W. Allen Wallis, Pres.
and LeRoy B. Thompson, V.P. & Treas.
Endowment: $82,395,000 (B)*
$165,200,000 (M)**
Gifts: $2,830,000

Vassar College
Poughkeepsie, N.Y.
Financial Officers: Sarah Gibson Bland-
ing, Pres. and Louis L. Brega,
Bus. Mgr.
Endowment: $28,857,000 (B)*
$34,700,000 (M)**
Gifts: $2,100,000

NORTH CAROLINA

Davidson College
Davidson, N.C.
Financial Officers: David Grier Martin,
Pres. and Robert A. Currie, Bus. Mgr.
Endowment: $9,512,000 (B)*
$10,600,000 (M)**
Gifts: $1,020,000

Duke University
Durham, N.C.
Financial Officers: Deryl Hart, Pres. and
G. C. Henricksen, V.P. Fin.
Endowment: $52,252,000 (B)*
$75,030,000 (M)**

University of North Carolina
Chapel Hill, N.C.
Financial Officers: William Friday, Pres.
and A. H. Shepard, Treas.
Endowment: $5,268,000 (B)*
$6,700,000 (M)**
Gifts: $5,100,000

NORTH DAKOTA

University of North Dakota
University Station
Grand Forks, N.D.
Financial Officers: George W. Starcher,
Pres. and E. W. Olson, Bus. Mgr.
Endowment: $2,221,000 (B)*

OHIO

Antioch College
Yellow Springs, Ohio
Financial Officers: James P. Dixson, Pres.
and Morton Rauh, V.P. Bus.
Endowment: $4,451,000 (B)*
$5,230,000 (M)**

Case Institute of Technology
University Circle
Cleveland 6, Ohio
Financial Officers: T. Keith Glennan,
Pres. and Clifford L. Nelson, V.P. Fin.
Endowment: $10,718,000 (B)*
$21,448,000 (M)**
Gifts: $1,100,000

College of Wooster
Wooster, Ohio
Financial Officers: Howard F. Lowry,
Pres. and Kermit Yoder, Treas.
Endowment: $6,410,000 (B)*
$8,880,000 (M)**
Gifts: $1,400,000

Denison University
Granville, Ohio
Financial Officers: A. Blair Knapp, Pres.
and A. J. Johnson, Bus. Mgr.
Endowment: $8,311,000 (B)*
$11,142,000 (M)**
Gifts: $1,300,000

Kenyon College
Gambier, Ohio
Financial Officers: F. Edward Lund, Pres.
and Shaler Bancroft, Compt.
Endowment: $4,252,000 (B)*
$5,520,000 (M)**

Oberlin College
Oberlin, Ohio
Financial Officers: Robert K. Carr, Pres.
and Lewis R. Tower, Bus. Mgr.
Endowment: $35,676,000 (B)*
$60,100,000 (M)**

Ohio State University
N. High St.
Columbus 10, Ohio
Financial Officers: Novice G. Fawcett,
Pres. and Gordon B. Carson, V.P. Fin.
Endowment: $15,642,000 (B)*
$21,830,000 (M)**

Ohio Wesleyan
Delaware, Ohio
Financial Officers: Eldon T. Smith, Pres.
　and Robert W. Meyer, Treas.
Endowment: $7,635,000 (B)*
　　　　　　$8,500,000 (M)**

University of Cincinnati
Cincinnati 21, Ohio
Financial Officers: Walter G. Langsam,
　Pres. and Robert W. Hoefer, Compt.
Endowment: $16,373,000 (B)*
　　　　　　$30,170,000 (M)**
Gifts: $3,115,000

Western Reserve University
2040 Adelbert Rd.
Cleveland 6, Ohio
Financial Officers: John Schoff Millis,
　Pres. and Donald Faulkner, V.P. &
　Treas.
Endowment: $40,513,000 (B)*
　　　　　　$47,800,000 (M)**
Gifts: $1,200,000

Wittenberg University
Springfield, Ohio
Financial Officers: Clarence C. Stough-
　ton, Pres. and Roland C. Matthies,
　V.P. & Treas.
Endowment: $8,264,000 (B)*

OKLAHOMA

Oklahoma State University of Agriculture and Applied Science
Stillwater, Okla.
Financial Officers: Oliver S. Willham,
　Pres. and J. Lewie Sanderson, Compt.
Endowment: $7,878,000 (B)*

University of Oklahoma
Norman, Okla.
Financial Officers: G. L. Cross, Pres.
　and Horace B. Brown, V.P. Fin.
Endowment: $7,870,000 (B)*

University of Tulsa
600 S. College St.
Tulsa 4, Okla.
Financial Officers: Ben G. Henneke, Pres.
　and John A. Hayes, Treas.
Endowment: $5,194,000 (B)*
　　　　　　$7,950,000 (M)**

OREGON

University of Oregon
Eugene, Ore.
Financial Officers: Arthur S. Flemming,
　Pres. and J. Orville Lindstrom, Bus.
　Mgr.
Endowment: $3,390,000 (B)*
Gifts: $1,540,000 (M)**

PENNSYLVANIA

Academy of the New Church
Bryn Athyn, Pa.
Financial Officers: Rt. Rev. Willard P.
　Pendleton, Pres. and Leonard E.
　Gyllenhall, Bus. Mgr.
Endowment: $7,255,000 (B)*
　　　　　　$15,386,000 (M)**

Bryn Mawr College
Bryn Mawr, Pa.
Financial Officers: Katharine E. McBride,
　Pres. and Paul W. Klug, Compt.
Endowment: $17,020,000 (B)*
　　　　　　$22,500,000 (M)**

Bucknell University
Lewisburg, Pa.
Financial Officers: Merle M. Odgers,
　Pres. and John F. Zeller, III, V.P. Fin.
Endowment: $5,309,000 (B)*
　　　　　　$8,100,000 (M)**
Gifts: $1,900,000

Carnegie Institute of Technology
Pittsburgh 13, Pa.
Financial Officers: John C. Warner, Pres.
　and Richard D. Strathmeyer, V.P. Bus.
Endowment: $38,184,000 (B)*
　　　　　　$55,250,000 (M)**
Gifts: $3,375,000

Chatham College
Woodland Rd.
Pittsburgh 32, Pa.
Financial Officers: Edward D. Eddy, Jr.,
　Pres. and Burt E. Ashman, Bus. Mgr.
Endowment: $6,927,000 (B)*
　　　　　　$7,350,000 (M)**

Drexel Institute of Technology
32nd and Chestnut Sts.
Philadelphia 4, Pa.
Financial Officers: James Creese, Pres.
   and George A. Dix, Compt.
Endowment: $4,665,000 (B)*
             $8,200,000 (M)**

Haverford College
Haverford, Pa.
Financial Officers: Hugh Borton, Pres.
   and Aldo Casselli, Compt.
Endowment: $11,283,000 (B)*
             $17,519,000 (M)**

Lafayette College
Easton, Pa.
Financial Officers: K. Roald Bergethon,
   Pres. and John N. Schlegel, Treas.
Endowment: $18,000,000 (B)*
             $22,910,000 (M)**
Gifts: $5,100,000

Lehigh University
Bethlehem, Pa.
Financial Officers: Harvey A. Neville,
   Pres. and Elmer W. Glick, Treas.
Endowment: $14,569,000 (B)*
             $24,400,000 (M)**

Pennsylvania State University
University Park, Pa.
Financial Officers: Eric A. Walker, Pres.
   and McKay Donkin, V.P. Fin.
Endowment: $2,218,000 (B)*
Gifts: $14,400,000

Swarthmore College
Swarthmore, Pa.
Financial Officers: Courtney Smith, Pres.
   and Edward K. Cratsley, V.P. Fin.
Endowment: $15,277,000 (B)*
             $23,300,000 (M)**
Gifts: $1,960,000

Temple University
Broad St. and Montgomery Ave.
Philadelphia 22, Pa.
Financial Officers: Millard E. Glatfelter,
   Pres. and Sterling K. Atkinson, V.P.
   & Treas.
Endowment: $4,263,000 (B)*
             $5,040,000 (M)**

University of Pennsylvania
34th St. and Woodland Ave.
Philadelphia 4, Pa.
Financial Officers: Gaylord P. Harnwell,
   Pres. and Henry R. Pemberton, V.P.
   Fin.
Endowment: $65,000,000 (B)*
Gifts: $10,000,000 (M)**

RHODE ISLAND

Brown University
Providence 12, R.I.
Financial Officers: Barnaby C. Keeney,
   Pres. and F. Morris Cochran, V.P. Bus.
Endowment: $27,800,000 (B)*
             $39,000,000 (M)**
Gifts: $2,700,000

SOUTH CAROLINA

Furman University
Greenville, S.C.
Financial Officer: John L. Plyler, Pres.
Endowment: $5,324,000 (B)*
             $5,500,000 (M)**
Gifts: $1,050,000

TENNESSEE

Fisk University
Nashville 8, Tenn.
Financial Officers: Stephen J. Wright,
   Pres. and Isaiah T. Creswell, Compt.
Endowment: $7,145,000 (B)*
             $8,130,000 (M)**

University of the South
Sewanee, Tenn.
Financial Officers: Edward McCrady,
   Pres. and Douglas L. Vaughan, Treas.
Endowment: $7,000,000 (B)*
             $9,000,000 (M)**

Vanderbilt University
Nashville 4, Tenn.
Financial Officers: Alexander Heard,
   Chancellor and Edwin S. Gardner,
   Treas.
Endowment: $47,261,000 (B)*
             $63,790,000 (M)**

TEXAS

Baylor University
Waco, Tex.
Financial Officers: W. R. White,
 Chancellor and Roy J. McKnight, V.P.
 Fin.
Endowment: $10,704,000 (B)*
            $11,770,000 (M)**

Rice Institute
6100 Main St.
Houston 1, Tex.
Financial Officers: K. S. Pitzer, Pres. and
 L. S. Shamblin, Treas.
Endowment: $89,700,000 (B)*

Southern Methodist University
Dallas 5, Tex.
Financial Officers: Willis M. Tate, Pres.
 and Trent C. Root, V.P. & Compt.
Endowment: $10,716,000 (B)*
            $13,680,000 (M)**
Gifts: $1,000,000

Texas Christian University
University Dr.
Fort Worth 29, Tex.
Financial Officers: M. F. Sadler, Chan-
 cellor and L. C. White, Vice-Chancellor
 Fin.
Endowment: $22,000,000 (B)*
            $1,000,000 (M)**

University of Texas
Austin 12, Tex.
Financial Officers: Harry Ransom,
 Chancellor and James C. Dolley,
 Vice-Chancellor Fin.
Endowment: $357,337,000 (B)*
Gifts: $9,100,000

VERMONT

Middlebury College
Middlebury, Vt.
Financial Officers: Samuel S. Stratton,
 Pres. and Carroll Rikert, Bus. Mgr.
Endowment: $10,464,000 (B)*
            $12,900,000 (M)**

University of Vermont
Burlington, Vt.
Financial Officers: John T. Fey, Pres.
 and Melvin A. Dyson, Compt.
Endowment: $7,203,000 (B)*
            $9,210,000 (M)**

VIRGINIA

Hampton Institute
Hampton, Va.
Financial Officers: Jerome H. Holland,
 Pres. and James W. Bryant, Bus. Mgr.
Endowment: $18,255,000 (B)*
            $20,160,000 (M)**

University of Richmond
Richmond, Va.
Financial Officers: George M. Modlin,
 Pres. and Chas. H. Wheeler, III, Treas.
Endowment: $5,262,000 (B)*
            $6,360,000 (M)**

University of Virginia
Charlottesville, Va.
Financial Officers: Edgar F. Shannon, Jr.,
 Pres. and Vincent Shea, Compt.
Endowment: $21,466,000 (B)*
            $45,000,000 (M)**
Gifts: $4,400,000

Washington & Lee University
Lexington, Va.
Financial Officers: Fred C. Cole, Pres.
 and E. S. Mattingly, Treas.
Endowment: $8,442,000 (B)*
            $14,150,000 (M)**

WASHINGTON

University of Washington
Seattle 5, Wash.
Financial Officers: Charles E. Odegaard,
 Pres. and John M. Look, Compt.
Endowment: $4,637,000 (B)*
            $5,760,000 (M)**
Gifts: $5,100,000

Washington State University
Pullman, Wash.
Financial Officers: C. Clement French,
    Pres. and C. A. Pettibone, Bus. Mgr.
Endowment: $26,200,000 (B)*
Gifts: $12,400,000

WEST VIRGINIA

Bethany College
Bethany, W. Va.
Financial Officers: Perry Epler Gresham,
    Pres. and Warner G. Peterson, V.P.
    & Treas.
Endowment: $5,047,000 (B)*
              $7,100,000 (M)**

WISCONSIN

University of Wisconsin
Madison 6, Wis.
Financial Officers: Fred H. Harrington,
    Pres. and Neil G. Cafferty, V.P. Bus.
Endowment: $13,180,000 (B)*
              $15,900,000 (M)**
Gifts: $3,800,000

WYOMING

University of Wyoming
Laramie, Wyo.
Financial Officers: G. D. Humphrey, Pres.
    and E. G. Hays, Dir. Fin.
Endowment: $7,744,000 (B)*
              $8,300,000 (M)**
Gifts: $1,330,000

INDUSTRIAL DEVELOPMENT ORGANIZATIONS

ARRANGED BY COMMUNITIES

Inquiries for financing or information should be addressed to the Managing Director of the Industrial Development Organization.

ALABAMA

**Industrial Development Association of
    Clayton**
Clayton

Montgomery Industries, Inc.
Montgomery

New Industries Committee of Tuscaloosa
Tuscaloosa

Note.—In Alabama, municipalities are empowered to issue revenue bonds (under the Wallace and Cater Acts) for industrial development. To date the following communities have raised an aggregate of $13,444,000 by revenue bond issues: Albertville, Alexander City, Andalusia, Blountsville, Brent, Boaz, Brewton, Brundidge, Centerville, Centre, Cullman, Decatur, Dothan, Fayette, Florence, Guin, Guntersville, Hamilton, Lafayette, Leeds, Linden, Luverne, Reform, Selma, and Thorsby.

ARIZONA

Casa Grande Chamber of Commerce
Casa Grande

Chandler Development Foundation
Chandler

Douglas Industrial Development Corp.
Douglas

Eloy Development Corp.
Eloy

Coolidge Industrial Development Corp.
Coolidge

Florence Development, Inc.
Florence

Prescott Foundation for Industrial Development
Prescott

Tempe Chamber of Commerce
Tempe

Tucson Chamber of Commerce
Tucson

Winslow Chamber of Commerce
Winslow

Colorado River Foundation for Industrial Development
Yuma

ARKANSAS

First Arkadelphia Industrial Development Corp.
Arkadelphia

Second Arkadelphia Industrial Development Corp.
Arkadelphia

Ashdown Industrial Development Corp.
Ashdown

Atkins Industrial Development Corp.
Atkins

Augusta Industrial Development Corp.
Augusta

Baxter County Industrial Development Corp.
Mountain Home

Bald Knob Industrial Development Corp.
Bald Knob

Bay Industrial Development Corp.
Bay

Beebee Industrial Development Corp.
Beebee

Bentonville Industrial Development Corp.
Bentonville

Berryville Industrial Development Corp.
Berryville

Blytheville Industrial Development Corp.
Blytheville

Boone County Industrial Development Corp.
Harrison

Booneville Industrial Development Corp.
Booneville

Brinkley Industrial Development Corp.
Brinkley

Calico Rock Industrial Development Corp.
Calico Rock

Camden Industrial Development Corp.
Camden

Clark County Industrial Development Corp.
Arkadelphia

Clarendon Industrial Development Corp.
Clarendon

Clinton Industrial Development Corp.
Clinton

Columbia County Industrial Development Corp.
Magnolia

Conway County Industrial Development Corp.
Morrilton

Corning Industrial Development Corp.
Corning

Cotter Industrial Development Corp.
Cotter

Crossett Industrial Development Corp.
Crossett

Dallas County Industrial Development Corp.
Fordyce

Danville Industrial Development Corp.
Danville

Desha County Industrial Development Corp.
McGehee

Des Arc Industrial Development Corp.
Des Arc

DeWitt Industrial Development Corp.
DeWitt

Dumas Industrial Foundation
Dumas

Earle Arkansas Industrial Development Corp.
Earle

East Poinsett County Industrial Corp.
Marked Tree

Elaine Industrial Development Corp.
Elaine

El Dorado Industrial Development Corp.
El Dorado

Eudora Industrial Development Corp.
Eudora

Eureka Springs Agriculture & Industrial Development Corp.
Eureka Springs

Faulkner County Industrial Development Corp.
Conway

Fayetteville Industrial Development Corp.
Fayetteville

Foreman Industrial Development Corp.
Foreman

Forrest City Industrial Development Corp.
Forrest City

Fort Smith Industrial Development Corp.
Fort Smith

Garland County Industrial Development
Corp.
Hot Springs

Glenwood Industrial Development Corp.
Glenwood

Grant County Industrial Development Corp.
Sheridan

Green County Industrial Development Corp.
Paragould

Green Forest Industrial Development Corp.
Green Forest

Hamburg Industrial Development Corp.
Hamburg

Harrisburg Industrial Development Corp.
Harrisburg

Heber Springs Industrial Development
Corp.
Heber Springs

Helena Industrial Development Corp.
Helena

Hempstead County Industrial Development
Corp.
Hope

Hot Springs County Industrial Development
Corp.
Malvern

Hughes Industrial Development Corp.
Hughes

Huntsville Industrial Development Corp.
Huntsville

Independence County Industrial Development Corp.
Batesville

Jackson County Industrial Development
Corp.
Newport

Jacksonville Industrial Development Corp.
Jacksonville

Johnson County Industrial Development
Corp.
Clarksville

Joiner Industrial Development Corp.
Joiner

Jonesboro Industrial Development Corp.
Jonesboro

Judsonia Industrial Development Corp.
Judsonia

Junction City Industrial Development Corp.
Junction City

Lake Village Industrial Development Corp.
Lake Village

Lawrence County Industrial Development
Corp.
Walnut Ridge

Leachville Industrial Development Corp.
Leachville

Lepanto Industrial Development Corp.
Lepanto

Logan County Industrial Development
Corp.
Booneville

McCrory Industrial Development Corp.
McCrory

McGehee-Dermott Industrial Development
Corp.
McGehee

Magnolia Industrial Development Corp.
Magnolia

Malvern Industrial Development Corp.
Malvern

Mammoth Springs Industrial Development
Corp.
Mammoth Springs

Manila Industrial Development Corp.
Manila

Mansfield Industrial Development Corp.
Mansfield

Marion County Industrial Development
Corp.
Yellville

Marion Industrial Development Corp.
Marion

Marvell Community Industrial Development Corp.
Marvell

Melbourne Industrial Development Corp.
Melbourne

Metropolitan Industrial Development Corp. of Little Rock
Little Rock

Mineral Springs Industrial Development Corp.
Mineral Springs

Montgomery County Industrial Development Corp.
Mount Ida

Monticello Industrial Development Corp.
Monticello

Mulberry Industrial Development Corp.
Mulberry

Murfreesboro Industrial Development Corp.
Murfreesboro

Nashville Industrial Development Foundation
Nashville

North Logan County Industrial Development Corp.
Paris

North Little Rock Industrial Development Corp.
North Little Rock

Osceola Industrial Development Corp.
Osceola

Ozark Industrial Development Corp.
Ozark

Parkin Industrial Development Corp.
Parkin

Piggott Industrial Development Corp.
Piggott

Pocahontas Industrial Development Corp.
Pocahontas

Polk County Industrial Development Corp.
Mena

Prescott Industrial Development Corp.
Prescott

Rector Industrial Development Corp.
Rector

Rogers Industrial Development Corp.
Rogers

Russellville Industrial Development Corp.
Russellville

Salem Industrial Development Corp.
Salem

Saline County Industrial Development Corp.
Benton

Scott County Industrial Development Corp.
Waldron

Searcy Industrial Development Corp.
Searcy

Sharp County Industrial Development Corp.
Hardy

Siloam Springs Industrial Development Corp.
Siloam Springs

Smackover Industrial Development Corp.
Smackover

Sparkman Industrial Development Corp.
Sparkman

Springdale Industrial Development Corp.
Springdale

Strong Industrial Development Corp.
Strong

Stuttgart Industrial Development Corp.
Stuttgart

Traskwood Industrial Development Corp.
Traskwood

Trumann Industrial Development Corp.
Trumann

Tuckerman Industrial Development Corp.
Tuckerman

Turrell Industrial Development Corp.
Turrell

Van Buren Industrial Development Corp.
Van Buren

Warren Industrial Development Commission
Warren

West Memphis Industrial Development Corp.
West Memphis

White and Woodruff Counties Industrial Development Corp.
Searcy

The Industrial Development Corp. of Wynne.
Wynne

CALIFORNIA

Delano Developments, Inc.
Delano

Fresno Industrial Site Development Foundation
Fresno

Antelope Valley Association
Lancaster-Palmdale

Madera County Industrial Development Corp.
Madera

Contra Costa County Development Association
Martinez

Merced Development Association, Inc.
Merced

Shasta County Economic Commission
Redding

Monterey County Industrial Development, Inc.
Salinas

San Jose Industrial Foundation
San Jose

San Luis Obispo County Development Association
San Luis Obispo

San Mateo County Development Association
San Mateo

Marin County Development Foundation, Inc.
San Rafael

Sanger Industrial Foundation
Sanger

COLORADO

Boulder Industrial Development Corp.
Boulder

Brighton Industrial Development Corp.
Brighton

Holland Industrial Center
Colorado Springs

Industries for Jefferson County, Inc.
Lakewood

Chamber of Commerce Industrial Committee, Inc.
Englewood

Greeley Chamber of Commerce, Industrial Committee, Inc.
Greeley

Loveland Development Fund, Inc.
Loveland

Huerfano Development Corp.
Walsenburg

Sterling Industrial Promotion Fund, Inc.
Sterling

CONNECTICUT

Bristol Industrial Development Corp.
Bristol

Canaan Industrial Development Association
Canaan

Danbury Industrial Foundation
Danbury

Danielson Industrial Foundation
Danielson

Kent Industrial Foundation
Kent

Middletown Industrial Foundation
Middletown

Norwich Industrial Foundation
Norwich

Putnam Area Foundation
Putnam

Rockville Industrial Foundation
Rockville

Stafford Springs Industrial Foundation
Stafford Springs

South Willington Industrial Foundation
South Willington

North Grosco Realty Corp.
Thompson

Torrington Development Corp.
Torrington

Greater Waterbury Area Industrial Development Corp.
Waterbury

Winsted Area Industrial Foundation
Winsted

DELAWARE

The Delaware State Development Department reports no community development corporations. The promotion of industrial development is carried on by the Governor's Committee to Promote Delaware, Inc. and by local chambers of commerce.

FLORIDA

Gilchrist-on-the-Suwannee Development Association
Bell

Calhoun County Industrial Development Corp.
Blountstown

Manatee County Committee of 100
Bradenton

Washington County Industrial Development Corp.
Chipley

Industrial Payrolls, Inc.
Daytona Beach

Lauderdale Industrial Corp.
Fort Lauderdale

Inverness Development Council
Inverness

Jacksonville Chamber of Commerce, Committee of 100
Jacksonville

Jasper Industrial Development Corp.
Jasper

Industrial Development Committee of 100
Lakeland

Baker County Development Commission
MacClenny

Madison Industries, Inc.
Madison

Miami-Dade County Chamber of Commerce
Miami

Marion County Chamber of Commerce, Committee of 100
Ocala

Orlando Industrial Board
Orlando

Industrial Development Corp.
Panama City

Industries Unlimited, Inc.
Pensacola

St. Augustine Committee of 100
St. Augustine

Pinellas County Industrial Council
St. Petersburg

Sarasota Industrial Council
Sarasota

Sebring Development Commission
Sebring

Greater Tampa Chamber of Commerce, Committee of 100
Tampa

Gilchrist County Development Commission
Trenton

Palm Beach County Resources Development Board
West Palm Beach

Industrial Development Commission
Wildwood

Williston Development Commission
Williston

GEORGIA

Abbeville Development Association
Abbeville

Cook County Enterprise, Inc.
Adel

Wheeler County Development Corp.
Alamo

Albany, Inc.
Albany

Industrial Development Corp.
Alexander

Bacon County Industrial Association, Inc.
Alma

Americus-Sumter County Development Corp.
Americus

Industrial Development for Ashburn
Ashburn

Industrial Development Corp.
Athens

Augusta Committee of 100
Augusta

Bainbridge-Decatur County Industrial Corp.
Bainbridge

Ball Ground Industrial Development Corp.
Ball Ground

Appling Industries, Inc.
Baxley

Industrial Development Corp.
Blackshear

Blairsville Industries, Inc.
Blairsville

Blakely Builders & Manufacturers Corp.
Blakely

Buchanan Building Co.
Buchanan

Marion County Improvement Corp.
Buena Vista

Grady County Industrial Development Corp.
Cairo

Gordon County Promotion & Development Association
Calhoun

Greater Camilla, Inc.
Camilla

Carroll County Development Corp.
Carrollton

Cartersville Industries, Inc.
Cartersville

Cave Spring Industrial Development Corp.
Cave Spring

Cedartown Industrial Development Corp.
Cedartown

Chatsworth Industries, Inc.
Chatsworth

Clarkesville Improvement Association
Clarkesville

Claxton-Evans Development Corp.
Claxton

Clayton Industrial Development Board
Clayton

Industrial Development Corp.
Cleveland

Cochran Development Co.
Cochran

Colbert Industrial Corp.
Colbert

Miller County Industrial Board
Colquitt

Columbus Industrial Development Corp.
Columbus

Crisp County Development Co., Inc.
Cordele

Cornelia Area Industrial Corp.
Cornelia

Dahlonega Enterprise, Inc.
Dahlonega

Dalton-Whitefield County Industrial Corp.
Dalton

Terrell County Development Corp.
Dawson

De Kalb Industrial Development Board, Inc.
Decatur

Seminole Industries, Inc.
Donalsonville

Coffee County Chamber of Commerce Industrial Corp.
Douglas

Dublin Investment Corp.
Dublin

Dodge County Industrial Development Corp.
Eastman

Elberton Development Corp.
Elberton

Schley County Industrial Corp.
Ellaville

Ellijay Industrial Development Corp.
Ellijay

Fitzgerald Civic Corp.
Fitzgerald

Chamber of Commerce Industrial Fund
Forsyth

Fort Valley Industrial Development Corp.
Fort Valley

Gainesville-Hall County Development Corp.
Gainesville

Tattnall County Development Corp.
Glenville

Greenville Industrial Development Corp.
Greenville

Greensboro Industrial Corp.
Greensboro

City-County Industrial Development Corp.
Griffin

Hartwell Industrial Committee, Inc.
Hartwell

Pulaski Development Co., Inc.
Hawkinsville

Clinch Industrial Association
Homerville

Butts County Development Corp.
Jackson

Twiggs County Development Corp.
Jeffersonville

Jesup Industrial Development Corp.
Jesup

Junction City Industrial Development
Club, Inc.
Junction City

Lafayette Industrial Development Corp.
Lafayette

La Grange Industries, Inc.
La Grange

Lanier County Development Corp.
Lakeland

Lavonia Development Corp.
Lavonia

Gwinett County Development Corp.
Lawrenceville

Lincoln County Industrial Corp.
Lincolnton

Logansville Industrial Development Corp.
Logansville

Lumpkin Development Corp.
Lumpkin

Lyons Development Corp.
Lyons

Macon Area Development Commission,
Inc.
Macon

Madison-Morgan County Industrial
Development Board, Inc.
Madison

Manchester Industrial Corp.
Manchester

Marietta Industrial Association, Inc.
Marietta

Telfair Industrial Development Corp.
McRae

Menlo Development Association
Menlo

Candler County Development Corp.
Metter

Millen Development Corp.
Millen

Milledgeville and Baldwin County
Development Corp.
Milledgeville

Monroe-Walton Co.
Monroe

Monticello Industrial Development Corp.
Monticello

Montezuma Industrial Development Corp.
Montezuma

Moultrie Development Commission
Moultrie

Mount Zion Development Corp.
Mount Zion

Newnan Industries, Inc.
Newnan

Irwin County Industrial Development Corp.
Ocilla

Bryan County Development Corp.
Pembroke

Perry Industrial Development Corp.
Perry

Brooks County Industrial Development
Corp.
Quitman

Rhine Industrial Council
Rhine

Richland Industrial Corp.
Richland

Crawford County Development Corp.
Roberta

Rockmart Industrial Development Corp.
Rockmart

Rome Chamber of Commerce Development
Commission
Rome

Royston Development Corp.
Royston

Sandersville Improvement Co.
Sandersville

Savannah District Authority
Savannah

Smyrna Development
Smyrna

Social Circle Development Corp.
Social Circle

Treutlen Development Corp.
Soperton

Hancock County Development Co.
Sparta

Bullock County Development Corp.
Statesboro

Summerville Industrial Development
Corp., Inc.
Summerville

Emmanuel County Development Corp.
Swainsboro

Sylvester-Worth County Development Corp.
Sylvester

Tallapoosa Realty Corp.
Tallapoosa

Stephens County Development Corp.
Toccoa

Thomasville-Thomas City Industrial
Development Corp.
Thomasville

Thomaston & Upson County Industries,
Inc.
Thomaston

Tifton Industrial Corp.
Tifton

Unadilla Development Corp.
Unadilla

Valdosta Industries, Inc.
Valdosta

Vidalia Development Authority
Vidalia

Warren County Promotion, Inc.
Warrenton

Waverly Hall Development Co.
Waverly Hall

Wilkes County Industries, Inc.
Washington

Ware County Industrial Development
Association, Inc.
Waycross

Waynesboro Development Corp.
Waynesboro

Valley Industrial Council
West Point

Winder-Barrow Industrial Development
Corp.
Winder

Wrens Industrial Committee, Inc.
Wrens

Johnson County Industrial Development
Association
Wrightsville

IDAHO

Boise Industrial Foundation, Inc.
Boise

Caldwell Industrial Corp.
Caldwell

Nampa Industrial Corp.
Nampa

North Idaho Industrial Corp.
Coeur d'Alene

Weiser Industrial Corp.
Weiser

Gooding Industrial Development Co., Inc.
Gooding

Twin Falls Industrial Development
Commission
Twin Falls

ILLINOIS

Belleville New Industries, Inc.
Belleville

Canton Industries, Inc.
Canton

Centralia Industries, Inc.
Centralia

Charleston Industries, Inc.
Charleston

New Industries, Inc.
Danville

Dixon Development Co.
Dixon

Clay-Wayne Trade Development Corp.
Flora

Freeport Industrial Expansion Corp.
Freeport

Galesburg Development Foundation, Inc.
Galesburg

Benlo-Gillespie Development Association
Gillespie

Hanover Commercial Club, Inc.
Hanover

Herrin Community Council
Herrin

Shares in Kewanee, Inc.
Kewanee

Shares in Litchfield
Litchfield

McLeansboro Golf Club
McLeansboro

New Industries of Moline
Moline

Mount Vernon New Industries Inc.
Mount Vernon

Murphysboro Community Enterprises
Murphysboro

Olney Booster, Inc.
Olney

American Community Builders, Inc.
Park Forest

Rantoul Industrial Development Corp.
Rantoul

Shelbyville Development Corp.
Shelbyville

Modern Research Industries, Inc.
Urbana

West Frankfort Community Council, Inc.
West Frankfort

INDIANA

Bloomington Advancement Association
Bloomington

Clinton Community Club
Clinton

New Industries, Inc.
Connersville

Elkhart New Industries Trust Fund
Elkhart

Chamber of Commerce
Evansville

Greater Fort Wayne Development Corp.
Fort Wayne

Frankfort Industrial Land Trust Fund
Frankfort

Gary Industrial Foundation, Inc.
Gary

Goshen Industrial Club
Goshen

Committee of 100, Inc.
Huntington

Kepner Tract (industrial subdivision)
Lafayette

Greater Linton Club
Linton

Industrial Development Corp.
Michigan City

North Vernon Industries, Inc.
North Vernon

Richmond's Committee of 100, Inc.
Richmond

Committee of 100 of South Bend and
    Mishawaka
South Bend and Mishawaka

Sullivan County Civic Employment Corp.
Sullivan

Vincennes Industry Expansion Corp.
Vincennes

Plymouth Industrial Development Corp.
Plymouth

Industrial Foundation of North Manchester
North Manchester

Rockville Improvement Association
Rockville

Greensburg New Industries, Inc.
Greensburg

Shelbyville Industrial Committee,
    Chamber of Commerce
Shelbyville

Madison Frontliners
Madison

Washington Industrial Expansion
    Committee
Washington

IOWA

Chamber of Commerce
Ames

Anamosa Improvement Corp.
Anamosa

Chamber of Commerce
Ackley

Chamber of Commerce
Albia

Chamber of Commerce
Algona

Chamber of Commerce
Alton

Chamber of Commerce
Atlantic

Audubon Industrial Development Corp.
Audubon

Chamber of Commerce
Burlington

Britt Industrial Development Corp.
Britt

Chamber of Commerce
Bettendorf

Chamber of Commerce
Boone

Community Development Commission
Clarion

Clinton Development Co.
Clinton

Chamber of Commerce
Council Bluffs

Chamber of Commerce
Creston

**Carlisle Construction & Development
Corp.**
Carlisle

Chamber of Commerce
Carroll

Chamber of Commerce
Cedar Rapids

Centerville Chamber of Commerce
Centerville

Chariton Development Co.
Chariton

Charles City Industrial Development Corp.
Charles City

Chamber of Commerce
Cherokee

Clarinda Industrial Board
Clarinda

**Crawford County Industrial Development
Corp.**
Denison

Chamber of Commerce
Dubuque

Chamber of Commerce
Davenport

Decorah Development Co.
Decorah

Des Moines Industrial Bureau
Des Moines

DeWitt Industrial Board
DeWitt

Chamber of Commerce
Eagle Grove

Chamber of Commerce
Emmetsburg

Chamber of Commerce
Estherville

Forest City Development, Inc.
Forest City

Business Industrial Committee
Fort Madison

Development Corp.
Fairfield

Grinnell Industrial Development Corp.
Grinnell

Grand Junction Development Association
Grand Junction

Community Development Corp.
Holstein

Chamber of Commerce
Harlan

Humboldt County Development Corp.
Humboldt

Independence Building Corp.
Independence

Development Corp.
Indianola

Chamber of Commerce
Iowa City

Iowa Falls Industrial Development Corp.
Iowa Falls

Chamber of Commerce
Jefferson

Chamber of Commerce
Keokuk

Industries Committee
Leon

Le Mars Development Commission
Le Mars
Lake Park
Laurens

Community Enterprises, Inc.
Le Grand

The Lenox Development Corp.
Lenox

Chamber of Commerce
LuVerne

Chamber of Commerce
Muscatine

Industrial Development Board
Mount Pleasant

Monona Development Corp.
Monona
Manchester

Chamber of Commerce
Marshalltown

Chamber of Commerce
Mason City

Manson Industrial Development
Commission
Manson
McGregor

Malvern Builders, Inc.
Malvern

Monticello Development Corp.
Monticello

Industrial Committee
Mount Ayr

Industrial Committee
Mediapolis

New Hampton Industrial Corp.
New Hampton

Chamber of Commerce
Newton

Community Development Corp.
North English

Chamber of Commerce
Ottumwa

Industrial Committee
Oskaloosa

Industrial Committee
Osceola

Industrial Development Committee
Osage

Chamber of Commerce
Oelwein

Chamber of Commerce
Perry

Community Development Commission
Rockwell City

Greater Rolfe Club
Rolfe

Chamber of Commerce
Red Oak

Rock Rapids Development Committee
Rock Rapids

Chamber of Commerce
Sac City

Sheldon Chamber of Commerce
Sheldon

Shenandoah Chamber of Commerce
Shenandoah

Community Development Corp.
Sidney

Idea Industries
Sioux City

Stanwood Development Association, Inc.
Stanwood

Spencer Chamber of Commerce
Spencer

Storm Lake Chamber of Commerce
Storm Lake

Sumner Development Corp.
Sumner

Washington Industrial Corp.
Washington

Chamber of Commerce
Waterloo

Chamber of Commerce
Waverly

Industrial Go-Ahead, Inc.
Webster City
West Liberty
Winterset

KANSAS

Anthony Industrial Development Corp.
Anthony

Arkansas City Industries, Inc.
Arkansas City

Baxter Springs Industrial Development
Corp., Inc.
Baxter Springs

Caney Industries, Inc.
Caney

Chanute Development Co.
Chanute

Clay Center Industrial Development Corp.
Clay Center

Coffeyville Industries, Inc.
Coffeyville

Columbus Industrial Development, Inc.
Columbus

Concordia Development Company, Inc.
Concordia

Development, Inc.
Garden City

Dodge City Industrial Development Corp.
Dodge City

Downs Enterprises, Inc.
Downs

El Dorado Development Co.
El Dorado

Emporia Enterprises, Inc.
Emporia

Eureka Industrial Development, Inc.
Eureka

Fort Scott Investment Co., Inc.
Fort Scott

Garnett Industrial Development Corp.
Garnett

Halstead Industrial Foundation
Halstead

Hanover Industrial Development Corp., Inc.
Hanover

Hiawatha Industrial Development, Inc.
Hiawatha

Hoisington Development, Inc.
Hoisington

Hutchinson Industrial Development Corp.
Hutchinson

Independence Industries, Inc.
Independence

Industry, Inc.
Atchison

Iola Industries, Inc.
Iola

Junction City Industrial Development, Inc.
Junction City

Lawrence Industrial Development Co., Inc.
Lawrence

Leavenworth Community Hotel, Inc.
Leavenworth

Manfax, Inc.
Manhattan

Marysville Industrial Development Corp.
Marysville

McPherson Foundation
McPherson

Neodesha Industries, Inc.
Neodesha

Newton Industrial Foundation, Inc.
Newton

Onaga Development Co., Inc.
Onaga

Osage City Industries, Inc.
Osage City

Ottawa Industrial Development, Inc.
Ottawa

Paolo Industrial Corp.
Paola

Pittsburg Industrial Development Corp.
Pittsburg

Russell Industries, Inc.
Russell

Salina, Inc.
Salina

Seneca Industrial Development Corp., Inc.
Seneca

Southwest Development Co., Inc.
Liberal

Tonganaxie Development Co., Inc.
Tonganaxie

Wamego Industrial Development Corp.
Wamego

Wellington Industrial Development Corp.
Wellington

Winfield Development Corp., Inc.
Winfield

KENTUCKY

Anthony Industrial Development Corp.
Ashland

**Bowling Green Industrial Development
  Association**
Bowling Green

**Trigg County Planning & Development
  Association**
Cadiz

**Taylor County Area Development
  Association**
Campbellsville

Carroll County Industrial Foundation
Carrollton

Central City-Muhlenberg County
  Development Association
Central City

Clinton Development Foundation, Inc.
Clinton

Columbia-Adair County Development
  Association
Columbia

Kenton Lands, Inc.
Covington

Danville Chamber of Commerce
Danville

Elizabethtown Industrial Foundation
Elizabethtown

Eminence Improvement Co., Inc.
Eminence

Franklin Industrial Development Board
Franklin

Georgetown Improvement Co., Inc.
Georgetown

Glasgow Development Corp.
Glasgow

Greensburg Industrial Foundation
Greensburg

Harrodsburg Industrial Development
  Committee
Harrodsburg

Henderson Committee of 25
Henderson

Hickman Development Corp.
Hickman

Hopkinsville Chamber of Commerce
Hopkinsville

City of Horse Cave Industrial Foundation
Horse Cave

Anderson County Industrial Development
  Association
Lawrenceburg

Lexington Industrial Foundation
Lexington

London-Laurel County Development
  Association
London

Louisville Industrial Foundation
Louisville

Maysville-Mason County Development Co.
Maysville

Middlesboro-Bell County Area Development
  Association
Middlesboro

Monticello Industrial Development Co., Inc.
Monticello

Montgomery County Investment Co.
Mount Sterling

Mundfordville Industrial Foundation
Mundfordville

Owensboro Industrial Foundation
Owensboro

Industrial Co.
Paintsville

Paris-Bourbon County Chamber of
  Commerce
Paris

McCreary County Chamber of Commerce
Pine Knot

Russellville-Logan County Civic
  Development Corp.
Russellville

Shelbyville Industrial Foundation
Shelbyville

Somerset Chamber of Commerce
Somerset

Stanford Industrial Foundation
Stanford

Tompkinsville Chamber of Commerce
Tompkinsville

Vanceburg Industrial Development Corp.
Vanceburg

Versailles Improvement Co., Inc.
Versailles

LOUISIANA

Arcadia Development Co., Inc.
Arcadia

North Baton Rouge Development Co., Inc.
Baton Rouge

Delhi Development Council
Delhi

Greater Elton Industrial Corp.
Elton

South Rapides Industrial Development
  Association
Glenmora

Gonzales Industrial Development Co., Inc.
Gonzales

Homer Development Co., Inc.
Homer

Marksville Development Association, Inc.
Marksville

Minden Industrial Development Corp.
Minden

Monroe Area Industrial Development Corp.
Monroe

Natchitoches Industries, Inc.
Natchitoches

Greater New Orleans, Inc.
New Orleans

Melville Development Corp.
Opelousas

Ruston Industries, Inc.
Ruston

Winnsboro Businessmen's Association, Inc.
Winnsboro

MAINE

Auburn Business Development Corp.
Auburn

Mount Desert Development Corp.
Bar Harbor

Bridgton Industrial Development Corp.
Bridgton

Brunswick Industrial Development Corp.
Brunswick

Calais Industries, Inc.
Calais

Penquis Development Association
Dover-Foxcroft

Ellsworth Industrial Development Corp.
Ellsworth

Farmington Development Co.
Farmington

Freeport Industrial Development Co.
Freeport

Gardiner Building Corp.
Gardiner

Houlton Regional Development Corp.
Houlton

Kennebunk Industrial Corp.
Kennebunk

Lewiston Development Corp.
Lewiston

Lincoln Citizens, Inc.
Lincoln

Livermore Falls Development Corp.
Livermore Falls

Ossipee Valley Development Association
Newfield

Patten Development Corp.
Patten

Knox Industries, Inc.
Rockland

Saco Industrial Corp.
Saco

Sanford-Springvale Chamber of Commerce
Sanford

South Paris Development Co.
South Paris

Waldoboro Industrial Realty Co.
Waldoboro

Waterville Industrial Development Corp.
Waterville

MARYLAND

The Industrial Corp. of Baltimore
Baltimore

Industrial Development Commission
Brunswick

Beltsville Industrial Center
Beltsville

Hartford Industrial Council
Bel Air

Dorchester Chamber of Commerce, Inc.
Cambridge

Industrial Procurement Committee of Centerville
Centerville

Kent County Development Council
Chestertown

Crisfield Industrial Development Corp.
Crisfield

Washington County Development Association
Hagerstown

Pocomoke Chamber of Commerce, Inc.
Pocomoke City

New Industry Committee of Salisbury
 Chamber of Commerce, Inc.
Salisbury

Carroll County Development Corp.
Taneytown

MASSACHUSETTS

Barrington Industrial Corp.
Barrington

Chicopee Industrial Building Corp.
Chicopee

Dighton Industries
Dighton

Gardner Industrial Foundation
Gardner

Greater Fall River Development Corp.
Fall River

Maynard Industries
Fitchburg

Greenfield Industrial Development Area
 Corp.
Greenfield

Haverhill Industrial Foundation
Haverhill

Holyoke Regional Business Development
 Corp.
Holyoke

Greater Lawrence Industrial Corp.
Lawrence

New Industrial Plants Foundation of
 Lowell, Inc.
Lowell

Greater New Bedford Industrial Foundation
New Bedford

Northampton Industrial Realty
 Development Corp.
Northampton

Northern Berkshire Development Corp.
North Adams

Pittsfield Industrial Development Corp.
Pittsfield

Southbridge Industrial Development
 Corp., Inc.
Southbridge

Spencer Development Corp.
Spencer Industries, Inc.
Spencer

Springfield Area Development Corp.
Springfield

Taunton Industrial Development Corp.
Taunton

Ware Industries, Inc.
Ware

Winchendon Development Corp.
Winchendon

Westfield Development Corp.
Westfield

MICHIGAN

Adrian Industrial Development Corp.
Adrian

Aus-Coda Development Corp.
Au Sable and Oscoda

Bad Axe Industrial Development Corp.
Bad Axe

Battle Creek Area Development Corp.
Battle Creek

Bay City Development Corp.
Bay City

Bellaire Industrial Development Corp.
Bellaire

Big Rapids Industrial Development Corp.
Big Rapids

Blissfield Industrial Development Corp.
Blissfield

Boyne City Industrial Development Corp.
Boyne City

Benton Harbor Industrial Development
 Corp.
Benton Harbor

Byron Industrial Development Corp.
Byron

Cadillac Industrial Development Corp.
Cadillac

Caro Industrial Development Corp.
Caro

Cass City Industrial Development Corp.
Cass City

Cassopolis Industrial Development Corp.
Cassopolis

Central Lake Industrial Development Corp.
Central Lake

Charlevoix Industrial Development Corp.
Charlevoix

Cheboygan Industrial Development Corp.
Cheboygan

Coldwater Industrial Corp.
Coldwater

Corunna Industrial Development Corp.
Corunna

Crosswell Industrial Development Corp.
Crosswell

Greater Dowagiac Association
Dowagiac

Durand Industrial Development Corp.
Durand

East Jordan Industrial Development Corp.
East Jordan

Elk Rapids Industrial Development Corp.
Elk Rapids

Ellsworth Industrial Development Corp.
Ellsworth

Escanaba Industrial Development Corp.
Escanaba

Frankfort Industrial Development Corp.
Frankfort

Gagetown Industrial Development Corp.
Gagetown

Gladstone Industrial Development Corp.
Gladstone

Grand Rapids Industrial Corp.
Grand Rapids

Harbor Beach Industrial Development Corp.
Harbor Beach

Harrison Industrial Development Corp.
Harrison

Harrisville Industrial Development Corp.
Harrisville

Hastings Industrial Development Corp.
Hastings

Hillsdale County Development Corp.
Hillsdale

Homer Industrial Development Corp.
Homer

Hudson Industrial Improvement Corp.
Hudson

Imlay City Industrial Development Corp.
Imlay City

Dickinson County Industrial Development Corp.
Iron Mountain

Iron River Industrial Development Corp.
Iron River

Ironwood Industrial Development Corp.
Ironwood

Ithaca Industrial Development Corp.
Ithaca

Jackson Area Industrial Development Corp.
Jackson

Kalkaska Industrial Development Corp.
Kalkaska

Lawrence Industrial Development Corp.
Lawrence

Lexington Industrial Development Corp.
Lexington

Lowell Industrial Development Corp.
Lowell

Ludington Industrial Development Corp.
Ludington

Manistique Industrial Development Corp.
Manistique

Marshall Industrial Development Corp.
Marshall

Mayville Industrial Development Corp.
Mayville

Menominee Industrial Development Corp.
Menominee

Mesick Industrial Development Corp.
Mesick

Millington Industrial Development Corp.
Millington

Morenci Industrial Development Corp.
Morenci

Morley Industrial Development Corp.
Morley

Greater Muskegon Industrial Foundation
Muskegon

Olivet Industrial Development Corp.
Olivet

Ovid Industrial Development Corp.
Ovid

Owosso Industrial Development Corp.
Owosso

Pentwater Industrial Development Corp.
Pentwater

Pigeon Industrial Development Corp.
Pigeon

Pontiac Industrial Development Corp.
Pontiac

The Industrial Development Corp. of the
    Port Huron-Marysville Area
Port Huron-Marysville

Presque Isle County Industrial
    Development Corp.
Roger City

Reed City Industrial Development Corp.
Reed City

Sandusky Industrial Development Corp.
Sandusky

Community Industrial Development Corp.
Sault Ste. Marie

Scottville Industrial Development Corp.
Scottville

South Haven Industrial Fund, Inc.
South Haven Industrial Development Corp.
South Haven

St. Louis Industrial Development Corp.
St. Louis

Stephenson Development Corp.
Stephenson

Sturgis Improvement Association
Sturgis

Traverse City Industrial Development Corp.
Traverse City

Union City Industrial Development Corp.
Union City

Vassar Industrial Development Corp.
Vassar

Vermontville Industrial Development Corp.
Vermontville

Yale Industrial Development Corp.
Yale

MINNESOTA

Ada Industries, Inc.
Ada

Jobs Buildings, Inc.
Albert Lea

Alexandria Developers, Inc.
Alexandria

Appleton Business Association
Appleton

Atwater Development Association
Atwater

Austin Development Corp.
Austin

Barnum Development Corp.
Barnum

Battle Lake Civic & Commerce
    Industrial Development Committee
Battle Lake

New Industries Committee
Bemidji

Industrial Development Committee
Benson

Bird Island Development Corp.
Bird Island

New Enterprise Committee
Blackduck

Blue Earth Industrial Service Co.
Blue Earth

Building Brainerd, Inc.
Brainerd

Breckenridge Industrial Development
    Corp.
Breckenridge

Cambridge Business Development Corp.
Cambridge

New Industry Committee of the Cannon
    Falls Commercial Club
Cannon Falls

Industrial Development Committee
Cass Lake

Greater Chaska, Inc.
Chaska

Community Development Organization
Chatfield

Business Development Committee
Chokic

New Industries Committee Cokato
    Association
Cokato

Crookston Jobs, Inc.
Crookston

Area Development Committee
Crosby

Delano Industrial Opportunities, Inc.
Delano

Detroit Lakes Development Corp.
Detroit Lakes

Dodge Center Industries, Inc.
Dodge Center

Elk River Associated Investors
Elk River

Ellendale Industries, Inc.
Ellendale

Fairfax Development Committee
Fairfax

Fairmont New Industries Committee
Fairmont

Faribault Industrial Corp.
Faribault

Industrial Development Association
Farmington

Fergus Falls Industrial Corp.
Fergus Falls

Greater Forest Lake Association
Forest Lake

Fosston Business Development Association
Fosston

Fridley Industrial Development Corp.
Fridley

Glencoe Development Association, Inc.
Glencoe

Business Development of Graceville
Graceville

Granite Falls Jobs & Industries
Granite Falls

Hayfield Development Council
Hayfield

Hubbard County Rural Development Committee
Hubbard County

Industrial Committee
Hutchinson

Jackson Industries, Inc.
Jackson

Kenyon Development Corp.
Kenyon

Kerkhoven Development Committee
Kerkhoven

Lafayette Industries, Inc.
Lafayette

Industrial Development Committee of Lake County
Lake County

Lewiston Industrial Development Association
Lewiston

The Lewisville Business & Research Development Committee
Lewisville

Litchfield Industries, Inc.
Litchfield

Luverne Business Development Organization
Luverne

Mankato Area Promotions, Inc.
Mankato

Marshall Industries Foundations
Marshall

McGregor Development Corp.
McGregor

Minneapolis Area Development Corp.
Minneapolis

Montevideo Development Corp.
Montevideo

Jobs & Building, Inc.
Montgomery

The Greater Moorhead Development Corp.
Moorhead

Mountain Lake Industrial Committee
Morris

Community Industrial Development Corp.
Mountain Lake

Nevis Development Association
Nevis

New Prague Development Committee
New Prague

New Richland Development Corp.
New Richland

New Ulm Industries, Inc.
New Ulm

Industrial Development, Inc., of New York Mills
New York Mills

Northfield Development Corp.
Northfield

Olivia Development Corp.
Olivia

Orono Development Corp.
Orono

Ortonville Civic & Commerce Business
   Research Committee
Ortonville

Osakis Jobs, Inc.
Osakis

Owatonna Industrial Development
   Committee
Owatonna

Industries for Park Rapids, Inc.
More Jobs for Park Rapids Area
Park Rapids

Perham Chamber of Commerce
Perham

Pine City Development Co.
Pine City

Pipestone Industries, Inc.
Pipestone

Plainview Enterprise Development Corp.
Plainview

Princeton Development Corp.
Princeton

Red Wing Industrial Development Corp.
Red Wing

Redwood Industries, Inc.
Redwood Falls

Industrial Opportunities, Inc.
Rochester

Rushford Business Development Corp.
Rushford

Sacred Heart Building Corp.
Sacred Heart

St. Cloud Opportunities
St. Cloud

St. James Industries Foundation
St. James

St. Peter Industries Foundation
St. Peter

Sauk Centre Industries, Inc.
Sauk Centre

Limit Products, Inc.
Slayton

Business Development Committee
South St. Paul

Spring Valley Area Development Corp.
Spring Valley

Springfield Business & Industrial
   Development Committee
Springfield

Business & Industrial Development
   Committee
Stillwater Development Corp.
Stillwater

Thief River Falls Jobs, Inc.
Thief River Falls

Tracy Enterprises, Inc.
Tracy

Truman Business & Industrial Development
   Committee
Truman

New Industry Committee
Tyler

Virginia Chamber of Commerce Industrial
   Committee
Virginia

Wabasha Industries, Inc.
Wabasha

Waconia Improvement Association, Inc.
Waconia

Wadena Industrial Corp.
Wadena

Walkerites Associated
Walker

Wells Development Corp.
Wells

White Bear Lake Area Development Corp.
White Bear Lake

Willmar Industries, Inc.
Willmar

Industrial Development Committee
Windom

Winnebago Development Co.
Winnebago

Winona Industrial Development
   Association
Winona

Worthington Industries, Inc.
Worthington

Zumbrota Development Corp.
Zumbrota

MISSISSIPPI

Greenville Industrial Development Council
Greenville

Industrial Development Corporation of
   Greater Jackson
Jackson

Pontotoc County Development Foundation
Pontotoc County

Community Development Foundation
Tupelo

Chickasaw County Development Foundation
Houston

Yazoo County Industrial Development Corp.
Yazoo

Industrial Development Corp.
Greenwood-Le Flore

Jackson County Industrial Development Foundation
Pascagoola

Union County Development Foundation
New Albany

MISSOURI

Adrian Development Corp.
Adrian

Industrial Development Corp.
Albany

Industrial Development Corp.
Arcadia

Ash Grove Industrial Development Corp.
Ash Grove

Ava Industrial Development Corp.
Ava

Belle Builders
Belle

Bernie Development Corp.
Bernie

Bethany Industrial Development Corp.
Bethany

Bolivar Industrial Development Corp.
Bolivar

Boonville Industrial Corp.
Boonville

Industrial Development Corp.
Bourbon

Bowling Green Industrial Development Co., Inc.

Bowling Green Building Corp.
Bowling Green

Branson-Hollister Industrial Development Corp.
Branson-Hollister

Industrial Development Corp.
Barymer

Brookfield Industrial Development Corp.
Brookfield

Buffalo Industrial Development Corp.
Buffalo

Butler Industrial Development Corp.
Butler

Cabool Development Corp.
Cabool

California Industrial Development Corp.
California

Camdenton Industrial Development Corp.
Camdenton

Cameron Industrial Development Corp.
Cameron

Community Industrial Development Corp.
Cape Girardeau

Carl Junction Industrial Development Corp.
Carl Junction

Carrollton Development Company
Carrollton

Carthage Industrial Development Corp.
Carthage

Caruthersville Industrial Development Corp.
Caruthersville

Cassville Industrial Development Corp.
Cassville

Centralia Industrial Development Corp.
Centralia

Chaffee Industrial Development Association
Chaffee

Charleston Industrial Development Co.
Charleston

Chillicothe Industrial Development Corp.
Chillicothe

Clinton Industrial Development Corp.
Clinton

Columbia Industrial Development Corp.
Columbia

Concordia Industrial Development Co.
Concordia

Crocker Industrial Corp.
Crocker Industrial Building Corp.
Crocker

Cuba Development Co.
Cuba

De Soto Industrial Development Corp.
De Soto

Dexter Development Corp.
Dexter

Dixon Factories, Inc.
Dixon

East Prairie Business Men's Association, Inc.
East Prairie

Marshfield Development Corp.
Eldon

Marshfield Development Corp.
El Dorado Springs

Ellington Industries, Inc.
Ellington

Farmington Expansion Corp.
Farmington

Howard County Development Corp.
Fayette

Fulton Industrial Development Corp.
Fulton

Gallatin Industrial Development Corp.
Gallatin

The Gasconade Industrial Development Corp.
Gasconade

Industrial Development Corp.
Gilman City

Granby Development Corp.
Granby

Greenfield Industrial Development Corp.
Greenfield

Hamilton Development Corp.
Hamilton

Hannibal Industrial Development Co.
Hannibal

Harrisonville Civic Association, Inc.
Harrisonville

The Hermann Industrial Development Corp.
Hermann

Higginsville Development Co.
Higginsville

Holden Industrial Committee
Holden

Houston Development Co.
Houston

Illmo Development Corp.
Illmo

Independence Area Development Corp.
Independence

Irondale Industrial Development Corp.
Irondale

Capital City Industrial Corp.
Jefferson City

Joplin Industrial Development Corp.
Joplin

Kahoka Industrial Development Organization, Inc.
Kahoka

Kennett Development Corp.
Kennett

Kirksville Industrial Development Corp.
Kirksville

Lebanon Industrial Corp.
Lebanon

Lee's Summit Industrials
Lee's Summit

Lexington Industrial Development Corp.
Lexington

Lilbourn Industrial Corp.
Lilbourn

Licking Development Corp.
Licking

Linn Industrial Development Corp.
Linn

Louisiana Industrial Development Corp.
Louisiana

Macon Industrial Development Corp.
Macon

Malden Industrial Commission
Malden

Mansfield Industrial Development Corp.
Mansfield

Marshall Industrial Development Corp.
Marshall

Marshfield Development Corp.
Marshfield

Industrial Development Corp.
Maryville

Memphis Industrial Development Corp.
Memphis

Mexico Industrial Corp.
Mexico

Moberly Development Co.
Moberly

Montgomery Industrial Corp.
Montgomery

Morrison Industrial Development Corp.
Morrison

Mound City Industrial Development
    Corp.
Mound City

Mountain Grove Industrial Development
    Association
Mountain Grove

Industrial Development Corp.
Mountain View

Neosho Industrial Development Corp.
Neosho

Nevada Industrial Development Corp.
Nevada

Newburg Development Co.
Newburg

New Madrid Development Co., Inc.
New Madrid

Norborne Development Co.
Norborne

North Kansas City Development Co.
North Kansas City

Odessa Development Co., Inc.
Odessa

Owensville Industrial Corp.
Owensville

Industrial Development Corp.
Palmyra

Platte County Development Association
Parkville

The Parma Industrial Committee
Parma

Pattonsburg Industrial Development Corp.
Pattonsburg

Perryville Development Corp.
Perryville

Industrial Development Corp.
Piedmont

Pineville Industrial Corp.
Pineville

Poplar Bluff Industries, Inc.
Poplar Bluff

Portageville Development Corp.
Portageville

Puxico Industrial Development Corp.
Puxico

Rich Hill Development Co.
Rich Hill

Richland Development Corp.
Richland

Rolla Industries, Inc.
Rolla

St. Joseph Industrial Development Corp.
St. Joseph

Salem Industrial Building Corp.
Salem

Salisbury Development Co.
Salisbury

Sarcoxie Industrial Co.
Sarcoxie

Senath Industrial Development
    Commission
Senath

The Seymour Industrial Development
    Corp.
Seymour

Sikeston Industrial Development Co.
Sikeston

Slater Development Corp.
Slater

Industrial Development of Springfield
Springfield

Stanberry Development Corp.
Stanberry

Steele Factory Committee
Steele

Thayer Development Co., Inc.
Thayer

Tipton Realty Co.
Tipton

Troy Realty Co.
Troy

Union Development Corp.
Union

Unionville Industrial Development Corp.
Unionville

Vandalia Industrial & Development Corp.
Vandalia

Warrensburg Industrial Development Corp.
Warrensburg

Warrenton Development Co.
Warrenton

Washington Civic Industrial Corp.
Washington

Webb City Factory Holding Corp.
Webb City

West Plains Development Corp.
West Plains

Willow Springs Development Corp.
Willow Springs

Winona Industrial Development Corp.
Winona

Carter Industrial Corp.
Carter

Steelville Enterprises, Inc.
Steelville

United Commercial Co. of Rich Hill, Inc.
Rich Hill

Sedalia Improvement Association, Inc.
Sedalia

Bell City Industrial Development Corp.
Bell City

Brunswick Development Co.
Brunswick

Canton Development, Inc.
Canton

New Haven Industrial Development Corp.
New Haven

St. Louis Chamber of Commerce Industrial Park Corp.

St. Louis Chamber of Commerce Industrial Development Corp.
St. Louis

Windsor Development Corp.
Windsor

Elsberry Industrial Development Corp.
Ellsberry

Jackson Industrial Development Corp.
Jackson

East Perry Development Association
Frohna

Jonesburg Enterprise, Inc.
Jonesburg

Joplin-Southern Corp.
Joplin

Marceline Development Corp.
Marceline

Civic Industrial Association
St. Joseph

MONTANA

Havre Development Co.
Havre

Flathead Development Committee, Inc.
Kalispell

Whitefish Development Co., Inc.
Whitefish

NEBRASKA

Albion Industrial Development Corp.
Albion

Alliance Development Corp.
Alliance

Lincoln Industrial Development Corp.
Aurora

Beatrice Development Corp.
Beatrice

Blair Industrial Development Corp.
Blair

Bridgeport Industrial Corp.
Bridgeport

Chadron Industrial Development Committee
Chadron

Industries, Inc.
Columbus

Cozad Industrial Development Corp.
Cozad

Crete Industries, Inc.
Crete

Fairbury Industrial Development Corp.
Fairbury

Falls City Improvement Corp.
Falls City

Fremont Industries, Inc.
Fremont

Gering Industrial Development Corp.
Gering

Gothenburg Industrial Development Corp.
Gothenburg

Grand Island Industrial Foundation
Grand Island

Hastings Corp.
Hastings

Holdrege Industrial and Development Corp.
Holdrege

Imperial Industrial Development Corp.
Imperial

Greater Kearney Corp.
Kearney

Lincoln Industrial Development Corp.
Lincoln

McCook Corp.
McCook

Minden Industrial Corp.
Minden

Nebraska City Industries, Inc.
Nebraska City

Greater Norfolk Corp.
Norfolk

North Platte Development Corp.
North Platte

Oakland Industrial Development Corp.
Oakland

Omaha Industrial Foundation
Omaha

Scotts Bluff Industrial Development Corp.
Scotts Bluff

Sidney Industrial Development Corp.
Sidney

Wahoo Industries, Inc.
Wahoo

Wayne Industries, Inc.
Wayne

York Industries, Inc.
York

NEVADA

Southern Nevada Industrial Foundation
Las Vegas

NEW HAMPSHIRE

Berlin Industrial Realty Corp.
Berlin

Claremont Industrial Parks, Inc.
Claremont

Concord Regional Development Corp.
Concord

New Hampshire Business Development Corp.
Concord

Conway Industrial Development Corp.
Conway

Derry Industrial Development Corp.
Derry

Dover Development Corp.
Dover

Exeter Industrial Development Corp.
Exeter

Franklin Developments, Inc.
Franklin

Franklin Savings Bank
Franklin

Farmington Industrial Development Corp.
Farmington

Greenville Development Corp.
Greenville

Hillsboro Industries, Inc.
Hillsboro

Keene Development Co.
Keene

Laconia Industrial Development Co., Inc.
Laconia

Lebanon Industrial Development Association
Lebanon

Lisbon Development Co., Inc.
Lisbon

Amoskeag Industries, Inc.
Manchester

Nashua-New Hampshire Foundation
Nashua

Newmarket Industrial Associates, Inc.
Newmarket

Newport Industries, Inc.
Newport

Plymouth Industrial Development Corp.
Plymouth

Chamber of Commerce
Portsmouth

Raymond Industrial Associates
Raymond

Greater Rochester Development Corp.
Rochester

Sunapee Corp.
Sunapee

Tilton-Northfield Development Association
Tilton

Whitefield Industrial Corp.
Whitefield

Woodsville Area Industries, Inc.
Woodsville

NEW JERSEY

The New Jersey Department of Conservation and Economic Development reports that there are no incorporated (private) community groups in New Jersey that have capital funds for investment in industrial development. A recently enacted law, however, authorizes the establishment of local business development corporations in the state.

NEW MEXICO

Alamagordo Industrial Development Corp.
Alamogordo

NEW YORK

Industries for Amsterdam, Inc.
Amsterdam

Antwerp Development Corp.
Antwerp

Industrial Development Foundation of Auburn, Inc.
Auburn

New Industries for Binghamton, Inc.
Binghamton

Rockland Industrial Center, Inc.
Blauvelt

Bolivar Industrial Development Corp.
Bolivar

Canandaigua Industrial Development Corp.
Canandaigua

Catskill Industrial Development Co., Inc.
Catskill

Cohoes Industrial Terminal, Inc.
Cohoes

Cortland County Industrial Development Co., Inc.
Cortland

Dolgeville Realty Corp.
Dolgeville

Elmira-Corning Industrial Development, Inc.

Elmira Association of Community Industrial Development Council

Elmira Enterprises, Inc.
Elmira

Fort Plain-Nelliston Industrial and Development Corp.
Fort Plain

Long Island Association
Garden City

Garnerville Holding Co., Inc.
Garnerville

Geneva Industrial, Inc.
Geneva

Fulton County Community Development Corp.
Gloversville

Hoosick Falls Committee for Industry, Inc.
Hoosick Falls

Hornell Enterprises, Inc.
Hornell

Horseheads Industrial Center
Horseheads Industrial Development Corp.
Horseheads

Industries for Columbia County, Inc.
Hudson

Ithaca Enterprise, Inc.
Ithaca

Jamestown Area Development Corp.
Jamestown

Fulton County Community Development Corp.
Johnstown

Industries for Columbia County, Inc.
Kinderhook

Kingston Industrial Development Corp.
Kingston

Federated Communities, Inc.
Lake George

Liberty Industries Development Corp.
Liberty

Twin Cities Development Corp.
Manchester-Shortsville

General Industrial Development Corp.
Manhasset

Middletown Community Development Corp.
Middletown

Orange County Industrial Site Placement Service, Inc.
Monroe

Wallkill Valley Industrial Development Association
Montgomery

Monticello Industrial Development Corp.
Monticello

Mount Kisco Project Corp.
Mount Kisco

Greater Newburgh Industrial Development Corp.
Newburgh

Civic and Community Association
New Rochelle

Chenango County Industrial Fund, Inc.
Norwich

Olean Development Corp.
Olean

Oneida Area Industrial Development Fund, Inc.
Oneida

Operation Oswego, Inc.
Oswego

New Industries for Plattsburgh, Inc.
Plattsburgh

Port Jervis Community Development, Inc.
Port Jervis

Rochester Industrial Terminal Corp.
Rochester

Saranac Lake Industrial Development Realty Corp.
Saranac Lake

Schenectady Industrial Development Corp.
Schenectady

Utica Industrial Corp.
Utica

New Industries for Vestal, Inc.
Vestal

Walton Industrial Development, Inc.
Walton

Warsaw Community Development Co., Inc.
Warsaw

Jefferson County Development Corp.
Watertown

Valley Economic Development Association, Inc.
Waverly

Home Town Improvement Corp.
Whitehall

NORTH CAROLINA

Ahoskie Development Corp.
Ahoskie

Stanly County Development Corp.
Albemarle

Angier Development Co.
Angier

Burlington Industrial Development Corp.
Burlington

Chadbourn Development Corp.
Chadbourn

Clarkton Community Development Corp.
Clarkton

Clinton Development Corp.
Clinton

Dobson Realty Co.
Dobson

Dunn Investors, Inc.
Dunn

Durham Committee of 100
Durham

Albemarle Industries, Inc.
Elizabeth City

Elizabethtown Development Corp.
Elizabethtown

Edenton Development Corp.
Edenton

Fairmont Development Corp.
Fairmont

Farmville Economic Council, Inc.
Farmville

Fayetteville Area Industrial Development Corp.
Fayetteville

The Forest City Co., Inc.
Forest City

Garland Development Corp.
Garland

Gastonia Industrial Realty Corp.
Gastonia

Goldsboro Industries, Inc.
Goldsboro

Greenville Industries, Inc.
Greenville

Hamlet Industrial Development Corp.
Hamlet

Hickory Development Corp.
Hickory

Agricultural and Industrial Commission
   for Orange County
Hillsboro

Ashe County Development Corp.
Jefferson

Kernersville Industrial Development Corp.
Kernersville

Kinston Development Corp.
Kinston

Lexington Industrial Corp.
Lexington

Lillington Industrial Development Co., Inc.
Lillington

Lincoln County Development Corp.
Lincolnton

Littleton Development Corp.
Littleton

Lumberton Development Co.
Lumberton

Marshville Development Corp.
Marshville

Maxton Development Corp.
Maxton

Middlesex Development Corp.
Middlesex

Mocksville Development Corp.
Mocksville

Union County Industrial Development
   Commission
Monroe

Mooresville Development Corp.
Mooresville

Mount Holly Industrial Development Corp.
Mount Holly

Nashville Industrial Development Corp.
Nashville

New Bern Industries, Inc.
New Bern

Wilkes County Industrial Development
   Corp.
North Wilkesboro

Oxford Future Industries
Oxford

Pittsboro Development Corp.
Pittsboro

Raleigh Industrial Building Corp.
Raleigh

Red Springs Development Corp.
Red Springs

Reidsville Development Corp.
Reidsville

Rich Square Improvement Corp.
Rich Square

Robbins Development Corp.
Robbins

Industrial Development Corp.
Rockingham

Rocky Mount Industrial Development Corp.
Rocky Mount

Roxboro Development Corp.
Roxboro

Salemburg Industrial Council
Salemburg

Shelby Industrial Development, Inc.
Shelby

Spring Hope Development Co.
Spring Hope

Smithfield Development Corp.
Smithfield Industrial Development Corp.
Smithfield

Jackson County Industries, Inc.
Sylva

Tabor Industrial Development Enterprises,
   Inc.
Tabor City

Alexander Development Corp.
Taylorsville

Valdese Industrial Development Board,
   Inc.
Valdese

Anson Industrial Corp.
Wadesboro

Wake Forest Industrial Corp.
Wake Forest

Warren County Development Co.
Warrenton

Duplin County Industrial Council
Warsaw

Washington Industrial Development Corp.
Washington

Waxhaw Development Corp.
Waxhaw

Haywood Industrial Development Corp.
Waynesville

Industrial Development Corp.
Williamston

Wingate Development Corp.
Wingate

NORTH DAKOTA

Bismarck Industries, Inc.
Bismarck

Devils Lake Community Development Corp.
Devils Lake

Fargo Development Corp.
Fargo

Grand Forks Industrial Foundation, Inc.
Grand Forks

Grafton Development Corp.
Grafton

Hatton Development Corp.
Hatton

Jamestown Industrial Development Corp.
Jamestown

Mayville Development Corp.
Mayville

Rugby Economic Development Corp.
Rugby

Valley City Development Corp.
Valley City

Wahpeton Commercial Development Corp.
Wahpeton

Three additional communities are in the process of organizing development corporations, Williston, Minot, and Dickinson.

OHIO

Alliance Development Corp.
Alliance

Ashland Industrial Development Corp.
Ashland

Ashtabula Industrial Corp.
Ashtabula

Bellaire New Industries, Inc.
Bellaire

Cambridge Community Industrial Association
Cambridge

Canton Development Corp.
Canton

Carey Industrial Development Organization
Carey

Carroll County Industrial Council
Carrollton

Ohio Valley Improvement Association, Inc.
Cincinnati

Dresser Industries, Inc.
Cleveland

Clyde, Ohio, Community Development Corp.
Clyde

Peoples Development Co.
Columbus

Conneaut Buildings, Inc.
Conneaut

Delta Industrial Development Association
Delta

Deshler Industrial Development Co.
Deshler

Tuscarawas Valley Development Committee
Dover

Lorain County Development Committee, Inc.
Elyria

Fostoria Community Industrial Association
Fostoria

Genoa Development Co.
Genoa

Greenville Chamber of Commerce, Inc.
Greenville

Hillsboro Industrial Development Council
Hillsboro

Jackson Chamber of Commerce
Jackson

Jefferson Development Corp.
Jefferson

Leipsic Industrial Development Co.
Leipsic

Lodi Development Corp.
Lodi

Massillon Industrial Development Corp.
Massillon

Mount Vernon Area Development
Foundation, Inc.
Mount Vernon

Newcomerstown Industrial Corp.
Newcomerstown

New Paris Development Council
New Paris

New Philadelphia Industrial Building
Corp.
New Philadelphia

New Washington Industrial Development
Corp.
New Washington

Oak Harbor Development Co.
Oak Harbor

Oakwood Development Co.
Oakwood

Pierpont Development Co.
Pierpont

Perry County Development Council
New Lexington

Port Clinton Development Co.
Port Clinton

Portsmouth Industrial Development Corp.
Portsmouth

Shelby Industrial Development
Shelby

Springeld Development Council
Springfield

Tiffin Industrial Council, Tiffin Chamber
of Commerce
Tiffin

Toledo Industrial Council, Inc.
Toledo

Wadsworth Development Corp.
Wadsworth

Washington Court House Industrial
Development Corp.
Washington Court House

Wellston Development & Improvement Co.
Wellston

Wellshire Development Corp.
Wellshire

Willard Industrial Development Co.
Willard

Lake County Industrial Development
Council, Inc.
Willoughby

Wooster Expansion Corp.
Wooster

Greater Youngstown Area Foundation
Youngstown

OKLAHOMA

Ada Industrial Development Corp.
Ada

Alva Industrial Foundation, Inc.
Alva

Anadarko Industries, Inc.
Anadarko

Pushmataha Foundation
Antlers

Ardmore Industrial Development Corp.
Ardmore

Bartlesville Industrial Development Corp.
Bartlesville

Chandler Industrial Foundation
Chandler

Cherokee Industries, Inc.
Cherokee

Grady Industries, Inc.
Chickasha

Claremore, Inc.
Claremore

Cleveland Industrial Corp.
Cleveland

Cordell Industrial Foundation
Cordell

Cushing Development Trusteeship
Cushing

Duncan Industrial Foundation
Duncan

Durant Industrial Foundation, Inc.
Durant

Eldorado Industrial Association
Eldorado

Elk City Industrial Foundation
Elk City

El Reno Industrial Foundation, Inc.
El Reno

Enid Industrial Development Corp.
Enid

Fairview Industrial Foundation, Inc.
Fairview

Frederick, Inc.
Frederick

Guthrie Foundation, Inc.
Guthrie

Hobart Industrial, Inc.
Hobart

**Industrial Development Corp. of Hugo
Choctaw County Industrial Foundation,
Inc.**
Hugo

Greater Lawton, Inc.
Lawton

Mangum Industrial Foundation
Mangum

Greater Marlow, Inc.
Marlow

**McAlester Foundation
McAlester Industries, Inc.**
McAlester

Miami Industrial Development Corp.
Miami

Muskogee Industrial Foundation, Inc.
Muskogee

Nowata Industrial Foundation
Nowata

Oklahoma Industries, Inc.
Oklahoma City

**Pauls Valley Industrial Development
Foundation**
Pauls Valley

Ponca City Industrial Foundation, Inc.
Ponca City

Poteau Industrial Corp.
Poteau

**Purcell Industrial Development Council,
Inc.**
Purcell

Sayre Industrial Foundation, Inc.
Sayre

Seminole Industrial Foundation, Inc.
Seminole

Stillwater Industrial Foundation, Inc.
Stillwater

Vinita Industries, Inc.
Vinita

Greater Tulsa, Inc.
Tulsa

Walters Industrial Foundation
Walters

Watonga Industries, Inc.
Watonga

Woodward Industrial Development Corp.
Woodward

OREGON

Astoria Industrial Development Corp.
Astoria

The Benton Industries Foundation, Inc.
Corvallis

**Forest Grove Industrial Development
Committee, Inc.**
Forest Grove

**Josephine County Development
Commission**
Grants Pass

Hillsboro Industrial Development Corp.
Hillsboro

LaGrande Industrial Promotions, Inc.
LaGrande

**Lebanon Industrial Development
Foundation**
Lebanon

McMinnville Industrial Promotions, Inc.
McMinnville

Newberg Industrial Development Corp.
Newberg

Sheridan Industrial Promotions, Inc.
Sheridan

PENNSYLVANIA

Altoona Enterprises, Inc.
Altoona

Ashland Industrial Promotion Corp.
Ashland

Slate Belt Development Corp.
Bangor

Bellefonte Industrial Development Corp.
Bellefonte

Berwick Industrial Plan, Inc.
Berwick

**Cambridge Springs Area Industrial
Development Corp.**
Cambridge Springs

Carbondale-Lackawanna Industrial
Development Co., Inc.
Carbondale

Connellsville Chamber of Commerce
Connellsville

Corry Building Corp.
Corry

Dushore Industries, Inc.
Dushore

Ellwood City Industrial Development Corp.
Ellwood City

Greater Erie Industrial Development Corp.
Erie

Franklin Chamber of Commerce
Franklin

Freeland Industrial Development Corp.
Freeland

Reynolds Development Corp.
Greenville

The Grove City Industrial Development
Corp.
Grove City

Hastings Area Development Association
Hastings

Greater Hazleton Community Area New
Development Organization, Inc.
Hazleton

Industrial Development Commission of the
Chamber of Commerce
Huntingdon

Indiana Development Corp.
Indiana

Industrial Association of Jim Thorpe
Jim Thorpe

Johnstown Industrial Development Corp.
Johnstown

Lebanon County Chamber of Commerce
Lebanon

Lewistown Industrial Development Corp.
Lewistown

Littlestown Industrial Development Corp.
Littlestown

Mahonoy City Industrial Corp.
Mahonoy

Meadville Industrial Development Corp.
Meadville

Mount Carmel District Industrial Fund,
Inc.
Mount Carmel

Industrial Real Estate Co.
Mount Pleasant

Greater Huntingdon County Industrial
Development Council
Mount Union

Nanticoke Industrial Development Fund,
Inc.
Nanticoke

New Bethlehem Area Development Corp.
New Bethlehem

Oil City Chamber of Commerce
Oil City

Patton Industrial Commission; Chamber of
Commerce
Patton

New Industries Commission, Greater
Pittston Chamber of Commerce
Pittston

Tawney Industrial Development Corp.
Punxsutawney

Greater Pottsville Industrial Development
Corp.
Pottsville

Greater Berks Development Fund, Inc.
Reading

Area Industrial Development Corp.
Saltsburg

Lackawanna Industrial Fund Enterprises
Scranton

Shamokin and Coal Township Chamber of
Commerce
Shamokin

Industrial Promotion Committee of the
Chamber of Progress
Shenandoah

Smethport Chamber of Commerce
Smethport

Monroe County Industry, Inc.
Stroudsburg

Sunbury Area Industrial Development Plan
Sunbury

Tamaqua Chamber of Commerce
Tamaqua

Greater Uniontown Industrial Fund
Uniontown

Green County Industrial Developments, Inc.
Waynesburg

Industrial Commission of the Chamber of Commerce
Wellsboro

Greater Wilkes-Barre Industrial Fund, Inc.
Wilkes-Barre

Greater Williamsport Chamber of Commerce
Williamsport

Windber Community Development Association
Windber

RHODE ISLAND

Coventry Industrial Foundation
Coventry

Portsmouth Development Corp.
Portsmouth

Industrial Development Foundation of Greater Woonsocket
Woonsocket

SOUTH CAROLINA*

I. County development boards (established by law): Abbeville, Aiken, Bamberg, Beaufort, Calhoun, Charleston, Cherokee, Chester, Darlington, Fairfield, Georgetown, Greenwood, Horry, Jasper, Laurens, Lexington, Newberry, Oconee, Orangeburg, Pickens, Richland, Spartanburg, Williamsburg, York.
II. Local chamber of commerce development committees: Allendale, Anderson, Barnwell, Berkeley, Chesterfield, Clarendon, Colleton, Dillon, Dorchester, Florence, Greenville, Kershaw, Lancaster, Sumter.
III. Private community development committees: Edgefield, Hampton, Lee, Marlboro, Saluda, Union.
* The State Development Board reports no local development corporations. Development activities are carried on by the county development boards (established by law) and by the chamber of commerce and private development committees listed above.

SOUTH DAKOTA

Aberdeen Development Corp.
Aberdeen

Brookings Industrial Development Corp.
Brookings

Flandreau Development Corp.
Flandreau

Hayti Improvement Corp.
Hayti

Huron Industries Foundation, Inc.
Huron

Madison Industrial Foundation
Madison

Mitchell Industrial Development Corp.
Mitchell

Pierre Progress, Inc.
Pierre

Rapid City Industries, Inc.
Rapid City

Sioux Falls Industrial and Development Foundation, Inc.
Sioux Falls

Watertown Development Corp.
Watertown

Greater Woonsocket Industrial Development Foundation
Woonsocket

Greater Yankton Industries
Yankton

TENNESSEE

Alamo Development Corp.
Alamo

Alexandria Industrial Development Corp.
Alexandria

Ashland City Industrial Corp.
Ashland City

Athens Industrial Development Corp.
Athens

Baxter Industrial Development Corp.
Baxter

Cherokee Industrial Development Corp.
Benton

Bolivar Development Corp.
Bolivar

Bradford Investment Co.
Bradford

Bristol Industrial Development Corp.
Bristol

Benton County Development Association
Camden

Carthage Industries, Inc.
Carthage

Chapel Hill Industrial Development Corp.
Chapel Hill

Industrial Committee of 100
Chattanooga

Clairborne County Industrial Corp.
Clairborne

Greater Clarksville Foundation
Clarksville

Anderson County Industrial Development Commission
Clinton

Collierville Industrial Committee
Collierville

Maury Industrial Development Corp.
Columbia

Putnam Industrial Association, Inc.
Cookeville

Cordova Industrial Development Co.
Cordova

Covington Development Corp.
Covington

Agricultural, Industrial & Tourist Development Committee
Crossville

Meigs County Agricultural & Industrial Improvement Association
Decatur

Peoples Industrial Development Corp.
Decaturville

Dickson Industrial Trust
Dickson

Steward County Industrial Development Corp.
Dover

Dresden Development Corp.
Dresden

Dunlap Bldg. & Real Estate Co.
Dunlap

Dyer County Foundation, Inc.
Dyersburg

Carter County Foundation
Elizabethton

Englewood Industrial Development Association
Englewood

Erin Industrial Committee
Erin

Etowah Building & Developers, Inc.
Etowah

Franklin Industrial Corp.
Franklin

Gallatin Industrial Development Association
Gallatin

Goodlettsville Improvement Co.
Goodlettsville

Grand Junction Industrial Corp.
Grand Junction

Greene County Foundation, Inc.
Greeneville

Greenfield Development Co., Inc.
Greenfield

Halls Industrial Commission & Development Co.
Halls

Hartsville Businessmen's Association
Hartsville

Humboldt Jobs & Industries, Inc.
Humboldt

Huntland Development Corp.
Huntland

The Jackson Foundation
Jackson

Fentress Development Corp.
Jamestown

Jellico Development Association, Inc.
Jellico

Johnson City Industrial Development Corp.
Johnson City

Kenton Development Corp.
Kenton

Greater Knoxville Development Corp.
Knoxville

Macon Industrial Corp.
Lafayette

La Follette Development Corp.
La Follette

Lake City Development Corp.
Lake City

Lexington Industrial Improvement Association, Inc.
Lexington

Overton County Development Corp.
Livingston

Loudon Development Corp.
Loudon

Madisonville Developers Club
Madisonville

Manchester Industrial Corp.
Manchester

Martin Development Corp.
Martin

McMinnville Development Corp.
McMinnville

Mount Pleasant Industrial Development Corp.
Mount Pleasant

Murfreesboro Industrial Development Corp.
Murfreesboro

Nashville Industrial Development Co.
Nashville

Newbern Industrial Development Corp.
Newbern

Industrial Promotion, Inc.
New Tazewell

Norris Corp.
Norris

Obion Industrial & Development Corp.
Obion

Paris Industries, Inc.
Paris

Petersburg Community Corp.
Petersburg

Bledsoe Manufacturers, Inc.
Pikesville

Ashland City Industrial Corp.
Pleasant View

Portland Development Corp.
Portland

Pulaski Industrial Commission
Pulaski

Ridgely Development Corp.
Ridgely

Ripley Industrial Corp.
Ripley

Hardin County Industrial Committee
Saltillo

Scotts Hill Industrial Corp.
Scotts Hill

Sevierville Industries, Inc.
Sevierville

Sharon Development Corp.
Sharon

Industrial Service-Development Corp.
Shelbyville

Epiphany Corp.
Sherwood

Somerville Building Corp.
Somerville

Sparta Industrial Development Corp.
Sparta

Spring City Industrial Development Committee
Spring City

Springfield Industrial Development Corp.
Springfield

Sweetwater Industrial & Agricultural Development Association
Sweetwater

Lake County Development Corp.
Tiptonville

Toone Industrial Development Corp.
Toone

Trenton Agricultural & Industrial Corp.
Trenton

Tullahome Development Co.
Tullahoma

Obion County Industrial Corp.
Union City

Morgan County Industrial Development Association
Wartburg

Franklin County Development Corp.
Winchester Merchants Association
Winchester

TEXAS

Alice Industrial Foundation
Alice

Atlanta Industrial Foundation, Inc.
Atlanta

Belton Industrial Board
Belton

Big Spring Industrial Foundation, Inc.
Big Spring

Bonham Industrial Foundation, Inc.
Bonham

Bowie Industrial Foundation, Inc.
Bowie

Brenham Industrial Foundation, Inc.
Brenham

Chamber of Commerce Industrial and
  Development Fund
Brownwood

Bryan Industrial Foundation, Inc.
Bryan

Cameron Industrial Foundation
Cameron

Center Development Foundation
Center

Childress Industrial Corp.
Childress

Cisco Foundation, Inc.
Cisco

Red River County Industrial Foundation
Clarksville

Columbus Industrial Foundation
Columbus

Commerce Industrial Development
  Association
Commerce

Conroe Industrial Foundation, Inc.
Conroe

Corsicana Industrial Foundation, Inc.
Corsicana

Crockett Industrial Foundation, Inc.
Crockett

Denton Industrial, Inc.
Denton

Maverick County Development Corp.
Eagle Pass

Edinburg Industrial, Inc.
Edinburg

Industrial Fund of the Ennis Chamber
  of Commerce
Ennis

Gainesville Industrial Foundation, Inc.
Gainesville

Grandview Industrial Foundation
Grandview

Grapeland Industrial Foundation, Inc.
Grapeland

Greenville Industrial Development
  Fund, Inc.
Greenville

Groesbeck Industrial Foundation, Inc.
Groesbeck

Henderson Industrial District
Henderson

Hill County Industrial Development
  Foundation, Inc.
Hillsboro

Jacksonville Municipal Development
  Fund
Jacksonville

Jasper Industrial Development Corp.
Jasper

Kernes Industrial Foundation
Kernes

Kilgore Industrial Foundation, Inc.
Kilgore

Killeen Industrial Foundation, Inc.
Killeen

La Grange Industrial Foundation
La Grange

Lufkin Industrial Foundation, Inc.
Lufkin

Marlin Civic Industrial Corp.
Marlin

Marshall Industrial, Inc.
Marshall

Mart Industrial Association
Mart

McGregor Civic Enterprises, Inc.
McGregor

Mexia Industrial Foundation
Mexia

The Midland Industrial Plan, Inc.
Midland

Mineola Industrial Foundation
Mineola

Mineral Wells Industrial Foundation
Mineral Wells

Mount Pleasant Industrial Foundation
Mount Pleasant

Franklin County Industrial Foundation
Mount Vernon

Nacogdoches County Industrial Foundation
Nacogdoches

Navasota Industrial Foundation
Navasota

Palestine Industrial Foundation, Inc.
Palestine

Paris Texas Industrial Foundation, Inc.
Paris

Pittsburg Industrial Foundation
Pittsburg

Raymondville Industrial Foundation, Inc.
Raymondville

Robstown Industrial Foundation, Inc.
Robstown

San Angelo Industrial, Inc.
San Angelo

San Marcos Industrial Foundation, Inc.
San Marcos

Texas Industrial and Development Foundation, Inc.
Sequin

Sherman Industrial Foundation, Inc.
Sherman

Smithville Industrial Foundation
Smithville

Hopkins County Industrial Foundation
Sulphur Spring

Taylor Agricultural and Industrial Foundation
Taylor

Temple Industrial Development Corp.
Temple

Terrell Industrial Foundation, Inc.
Terrell

Texarkana Industrial Foundation, Inc.
Texarkana

Tyler Industrial Foundation, Inc.
Tyler

Vernon Industrial Foundation, Inc.
Vernon

Weatherford Industrial Plan, Inc.
Weatherford

Wharton Civic Development Foundation
Wharton

Chamber of Commerce Industrial Fund
Whitesboro

Wichita Falls Industrial Foundation
Wichita Falls

Winnsboro Industrial Foundation
Winnsboro

UTAH

Davis County Industrial Bureau
Layton

Sanpete County Industrial Development Committee
Manti

Weber County Industrial Bureau
Ogden

Eastern Utah, Inc.
Price

VERMONT

{**Big Mill, Inc.**
Industrial Development Committee of Chamber of Commerce
Bennington

New Industries Committee
Brattleboro

Greater Burlington Industrial Corp.
Burlington

Ludlow Industries Group, Inc.
Ludlow

Montpelier Area Development Association
Montpelier

Chamber of Commerce
Poultney

Border Towns Development Corp.
Richford

New Industries, Inc.
Rutland

St. Albans Industries, Inc.
St. Albans

Industrial Development Fund
St. Johnsbury

{**Chamber of Commerce**
Industrial Development Committee
Winooski Development Corp.
Winooski

VIRGINIA

Abingdon Industrial Development Corp.
Abingdon

Alberta Industrial Development Association
Alberta

Alexandria Area Industrial Development
Foundation, Inc.
Alexandria

Amelia County Development Association
Amelia

Amherst Industrial Development Corp.
Amherst

Powell River Industrial Development Corp.
Appalachia

Bedford Builders, Inc.
Bedford

Blackstone Industrial Development, Inc.
Blackstone

Bluefield Industrial Development Corp.
Bluefield

Caroline County Development Corp.
Bowling Green

Boykins-Branchville Industrial Committee
Boykins

Bristol Industrial Development Corp.
Bristol

Buena Vista Development Corp.
Buena Vista

Clarksville Industrial Development Corp.
Clarksville

Clifton Forge Development Corp.
Clifton Forge

Culpeper Industrial Corp.
Culpeper

Damascus Industrial Development Corp.
Damascus

Danville Industrial Development, Inc.
Danville

Middlesex County Corp.
Deltaville

Dungannon Development Commission
Dungannon

Emporia Industrial Development Corp.
Emporia

Farmville Area Development Corp.
Farmville

Floyd County Industries, Inc.
Floyd

Fredericksburg Area Development
Committee
Fredericksburg

Front Royal-Warren Co. Development
Corp.
Front Royal

Galax Holding Corp.
Galax

Giles-New River Development Corp.
Giles.

Gordonsville Development Corp.
Gordonsville

Rockingham Development Corp.
Harrisonburg

Carroll Industrial Land Corp.
Hillsville

Kenbridge Industries, Inc.
Kenbridge

Lawrenceville Industries, Inc.
Lawrenceville

Little Cedar Building Corp.
Lebanon

Leesburg Industrial Development Corp.
Leesburg

Louisa Co. Industrial Development Corp.
Louisa

Luray Civic League, Inc.
Luray

Lynchburg Area Development Corp.
Lynchburg

Smyth County Development Corp.
Marion

Martinsville & Henry Co. Development
Association
Martinsville

McKinney Industrial & Development
Association
McKenney

New Market Industrial Development Corp.
New Market

Tidewater Virginia Development Council,
Inc.
Norfolk

Orange County Industrial Development
Corp.
Orange

Portsmouth Industrial Foundation, Inc.
Portsmouth

Powhatan Holding Corp.
Powhatan

Pulaski Development Corp.
Pulaski

Montgomery-Radford Industrial Development Corp.
Radford

Roanoke Valley Development Corp.
Roanoke

Community Industrial Development Corp.
Richlands

Campbell County Industrial Development Corp.
Rustburg

South Hill Industrial Development Corp.
South Hill

Strasburg Industrial Development Corp.
Strasburg

Essex County Development Corp.
Tappahannock

Victoria Development Corp.
Victoria

Wythe Industrial Development Corp.
Wytheville

WASHINGTON

Centralians, Inc.
Centralia

Chehalis Community Development
Chehalis

Longview Industrial Corp.
Longview

Olympia Industrial Sites, Inc.
Olympia

South Bend Industries, Inc.
South Bend

Tacoma Industrial Fund
Tacoma

Industrial Development Fund
Walla Walla

WEST VIRGINIA

Belington Industries
Belington

Bluefield Area Development Corp.
Bluefield

Bramwell Development Association
Bramwell

Grant District Improvement Association
Cairo

Jefferson County Chamber of Commerce
Charles Town

North Hancock County Development Association
Chester

Clarksburg Chamber of Commerce
Clarksburg

Wirt County Industries
Elizabeth

Elkins Industries, Inc.
Elkins

Greater Fairmont Development Association
Fairmont

Franklin Community Development Committee
Franklin

Gassaway Industrial Development Committee
Gassaway

Talyor County Board of Trade
Grafton

Calhoun Recreational and Development Center
Grantsville

Hamlin Industrial Development Association
Hamlin

Jane Lew Development Association
Jane Lew

Greenbrier Valley Industrial Association
Lewisburg

Logan County Development Corp.
Logan

Marlinton Chamber of Commerce
Marlinton

Martinsburg Development Corp.
Martinsburg

Milton Industrial Association
Milton

Moorefield Industrial Development Association
Moorefield

Morgantown Chamber of Commerce
Morgantown

Pennsboro Area Industrial Association
Pennsboro

Petersburg Development Association
Petersburg

Piedmont Industrial Development Group
Piedmont

Ravenswood Chamber of Commerce
Ravenswood

Shinnston Area Development Corp.
Shinnston

Tyler County Board of Trade
Sistersville

Roane County Chamber of Commerce
Spencer

Braxton County Development Association
Sutton

Terra Alta Development Credit Corp.
Terra Alta

Blackwater Civic Association
Thomas

Webster Springs Industrial Development
   Organization
Webster Springs

Doddridge County Development Corp.
West Union

Weston Development Corp.
Weston

Ohio Valley Industrial Corp.
Wheeling

White Sulphur Springs Industrial Corp.
White Sulphur Springs

Tug Valley Chamber of Commerce
Williamson

WISCONSIN

Abbotsford Development Corp.
Abbotsford

Algoma Industrial Development Corp.
Algoma

Amery Industrial Development Corp.
Amery

Amherst Industrial Development Corp.
Amherst

Antigo Industrial Corp.
Antigo

Appleton Industrial Development Corp.
Appleton

Arcadia Projects, Inc.
Arcadia

Ashippun Industrial Corp.
Ashippun

Ashland Area Industrial Development
   Corp.
Ashland

Baraboo Industrial Expansion Corp.
Baraboo

Barron Development Corp.
Barron

Beaver Dam Industrial Development
   Corp.
Beaver Dam

Belleville Industries, Inc.
Belleville

Berlin Industrial Development Corp.
Berlin

Birnamwood Industries, Inc.
Birnamwood

Blair Development Corp.
Blair

Blanchardville Industrial Development
   & Civic Improvement Corp.
Blanchardville

Bloomer Industrial Development Corp.
Bloomer

Blue River Community Industrial Corp.
Blue River

Boaz Development Corp.
Boaz

Bonduel Community Industries, Inc.
Bonduel

Boscobel Industrial Development Corp.
Boscobel

Boyceville Development Corp.
Boyceville

Brandon Development Corp.
Brandon

Brodhead Industrial Development, Inc.
Brodhead

Cambria Area Corp.
Cambria

Campbellsport Area Industrial
   Development Corp.
Campbellsport

Chetek Development Foundation
Chetek

Chilton Area Development Corp.
Chilton

Chippewa Falls Industrial Development Corp.
Chippewa Falls

(Greater) Clintonville, Inc.
Clintonville

Coleman Industrial Development Corp.
Coleman

Coloma Community Development Corp.
Coloma

Columbus Advancement Association
Columbus

Crandon Industries, Inc.
Crandon

Crivitz Community, Inc.
Crivitz

Cuba City Industrial Development Corp.
Cuba City

Darlington Industrial Development Corp.
Darlington

Delavan Development Co., Inc.
Delavan

Dousman Industrial Development Corp.
Dousman

Durand Area Industrial Development Corp.
Durand

Eagle Advancement Corp.
Eagle

Eagle River Area Development Corp.
Eagle River

Eau Claire Industrial Development Corp.
Eau Claire

Edgar Industrial Development Corp.
Edgar

Edgerton Industrial Development Corp.
Edgerton

Elkhorn Development Co.
Elkhorn

Ellsworth Industrial Development Corp.
Ellsworth

Elroy Industrial Development Corp.
Elroy

Endeavor Industrial Development Corp.
Endeavor

Evansville Development Corp.
Evansville

Fennimore Industrial Development Corp.
Fennimore

(Greater) Fond du Lac Corp.
Fond du Lac

Footville Development Corp.
Footville

Fort Atkinson Realty Corp.
Fort Atkinson

Fox Lake Advancement Association, Inc.
Fox Lake

Frederic Industrial Development Corp.
Frederic

Friesland Area Development Corp.
Friesland

Galesville Industrial Development Corp.
Galesville

Genoa City Industrial Expansion, Inc.
Genoa City

Gillett Industrial Development Corp.
Gillett

Glenwood City Cooperative Industrial Development Association
Glenwood City

Grafton Development Corp.
Grafton

Grantsburg Development Corp.
Grantsburg

Green Lake Development Corp.
Green Lake

Hancock Industrial Development Corp.
Hancock

Hartland Community Industrial Development Corp.
Hartland

Hayward Development Corp.
Hayward

Horicon Community Development Corp.
Horicon

Hudson and North Hudson Development Corp.
Hudson and North Hudson

Iola Area Development Corp.
Iola

Iron Ridge Development Corp.
Iron Ridge

Jackson County Development Corp. (Black River Falls)
Jackson County

Janesville Industrial Development Corp.
Janesville

Johnson Creek Area Development Corp.
Johnson Creek

Juneau Industrial Development Corp.
Juneau

Keosha Industrial Development
Foundation, Inc.
Kenosha

La Crosse County Industrial Association
La Crosse

Lake Geneva Development Corp.
Lake Geneva

Lake Mills Area Development Corp.
Lake Mills

Lancaster Industrial Development Corp.
Lancaster

Lomira Area Industrial Development Corp.
Lomira

Loyal Industries, Inc.
Loyal

Luxemburg Industrial Development Corp.
Luxemburg

Madison Improvement Corp.
Madison

Manawa Industries, Inc.
Manawa

Manitowoc Industrial Development Corp.
Manitowoc

Markesan Industrial Development
Markesan

(Greater) Marshfield, Inc.
Marshfield

Mauston Industries, Inc.
Mauston

McFarland Industrial Development Corp.
McFarland

Medford Industrial Development Corp.
Medford

Melrose Development Co., Inc.
Melrose

Menomonie Development Corp.
Menomonie

Merrill Area Development Corp.
Merrill

Middleton Industrial Development Corp.
Middleton

Milltown Development Corp.
Milltown

Mondovi Area Development Corp.
Mondovi

Monroe Industrial Development Corp.
Monroe

Montello Community Investors, Inc.
Montello

Mosinee Development Corp.
Mosinee

Mount Horeb Industrial Development Corp.
Mount Horeb

Muscoda Industrial Development Corp.
Muscoda

Necedah Development Co., Inc.
Necedah

Neillsville Industrial Development Corp.
Neillsville

New Auburn Development Association
New Auburn

New Glarus Business Association
Industrial Corp.
New Glarus

New Lisbon Industrial Development Corp.
New Lisbon

New London Industrial Opportunities, Inc.
New London

New Richmond Development Corp.
New Richmond

North Fond du Lac Area Industrial Corp.
North Fond du Lac

Oconto Development Corp.
Oconto

Ogema Area Development Corp.
Ogema

Omro Area Development Corp.
Omro

Oshkosh Industrial Development, Inc.
Oshkosh

Oxford Development Corp.
Oxford

Palmyra Area Co., Inc.
Palmyra

Pardeeville Industrial Development Corp.
Pardeeville

Park Falls Area Industrial Development
Corp.
Park Falls

Pewaukee Area Development Corp.
Pewaukee

Phillips Industrial Development Corp.
Phillips

Plainfield Industrial Development Corp.
Plainfield

Platteville Area Industrial Development Corp.
Platteville

Plymouth Industrial Development Corp.
Plymouth

Polk County Industrial Development Corp. (Osceola)
Polk

Portage Industrial Development Corp.
Portage

Port Washington Industrial Development Corp.
Port Washington

Prairie du Chien Industrial Development Corp.
Prairie du Chien

Prentice Industrial Development Corp.
Prentice

Pulaski Industries, Inc.
Pulaski

Random Lake Development Corp.
Random Lake

Redgranite Community Co., Inc.
Redgranite

Reedsburg Development Corp.
Reedsburg

Reedsville Industrial Development Corp.
Reedsville

Reeseville Community Development Corp.
Reeseville

Rice Lake Industrial Corp.
Rice Lake

Richland (Center) Development Credit Corp.
Richland

River Falls Industrial Civic Development Corp.
River Falls

Seymour Industrial Development Corp.
Seymour

Shawano Economic Development, Inc.
Shawano

Siren Industrial Development Corp.
Siren

Sparta Industrial Foundation, Inc.
Sparta

Stevens Point Industrial Development Corp.
Stevens Point

Stoughton Industrial Development Corp.
Stoughton

Stratford Industrial Corp.
Stratford

Sturgeon Bay Development Corp.
Sturgeon Bay

Sun Prairie Development Corp.
Sun Prairie

Superior Industrial Development Corp.
Superior

Suring Development, Inc.
Suring

Theresa Industrial Development Corp.
Theresa

Tomah Advancement Association
Tomah

Tomahawk Area Corp.
Tomahawk

Two Rivers Industrial Development Corp.
Two Rivers

Valders Improvement Corp.
Valders

Verona Development Corp.
Verona

Viroqua Development Association
Viroqua

Waterloo Industrial Development Corp.
Waterloo

Watertown Association of Commerce Promotive Corp.
Watertown

Waupaca Industrial Development, Inc.
Waupaca

Wautoma Industrial Development Corp.
Wautoma

Weyauwega Industrial Development Corp.
Weyauwega

Whitewater Industrial Development Corp.
Whitewater

Wild Rose Community, Inc.
Wild Rose

Winter (South Sawyer County) Industrial Development Corp.
Winter

Wisconsin Dells Area Building Co.
Wisconsin Dells

Wittenberg Industrial Development Corp.
Wittenberg

Wonewoc Development Corp.
Wonewoc

Woodville Community Industrial Corp.
Woodville

WYOMING

Laramie Developments, Inc.
Cheyenne

Albany County Industrial Fund
Laramie

CAPITAL SOURCES OF SPECIAL INTEREST

American Express Co.
65 Broadway
New York 6, N.Y.
Financial Officer: Clark B. Winter, V.P. & Treas.
Operates a worldwide specialized banking service through 400 offices in 33 countries, with correspondents in 141 other countries. Provides a variety of banking and financial services, including money orders, drafts, letters of credit, traveler's checks. Has liquid resources of over $400,000,000, including time deposits, U.S. Treasury, and corporate securities

American Research & Development Corp.
200 Berkeley St.
Boston 16, Mass.
Financial Officer: Georges Doriot, Pres.
Provides venture capital and financial backing for new and established businesses as well as for individuals and groups of individuals with new inventions, processes, etc.

Amsterdam Overseas Corp.
70 Pine St.
New York 5, N.Y.
Financial Officer: Peter Fleck, Esq., Special Agent
Financial agents for Rothschild banking interests

D. H. Blair Corp.
66 Beaver St.
New York 4, N.Y.
Financial Officer: Charles Miller, V.P.
Provides capital for variety of corporate purposes and makes collateral and "call" loans

Deak & Co.
26 Broadway
New York 4, N.Y.
Financial Officer: Otto Rothemund, V.P.
International private banking firm. Specializes in foreign exchange, international commercial banking specialties, arranging deposits and other services with Swiss banks

Deltec Panamerica, S.A.
72 Wall St.
New York 5, N. Y.
Financial Officer: Clarence Dauphinot, Jr.
Has close connections with banks, institutions and commercial and industrial interests in Mexico and other Latin-American nations; provides financing for projects in these countries

Discount Corporation
50 Pine St.
New York 5, N. Y.
Financial Officer: Andrew K. Markwald, Sr. V.P.
A special agency for banks, institutions and other financial interests in purchase and sale of bankers' acceptances, certificates of time deposit, Treasury bills and other short-term banking instruments

Empire Trust Co.
20 Broad St.
New York 4, N. Y.
Financial Officer: Berry O. Baldwin, Sr. V.P.
A commercial bank (deposits of $250,-355,000) which provides services be-

yond the range of usual commercial banking; has a wholly-owned subsidiary, Empire Resources Cor., which provides financing for selected oil, natural gas and other natural resource projects; maintains special departments for financing oil and gas situations, electronics projects, chemical programs and real estate; also maintains a Canadian department

First Boston Corp.
20 Exchange Pl.
New York 5, N. Y.
Financial Officer: Charles C. Glavin, Sr. V.P.
One of the largest publicly-owned securities underwriting and investment banking organizations; also purchases and sells certificates of time deposit, bankers' acceptances, Treasury bills and other banking and investment instruments; underwrites commercial paper

Garvin, Bantel & Co.
120 Broadway
New York 5, N. Y.
Financial Officer: George K. Garvin
Makes collateral and "call" loans

Goldman Sachs & Co.
20 Broad St.
New York 4, N. Y.
Financial Officer: John W. Callaghan
Investment bankers and underwriters; also a prominent underwriter of commercial paper

Frederick Hatch & Co.
72 Wall St.
New York 5, N.Y.
Financial Officer: James W. Johnson, Pres.
U.S. Affiliate and Representative of Pan Americana, S.A. Arranges financing in Mexican and other Latin-American short-term and intermediate-term notes and construction loans

Carl Marks & Co.
20 Broad St.
New York 4, N.Y.
Financial Officer: Robert Boas

One of the largest investment firms specializing primarily in foreign securities. Also arranges for financing of certain foreign private placements and loans

New York Hanseatic Corp.
60 Broad St.
New York 4, N.Y.
Financial Officer: William O'Kolski, Sr. Exec. V.P.
Investment banking and securities brokerage firm, also has a subsidiary, NYHACO, which provides financing for Mexican and other Latin American short-term and intermediate-term loans

Salomon Bros. & Hutzler Co.
60 Wall St.
New York 5, N.Y.
Financial Officer: Burton R. Bachrach (Commercial Paper Dept.)
Investment bankers and underwriters, also major underwriters of commercial paper

Tobey & Kirk
52 Wall St.
New York 5, N.Y.
Financial Officers: Herbert Buschman and Robert D. Hill
Investment brokers. Corporate Department arranges private placement, and financing for special situations and various corporate requirements. Also negotiates corporate mergers, acquisitions, etc.

Truman & Co.
70 Pine St.
New York 5, N.Y.
Financial Officer: Dr. Bonifacio Hassan
Private banking firm, arranges financing for various domestic and international projects

Wertheim & Co.
One Chase Manhattan Plaza
New York 5, N.Y.
Financial Officer: Frank Schoetz, Mgr. Foreign Dept.
Investment bankers and security brokers, also prominent in foreign securities

Allan S. Wieder
30 Broad St.
New York 4, N.Y.
Provides financing for various corporate
and realty situations, domestic and
international. Funds available for time
deposits

B. C. Ziegler & Co.
Security Bldg.
West Bend, Wis.
Financial Officers: Delbert J. Kenny,
Pres. and Dean W. Clausen, Research
Mgr.
Largest underwriter of loans and financ-
ing for churches, hospitals, parochial
schools and church-related institu-
tions

UNITED STATES GOVERNMENT SOURCES OF CAPITAL, CREDIT AND GUARANTEES AND QUASI-GOVERNMENT INTERNATIONAL FINANCE AGENCIES

**International Bank for Reconstruction
and Development (World Bank)**
1818 H. Street, N.W.
Washington 25, D.C.
Financial Officers: George Woods, Pres.,
Sir William Iliff, V.P., and J. Burke
Knapp, V.P.

Export-Import Bank of Washington, D.C.
811 Vermont Ave. N.W.
Washington 25, D.C.
Financial Officers: Harold F. Linder, Pres.,
Walter C. Sauer, First V.P., R. H. Rown-
tree, Exec. V.P., Raymond L. Jones, V.P.
for Exporter Credits, Guarantees and
Insurance, and Glenn E. McLaughlin,
V.P. for Program Planning and Informa-
tion

AID REGIONAL OFFICES, WASHINGTON

For countries in Africa-Europe:
Office of Capital Development and Finance
Bureau for Africa-Europe
Agency for International Development
Washington 25, D.C.

For countries in Far East:
Capital Development and Finance Staff
Bureau for Far East
Agency for International Development
Washington 25, D.C.

For countries in Latin America:
Assistant Administrator
Bureau for Latin America
Agency for International Development
Washington 25, D.C.

For countries in Near East and South Asia:
Office of Capital Development and Finance
Bureau for Near East and South Asia
Agency for International Development
Washington 25, D.C.

INTER-AMERICAN DEVELOPMENT BANK
808 17th St. N.W.
Washington 25, D.C.
Financial Officers: Felipe Herrera, Pres.
and T. Graydon Upton, Exec. V.P.

**HOUSING AND HOME FINANCING
AGENCY**
1626 K St. N.W.
Washington 25, D.C.
Administrator: Robert K. Weaver and
J. T. Conway, Dep. Adm.

FARM CREDIT ADMINISTRATION
Washington 25, D.C.

Federal Farm Credit Board
Glen R. Harris, Chairman. Regional Admin-
istrators: Julian B. Thayer, Middlefield,
Conn.; Joe B. Zeug, Walnut Grove, Minn.;
William T. Steele, Jr., Richmond, Va.;
J. B. Fuller, Torrington, Wyo.; Marshall
H. Edwards, Bartow, Fla.; George W.
Lightburn, Capron, Okla.; Marvin J.
Briggs, Indianapolis, Ind.; Frank Stubbs,
Corpus Christi, Tex.; J. Pittman Stone,
Coffeeville, Miss.; Glen R. Harris, Rich-
vale, Calif.; L. C. Carter, Stuttgart, Ark.;
Robert T. Lister, Prineville, Oreg.; and
Murray D. Lincoln, Columbus, Ohio

Commodity Credit Corporation
Washington 25, D.C.
Financial Officers: Charles S. Murphy, Pres. and Under Secretary, Department of Agriculture; Horace D. Godfrey, Exec. V.P. and Administrator, Agricultural Stabilization and Conservation Service; and Raymond A. Ioanes, V.P. and Administrator, Foreign Agricultural Service

FARM CREDIT BANKS

Farm Credit Banks of Baltimore
Baltimore 3, Md.
Financial Officer: Hugh S. Mackey, General Agent

Farm Credit Banks of Berkeley
Box 525
Berkeley 1, Calif.
Financial Officer: Wallace E. York, Chm. Management Comm.

Farm Credit Banks of Columbia
Box 1499
Columbia 1, S.C.
Financial Officer: Robert A. Darr, General Agent

Farm Credit Banks of Houston
Houston 1, Tex.
Financial Officer: William N. Stokes, Jr., General Agent

Farm Credit Banks of Louisville
P.O. Box 239
Louisville 1, Ky.
Financial Officer: J. Kenneth Ward, General Agent

Farm Credit Banks of New Orleans
P.O. Box 50590
New Orleans 50, La.
Financial Officer: John L. Ryan, General Agent

Farm Credit Banks of Omaha
Box 1229
Omaha 1, Nebr.
Financial Officer: Thomas A. Maxwell, Jr. General Agent

Farm Credit Banks of St. Louis
St. Louis 66, Mo.
Financial Officer: Stanley A. Morrow, General Agent

Farm Credit Banks of St. Paul
St. Paul 1, Minn.
Financial Officer: Lloyd L. Ullyot, General Agent

Farm Credit Banks of Spokane
Spokane 1, Wash.
Financial Officer: Fred A. Knutsen, General Agent & General Counsel

Farm Credit Banks of Springfield
Springfield 2, Mass.
Financial Officer: Gordon Cameron, Pres.

Farm Credit Banks of Wichita
Wichita 2, Kan.
Financial Officer: James R. Williams, General Agent